# PROSTITUTION AND THE ENDS OF EMPIRE

# PROSTITUTION AND THE **ENDS** OF **EMPIRE**

SCALE, GOVERNMENTALITIES,
AND INTERWAR INDIA

STEPHEN LEGG

DUKE UNIVERSITY PRESS   DURHAM AND LONDON   2014

Library of Congress Cataloging-in-Publication Data
Legg, Stephen.
Prostitution and the ends of empire : scale,
governmentalities, and interwar India / Stephen Legg.
pages
Includes bibliographical references and index.
ISBN 978-0-8223-5759-9 (cloth : alk. paper)
ISBN 978-0-8223-5773-5 (pbk. : alk. paper)
1. Prostitution—Government policy—India—History—
20th century.
2. Prostitution—India—History—20th century.   I. Title.
HQ125.I4L44 2014
364.15'3409540904—dc23
2014012188

Cover art: Indian prostitutes peeking out from doorways of their brothel, circa 1946.
Photo by Margaret Bourke-White/Time & Life Pictures/Getty Images.

# CONTENTS

———•———

# PREFACE

―――•―――

In 2003 I visited Delhi as part of a postdoctoral fellowship, working toward what became my *Spaces of Colonialism* book on India's interwar capital. While chasing up a building regulation in the manual *Delhi Municipality: Bye Laws, Rules and Directions* (1933), I came across a table listing "Prohibited areas for the residence of public prostitutes and the keeping of brothels." Having studied the historical geographies of prostitution regulation with Philip Howell at Cambridge, this tabulation caught my eye. I chased up the reference as a complement to my interests in the landscapes of residential segregation, the police, and urban improvement in the new and old cities. The seam of files at the Delhi State Archives was incredibly rich, detailing the turn of the city against its "prostitutes." This was, to a greater degree than in the other forms of political landscaping that had attracted me, a process incorporating popular petitioning and campaigns, voluntary groups and charities, as well as the Municipal Committee and Delhi administration. I wrote up this material as the fourth chapter to my Delhi book, focusing on the blurred boundary between the state and civil society and the sexual intersection of the individual and public body.

The chapter, however, didn't work. While the other case studies on accommodation, policing, and urban infrastructure required national and imperial contextualization, they presented stories that could be sufficiently told within a Delhi frame. Many of their spatial innovations originated within Delhi though, of course, drawing upon lessons, parallels, and warnings from without. Prostitution policy in Delhi, however, seemed behoven to objects, people, and developments from beyond the city limits. A Suppression of Immoral Traffic Act was debated in the late 1930s, emerging near-fully formed from the legislative spaces beyond Delhi Province. The irrepressible voice of a female campaigner, named Meliscent Shephard, announced itself through letters, petitions, questionnaires, notes, and chits in the early 1930s, while the League of Nations and the hopes of internationalism increasingly found their way into governmental debates on the fate of Delhi's prostitutes through the 1920s. Tracking these actors required the use of, among others, national archives in India, feminist archives in London, and internationalist archives in Geneva.

The last chapter of my first book slowly morphed into the first chapter of this one. That Delhi should come first was obvious to me, and not merely because it was the departure point for my archival rovings. In each archive I visited, no matter how grand or global, my interest had always been in the local tolerated brothel zone, or the "red-light district." How was it depicted? How was it managed? How did it exploit women? How did it not?

Keeping Delhi first was a reminder to myself, and hopefully to the reader, that the national, the imperial, and the international are always experienced at the level of the body, the encounter, and the local. But this does not, for a second, diminish the power of distant geographies. If the first book faced the challenge of explaining the power relations of space, then this book would have to contemplate the power relations of scale. How, like space, was scale constructed? Who could use it? How did it collapse? How was it resisted or used? And how did scales tumble into one another? My grapplings with scale were informed by a long and complex tradition of writing, in geography and beyond, on scale itself. But each chapter progressively took me beyond my training in colonial urbanism to the literatures on South Asian feminism, hygiene and sexology, law and international relations, and, most centrally, sexuality. Each of these historiographies dealt with scale, even if not through scalar terminologies. But a recurrent focus was on influence: how it traveled over scale, how it was made through scale, and how scalar positioning made some people more vulnerable to being influenced than others.

Just as the first book had plotted three paths through the colonial spaces of Delhi (geographical, historiographical, and theoretical), so this book treks beyond Delhi and colonial urbanism, but also beyond the established framework of colonial governmentality studies. At the center of this book are clearly a scalar study of the tolerated brothel and a temporal examination of the turn from segregation to suppression in the interwar years. But, and without wishing to diminish the significance of the empirical material here presented or the lives of the men and women here recounted, the book also continues a broader attempt to critically examine the excesses and neglects of colonial power relations. The challenge is, therefore, to somehow reproduce the Foucauldian feat of respecting an archival story while also outlining a broader narrative regarding power, the self, and others. As Arnold Davidson (2006, 123) put it: "Volumes 2 and 3 of *The History of Sexuality* are about sex in roughly the way that *Discipline and Punish* is about the prison." Michel Foucault himself put it more pointedly: "I must confess that I am much more interested in problems about techniques of the self and things like that rather than sex . . . sex is boring" (Foucault et al., 1983, 229). While one doesn't have to agree with the latter point to accept the former, this book offers few insights into the sexual lives of "prostitutes" and their clients in interwar India. But what it does offer is a critical apparatus with which to explore the ongoing exploitation, displacement, and silencing of women classed as prostitutes. The book continues a critical engagement with the work of Giorgio Agamben, appropriating his topological work on sovereignty and the in/outside. It combines this with Foucault's thoughts on governmentalized society and the governmentalization of the state to explore the "civil abandonment" of prostitutes in cities across India. Just as *Spaces of Colonialism* drew its theoretical frame from Foucault's Security Territory Population lecture course, so here I provide a detailed reading of the Birth of Biopolitics lectures to facilitate a deeper understanding of the scalar politics of governmentalities. The book, in this sense, extends Foucault's antiessentialist project to that of scale, arguing that: scales do not have natural processes, whether economic, social or political; that scales are networked into existence; and that they also operate through the awesome power of naming.

My long list of indebtedness charts the financial, emotional, and institutional props, ladders, lifts, tugs, hands, and help that got me over, under, through, around, and into scale. My trips to India in 2003, 2006–7, and 2011 were funded by, respectively: a Junior Research Fellowship at Homerton College, University of Cambridge, and an ESRC Postdoctoral Fellowship I took while based there; the University of Nottingham New Lecturer Fund and a Royal Geographical Society Small Research Grant; and a Philip Leverhulme Prize. The project has benefited from discussions at dozens of conferences and seminars, and I cannot do justice to the profound effect of them all here. Especially formative, however, were discussions during the Spaces of Civil Society panels organized by Gerry Kearns at the European Social Sciences History Conference in 2008; Anne Hardgrove's session on "Interwar India: The League of Nations and Sexuality in India" at the Madison Annual Conference on South Asia in 2009; two workshops on South Asian gender (2008) and sexuality (2011) formations co-organized at Nottingham with Srila Roy and generously funded by the university and BASAS; two workshops co-organized with Deana Heath on "South Asian Governmentalities" at Jawaharlal Nehru University (JNU) in New Delhi (2011) and the British Academy in London (2012); and conversations had during visiting fellowships at Queen Mary, University of London, and the Jawaharlal Nehru Institute of Advanced Studies at JNU in 2011.

Various people and institutions have been vital to the book's coming into being. At Duke University Press my thanks to Valerie Millholland and Gisela Fosado for their editorial skills and to the five external readers for their comments during the four rounds of external review. Thanks also to Anitra Grisales for her development editing. The giving and keeping of the archivists at the following institutions made this book possible: Delhi State Archives, the National Archives of India, the Women's Library at London Metropolitan University (now at LSE), the Asia and Africa Collections room at the British Library, the Centre of South Asian Studies at the University of Cambridge, and the League of Nations Archive at the United Nations Office at Geneva. I have been lucky enough to forge and draw upon an extensive range of colleagues and friends beyond my geographical kin over the last ten years. Heartfelt thanks to David Arnold, Anjali Arondekar, Pratiksha Baxi, Rachel Berger, Faisal Devji, Will Glover, Will Gould, Deana Heath, Sarah Hodges, Shruti Kapila, Prashant Kidambi, Elizabeth Kolsky, Philippa Levine, Stephanie Limoncelli, Janaki Nair, Eleanor Newbigin, Veena Oldenberg, David Pomfret, Srila ("friend of friends") Roy, Svati Shah, Awadhendra (Dipu) Sharan, Minnie Sinha, Ashwini Tambe, and Priscilla Wald. Within geography I continue to benefit from a broad and brilliant family of colleagues including, but not limited to, Michael Brown, Kath Browne, Dan Clayton, Ruth Craggs, Louise Crewe, Felix Driver, Jim and Nancy Duncan, Stuart Elden, Derek Gregory, Matt Hannah, Phil Hubbard, Tariq Jazeel, Craig Jeffrey, Gerry Kearns, Alan Lester, Colin McFarlane, David Nally, Andre Reyes Novaés, Miles Ogborn, Chris Philo, and Michael Samers. At Nottingham I have had the pleasure of acting as doctoral supervisor to (and learning a lot from) Kate Lynch, Amber Martin, Jo Barnard,

Jake Hodder, Reshaad Durgahee, and Ben Thorpe. The Nottingham cultural and historical geography research group has proved to be a brilliant home. Thank you to Stephen Daniels, Georgina Endfield, Mike Heffernan, Dave Matless, Susanne Seymour, and (especially) Alex Vasudevan and Charles Watkins for inspiring me, challenging me, supporting me, and, most heroically of all, putting up with me. Special awards go to my friends who have liberally allowed me to chew their collective ear over the years during the book's long gestation: to Mitu Sengupta and Sumit Baudh's hospitality in Delhi; in Nottingham to Gary, Jamie, Lesley, Mark, Martin, Ryan, and Srila's patient listening; and in London to the continued love (not to mention free accommodation) of Rosy and Ed, Mark and Sacha, and Jon and Amber.

Almost finally, a very special thank you is owed to Phil Howell. He introduced me to Foucault and the study of prostitution as an undergraduate and has been an invaluable colleague and friend ever since, bearing my questioning (and poaching) of his work, while cajoling, reprimanding, and generally encouraging me, all at the right times. And, lastly, thank you to my brilliant family. This research was undertaken and written up on a solid foundation of lovingly given and gratefully received Sunday roasts. I dedicate this book to Lucas and Chloe, for bearing their perambulations around the University Lake with good humour and for teaching me that we are more than just subjects.

# INTRODUCTION

―――・―――

SPATIAL GENEALOGIES FROM
SEGREGATION TO SUPPRESSION

*Burma*—On September 8th, 1930, the police received information to the effect that a Burmese girl had been thrown out
of the window from a building into the back drainage space
between 29th Street and Mogul Street. The police at once
proceeded there and saw a girl about 13 years old lying on
her back with a broken arm. She was speedily conveyed to
the General Hospital and on examination it was found that
her spinal cord was also broken. On regaining consciousness, she told her story, which was to the effect that she
was seduced by a young Burman and was sold for Rs.20 to
a brothel-keeper in 29th Street. She was forced to prostitution and finally, when she refused to obey the keepers of the
house, she was thrown out of the window.[1]

Besides the anatomical precision of its violent description, the
above report on the injuries to a girl in 1930s Rangoon is not
unique. It relates the misfortune of the numberless women and
children who were enticed, coerced, or trafficked into prostitution,
and subjected to sexual violence in their everyday economies. It
also tells of the extreme physical violence in the exceptional cases

in which these women tried to escape. But in addition to not being unique, the report is also generic. It contains various discursive tropes that recur in narratives of trafficking and violence against women in colonial India more generally (Mani 1998, 12): the heroic, rescuing authority figure; the dastardly perpetrators; the naïve victim. Similarly, there is an affective grammar and vocabulary at play: the police rushed *at once* to the girl's aid; she had been *seduced, sold,* and *forced* into prostitution; but she failed to *obey.* Her price was cheap, and the sewer she was thrown to invoked the Augustinian metaphorical linkage (revived by Alexandre Parent-Duchâtelet in Paris, see Corbin 1978 [1990], 62) of the prostitute as the sewer that cleansed mankind's morality. The assemblage of language and narrative plays across time, chiming with affective dispositions against child labor, sexual exploitation, and physical abuse. But was the girl pushed, or did she jump from the window? Was she seduced, or did she voluntarily opt for life in Burma's cosmopolitan capital port city? And why should these questions matter when her victimhood seems so complete?

They matter because the horror this case induces and the contemplative methodological questions it raises are both at the center of contemporary debates in colonial historiography and at the core of this book's attempt to understand the shift from the segregation and toleration of brothels in interwar India to their abolition and suppression. The seemingly transparent archival window into the true experiences of prostitutes in colonial India gives way to the smoke and mirrors of subaltern feminist theory: the constructed image of the victim reveals itself to be as much a reflection of the researcher, the governor, and the archivist, as of the historical subject herself. The confusions of representation and interpretation are just as present in the visual as the textual or the material (as Margaret Bourke-White's photograph on this book's cover makes clear).[2]

This occlusion is not merely a question of class; the individualized registration and policing of prostitutes in Paris (Corbin 1978 [1990]) or London (Laite 2012), for instance, provide a much more detailed archival sociology of their brothels, streetwalkers, and madams. The insights of subaltern studies, or at least the attention they draw to obscurity and occlusion, highlight how the governing of Indian prostitutes as a racialized and sexualized class was, at every stage, inflected by questions of difference: of oriental bodies, of tradition, of caste, of demand, and of tropically pathological disease.

But if the assemblage of emotions, facts, events, and discursive tropes contained in the Rangoon report appeals to us across time, this is because it was assembled to appeal across geographical space. For this archival trace was not found in the Rangoon police archives, or in the National Archives Department of the Government of the Union of Myanmar. It was not read in the National Archives in Delhi, or the imperial repository of the India Office Records in London. The report was read in the Official Publications room in Cambridge University's Library, reprinted in a League of Nations summary of reports on the traffic in women and children. As such, it could be read, and doubtless has been read repeatedly, in the libraries of Buenos Aires, Berlin, Tokyo, Canberra, or Mexico City. The report continues that while the alleged husband of the girl had absconded, a forty-eight-year-old and a twenty-eight-year-old had been charged under section 373 (buying a minor) and 325 (grievous hurt) of the Indian Penal Code, which the government of India had compiled in 1860 to bring legal homogeneity to its willfully heterogeneous territories. The very existence of the house was a sign of the failure of the Burma Suppression of Prostitution Act (1921), under which the report indicated that two other people had been convicted in 1930 of keeping a brothel. This act had been modeled on Britain's Criminal Law Amendment Act of 1912, which provided powers to clamp down on areas of segregated prostitution in the hope of reducing the "white slave trade," which so excited the salons of middle-class England, and so profited the newspaper account sheets of Fleet Street.

The Burmese Act turned out to be the first experimental site in a legislative network that eventually covered much of British India. It was designed to close down the routes through which women and girls could be trafficked into and around India, and the spaces in which they could be sexually exploited. During the years leading up to the First World War in India, the government accepted segregated zones of tolerated brothels as the safest way of dealing with the social and biological risk posed by prostitutes (see Legg 2012b). Broader shifts in science and society initiated a turn against the brothel, while the scandalous sites I will describe in chapter 2 discredited the segregationist system and spurred the development of legislation to suppress trafficking and neutralize the prostitute's perceived risk. In this book I set out to explain this shift from segregation to the suppression of tolerated brothels in interwar India, which approached the intimate space of the brothel as a local, national, imperial, and international problem. This book places scale at the heart of its methodology, showing how the most intimate spaces of desire and intercourse were forever enframed in broader scales of politics, terminology, and movement.

The league report on the unnamed Burmese girl, then, must be situated among the histories of prostitution and its policing through time. But the report also points to diverse geographical origins: where these people originally came from, from where the laws, sentiments, and science against prostitution were derived, and the archival repositories that provide access to this event. That is, the report directs us to the spatial genealogy of prostitution and its governmentalities.

Drawing on analyses of colonial rationalities, materialities, and practices, this book moves beyond my previous analysis of external influences on state apparatuses (Legg 2007b) to examine critically the governmentalities of local civil society, provincial governments, imperial humanitarian bodies, and international organizations. (For further work on (post) colonial governmentality, see Birla 2009; Chatterjee 2011; and Heath 2010.) While posing the question of imperial and international governmentalities, I will retain the urge to consider governmentalities critically, with an eye to their ethos and problematization, their excess and neglect. These observations serve to continue the critical dialogue with Foucault and his Eurocentric blind spots. But they also continue the critical engagement with the colonial state, which through this engagement with Foucault (and Agamben) is brought into focus as an agent of civil abandonment rather than of social uplift.

In this book I expand colonial governmentality analytics through two engagements. The first, more theoretical engagement draws upon the concepts of "apparatuses" and "assemblages," from Foucault and Gilles Deleuze, respectively, to complicate the way we think about scale, power, resistance, stability, and instability in colonial governmentalities. Methodologically, I draw upon an implicit logic in Foucault's *Birth of Biopolitics* (1978–79 [2008]) lecture course to suggest that we should be wary of claims to natural orderliness and should challenge such claims with an analysis of the existence and effects of networks and nominalism. In short, I suggest that we scrutinize *naturalistic* claims (for instance, that economies, populations, societies, or sexualities have "natural," and thus proper, orders) and insist that we think about scales as *networks* of differing lengths (such as intimate, local, regional, national, and imperial) and as the *nominalist* effects of naming (such as the body, the city, the province, the nation-state, and the empire).

The former, theoretical engagement will be outlined below and then demonstrated in practice through the introduction of the temporal and spatial scales of this study; namely, the interwar, the city/urban, the government of India/Raj, and the empire/imperialism. The methodological analytics of natures, networks, and nominalism will also be picked out in the literature that follows, while their origins in the second of Foucault's "governmentality" lecture courses will then emerge through the detailed reading of the *Birth of Biopolitics* with which this chapter concludes. These lectures present a major shift in Foucault's governmentality thinking. A detailed reading presents an opportunity to invigorate colonial governmentality analyses with the attention to scale and the social, which has been explicitly lacking in most postcolonial theory, and to continue the now widespread evaluation of the applicability of Foucault's concepts and observations to the colonial world.

### Assemblage/Apparatus

In Foucault's famously controversial *History of Sexuality, volume 1: The Will to Knowledge* (1979), he suggests that sexuality was constructed through a *dispositif* (apparatus) as much as through nature, and that sexual freedoms could very well be the most intimate and persuasive forms of control. This conscribing of sexuality to apparatuses of control contrasts starkly with Deleuze's situating of desire within an overarching *agencement* (assemblage), of which power is only a secondary effect (Grace 2009, 72). Foucault would later explore pleasure as a means of escaping the mind-set of sexual apparatuses, an approach that avoids what he felt were the medico-psychological presuppositions of Deleuze and Félix Guattari's emphasis on desire (Foucault et al. 2011, 389). This productive tension between sexuality/pleasure apparatuses and desire assemblages is just one dimension of a broader intellectual dialogue.

Beyond the specific debate regarding sexuality and desire, the intersection and distinctions between apparatuses and assemblages are gaining increasing attention (Legg 2009b). Apparatuses can be described as the governing discursive network between propositions, institutions, laws, and scientific statements that serve a dominant strategic function (Macey 1993, 355), such as absorbing a surplus population, regulating sex, ordering a city square, or normalizing bodily habits. As with Foucault's broader definition of discourse, apparatuses span text and performance, materialism and hermeneutics, embodiment and thought, but functionally focus around a purpose, usually of security. In contrast, Deleuze's assemblages focus on crossing borders, disassembling organs and bodies, tracing nomadic thought, lines of flight, and de-territorialization (Deleuze and Guattari 1987). As Ben Anderson and Colin McFarlane (2011, 124) explain, assemblage "is often used to emphasise emergence, multiplicity and indeterminacy, and connects to a wider redefinition of the socio-spatial in terms of the composition of diverse elements into some form of provisional socio-spatial formation." However, I argue that we must think of assemblages and apparatuses together, as creating the conditions for each other's emergence and dissolution (Legg 2011a). Neither concept has a monopoly on power or resistance, scaling or de-scaling, stratifying or smoothing space. However, in this book I will refer to apparatuses as those governing networks with a strategic function and ordering intent, while I characterize assemblages by their gatherings, heterogeneous groupings, and emergences. I will use the relationship between apparatus/assemblage to explore the dialectics of city/urban, government of India/Raj and empire/imperialism below. By paying attention to assemblage theory we can think beyond Foucault's ordering categories and norms. Though he developed governmentality, as a concept device, with the intention of exposing and unmasking apparatuses, when we apply it we often reinscribe the power of those apparatuses by making our thought and investigations equally neat and containable.

Because they are also resisted and contested, we must think about sexual apparatuses (such as the regulation of prostitution) alongside assemblages of their unraveling, expansion, and dissolution. Some women labeled as "prostitutes" in Delhi, for example, refused to move from their centrally located brothels and directly petitioned the chief commissioner in person, invoking complex assemblages of artistry, rights, and precarity. Women's reform groups campaigned at the provincial level to secure "social legislation" to rescue exploited women from pimps and brothels, and international humanitarian bodies pressed the government to restrain its military and to bring tolerated brothel zones within the purview of a reluctantly interventionist state, mobilizing texts, theories, and statistics from sexology, hygiene science, and anticolonial nationalism. These forms of resistance signpost a route that we can follow today to trace the colonial state's exploitation and neglect of the Indian population and territory. This will expose a state that outsourced the regulation of prostitution to a ruthlessly reformative civil society, yet refused to fund "rescue work"; that encouraged provincial suppressionist legislation but refused to support it centrally; that tactically supported imperial campaigns against tolerated brothels while failing to effectively police military prostitution or fund preventative and curative medicine for the Indian population; and that signed international agreements against trafficking but blocked any measures thought to impinge upon its "scalar sovereignty" (Legg 2009b).

To construct a *spatial* genealogy of this history, this book takes up Foucault's concerns with bodies, power, knowledge, security, and liberalism.

Rather than taking a body or event and moving *back* through time, it takes a place (Delhi) and moves *out* through space to explain the shift in the interwar years from segregationist to suppressionist legislation and attitudes regarding the brothel. As these scales of study expand, however, the space at the center of this study does not; rather, increasing scales are used to recast the brothel as a local, national, imperial, and international space.

## Histories and Geographies of Sexuality
### *From the Colonial Brothel to the Imperial Globe*

Worldwide research into colonial prostitution, and historical studies of colonial Indian sexuality in particular, is still very much indebted to Kenneth Ballhatchet's (1980) pathbreaking work on the introduction in 1868 of the Indian Contagious Diseases Acts (CDAs), the forcible registration of prostitutes serving the military, the acts' repeal in 1888, the military regulations which preceded and succeeded them, and the politics of European sexuality in India. In the thirty years since Ballhatchet's publication, historical studies of prostitution have been accepted as legitimate subjects of inquiry and have moved beyond a sole emphasis on regulation. Such research has explored methodologies from social and women's history, examining the structure and organization of commercial sex, to cultural and literary studies that analyze the symbolic and discursive construction of the prostitute (Gilfoyle 1999). Recurring tropes in investigations of prostitution in Russia, Europe, Nairobi, and Argentina after 1800 include the increasing dominance of sexual, over companionship, relationships in prostitution as the modern age progressed. Social analysis has proffered increasingly broad explanations for this phenomenon, while evangelical Christianity globalized its attack on legal brothels. Yet this literature also warns against simplistic generalizations regarding modern trends toward or away from oppression. For example, prostitution regulation in London between 1885 and 1930 increased repressive measures even as social purity arguments declined in force (Laite 2012). The criminalization and pathologization of the prostitute made her the subject of increasing control, yet definitions of "brothels" were worked around by prostitutes and pimps, while the police were loath to enforce the powers they acquired.

Attention to the international geographies of prostitution also reveals diverse connections between nations, states, and colonies (for an early review, see Bryder 1998). Rich contrasts have been drawn, for instance, between debates across the British Empire over age-of-consent legislation, homosexuality, and the regulation of prostitution (Phillips 2006). There were complex variations in regulatory policies regarding prostitution in the empire before the CDAS (Howell 2000), while British feminism itself was deeply imbricated with the imagined lives of Indian women (Burton 1994). Philippa Levine's (2003) brilliantly detailed comparative work has examined contagious diseases laws and broader cultural and political practices in Queensland, the Straits Settlements, Hong Kong, and India. She displays a keen awareness of each site's complexity and reflects at the end of the book on the landscapes and micro-spaces of selling colonial sex, yet the emphasis is very much "out" from each site toward comparison. While displaying similar interests and frames of reference, Howell's *Geographies of Regulation* (2009) is sensitive to the politics of place, which inspires the methodology I follow throughout this book; his work both goes "in" to the local spatial policing of sexuality and "out" to the geopolitics of the imperial state at the global scale.

While Howell expands from Britain out to its empire, showing that the flow of regulation was bidirectional across the borders of the United Kingdom, this book moves from Delhi to the national, imperial, and international contexts that frame the move from the segregation and toleration of brothels at the turn of the century to the abolition and suppression of brothels in the interwar period. Other scholarship has noted this shift in different parts of Asia. The commercialization of sex in twentieth-century Shanghai mapped itself onto the specific cultural geographies of the treaty port (Hershatter 1997). In Malaysia the state was involved in the medical inspection of brothels until 1907, and it was only with the international shifts in the 1920s in thinking on medical health, the protective role of the state in terms of the abuse of women and minors, and concerns over reproduction that the colonial government turned against brothels (Manderson 1996). Few investigations, however, focus on interwar prostitution in Asia. South Asian scholarship, like that of Levine and Howell, tends to end its investigations at the start of the First World War. There has also been a broader tendency to lapse into lazy orientalist assumptions about Hindu religion as a cause of Indian prostitution (Ringdal 2004), or that brothels in the "East" had not changed in several centuries (Simon 1975, 88).

There is, however, a rich body of work on nineteenth-century prostitution to draw on. This covers the different ways in which prostitutes could use and subvert the CDAS (Hodges 2005); the evolving rates of, and discussions about, venereal disease (Arnold 1993b; Levine 1994, 1996); the changing fortunes of courtesan culture (Oldenburg 1990); and the gradual association of the *devadasi* tradition with prostitution (Jordan 2003). In this book I am concerned almost entirely with urban prostitution, not the traditional courtesan or devadasi cultures that exceeded both the commercial purchase of sex and the capacities of colonial orientalist sociology to comprehend alternative sexual economies (Kumar 1993, 35). Erica Wald (2009) has outlined the nineteenth-century naming practices through which an increasing range of women were comprehended as "prostitutes." Rather than substituting a more contemporary term like "sex worker," I retain the term "prostitute" throughout this book. However, the creation of the prostitute through different apparatuses of regulation will highlight how constructed and contested this name was. In this book, as in the vast majority of documents consulted, "prostitutes" are presumed to be female. The League of Nations inquiry into trafficking in the East found almost no evidence of male prostitution, although "homo-sexual prostitution" was suspected among some Indian boys in Karachi. It was suggested that some of them had been trafficked to Basra and the pearl-fishing islands of the Gulf for immoral purposes.[3] Where homosexuality occurs within these texts, it is usually mobilized as a fear of what might result from depriving men of their brothels (a view that was fast falling out of favor; see Legg 2012b). The term "brothel" was likewise constructed and contested. It was a global term that came to encompass the range of *kothas* (apartments), *pukka* (well-built) huts, and *basti* (slum) shops in which women worked, but which was generalized to mean the prison and/or entrepôt of victimized women.

If brothels themselves have a complex nomenclature, so do the campaigns against them. The actions taken against segregated brothel zones in the interwar period built upon the successes of nineteenth-century campaigns against brothels that were registered, licensed, and inspected (embodied in the CDAS in the United Kingdom and across the British Empire; for broader examples, see Limoncelli 2010). This "regulationism" provoked a ferocious campaign to repeal the laws, spearheaded by Josephine Butler's Ladies National Association, which was later supplemented by the International Abolitionist Federation. The CDAS were repealed in 1886, a year after the Criminal Law Amendment Act (CLAA) introduced "abolitionist" legislation that increased penalties against brothels, procurement, and homosexuality. The campaign for such reforms continued throughout the empire.

Abolitionism did not, however, only campaign against registered brothels. In twentieth-century India we can identify at least three further, interlinked stages that targeted segregated brothel zones, brothels themselves, and trafficking. Prostitutes and local governments reformed their tactics

9

around the new landscapes of regulation that each abolitionist victory produced. The expulsion of prostitutes from registered houses led to the clustering of brothels in red-light districts (Legg 2012b). This system of segregation was accepted by the Indian government until the years of the First World War, when a series of scandals discredited it (as I explain in chapter 2). The abolition of segregated brothel zones, pioneered by Bombay and Rangoon, dispersed women into un-clustered brothels, the toleration of which became the subject of abolitionist campaigns in the 1920s and 1930s. Legislation passed from 1923 banned brothel keeping and forced women into apartments, to work by themselves, or onto the street, where they were said to be more vulnerable to pimps or traffickers. Ironically, these powers were contained in legislative acts designed to target trafficking itself. This fourth stage of abolitionism, however, took up the new mantle of "suppression."

The term "suppression" was not new; there had been British campaigns for the suppression of juvenile prostitution in the 1840s, while the CLAA (1885) aimed to "suppress brothels." By the turn of the century, however, the term had been appropriated by the sensationalist campaigns against the "white slave trade" (E. Bell 1909). International meetings for the "suppression" of this trade were held in 1899, 1904, and 1910, and their provisions were incorporated into the League of Nations' International Convention for the Suppression of the Traffic in Women and Children in 1921, to which India was a cosignatory. At the insistence of Japan, the terminology of the "white slave trade" was de-racialized and replaced with that of "trafficking of women and children," regardless of race. The following fifteen years would see an occasionally heated debate regarding the extent to which brothels (licensed, segregated, or tolerated) encouraged trafficking. Under pressure from its member states, the league classified India as abolitionist because it had no registered or inspected brothels. However, the provincial acts passed in the 1920s and 1930s were explicitly suppressionist because they targeted trafficking as well as abolishing (on paper) or even tolerated brothels.

Abolitionism evolved with regards to its approach to the prostitute, to morality, and to space. In terms of the prostitute, the Association for Moral and Social Hygiene championed her rights against the more punitive National Vigilance Association, for instance. In the moral debate a social-purist emphasis on chastity faced an increasing acceptance of women as desiring subjects. Regarding space, abolitionists targeting registered brothels identified certain buildings to close and laws to repeal. The abolition of segregated zones targeted particular localities through new laws, while tolerated brothels had a much more diffuse geography. The suppressionist phase of abolition had a relational geography that saw brothels as hubs of broader networks that had to be tackled in their entirety, which required the cooperation of organizations that could span nation-states with a concept and target that was more expansive than "prostitution."

In this book I combine an awareness of international networks with a committed focus on the city. Many insightful local studies of Indian brothels and their occupants bring to light the oral traditions and experiences of prostitutes in Calcutta (Banerjee 1998) and the shifting forms of regulation in Madras (Raj 1993). The latter strays into the twentieth century, but only Ashwini Tambe (2009a) has provided a thorough microanalysis of the shift from nineteenth-century regulation to the abolitionism of interwar Bombay. Chapter 2 will examine the cases that Tambe studied, including the murder of a young woman in the brothel district in 1917 and the template-setting legislation that followed, but it will work out from this site to provide a comparative analysis of suppressionist legislation across India in the fifteen years that followed. This time period, as much as the spatial scales that will narrate the shift from segregation to suppression, demands explanation.

### INTERWAR

"Interwar" is as unsuitable a category as "late colonial" for the period under study. These categorizations teleologically tether the 1920s and 1930s to a war and to decolonization that took appeasers and die-hard imperialists, respectively, by surprise. Similarly, there is a scalar assumption that ties the interwar to the international and the late colonial to the imperial state. And despite the radical newness of the violence and technological change provoked by the First World War, the cultural, political, and economic legacies of the previous era were not so quick to disintegrate as is often assumed. The monumental changes wrought by the two world wars do, however, justify this period as a time scale of investigation.

In terms of prostitution, the two world wars led to suspensions of usual practice across the world, as hundreds of thousands of troops were mobilized, increasing the demand for prostitutes. Under the Defence of India Act (1915), Regulation 12C was passed in 1918, providing powers to close down brothels in or nearby military camps (cantonments) for fear that they were infecting the troops. This marked the first of many surprising coalitions between feminist campaigners and military officials.[4] The Second World War would, however, see the faltering of the abolitionist drive among the armed forces and imperial campaigners, leaving the campaign to be taken forward by Indian social reformers and local groups. The gradual spread of penicillin as a treatment for syphilis after the war radically altered the perception of venereal diseases, if not the gendered and sexualized politics of policing prostitution.

Beyond policies regarding prostitution, the interwar period was also a dynamic time of rapid change and of the spectacular evolution of the spatial logics of imperialism, globalization, nationalism, and internationalism. India's support for the imperial war effort led to expectations of reward in terms of increased self-government that were only partly satisfied by the Montague-Chelmsford Report of 1918 and the Government of India Act (1919). The resulting constitutional improvisation was termed "dyarchy" and instituted a particularly scalar divide between essential and nonessential powers, associated with central and local government. While foreign policy, military, and financial subjects were reserved for central government, education, health, and statistical services were devolved to elected ministers in provincial government. The Government of India Act (1935) granted provincial autonomy, though with checks and controls for New Delhi, although the Congress Ministries resigned their posts in 1939 in opposition to the British decision to send India to war. The provincial geographies these constitutional reforms created were vital in providing the financial and governmental spaces of biopolitical experimentation that the Suppression of Immoral Traffic Acts (sitas) filled in regional Legislative Councils.

At the international scale, the First World War secured India's membership in the League of Nations, although, again, its representative capacities were heavily curtailed (Legg 2014). Though the Indian National Congress was founded in 1885, and the partition of Bengal in 1905 sparked *swadeshi* (self-made) and revolutionary movements, it was M. K. Gandhi's Rowlatt Satyagraha in 1919 that inaugurated the period of mass-movement nationalism in India that would reflect and provoke political and social reform throughout the 1920s and 1930s. The interwar period also saw new concerns emerge for all developed nations, ranging from the threat of Bolshevism, to women and labor movements, and revolutionary nationalism as well as constitutional anticolonialism (Sinha 2006, 33). These changes were, however, felt and responded to through the filters of scale (the local, the national, the world) and locality (between cities, provinces, and empires), as I explore below.

THE CITY AND THE URBAN

Current research on cities can be situated between two urges (see Legg and McFarlane 2008). The first is to appreciate cities as relational spaces, in which global cities sit at the center of vast networks (Sassen 1991), and in which even the homeliest of places is acknowledged to be constituted by its outsides (Massey 2005). At the other extreme is the urge to recognize all cities as "ordinary cities" (Robinson 2005) that deserve to be judged on their own terms, and in all their uniqueness and specificity. The happy medium is to attend to the specificities of city life while acknowledging the broader conditioning factors of city governance. A series of recent works has balanced these demands by, for instance, examining the networked port of colonial Bombay (Hazareesingh 2007), the architectural manifestations of British imperial power and its local hybridizations in Lahore (Glover 2008), or the municipal and local governmental efforts to modernize and securitize Mughal urban infrastructures (Hosagrahar 2005). While these apparatuses and ordering strategies are central to the management of the city, they should not be confused with the encompassing concept of the urban: "The urban is a myth, a desire and an ideal as well as a set of experiences; it is a kind of place, perhaps, but one that has a distinct temporalization; it is also a legal assemblage that has always been shot through with non-urban knowledges and powers and rationalities, both public and private" (Valverde 2009, 154). While cities perhaps lend themselves more easily to scalar delimitation—with city limits and definable authorities—the "urban" suggests a more radically open and enfolded assemblage, one linked to the broader world not just through capitalist accumulation or infrastructure, but through imagination, circulating ideas and designs, and mobile populations (McFarlane 2011). As such, the urban is a representational as much as a materialist category, as Swati Chattopadhyay (2005) has shown for Calcutta.

This book opens with a detailed case study of Delhi, which is fascinating precisely because it was *not* a scandalous or experimental site in terms of prostitution (as I explore in chapter 2). Though a fascinating local site of campaigning, controversy, and sex, all within the context of a sensitive and rapidly expanding capital, Delhi was largely influenced by innovations originating elsewhere and as such presents an ideal forum in which to first encounter emergent trends in prostitution regulation as governmental technologies that moved into Delhi and were gradually taken up in local governance, whoever those governors might be.

In chapter 1 Delhi will be presented as an urban sphere of rumor, myth, and desire, where injunctions to social and moral hygiene were persistently flaunted or ignored by a population increasingly attuned to the culture and politics of networks across national and international scales. But it was also a space that was claustrophobically penetrated by apparatuses of the colonial state (central, local, and municipal) as well as by civil society organizations of both imperial and nationalist sympathies, both of which abandoned the prostitute in different ways. Delhi was saturated with various organizations that brought demands for urban order. The central state was represented through the capital of British India in New Delhi; the Province was run by the Delhi administration under the command of centrally appointed European chief and deputy commissioners; and the "old city" was served by a partially elected Municipal Committee. Added to this were the demands of the Army Cantonment in the Fort, the Delhi Improvement Trust, the New Delhi Development Committee, and various other branches of the state.

The majority of the material informing chapter 1 is drawn from the Delhi State Archives, including the files of the deputy commissioner, the chief commissioner, and the Confidential Department. It was in this archive that this book project was conceived, as figures from ever more distant origins intruded into what I was reading about Delhi's local affairs: military orders from the commander in chief in New Delhi, amendments of municipal codes from the Punjab, scandals from Bombay, campaigners from London, questionnaires from Geneva. What the Delhi archives highlight is how this complex of "state" organizations was being governmentalized by an embryonic colonial civil society. For instance, the Delhi Health and Social Services Union was established in 1928 with the express support of the chief commissioner and the active participation of many members of Delhi's social elite.[5] It sought to coordinate existing organizations, like the Young Men's Christian Association (YMCA), and to investigate social ills. The union aimed to address people's conduct through seven subcommittees that would tackle maternity and child welfare, tuberculosis, education and publicity, the creation of acts to protect children, overcrowding and economic surveys, the beggar problem, houses of ill fame, and venereal diseases. This general organization was complemented by elitist women's organizations, most notably the Delhi Provincial Council of Women (DPCW).

The council had been formed in 1925 and operated under the presidency of Lady Grace Glancy from the prestigious address of 10 Queensway, New Delhi. Despite this high standing, it claimed to work among rich and poor, the English and the Indian.[6] This work was educational, through personal contact, social activities, and lectures, but also practical, by supplying garments for the poor and bandages to hospitals. By the late 1930s the council was also campaigning against the traffic in women and for a Delhi rescue home.

This approach to prostitution as a social and biological disease was very much opposed to that of the Delhi Women's League (DWL), which will emerge as a decisive actor in chapter 1. It had been founded in 1926 by Rameshwari Nehru as the local body of the All Indian Women's Council (AIWC).[7] The latter was the predominant forum of debate regarding the social, educative, political, and economic status of women in India. The DWL sent a representative and between five and ten delegates to each annual AIWC conference, drawing upon prominent women from Delhi's educational, political, commercial, and charitable spheres. While refusing to be dragged into the uptake of an anticolonial stance, many AIWC members were involved in the nationalist movement and, in response to inquiries being made by the chief commissioner in February 1944 the superintendent of police in the Criminal Investigation Department commented that the league did not "come to notice as an organisation for its political or communal affairs although many of its workers are known for their political views and activities."[8] In the late 1920s, however, the DWL focused its attentions on abolishing child marriage, undermining caste prejudice, and educating women.[9] In the early 1930s it organized various public lectures advising women on their electoral rights and duties, and encouraged their further education. The mid-1930s saw the league encourage swadeshi manufacture, a fundamental tenet of both economic regeneration and Gandhian nationalism. By 1939 the DWL had diversified and supported subcommittees that addressed famine relief, rural reconstruction, education, labor, legislation, medical issues, and indigenous industries, but it retained a subcommittee to investigate the traffic in women and children. This had been formed in the mid-1930s alongside DWL calls for the retraining of prostitutes and the creation of a rescue home (Basu and Ray 1990, 64, 77–81). On the recommendation of a specially convened subcommittee of 1937, all local branches of the DWL were urged to press for the application of a Suppression of Immoral Traffic Act and the creation of a state-aided rescue home. Not long after this, members of the DWL would clash with the British-born representative of the Association for Moral and Social Hygiene, who bluntly inserted the white authority of imperialism into Delhi's dense urban apparatuses of security (see below).

In terms of the broader theoretical and methodological argument, what we will see here is the nonnatural and agonistic functioning of urban "civil society," exposed as the product of dense and conflicting local networks that also provided the way for outside influence to enter and constitute the "local." It also named the city as sexually respectable and stigmatized the prostitute, while also hosting resistant acts of naming (the refusal of the term "prostitute" in favor of "radio artistes") and mobilization (most notably a procession to the deputy commissioner's home).

Chapter 1 examines Delhi's struggles to evict prostitutes from the walled city by, first, engaging Giorgio Agamben's work on abandonment, suggesting that this concept is more useful than abstract and nihilistic speculation over states of exception and bare life. It also helps us think about the closer imbrication of sovereign powers and biopowers in colonial governmentalities, in a way that is difficult to achieve through a simple transposition of Foucault's concepts to India. I combine this work with literature on the supposed *naturalness* of civil society and the "social" to present colonial voluntary organizations as agents of "civil abandonment." The first section looks at the exclusion of prostitutes from the walled city of old Delhi; this involves the *nominalist* process of their stigmatization, the petitioning against their central location, and the women's fight against this "purge." The second section focuses on the "rescue" of women and children and the debates between *networks* across the state-civil society divide to find a place to put them, their inclusion back into the city through a rescue home, and the Suppression of Immoral Traffic Act that was eventually introduced into Delhi to facilitate these inclusions. Chapter 2 traces the origins of the SITAs in nationwide networks of scandal, experimentation, and diffusion.

## THE GOVERNMENT OF INDIA AND THE RAJ

Viewed as an assemblage, the government of India stood as a construction of intimidating diversity and power: its military, civil service, wealth, architecture, geographical scope, literature, scientific output, spectacular violence, paintings, poetry, pageantry, and subject population popularly inspire an awe that even merits the assemblage its own name: the Raj. Viewed not as a semiautonomous domain of natural, colonial sovereignty but as an apparatus that created, emerged from, and had to support the edifice of the Raj, the government of India appears as a more fragile and less comprehensive network.

While "India" was associated with a subcontinent of territory, debate continues to rage about what India *was*: from Immanuel Wallerstein's (1991 [2001]) question of historiography and capitalist economy; to Manu Goswami's (2004) study of geography, pedagogy, and finance. As a League of Nations–sponsored report commented, the census of 1921 had shown that India included one-fifth of the world's population (320 million peoples, Hoops 1928). One-third dwelled in the "Native States," governed by royal families who were guaranteed their qualified independence in 1858. British India was divided into the nine major provinces of Bengal, Assam, Bihar and Orissa, Bombay, the United Provinces, Punjab, Madras, the Central Provinces, and Burma. Calcutta and Bombay were the largest cities, with over 1.25 million dwellers, while Madras had over half a million. Ten other cities had over 250,000 inhabitants (Delhi, Lahore, Ahmedabad, Lucknow, Cawnpore, Poona, Karachi, Rangoon, Hyderabad, and Bangalore). The administrative hierarchy ran from the king, to the secretary of state for India in London, to the viceroy and his six-member Executive Council in New Delhi. Under the dyarchy system following the Government of India Act (1919), the departments of local self-government, education, medical administration, public health, and agriculture were transferred to provincial administration, where they were run by Indian elected ministers, who took up further powers in the reforms of 1935. The Raj's attempts to name and network this heterogeneous space into a coherent state from its capital in New Delhi were often ineffective and became more difficult during dyarchy and provincial self-government, as progressive regional parties further exacerbated the contrasts between "local" governments.

The archive for the majority of the material in chapter 2 was the center of calculation through which the government of India attempted to reform, constitute, and marshal its regional provinces into some semblance of a colonial state. The National Archives of India (the old Imperial Archive, housed in part of the complex designed by Edwin Lutyens at the intersection of Kingsway and Queensway, the geometrical heart of New Delhi) allows one to trace central government attempts to encourage, coerce, stimulate, and suggest policies for regional governors who, from 1919, had control over most policies relating to prostitution. While provincial policies are also here studied using regional sources such as Madras's *Stri Dharma* or reportage from the Association for Moral and Social Hygiene's the *Shield*, the diverse channels through which the central state collected information on the provinces are daunting in their range. Annual police reports, CID information briefings, committee reports on proposed bills, governor summaries of provincial affairs, letters of complaint, voluntary association reports, and statistics that were forwarded on to the League of Nations in Geneva provide a phenomenally rich archive of sexual regulation, but also of the attempt to network together the regions, provinces, and cities of India itself.

The scalar tactics deployed in this attempt were, in part, repeated in different brands of South Asian historiography. The Cambridge school of imperial history analyzed the "vertical penetration of local elites by the colonial state," in contradistinction to the "horizontal affiliations of class," while studies of economic nationalism focused on the more abstract "epic battle between forces of nationalism and colonialism" (Chakrabarty 2000, 13). Bernard Cohn even provided a scalar typology of (precolonial) Indian state forms, from the imperial/Mughal to Mughal-governed secondary states, regional spheres, and local "little kingdoms" (see Ramusack 2004, 3–4). Subverting these scalar narratives, the subaltern studies school suggested an autonomous domain of the people, beyond the "vertical" mobilization of elite politics, and focused on "horizontal" affiliations of kinship and territory.[10] Recent literature has been pursuing a "flatter" epistemology within India's political networks beyond its shores. This asks how we can think beyond both the territory and the category of the nation to, for instance, the Indian Ocean arena (Tambe and Fischer-Tiné 2009). Such investigations highlight India's role as a sub-imperial metropolis, orchestrating colonial economies and administrations from west Africa to Malaysia (Metcalf 2007). But such histories are also part of a broader desire to destabilize core/periphery scalar divisions, as well as to consider links between colonies and empires.

Chapter 2 suggests that we need to extend this model to consider the internal political geographies of the colonial state itself and proceeds in two parts. After a summary of debates about the supposedly *naturalistic* orderings of colonial law and gender politics, and the sexological debate about the brothel, the first section examines the *nominalistic* discrediting of the segregated brothel system after the First World War in the scandalous sites of Rangoon and Bombay. These sites also provided the first experiments in suppressionist legislation, which informed the first SITA in 1923 in Calcutta. The second half of the chapter traces the diffusion of these acts through the dyarchical landscape of the 1920s and 1930s, stitching together India into a more and more comprehensive suppressionist *network*. This approach draws upon the histories Durba Ghosh and Dane Kennedy (2006) outline, which are attentive to the origins and implementations of differing types of colonial modernity as well as to the variety of forms that colonial governmentalities could take, and which stress that types of freedom and collective action also circulated through and across empires, that is, to India as part of a new imperial history.

## EMPIRE AND IMPERIALISM

As the assemblage out of which the apparatus of empire arose, imperialism defies neat definition in terms of period, place, content, or politics. Edward Said's definition (1993, 8: "the practice, the theory, and attitude of a dominating metropolitan centre ruling a distant territory") highlights how formal and informal imperial actions, intellectual justifications and investigations, dispositions, aesthetics, and representations were assembled into a world-spanning whole. The imperial domain was assumed to possess seminatural processes of trade, civilization, Christianity, and domination. Russia and the USSR, the United States (Stoler, McGranahan, and Perdue 2007), and British dominions in their regional spheres of influence (Pedersen 2006) took up imperial practices that were comparable to those of European states. Attention to these comparisons and connections has been central to the study of "new imperial histories" (Howe 2010), which denaturalizes imperial relations by emphasizing the contingent networking and naming of empire. Bringing the methodology and theoretical toolkits of postcolonial studies, gender and sexuality theory, race and identity politics to the study of imperial assemblages, these new histories also have specific geographies. As Alan Lester (2013) has made clear, previous debates about the core- or periphery-led nature of imperial expansion have been replaced with a network ontology that looks at the mutual constitution of the European self and colonial other. Augmenting interests in space and place with a concern for "levels and units of analysis" (Howe 2010, 11), methodological nationalism is here supplanted with a fluid sense of mobility and exchange within empires and, to a lesser extent, between them (Grant, Levine, and Trentmann 2007). The best of these analyses recognize that "imperial networks" are limited, grounded in competing discourses, and face appropriation and contestation in places such as the Cape Colony (Lester 2010), Morant Bay and Birmingham (Hall 2002), or seventeenth-century Madras (Ogborn 2007). In addition to this attentiveness to space, a scalar appreciation of the named divisions of the empire apparatus can make us more attentive to the problematized flows of technologies, people, and goods within the

"British space" of "World-Empire-Continent-Nation-Region-Locality" (Keith 2009). The forceful coherence of "empire," conceived not as a vertical hierarchy, but as a series of distanced networks spanning borders and boundaries, fragments under analysis into a haphazard collage of dominions, the Indian Empire, sixty colonies and protectorates, mandates, and a vast empire of informal influence.

The scalar constitution of the empire underwent major shifts in the interwar years in the face of debates over imperial overstretch, the emergence of the modern commonwealth, controversies of protectionism and economic integration, and the question of trusteeship (Butler 2002). However, to reduce imperialism to the acts of an empire would be to underestimate the diversity of its assembled parts. Trade and industry were symbiotic with the empire but in no way reducible to it, and neither were imperial social formations. The analysis of the latter has pushed Mrinalini Sinha (2006, 16) to "a simultaneous widening and deepening of a multiply scaled mode of analysis" that attends to how imperialism assembled different societies into relationships of interdependence and interconnection, and the uneven effects resulting from these connections. This combines an analysis of macro-political operations of empire with micro-political discourses operating within practice, that is, a "multiply scaled context" (Sinha 2006, 26). Such a framework can draw our attention to geographies of humanitarianism (Lambert and Lester 2004) or imperial feminism, both of which highlight tensions within what can still be termed an imperial project, as I will examine through imperial humanitarian anti-brothel campaigns in chapter 3. Here any sense of a natural and orderly imperial domain was fractured by the feminist and racial politics of the main campaigning body, the Association for Moral and Social Hygiene (AMSH).

The AMSH was formed in 1915 by the merger of the British, Continental, and General Federation for the Abolition of Government Regulation of Prostitution and Josephine Butler's Ladies National Association, the latter of which had campaigned so effectively against the Contagious Diseases Acts. The AMSH fought for gender equality through its general goals of achieving a high and equal standard of morality and sexual responsibility for men and women, the abolition of state-regulated prostitution, the suppression of profiteering from prostitution, and hygienic reform. Its journal, the *Shield*, documented its efforts throughout the United Kingdom, but also throughout the empire and beyond.

The *Shield* itself is a remarkably rich archive with which to examine the AMSH, but chapter 3 also makes use of the association's diverse collected records, stored at the Women's Library in London. As with the imperial archive in New Delhi, the AMSH had to string together representatives and issues across the empire into a coherent body that could be disciplined, defended, and funded. The data sources in the archive are phenomenally rich, as are the intensity of friendships and loyalties formed between women working across the globe. The achievements of these women can also be traced in the archives of their places of work. The AMSH appeared as a frequent correspondent in colonial archives and, in India, this left the indelible fingerprint of an astonishingly versatile, and controversial, figure. Meliscent Shephard was trained by the AMSH and sent out to Calcutta in 1928 on a three-year program, but went on to represent the AMSH in India until 1947. The influence and spread of the AMSH in India make it the main focus of chapter 3, but this necessarily becomes a study of Shephard and her controversial networking efforts in India.

As I will illustrate, there were also other British institutions vying for influence in India. Most notable of these was the British Social Hygiene Council (BSHC, named the National Council for Combating Venereal Disease between 1917 and 1925), which had been established to organize propaganda and education about sexually transmitted diseases (Legg 2013). Because it was established as a result of a Royal Commission in 1917 and funded by the British government until 1929, the organization was more aligned to the state and to curing disease scientifically than the AMSH was. The BSHC established initial but unsuccessful footholds in India in the early 1920s, ultimately being outpaced by Shephard's tireless campaigning. Both bodies were criticized for being complicit with the Indian government and of being first and foremost *white* organizations, for which social and moral hygiene was simply a new name for an older civilizing mission. This was, in large part, borne out by the groups' often racialist and arrogant practices, their determined name association with empire and London, and their refusal and inability to network themselves successfully with Indian social reform groups. This was reflected in their attachments not just to London, but also to the new experiments in internationalism emerging from Geneva.

Chapter 3 opens with a contextualization of the AMSH in debates about a naturally civilizing international civil society, colonial public health, and hygiene, and outlines how the analytical categories of governmentality analysis can be used to narrate institutional and individual biographies. It then proceeds in three parts, tracing Shephard's initial three-year stay in Calcutta, her four years of independent work in Delhi, and the four years in which she accepted a stipend from the government, leading to accusations of complicity with the colonial state that she had spent so long condemning. Each period is analyzed through the problematizations, ethos, nominalistic identities, and networked technes that allowed the AMSH to exert its influence so widely.

## RELATIONAL SPACE, SCALE, AND SEXUALITY

The scalar construction of the urban, the national, and the imperial are the focus here. This necessarily excludes an explicit focus on other scales, which will recur throughout and have been addressed elsewhere (on the brothel see Tambe 2006; on the provincial see Legg 2012b; and on the international see Metzger 2001). What is clear is that scalar terms and networks were fundamental to interwar India. But an emphasis on scale also serves as a useful corrective to an overly networked emphasis on mobility, flows, and transit across space. As Martin Jones (2009, 493) has stressed, the case for understanding spaces primarily through their relations with other spaces has been seriously overstated, neglecting the constraints and structuring influences on spatial relations. Territorial, cultural, and political strategies often close down these relations, lived experience is often woefully deprived of the chance for openness, and material and discursive effects of spatial permanence are powerfully enforced. But mobility and fluidity should not be seen in opposition to territory and borders. Philip Steinberg (2009), for instance, has shown that European state and territorial boundaries were solidified just as sixteenth-century merchant capitalism began regularly bypassing and transgressing these very borders. How, then, should such barriers be envisaged, if they function as much through their transgression as their containment?

A broader concern over the festishization of mobility and borderlessness, especially in writings on globalization, has prompted provisional debates over scale in a variety of disciplines. In ethnography, Jean Comaroff and John Comaroff (2003) have pondered the "awkward scale" of the local that contains social and economic forces from broader scales. Marilyn Strathern (1991 [2004], xv) has considered the problem of scalar organization and complexity in anthropology, while Antoinette Burton (2007) has called for a debate over method and scale in world history (also see Aslanian et al., 2013). Mariana Valverde (2009) has used scale theory to consider jurisdiction, security, and the law, just as Nancy Fraser (2010) has considered political spaces of globalization in *Scales of Justice*. It is from within the geographical discipline, however, that scale has received the most consistent, if not resolved, discussion. Moving beyond scale as a cartographic measure of representation, Peter Taylor (1982) established a materialist scalar framework for political and historical geographies of global capitalism, replacing Wallerstein's (1974) horizontal division of the world into core/semi-periphery/periphery with a vertical division into global/national/urban. The subsequent debates about scale in geography have been phenomenally rich (Moore 2008; Herod 2011) and informed by Marxist analyses of capitalist equalization/differentiation and uneven development (Smith 2004). Here scale has been envisaged as relational, in that it is a process that emerges through practices of capital accumulation, and as that which comes to provide a vertical and material framework linking global capital to local labor. While some have welded this vertical ontology to horizontal notions of network (Jessop, Brenner, and Jones 2008), others claim this verticalism is inseparable from scalar thought and discredits scalar analysis entirely (Marston, Jones, and Woodward 2005; see Legg 2009b, for further discussion). The suggestion is that scalar categories incorporate vertical assumptions about size or level, which map onto binaries of micro/macro, agency/structure, or local/global. As other critics have shown, this can pose the global as powerful beyond reach (Gibson-Graham 1996) and romanticize local struggles (Escobar 2001). However, while scale as "level" should be guarded against, the value of scalar narrations of networks of different lengths should not be dismissed (Jonas 2006), while the continued reality of scalar social constructions cannot be wished away.

This has been made abundantly clear in work on gender and sexuality where, for instance, we are warned against macro-generalizations and micro-romanticization that surface in assumptions about domination from "above" and resistance from "below" (Basu et al. 2001). Similarly, Kathleen Barry's (1995) radical work on prostitution strives from the outset to overcome the macro/micro, personal/political division. Ann Laura Stoler's (1995) reading of Foucault's work on sexuality alongside his lecture on race and society allowed her to think through the imperial circuits of sexuality. These networks linked metropolitan sexual identities and practices to imperial anxieties and encounters, overturning earlier suggestions of a mono-directional release of repressed European libidinal energies through colonial outlets (Hyam 1990). In Stoler's later work she moved from the discursive to the intimate realm, as defined by a series of micro-political sites such as those of parenting, nursing, and illicit sex, which also formed the "affective grid of colonial politics" (Stoler 2002, 7). Though she combined the imperial and intimate scales with great skill, these remain sites of

European privilege, involving the intense surveillance and pastoral concern for the elite population; intrusions into the sexual lives of the Dutch East Indies population (or the reasons for their absence) do not gain the attention attempted in this book, and in the broader field. While Stoler drew upon Foucault's (1975–76 [2003]) *Society Must Be Defended* lectures to re-read his *History of Sexuality* in terms of imperial circuits, I attempt a similar rereading of Foucault's sexuality work, but through the text of the *Birth of Biopolitics* and the geographical register of scale.

As widely acknowledged, Foucault's shift to a genealogical methodology brought his interest in power relations to bear directly onto the body (Foucault 1977b) and onto sexuality specifically. Bridging individual self-conduct and the reproduction of the species-body, sexuality was targeted by both disciplinary surveillance and the biopolitical guidance of freedoms. These practices produced sexuality, rather than repressing it, through apparatuses such as sexology (explored in chapter 2 to frame the shift in approaches to the brothel in interwar India) and hygiene science (which chapter 3 introduces in its moral and social hybridizations). While the *History of Sexuality* (Foucault 1979, 103) stressed the need to examine local geographies of sexuality, the book's broader geographies were largely underdeveloped (for contemporary work on geographies of sexuality, see Browne, Lim, and Brown 2007). As Howell (2007) has suggested, Foucault's speculations about the Eastern practice of *ars erotica* are saturated with a sensual orientalism, while the geopolitical ramifications of his work are not elaborated.

Yet a hint toward Foucault's more explicitly scalar work is embedded within his discussions of sexuality. In an interview from 1978 he suggested, "I think that, now, it will be necessary, in a sense, to take a jump backward— which does not mean to retreat but rather to retake the situation on a larger scale. And to ask, but what, in the end, is this notion of sexuality?" (Foucault et al. 2011, 387). This built upon his *History of Sexuality*, in which Foucault proposed four rules for analyzing power (Foucault 1979, 93). The rule of immanence warned against assuming that spheres, such as sexuality, existed that could be studied; this "sphere" itself would be a product of power relations that established the object of investigation in the first place. Better to study sexuality in "local centers" and study the subjugation and schemes of knowledge, what one might call networks and naming practices. The second rule reminded us of the continual variation of power, and the fourth of the tactical polyvalence of discourses, which were multiple and fragile. The third rule, however, referred to the relationship between the individual- and population-poles of biopower and dismissed any scalar association of the individual with the small and the social body with the large. For instance, the role of a father and a head of state as governing figures was not a representative one, nor were they projections of each other "on a different scale." Rather, they were linked through specific power mechanisms. Foucault presented the rule of "double conditioning" to address the relationship between local centers and overall strategy: "There is no discontinuity between them, as if one were dealing with two different levels (one microscopic and the other macroscopic); but neither is there homogeneity (as if the one were only the enlarged projection or the miniaturization of the other); rather, one must conceive of the double conditioning of a strategy by the specificity of possible tactics, and of tactics by the strategic envelopes that make them work" (Foucault 1979, 99–100).

How, then, do we think about and narrate geographical scale within a sexual and spatial genealogy? While attuned to the networking of body politics, genealogies resist the urge to situate dynamism, meaning, and explanation at a larger scale, reducing local examples to mere examples of a greater logic. Embedded within Foucault's Nietzschean turn, I suggest, is the latter's lament regarding the tendency to place "highest" and general theories or concepts first, as they often turn out to be the emptiest, or little more than the "last smoke of an evaporating reality. . . . That which is last, thinnest, and emptiest is put first, as the cause, as *ens realissimum*" (Nietzsche 1888 [2007], 19; cited in Philo 1992, 140). This is not the tale of a global structural shift, with national conjunctural movements and eventful brothel closures. The League of Nations, the British Empire, and the government of India are the elements, not origins, of the shift from segregation to suppression in interwar India. As such, the narrative methodology of this book stubbornly refuses to shunt the smaller scales of study, such as the city, to the back of the scalar hierarchy.

But why, then, not do away with scale in its entirety? First, I retain scale here because of the significance of distance; the sheer material and political energy involved in traveling over space lends scales of particular lengths particular importance. Secondly, the naming of people or things as local, national, or imperial has particular effects that must be acknowledged. These two facts lend scale a narrative role in this book that attests its historical significance, and its utility in the present, by allowing the past to be recounted in a coherent way (a historical geography of regulation in a city, a state, and an empire). But this narrative coherence of scale will be undermined by disrupting linkages between the local and the micro, the imperial and the macro. This will be done by highlighting first, the institutional struggles to create the impression of these scalar distinctions, and, secondly, the ways through which scales of different lengths and of different naming effects constantly intrude into any tidy sense of the local, national, imperial, or international, highlighting the significance of the macro in the local or the pivotal role of micro events in global forms. As such, scales are used and evoked here under "erasure" (see Spivak, xiv–xv, in Derrida 1976), just as Agamben (2005, 36) spoke of the "~~law~~" to denote "the force of law without law" (cited in Coleman 2011, 129). Here, this erasure acknowledges that as a local network and a name the city has great force, but that the ~~city~~ is always constituted by its outsides and is a radically unstable signifier, as are ~~states~~ and ~~empires~~.

The methodological categories I employ throughout this book have emerged from a detailed engagement with Foucault's governmentality lecture courses. I see this as forming part of a larger project to explicate colonial governmentality as a detailed analytical methodology. As a geographer, my aim is to contribute to thinking about Foucault's spatial (and scalar) politics in light of his recently translated works. I thus present the following reading, which provides a deeper theoretical analysis of my emphasis on natures, networks, and nominalism in relation to scale, which will hopefully be of interest to those pursuing a governmentality analysis of colonialisms, and to Foucauldians interested in the geographies of governance more broadly.

### Scalar Governmentalities
#### Nature: Scale as Domain

During his 1978–79 lecture courses Foucault explicitly used scalar terminology to describe the scope of European networks of governmentality, his methodological shift from micro to macro powers, and the domains (economy, population, society) that emerged in political thought as checks on overambitious sovereign powers. This marked an explicit turn away from his earlier scalar imagination. This element of his archaeological work has been criticized (summarized in Legg 2007b, chapter 2) for its suggestion of autonomous scalar domains of discourse. In *The Order of Things* Foucault (1970, xxii) established his object of inquiry to be the epistemological field (*episteme*) that lay between the empirical order of culture and the scientific or philosophical order of theory and interpretation. Despite his refutations, this period saw Foucault at his most verticalist and structuralist, etching out the synchronic connections in categorization between grammar and philology, natural history and biology, and wealth and economy. The synchronic connections were split by diachronic epochal ruptures between the classical age and the modern age in the early 1800s, the latter of which saw the emergence in the human sciences of "man." Foucault returned to these themes in the *Birth of Biopolitics* lectures, but with a different conception of man (*homo oeconomicus*) and of the historically contingent *production* of the *belief* in epistemic domains, not their use as a basis for methodological investigation. Yet, even in the volume that systematized this methodology, Foucault had begun his attack on scalar thinking in historiography, if not epistemology. In *The Archaeology of Knowledge* Foucault (1972, 10) famously insisted on the shift from total, civilizational, essentialist histories to general, dispersed, and local histories (see Philo 1992, 143).

This shift would eventually result in Foucault's Nietzschean turn to power, the body, and genealogy. The micro-political sites it discovered have been richly mined, but such studies have been criticized for neglecting attention to broader scales. It was, in part, to answer such criticisms that Foucault sought to connect changes in power over bodies to broader shifts in government, although his first attempts to do this retained his archaeological focus on epochal shifts (see Collier 2009). In his first *History of Sexuality* volume (published in France in 1976, translated in 1979, 25), Foucault linked changes in individuals' understandings of their sexuality to the emergence of "population" as an economic and political problem, in relation to wealth, manpower, and resources, in the eighteenth century. This domain was thought to have its own specific phenomena and peculiar variables (birth and death rates and life expectancy as related to diet and habitat). Sex linked these general processes to the individual, making it the target of individualizing, disciplinary surveillance and general, biopolitical measures to regulate the population. The scalar shift in Foucault's methodology is explicitly described in the contemporary *Society Must Be Defended* (Foucault 1975–76 [2003], 242) lectures, where his earlier focus on the disciplinary anatamo-politics of the individual was conjoined with an emphasis on man-as-species, or population, in biopolitics. The combination of these two scalar poles marked the emergence of biopower, power over life, not just territory. Yet, as Agamben (1998) famously critiqued, such powers were dissociated here from the sovereign's powers to "take life or let live," in pursuit of a modern age of normalization. Stephen Collier (2009, 85) has argued that the 1978–79 lectures elaborated biopower into a historically and methodologically complete concept of governmentality that was less epochal, relating sovereign power to biopower, and more attentive to spatial difference. But these lectures further elaborated the significance of the "emergence" of semiautonomous domains with their own logics, whose "naturalness" checked the ambitions of authoritarian governments and ushered in the conditions for liberal governmentalities.

In the *Security, Territory, Population* lectures, Foucault ([1977–78] 2007, 22) suggested that in the artificial milieu of the town, the problem of the "naturalness" of the human species in their milieu emerged (see Terranova 2009). Here it was acknowledged that interventions in the town were necessary to guarantee population processes. This logic was encapsulated more completely in physiocratic (literally rule [-*crat*] of nature [*physio*], 90) approaches to the economy that, again, detected regularities and processes (such as the price of grain) that demonstrated their own laws *but* were tied to the *realities* of grain (soil, climate, transport, demand; see Foucault [1977–78] 2007, 36). In place of an archaeology of physiocratic thought, Foucault's genealogy of their economic episteme led to technologies of power (the objectives, governing strategies, and program of political action that such thought initiated). This analysis of the economy inevitably led to the market, a self-curbing reality that provided a window onto the checks, balances, and laws of the economy, but which had to be maintained and protected (Mitchell 1999 [2006]). The domain of the economy was thus thought to be semiautonomous, to have a nature that needed sustaining. Bernard Harcourt's (2011) exploration of the "illusion of the free market" has detailed how the physiocratic belief in natural orderliness was revised through Adam Smith and Jeremy Bentham into eventual thinking on equilibrium theory, which sustains the idea of a realm of natural, economic order, and masks the regulation and disciplining of the market by the state that this nature requires.

Explicitly reflecting on the scalar consequences of this shift in thought, Foucault (1977–78 [2007], 42) identified two emergent "levels of phenomena": the population, for the government's economic-political action, and the multiplicity of individuals. The latter became pertinent to governmental thought only in that, if properly managed, maintained, and encouraged, they could produce effects at the scale of the population (see Selmeczi 2009, on the individual abandonment this can lead to). The processes that operated at the scale of the population were described as centrifugal and "aleatory" (dependent on uncertain events), and constituted their own "effective reality." The politics of this reality was the foundation of liberalism because, for such processes to work most effectively, they required a multiplicity of *free* individuals, the rational decisions of which were the reality upon which the laws of population, economy, and society were grounded.

Stressing again the links, and differences, to his archaeological work, Foucault ([1977–78] 2007, 77–78) revisited his *Order of Things* interests armed with the concept of population and found it to be central to the shifts he had earlier described: from grammar to popular philology; to evolutionary "populations" mediating organisms and milieu in biology; to the emergence of the sciences of life, language, labor, and production. The latter shift would become Foucault's central focus; the emergence of political economy as the science of government that instructed the sovereign to stand back, instead of intervening in the disposition of things. This would be the focus of the 1978–79 lectures, but even here Foucault drew attention to the parallel, potentially agonistic, emergence of the social: "It is society as a naturalness specified to man's life in common that the *économistes* ultimately bring to light as a domain, a field of objects, as a possible domain of analysis, knowledge and intervention. Society as a specific field of naturalness peculiar to man, which will be called civil society, emerges as the vis-à-vis of the state" (Foucault 1977–78 [2007], 349). Foucault concluded the 1978 lectures by defining the elements of the new governmentality as society, economy, population, security, and freedom. Liberty was the reality upon which the naturalness of the three scalar domains—analysis, knowledge, and intervention—depended; their processes, and a sufficient degree of freedom, would be guaranteed by security apparatuses whose purpose was precisely to bridge both the anatamo- and biopolitical poles of biopower, but also to both know and govern the multiplicity and the population. Foucault's *Birth of Biopolitics* expanded upon the scalar arguments made in the previous lectures, but addressed them much more explicitly:

> What I wanted to do—and this was what was at stake in my analysis— was to see the extent to which we could accept that the analysis of micro-powers, or of procedures of governmentality, is not confined by definition to a precise domain determined by a sector of the scale, but should be considered simply as a point of view, a method of decipherment which may be valid for the whole scale, whatever its size. In other words, the analysis of micro-powers is not a question of scale, and it is not a question of a sector, it is a question of point of view. (Foucault 1978–79 [2008], 186)

The above quote shows how directly the question of domain and scale was central to Foucault's self-description of his project by March 1979. This quote, however, is a direct adaptation of four pages that Foucault left out of the preceding year's lecture course, where the language was that of micro to macro, rather than of domains (see Foucault 1977–78 [2007], 119). But if these two lecture courses are linked by the analysis of governmentality, they are significantly different in certain ways. Foucault (1978–79 [2008], 2) opened his first lecture by stressing that he would be moving from an analysis of applications of the art of government to the reasoning behind and reflection upon government; that is, how a "domain of government" was established so as to improve governmental practice. As such, Mike Gane (2008, 361) sees the *Biopolitics* lectures as a top-down analysis of political-economic texts, while the *Security* lectures focused on a bottom-up analysis of liberalism. Collier (2009, 94), likewise, comments on the greater emphasis on "thinkers" in *Biopolitics*, but stresses how Foucault's understanding of thought had evolved. Against archaeological notions of autonomous discourses speaking through subjects, the later Foucault was concerned with ethical self-formation and critical thought. To understand, for instance, the "emergence of the market" in eighteenth-century thought requires a "polyhedral" appreciation of gold and monetary supply, demographic growth, changing agricultural production, and the technicalization of government, which were inseparable from the way economic problems were being given theoretical form (Foucault 1978–79 [2008], 33).

The recurrent analytical challenge in these lectures is to expose the domains and processes that are commonly assumed to constitute the primary nature of sovereignty, the state, or civil society as historically produced practices of government. As such, the existence of universal domains employed in sociology, history, or political philosophy is shown to be historical a priori, creations of a specific scalar imagination (Foucault 1978–79 [2008], 3). Yet such thought acted back on the realities it described, intervening through the application of rationalities from the natural sciences to "society" and "economy" (Foucault 1978–79 [2008], 115). Through recasting the *Security* lectures in this new perspective, sixteenth-century Raison d'État was said by Foucault to have imagined the state as an autonomous reality that was dominated by laws above or external to it. Yet while the European balance of power checked the state externally, mercantilism presented the police state with no internal check (Terranova 2009, 237). The emergence in the eighteenth century of a scale of economic processes, as defined by political economics, beyond the state provided this check, not through the dramatic, external language of rights or law that the sovereign *should* not transgress, but through the internal realization that the sovereign *could* not manage the laws better than they naturally managed themselves under conditions of sustained freedom. Liberal constitutionalism would thus work to displace the leader (in terms reminiscent of Carl Schmitt (1922 [2005]), who "in complete sovereignty and full reason, will decide on this internal limitation" (Foucault 1978–79 [2008], 12), with free discussion and conflict over how to govern. Sustained freedom provided the government's new role: the creation of *homo oeconomicus*, as exercised through the new reality of civil society (Foucault 1978–79 [2008], 295). Whilst checking overextensions of state sovereignty, civil society also allowed the state to access society and to mold a multiplicity capable of sustaining a healthy population and profitable economy. The latter would be accessed by government through the market, but the nature and complexity of the scalar domain the market revealed meant that the government itself would be judged by its truth-telling ("veridiction," Foucault 1978–79 [2008], 31; although see Walter 2008, for a critical reading of Foucault's periodization of the emergence of the "economy").

The existence of these domains was not, however, totally harmonious. (Neo-)liberal theorists in post–Second World War Germany argued that, just as classical liberalism in the eighteenth century had intervened into urban infrastructures to remedy the social breakdown and epidemiological disasters of Victorian cities, the state should intervene to buttress society from the untrammeled consequences of free market economics (an anti-naturalistic conception, for Lemke 2001, 193). However, the obverse to this investment was that heavy interventions would be made to guarantee conducive conditions for the market in "social factors" (technology, science, law, geography) but not in economic processes themselves (Foucault 1978–79 [2008], 141). American neoliberalism, however, viewed society as part *of* the economy and applied market logics across the range of governmental commitments. The historical span of this genealogy of liberalism is obviously extensive, but running through the 1978–79 lectures is a consistent narrative that returns to the analytical categories that have emerged from governmentality studies (see Legg 2007b, 12) (see table I.1).

Foucault thus provides a political theology of sorts: describing how domains of autonomous laws that should govern individual conduct, previously preserved for God and divine law, became secularized and operationalized to check the sovereign and limit government. But running throughout this work is Foucault's obsession in the late 1970s: power. Before his comment on the scalar point of view quoted above, Foucault (1978–79 [2008], 186) reflected that his object had been to find concrete content for the analysis of power relations. Indeed, power was said to constitute the domain of

**TABLE I.I Analytical categories for governmentality studies**

| | |
|---|---|
| Problematizations | The town, the unchecked sovereign |
| Ethos | Antieconomic-sovereignty, pro-circulation, pro-liberal freedoms |
| Techne | Security apparatuses of civil society, political economy, and biopolitics |
| Visibility | Statistics, social mapping |
| Identity | *Homo oeconomicus*, the liberal subject |
| Episteme | Domains of society, economy, population |

relations referred to as governmentality. This power was exercised by apparatuses of security, but this power was also "polyhedral," self-contradictory, and assemblage-like. One critical position would be to focus on such contradictions and resistances within the creation and governance of such domains. But another is to return to the mundane governmentalities at the level of "concrete analysis."

Given that Foucault remained committed to such analyses, what should we make of his obsession with the emergence of belief in scalar domains, social naturalness, and processes at levels removed from the multitude? I contend that this shift of attention from practice to thought was intended to show that many taken-for-granted assumptions about the ontological makeup of the world are historically contingent, and thus fragile and malleable. The project is one of de-reification, of examining scalar formations as networks of particular scopes, and which manifest themselves through particular naming effects.

Analyzing power thus involves de-reifying processes which are proclaimed to operate semiautonomously at particular scales. In the following chapters the natures that will be analyzed include those of society and the city, the supposedly civilizing law and order of the state, and the cleansing and uplifting nature of the British Empire. This scalar approach will be replaced with one which examines the networked relationships between actors over varying distances, and the attempts to name them into being.

Investigating these two alternative approaches to scale will provide us with a methodology for conducting a critical scalar analysis of governmentalities that raises fundamentally geographical questions, such as: Were geographical scalar domains (the international, imperial, national, or urban) thought to have their own processes? And how might analyzing scales as horizontal networks of distance provide a tool in the attempt to de-reify assumptions about scalar domains?

*Network: Scale as Distance*

Foucault's inattention to scales (of length) greater than the local or national has been well criticized, but the 1978–79 lectures marked a brief but significant engagement with the world outside of Europe. The potential of a governmentality approach to explore the "global" through micro-political sites and practices, combining an interest in local studies with an analytical focus on the links between micro and macro scales (Merlingen 2006), is one of the most interesting methodological developments to come out of the 1978–79 lecture courses. Hints at these trans-scalar ("domains") connections across space (distance) had been hinted at in previous works. Biopower was originally defined by its "lines of penetration" which incorporated both abnormal individuals and normal families. The latter were understood not as private domains beyond state sovereignty, but as devices of sexual saturation: "All this made the family, even when brought down to its smallest dimensions, a complicated *network*, saturated with multiple, fragmentary, and mobile sexualities" (Foucault 1979, 46, emphasis added). The *Security* lectures of 1978 had shown how the household was transformed from a model for the sovereign to a networked space to govern *through*, the ideal site to target the multiplicity in the hope of regulating the natural processes of the population. The *Biopolitics* lectures of 1978–79 continued this network approach to the home, by looking at how American neoliberalism extended market logic to all scalar domains. Families could thus be studied in terms of their investment strategies and as a series of interactions based on capital and calculation (Foucault 1978–79 [2008], 245). As the basis of the stable laws of economy, society, and population, the individual subject should not just be an introverted one, protecting his or her judicial *rights*, but must be an extroverted one of economic *interests*. The market and the social contract are thus spatially opposed: "In short, the individual's enjoyment is linked to a course of the world that outstrips him and eludes him in every respect" (Foucault 1978–79 [2008], 277). But if an individual's interests were increasingly networked, so were apparatuses of security; even Bentham's panopticon was returned to (Foucault 1978–79 [2008], 67), not as a regional mechanism, but as a general political formula for government. This was, however, an apparatus that detracted from freedom, rather than depended upon it.

The interconnections between governmentalities that networked across scalar domains and debates over freedom are at the center of current attempts to think of governmentalities beyond the scalar domain and territorial boundaries of the nation-state. The colonial governmentality school has made a substantial contribution to this debate, but has often focused on the micro-political application of governmentalities, in translated forms in colonial contexts, rather than on imperial or international governmentalities that circulated, compared, connected, and critiqued. Such injunctions have been made by the new imperial history school, but debates in international relations are also using Foucault's newly translated lectures to move beyond debates about discourse or biosecurity to consider global governmentalities (Kiersey and Weidner 2009), international law (Aalberts and Golder 2012), and the broader applicability of Foucault's theories of power (Kiersey 2009). Just as Foucault's genealogical lectures broke down reified domains through his historical research, Jan Selby (2007) has shown how Foucault has also been used to break down contemporary realist notions of sovereignty, anarchy, and state, exposing them as discursive constructs. Yet, this has usually been done by analyzing treatises rather than examining the procedures through which states were actually constituted, and how they gained the impression of stability and reality. As such, Halvard Leira (2009) has demonstrated the need for historically specific studies of interstate governmentality, recognizing the shifting sense of diplomacy (which Foucault neglected) as the administrative states (of c. 1580–1650) evolved, through the reason of state, into the liberal states of political-economy in the early 1800s. This specificity would also recognize that governmentalities were not just used to govern through freedom, that colonial states had to be made as much as governed through, and that liberalism and theories about it have always been directed beyond the domestic to the international (Hindess 2004).

Foucault recognized this in the 1978–79 lectures, which in some part rectify his previous neglect of both international relations and Europe's exploitative relationship with its constitutive outside (see Legg 2007a). The *Security* lectures positioned Europe itself as a postimperial space, establishing order following the breakdown of the Holy Roman Empire, but also as a state system dependent upon colonial conquest (Legg 2011b). After Spain and Portugal's quasi-monopolistic colonial and maritime empires, European states could re-envisage themselves, outside Europe, as operating within an open economic and political field (Foucault 1977–78 [2007], chapter 11; contrast to Schmitt 1950 [2003]). But the emphasis here was on how the diplomatic-military apparatus provided one of the three antecedents for modern security apparatuses of liberalism, having inward effects on states, their relations, and on the concept of Europe itself: "Europe as a geographical region of multiple states, without unity but with differences between the big and small and having a relationship of utilization, colonization, and domination with the rest of the world. That is what Europe is" (Foucault 1977–78 [2007], 354).

The *Biopolitics* lectures contain some scattered references to the influence of imperialism on British liberalism, and the internal threat of an over-expansive state establishing endogenous imperialism over civil society (Foucault 1978–79 [2008], 107, 187). But in terms of scalar networks, the most significant shift is the acknowledgment that the third characteristic of the liberal art of government was "international equilibriums, or Europe and the international space of liberalism" (Foucault 1978–79 [2008], 51). Whereas mercantilism had a zero-sum conception of national wealth (one state's wealth would increase only at the expense of another's), political economics suggested that through effective competition the buyer and seller could profit. Europe could thus progress beyond an imperial unity or a balanced peace to a world-dominating program of collective enrichment, as long as there were permanent and continuous inputs: "It is necessary to summon around Europe, and for Europe, an increasingly extended market and even, if it comes to it, everything in the world that can be put on the market. In other words, we are invited to a globalization of the market when it is laid down as a principle, and an objective, that the enrichment of Europe must be brought about as a collective and unlimited enrichment, and not through the enrichment of some and impoverishment of others" (Foucault 1978–79 [2008], 55). This marks, however, a critical failure in Foucault's analysis. As so often in the *Biopolitics* lectures, his refusal to adopt a critical standpoint often leaves his voice undifferentiated from the liberal theory he describes, despite acknowledging that the world becomes the "stake" for European "players." The zero-sum game remained, but it was the primitive accumulation of colonial resources and labor that supplied it, and the native dispossessed who paid the price. Foucault never mentions the violence inherent to this expansion of the lack of freedom of those encompassed by it (see Cooper 2004). It remains clear, however, in the lectures that the expanded scale of capitalism is a vital component to understanding liberal governmentalities: "I think there are many signs of this appearance of a new form of global rationality, of a new calculation on the scale of the world" (Foucault 1978–79 [2008], 56). The challenge is to consider these rationalities and their effects at the scale of the world, through networks of differing lengths within this recalculated world. These networks could function as apparatuses that securitized, regulated, and surveilled, but also as assemblages that fragmented borders, encouraged movements and migrations, and questioned the cartographic narrative of world spaces. In the chapters that follow these networks will be laid out in detail: the enmeshing of state and civil society in Delhi; the piecing together of the government of India out of its provincial governments; and the letters, mobilities, and ideas that Meliscent Shephard pulled together in her imperial campaign to rid India of brothels. This will put to use one critical methodology for challenging the impression that scales have domains and processes of their own. But these networks of different lengths were inseparable from their names. Examining this process of naming provides the second methodology with which to critically appraise scalar practices.

*Nominalism: Scale as Naming Effect*

According to Geoff Eley, "'globalization' as a socio-economic, cultural, and political postulate (as a set of powerful and insistent claims about changes in the really existing world) is just as crucial to the process of globalization as the existence of globalization as a demonstrable social fact (the supposed structural primacy of global integration)" (2007, 158). Eley encourages us to appreciate that globalization affects us as much through ordinary language as through the changes in capitalism and social formation that we can access through scientific analysis; that "intellectual" histories of globalization are as important as "actual" histories; and, most important, that phenomena, events, and trends exist in a dialectical relationship with the language of social understanding. Each historical phase of "globalization" and the terms used to comprehend it require attention, in addition to a horizontal analysis of geographical unevenness and differentiation (Eley 2007, 160).

Foucault presents us with an apposite framework for this project, having long insisted that discourses are as much material, performative, and institutional as they are textual, visual, or ideological. A "semiotics of materiality" in world history would, thus, not just examine texts or inscriptions of reality, but would examine technical realities and the interlinked constitution of these realities (Merlingen 2006). This is what Ian Hacking (2002, 2) refers to as dialectical realism (the interaction of what *is* and our *conceptions* of what is) or dynamic nominalism (the interaction of naming and the named). Drawing on Foucault, Hacking (2002, 40) showed that while natural scientific categories did not actually change the materials they described, social scientific categories could ontologically create people and actions, who would then alter the categories themselves. This was the new approach to the thinking subject that Collier noted in the *Biopolitics* lectures, and it gives us another tool to de-reify scales as domains and understand their impacts as networks.

Foucault (1978–79 [2008], 4) made the nominalist capacities of governmentalities apparent from the beginning of the 1978–79 lectures by stressing that a state is both an existential given, but also an objective to be constructed: "The state is at once that which exists, but which does not exist enough." It was the investigation of this dynamic that spanned Foucault's projects: not to expose a hidden object of knowledge, not to expose illusions, but to show "how a particular regime of truth, and therefore not an error, makes something that does not exist able to become something. It is not an illusion since it is precisely a set of practices, real practices, which established it and thus imperiously marks it out in reality" (Foucault 1978–79 [2008], 19). It was from this premise that Foucault's antirealist, antiessentialist approach to the state emerged (also see Harcourt 2011, 48). While without essence, the state does have a reality as the effect and profile of perpetual *statification*: "The state is nothing else but the mobile effect of a regime of multiple governmentalities" (Foucault 1978–79 [2008], 77). While the *Security* lectures had made this clear, the *Biopolitics* lectures extended this methodology to the scalar domains of economy, population, and society; none of these domains existed until they were imagined, but they gained a reality through this imagination. But how much? Civil society, for instance, was not a natural given, not a "primary and immediate reality" but a part of modern, governmental technology. But "to say that it belongs to governmental technology does not mean that it is purely and simply its product or that it has no reality" (Foucault 1978–79 [2008], 297). Like madness and sexuality, civil society is a "transactional reality," a transitional figure that is real, although it didn't always exist, "born precisely from the interplay of relations of power and everything which constantly eludes them, at the interface, so to speak, of governors and governed" (Foucault 1978–79 [2008], 297). While naming and language are subject to apparatuses of grammar, censoring, and discourse, language readily plays upon the assemblage-like potential of the imagination, mischievous word-play, and endless mutability.

While Foucault's analysis was usually endogenous to the state, such transactional realities also "function not so much to represent as to constitute the world of international politics" (Selby 2007, 326). The state-as-effect was not just a political technology of government. It was a governmentality imbricating biopower and sovereign power; the performance of the state enacted as much sovereign exclusivity over a bounded territory as it legitimized a bureaucracy or political philosophy. So with the city. Its culture, reputation, economy, and administration were consolidated into not just an intramural or regional persona, but a scale of subordinate but identifiable sovereignty. Engin Isin (2007) has identified how we should de-essentialize such relationships and expose them as the effects of scalar apparatuses of capture. But what of empires, or international leagues? How have they been orchestrated to create the impression of semiautonomous scales? How can we analyze their networks and nominalist effects to undercut this impression, exposing their nodes of violence, fragility, contradiction, and complexity? And what types of reality did they draw upon to continually re-territorialize and rescale their apparatuses in the face of both entropy and willed efforts at de-territorialization and descaling? The empirical material that follows will show how campaigns were launched to protect the name of respectable cities by stigmatizing prostitutes, how national sites of scandal were used to insist upon local interventions, and how the name of the British Empire was used to justify the eradication of the brothel as a way of life.

One of the complaints we can raise against the governmentality methodology is that it is too attentive to apparatuses and neglectful of the assemblages from which they arose. The "polyhedral" appreciation of the sheer diversity of assemblages often gives way to a Eurocentric and state-centric emphasis upon the stabilization of governing techniques into stratifying institutional apparatuses. In the chapters that follow, three scales of analysis will be used to show how apparatuses of ordering were constantly undoing and being undone. The stable impression of natural processes and domains (civil society and the urban, sexuality and the Raj, hygiene and imperialism) will be exposed through attention to the desperate and consuming efforts to create networks (the local, the national, and a British transnationalism) and evoke names (the city, the government of India, and the Empire) that would enable the switch from segregation to suppression as the solution to the problem of prostitution. Some of these features are picked out below: they will be referred to recurrently through the chapters and will be systematically drawn together in the conclusion (see table I.2).

The methodological question this raises, and which I will consistently return to throughout this book, is, why bother with scale? If the aim is to disprove that scalar processes exist in some semiautonomous, natural domain, and to show that they actually only exist in networked and nominal-

**TABLE I.2 Approach to natures, networks, and nominalism throughout the book chapters**

| | Chapter 1: Delhi | Chapter 2: SITA | Chapter 3: AMSH |
|---|---|---|---|
| NATURE (the challenge) | URBAN: expose production of civil society and sexuality | RAJ: expose law and ordering as power and governing | IMPERIAL: expose the myth of the cleansing empire |
| NETWORK (the features) | LOCAL: state and voluntary association alliances and resistance networks | NATIONAL: movement of legislation, traffickers, and prostitutes | WORLD: stringing together London, Delhi, and provincial centers |
| NOMINALISM (the naming) | CITY: stigmatization of women as threatening and mislocated | STATE: scandalous sites and central/local divisions | EMPIRE: an imperial morality of self-control |

ist processes that are produced "on the ground," why not just describe these sites? This is because scales cannot be wished away; their networked and nominalist effects, though transactional realities, are socially and spatially real. The methodological challenge is to represent this multidimensional reality in writing (which progresses unidirectionally from left to right, line after line). This is an intentionally unresolved tension that courses throughout the chapters that follow. The form of each chapter retains scale as a narrative device and focuses on a scale of a particular name and length. But the overtone of the chapter structure is productively undermined by two further scalar devices. First, each chapter constantly returns to a site, the brothel, and thus shows how this singular space encapsulated scales from the genital to the global. Secondly, the scalar overtone of each chapter is enlivened by perennial undertones of other scales: of national acts, imperial campaigners, and internationalist traveling commissions in Delhi; of local bill campaigns, imperial advocacy, and international surveillance of national legislation; and the domestic offices, national imaginaries, and global networks assembled by Meliscent Shephard. I hope that these natures, networks, and names, as well as these scales, apparatuses, and assemblages, provoke others to consider the scalar politics of the worlds they study and the words they write.

# One

# CIVIL ABANDONMENT

———•—

## THE INCLUSIVE EXCLUSION
## OF DELHI'S PROSTITUTES

### Governing Concepts

Between 1857, when Delhi was reclaimed from the "mutineers," and 1947, when it became the capital of independent India, the city saw the emergence of a class of "common prostitutes," whose existence posed the city's governors with challenging questions concerning the medical and moral security of the city. These new figures were reviled in biological terms, as contagion, and in social terms, as sexually licentious and transgressive, bearing, as always, the blame for satisfying the demands of their male clients. This revulsion was not *represented* in space, but constituted and *reproduced* in and through it. The bazaars in which prostitutes publicly solicited and enticed men into their brothels and kothas became the target of petitioning and reformatory zeal. The Municipal Committee selected particular places into which the women could be segregated, which sparked further protests from local residents unwilling to cohabitate with this abject community. This process did, at least, accept that the women had a right to dwell and work in this manner *somewhere* in the city. However, in the mid-1930s a new campaign in Delhi sought to abolish brothels and public soliciting in the city altogether.

These two campaigns, to segregate prostitutes into one part of the city or to abolish their infrastructures of support altogether, reflected the ideological positions that were struggling for supremacy in interwar India and the world at large. Broadly speaking, different branches of urban government in Delhi adopted these opposing measures. The partially elected Delhi Municipal Committee (DMC) responded to local complaints against prostitutes in bazaars by segregating the women in a series of locations, leaving them and their activities relatively unreformed. This resulted in the women's gradual *exclusion* from the confines of the walled city. In contrast, the centrally appointed Delhi administration began, in the 1930s, to support suppressionist legislation, in line with pressure from international campaigning groups and the military. To compensate for these measures, voluntary associations worked to provide basic infrastructures to socialize "rescued" women and children and to make prostitutes a topic of popular concern, thereby *including* these women in Delhi's emergent colonial civil society. The support for these women was, however, wholly inadequate and simply marked another stage in the persecution and punishment of prostitutes within patriarchal orders (British and Indian) that were already structured to exploit them to the fullest. This chapter will seek to explain the simultaneous processes of exclusion and inclusion operating through both civil society and the state, both of which came together to place Delhi's prostitutes in a state of civil abandonment.

This analysis will show how two imagined *natures*, or "domains," were central to this process: the city as a space of sexual propriety, and civil society as an ordering force. In terms of the specifically colonial context, the city apparently needed extra regulation while civil society had to be fostered *by* (not emerge in opposition *to*) the state. The attempts to rescue and include women and children in Delhi resulted in a dense *networking* effort, in an attempt to create the impression of a sexually civil city. But these networks clashed and betrayed the constant interventions of national and imperial people and ideas into the city. The parallel effort to exclude prostitutes *named* them as the problem, and too rarely as the victims, of the city. While the women resisted these categorizations, the need to protect Delhi's name was too great. The capital risked becoming, the Delhi YMCA had suggested, a "byeword for immorality." It appeared that Delhi was still, as Viceroy Hardinge (cited in Legg 2007b, 56) had insisted when he relocated the capital from Calcutta, a "name to conjure with."

Nikolas Rose (1999, 101) has described the domain of the "social" as the conceptual space through which intellectual, political, and moral authorities, in certain territories, think about and act upon collective experience. Most definitions describe a belief in an autonomous domain with lawful dynamics that inform social institutions and aggregate in social agents (Poovey 2002, 47), the emergence of which Foucault (1977–78 [2007]) described as central to the sciences of government. Definitions of the social have included eighteenth-century considerations of abstract human nature, nineteenth-century organicist and evolutionary models, and the more structural formulations of the interwar period (Joyce 2002, 11). This evolution involved a shift from seeing the social as a natural and material force to it being conceived of as a product of conscious will and purpose, maintained by people and associations that were encouraged and regulated by the state, yet existed outside of it. The term's complexity can be comprehended through the different levels of abstraction used to define the social. These include first order, "empty" units such as society and economy; second order, historically specific, narrative paradigms of the social; and third order, public dynamics and desires by which these abstractions are lived out (Poovey 2002).

Within these complex genealogies, and from Mary Poovey's second order, the concept of "civil society" must have a special place. Both Hegel and Marx agreed that the distinctive feature of political modernity was the separation of state and civil society. Hegel described the latter as a sphere that was neither the family nor the state, but where private individuals came together under the regulation of the state. As such, while conceptually distinct, the state exerted its authority in civil society through administrative mechanisms. Marx radicalized Hegel by attributing the production of poverty to civil society, a superstructural product of wage-labor relations (Neocleous 1996, 13). As such, Hegel's mediating institutions were reinscribed as tentacles of the state that subsumed social struggle into the administrative machinery. Antonio Gramsci (1971, 12) later made the distinction between "political society," which was characterized by these very institutions and coercively exerted direct domination through the state and juridical government, and civil society, which achieved hegemony noncoercively. Churches, schools, clubs, and political parties marked the latter; police, the government, armed forces, and legal apparatuses marked the former.

Foucault also considered civil society a means through which to govern, but one that involved a more decentered power dynamic (see Cohen and Arato 1994, 255–98). Mark Neocleous (1996, 58) has argued that Foucault's assertion depoliticized social relations by dissolving the state into the "social body" and law into administration. He also argued that Foucault dismissed the state/civil society division, focusing on the normalization of society through administration, and dismissing the cold monster of the state. This argument was made mostly on the basis of Foucault's (1977a) work on discipline and also assumed Foucault's lack of attention to different types of power, whether of the state and civil society or of the group or individual. At exactly this period, however, Foucault was turning his attention to the role of conflict: first, between civil society and the state or business; and, second, between groups within civil society. In the *Society Must Be Defended* lecture course (Foucault 1975–76 [2003], 18, 61), the formative and continuing role of conflict in civil society was stressed. Society was here posited as a new subject of history that emerged in the eighteenth century, but one that was quickly colonized by institutions that made race and class struggle function as a way to normalize this new social body. Civil society was later posed as a product of the state, a means of regulation and control (Foucault 1977–78 [2007], 349). The relationship of civil society to the social is thus parallel to the relationship between political economics and the economy, or biopolitics and the population. Such a visualization breaks down the imaginary boundaries between state and society, but also subverts the scalar ontology that sees the state above the population and embeds the state in the complex "power topographies" of the local (Ferguson 2004).

But Foucault's lectures also made clear, to a greater extent than his discussion of biopolitics, how civil society (also referred to as governmentalized society) organized the fragile and obsessive object called the state (Foucault 1977–78 [2007], 248). Foucault denied that civil society was an aboriginal, preexisting reality or a construct of the state. Rather, he argues, it was a correlate of a political technology of the state and, as such, was variable and open to constant modification: "For Foucault, the political objectification of civil society plays a central role in determining a relatively open-ended and experimental problem-space of *how* to govern: that is, of finding the appropriate techniques for a government oriented by a problematic of security. This 'transactional' domain at the frontier of political power and what 'naturally' eludes its grasp constitutes a space of problematisation, a fertile ground for experimental innovation in the development of political technologies of government" (Burchell 1991, 141). Tailoring these more abstract concepts to the spaces of the city, Patrick Joyce (2003, 172) has shown how the social took shape in direct relation to the threat that nineteenth-century urbanism posed. Cities would now be town-planned into order, creating an ideal demonstration testing ground for the new social sciences. Social processes, facts, and the bonds of people to society came to be explained by the now-established statistical machinery, which promised to make the population amenable to secure governance, while providing liberal checks against any over-intrusions of the state.

The boundary between the social, as conceived, and the state was complex and blurred. The social was never thought to be as much an autonomous force as the economy. This was not because it had been swallowed by a police state, but because the state began to become as complex *as* society, taking on new roles and interventions. Colin Gordon (1991, 34), drawing on Michel Foucault's lecture courses and the work of Jacques Donzelot, described the social as the field of governmental action operating within and upon the discrepancies between the economy and society, many of which had biopolitical manifestations and solutions. Social governmentalities were not persistent policies; instead, they responded to certain crises such as overcrowding, theft, and crime, but also to epidemics and diseases (Rose 1999, 101). The state did, from the late nineteenth century onward, begin to intervene more in the social sphere, in line with what Stuart Hall and Bill Schwarz (1985, 9) refer to as the replacement of laissez-faire liberalism with state interventionism. Colonial states, however, were differentiated by the excesses and neglects of their interventions. While it is an accepted feature of colonial governments that they were less liberal in terms of checks on the disciplinary actions of the state, their limited intervention on social issues was also a key feature. Whether from fear of offending "native" sentiment or a simple financial reluctance to invest, the colonial state recurrently displayed an unwillingness to intervene in the domain of the social.

This can be better understood by framing the social as a key domain in the liberal art of government. The social was not part of the state, but it was governed *through* (Joyce 2002, 10). Liberalism constitutes governance through freedom: of the self, the family, the economy, and society. Yet this freedom depends upon free and self-regulating individuals. As such, we must ask: What form does the social take in regimes of colonial governmentality? How was "oriental" society conceived of by an authoritarian liberalism that assumed the fundamental difference, rather than sameness, of the Indian people (Metcalf 1994)? And to what extent had Indian nationalists, by the interwar years, reimagined *samaj* as a non- and even anticolonial version of "society" that was consonant with the nation, even as "it retained the fault-lines of caste, community and gender throbbing right under the surface."[1]

Partha Chatterjee has complemented his earlier work on the colonial rule of difference (Chatterjee 1993) with further meditations on the relationship between the epistemological objects of the population and civil society in the colonial context. Chatterjee adopted Gramsci's distinction between political society (policies relating to the mass of the population) and civil society (the elite) and argued that, in the United Kingdom, modern forms of government arose following the spread of civil rights in civil society. However, in Asia and Africa, the techniques of governmentality preempted, and constituted, the nation-state (Chatterjee 2004, 36). As such, the mass of the population was conceived of as subjects, rather than citizens, to which the colonial state was determinedly external (also see Prakash 2002, 81). Contact with the population was maintained by ruling via the traditional social forms of the community, those collective bonds and rights based on imagined ties of kinship, religion, culture, and the past.

Building upon understandings of community and colonialism, Chatterjee (2004, 6) chose to stress the heterogeneity of the social, as against the supposedly homogenous, empty time of the nation-state. The multiple techniques of colonial governmentality created crosscutting and shifting classifications of the population: as criminals, residents, workers, or slum dwellers, for example. Yet beyond these considerations of political society, the colonial environment *did* foster a civil society. For most cases of the nineteenth century, Chatterjee (1993, 24) was right to claim that "the only civil society that the government could recognize was theirs; colonized subjects could never be its equal members." Yet, though without equality of status, Indian elites were incorporated into civil society, even as this society was itself colonized by nationalist sentiment (Kalpagam 2002). This increased the heterogeneity of the social through the formation of, for instance, a Hindi-language public sphere (Orsini 2002); philanthropic, educative, and religious institutions (Watt 2005); political organizations campaigning for self-government and political citizenship (McClelland and Rose 2006); and associations campaigning for women's rights (Basu and Ray 1990). In addition, during the twentieth century the government encouraged the formation of a civil society that could mediate the state and the social. The latter would be a domain in which subjects were encouraged to think of themselves as citizens with the obligation to work together in "social service."

Indeed, at the blurred boundary between the state and the social domain were independent reformers, charities, and voluntary associations who re-coded crises of government as moral problems with national consequences (Rose 1999, 102). In the twentieth century, the colonial Indian state was increasingly pressured to regulate the moral domain and encourage standards of self-conduct. This included intellectual education to encourage foresight, prudence, and planning, but also involved targeting the body to encourage hygiene, virtue, and normalized sexuality. Further confusing the scalar politics of the state/society boundary, voluntary associations involved in this endeavor were often international organizations that implanted transnational governmentalities into local contexts (Ferguson 2004). Attempts to normalize sexuality came to be conceived of in the dense and emotionally charged circuit of the sexual, which Frank Mort (1987) has argued constituted a governmental domain in itself. Yet this interest in sexuality must be framed within the particular articulation of sovereign power that the imperial context brought to the social and civil society in colonial India.

### Abandonment: Inclusive Exclusion

When thinking about how colonial civil society, in cooperation with the state, worked to govern the population, we must address the specific conditions of colonial governmentality. Beyond being conditioned by "race" (Chatterjee 1993), colonial governments were structured by a series of excesses and neglects (Legg 2007b, 21). Considering these over- and under-reachings reminds us, also, of Foucault's failure to theorize the colonial world. This is equally true of his writing on the social and civil society.

As I explained above, the state both limited and partly constituted colonial civil society. But we must also situate civil society within a colonial state that often ranked the powers and techniques of government and discipline beneath the exigencies of sovereign power. In my previous work I argued that the landscapes of ordering in Delhi displayed the ways in which sovereign power was imbricated with different types of power relation: from hierarchical categorization (New Delhi residential landscapes), to discipline (policing), and biopolitics (improvement of Old Delhi). This chapter extends that analysis to the study of civil society and its regulation of prostitution in Delhi.

Envisioning sovereign power through the lens of civil society raises several interesting questions: Who could use the language of rights against certain manifestations of exceptionalism? Did the colonial context increase the likelihood that the invocation of these rights would further embed sovereign powers within the institutions of the state? If we consider colonial states to be perpetually closer to states of exception (Hansen and Stepputat 2005; Gregory 2004), what does this mean for our considerations of civil society? How central, for instance, was colonial civil society in othering and outlawing forms of Indian violence, such as sati (widow immolation) or hook swinging (the suspension of men by iron hooks inserted through the skin of their backs), and did juridico-scalar concerns also play out here (Mani 1998)? How were simultaneous forms of violence, abuse, or even torture ignored and thus legitimated by the state? Does the incomplete spread of colonial civil society mean that these forms of exceptionalism were highly provisional, or longer lasting? And how did the state claim to be simultaneously the agent for spreading law and order in India, but also the body that could, and did, suspend that law in self-defined periods of emergency?

I still believe that Agamben's work on sovereignty must be adapted to take account of resistance, the complexity of sovereign powers' manifestations, its geographies, and its imbrications with disciplinary and governmental forms of power relation (Legg 2007b, 4–7). My intention here is not to summarize or survey the scope of Agamben's work, or the commentary on it (see Hussain and Ptacek 2000; Norris 2005; Calarco and DeCaroli 2007). Rather, I intend to select and scrutinize those analytical concepts that will enable us to examine civil society through the lens of exceptionalism. Claudio Minca (2006) has shown that Agamben adapted Carl Schmitt's claim that the sovereign is he or she who decides upon the exception, which is represented paradigmatically in the camp, and structured topologically by the ban. While the camp is interesting to scholars of sovereign power just as the Panopticon is interesting to scholars of disciplinary power, it is the ban that breaks free from the archipelago of sovereign power and courses through the capillaries of society (see Bigo 2008, 32, on the "ban-opticon"). Banned people, or groups, are not exiled or excluded; the law is removed from them, but through this decision they are necessarily produced by the law itself. They exist in a zone of indistinction between law and lawlessness that constitutes their "inclusive exclusion" (Agamben 1998, 27) from society: "He [sic] who is banned is not, in fact, simply set outside the law and made indifferent to it but rather *abandoned* by it, that is, exposed and threatened on the threshold in which life and law, outside and inside, become indistinguishable. It is literally not possible to say whether the one who has been banned is outside or inside the juridical order" (Agamben 1998, 28–29, original emphases).

The relation of exception, therefore, is defined as that which is included solely through its exclusion (Agamben 1998, 18). The abandoned is not simply cast away from the sovereign; on the contrary, the abandoned figure enters into an exceptionally intimate relationship to the sovereign because the ban can be rescinded at any time (Agamben 1998, 67). It is this precariousness of existence that resonates most clearly with the prostitutes of Old Delhi who were excluded from the walled city and denied permanent residence while the colonial state sought a(n impossible) place to abandon them.

But Agamben tempered Schmitt's emphasis on decisionism with Walter Benjamin's insistence that the exception can become the norm (Agamben 1998, 55), and thus extend beyond the adjudication of a single sovereign authority to become the prerogative of the swarming sovereigns within the population. This forces us to think of exceptionalism alongside the governmentalities that exert power through everyday rationalities of conduct. Exceptionalism has been studied in relation to, for example, the police (Secor 2007) and famine biopolitics (Kearns 2007), but has not been systematically thought through in relation to civil society. The first half of this chapter will show how different wings of the colonial state (the Delhi administration and the Delhi Municipal Committee) abandoned prostitutes by using the laws of the Punjab Municipalities Act to exclude them from the city, while using the same law to include them by dictating where they could live beyond the walled city. What we see here is the full nominalist force of stigmatizing women and certain places; this naming was driven by urban communities as much as a biopolitical state. The second half of the chapter will show how Delhi's emerging networks of colonial civil society partook of their own form of abandonment. This was achieved through naming and discussing the prostitute's fate, and in actually reclaiming her or her children into the Delhi Rescue Home, while lobbying the state to abolish tolerated brothels and to further exclude the prostitute from the city. This will involve further tailoring Agamben's initial work in light of ongoing revisions and critiques, which further impel us to think about the geographies, resistances, complexities, and imbrications of sovereign power.

While replete with spatial language, Agamben's (1998, 19–20) account insists that exceptionalism is "unlocalizable." Matthew Hannah (2008, 60–62) draws attention to the complex topologies of these exceptional *geographies*; outside/inside, exception/rule, exist as zones of indistinction, not clearly defined territories or spaces. Bare life, the vulnerable biology that exceptionalism forces forth, is said to have been normalized and thus exists well beyond the camp or the laboratory. As such, Oliver Belcher et al. (2008) variously describe geographies of the exception as topological, in process, as a set of dynamic techniques and emergent spatializations.

However, these exceptional spaces are not confined solely to the virtual; they *can* be actualized. As Hannah (2008, 62; drawing on Agamben 1998, 123) emphasized, the camp can be viewed as a paradigm of modern politics, but also one that exists as a pure biopolitical space. Agamben (1998, 19) immediately qualified his assertion that a state of exception is unlocalizable with the following rider: "(even if definite spatiotemporal limits can be assigned to it from time to time)." It thus seems important to acknowledge that the spatiality of the exception need not take material form, but that this "*need* not" should not be conflated with "*can* not." Exceptionalism, as Agamben (2005) develops in later work, operates as an "amorphous technology of security which infuses and envelops all spaces" (Coleman 2007, 190), imbuing them with the potential to territorialize into actual spaces of exception, as well as functioning in institutional spaces like the camp. To understand the problem of the state of exception, the challenge thus becomes to "determine its localization (or illocalization)" and to track the disputes "over its proper *locus*" (Agamben 2005, 24, original emphasis). Though the prostitutes of Delhi were forced to spend over twenty years in continually shifting sites of exclusion, their abandonment did ultimately result in their landing in a space of utter indistinction, neither within nor without the city, but on the site of the demolished wall that had once separated the two.

The conception of these spaces has important connections to concerns about *resistance*. As Hannah (2008, 63) asked, "what are the geographical presuppositions of our purported vulnerability, and how universally can they be said to apply?" While Foucault, belatedly at least, insisted upon the centrality of resistance to questions of power, Agamben's writings can lead to an obsession with thanatopolitics (the politics of death). As Paul Patton (2007) forcefully argues, Agamben conflates bare life with *homo sacer*, associating natural life with a historically and geographically specific, and by no means inevitable, fate.

Ernesto Laclau (2007) has made a similar point, stressing that the ban can lead to various possibilities, determined by the specific conditions of the individual in question. For instance, does the individual have a collective identity? Is he or she wholly exposed to violence, and without means of defense? What system of structural possibilities is opened up by each new situation? As such, Laclau (2007, 22) damningly concludes that Agamben fails to deconstruct the logic of political institutions and show which forms of struggle and resistance are possible: "Political nihilism is his ultimate message."

Jenny Edkins and Véronique Pin-Fat (2004) have hinted at ways of resisting the ban that would highlight the process of abandonment and the violence at its heart. Hannah (2008) has also shown that individuals and groups can successfully work to remain *un*exceptional and evade sovereign powers' attempts at inclusion and exclusion. This was especially evident in Delhi, where prostitutes consistently moved around, or simply ignored, the ban. They were also effective litigators, challenging the state's categorization of them as prostitutes, and petitioning the government to uphold its basic duty to provide them with somewhere habitable to live. This critique seared to the heart of colonial abandonment. It did not target a specific law aimed at prostitutes, but rather addressed the suspension of the most general "law" of government, which dictated that the population be granted the basic conditions of existence. This appeal was made as *zoē* (natural life) not as *bios* (political life).

Beyond this most fundamental of appeals, Delhi's prostitutes were also targeted in terms of their collective identity, that is, their sexuality, nation, and gender. This brings us to the absence of *complexity* in Agamben's conception of the ban, which must be worked out across the range of sovereign powers, subjectivities, and places of enactment. In terms of the former, the power of the sovereign was not simply to decide on abandonment, but also to administer tax, land, finances, and the spectacle of its own performance. In terms of subjectivity, Geraldine Pratt (2005, 1055), for instance, has insisted on combining feminist theorizations of gendered divisions of space with her study of the legal abandonment of sex workers and migrant domestic labor in Vancouver. The abandonment of Delhi's prostitutes was specifically gendered and sexualized, within contexts of both imperial and Indian reformist stigmatization of prostitutes, which increasingly worked to portray the prostitute as the outsider within. The prostitute in interwar India threatened not only British soldiers with venereal disease, but also the emergent nationalism with a radically "other" negotiation of the gendered division of public/private space, that is, the prostitute/brothel rather than the mother/home (Mufti 2000).

One must also retain a sense of the complexity of the authorities administering sovereign power (as explorations of feminist literature on sexuality, law, and the state in the next chapter will demonstrate). The chief commissioner, the deputy commissioner, and the Delhi Municipal Committee

(DMC) all, to some degree, represented the state in Delhi, but from very different (and often conflicting) perspectives. This complex arrangement also denies any essentialist division of colonizer/colonized, with the attendant moral judgments that accompany that binary. The DMC was partially elected and worked to represent the views of the population, but was also the foremost agent for expelling prostitutes from the walled city. In contrast, the British deputy commissioner, who conducted the day-to-day activities of the Delhi administration but was also president of the DMC, insisted that the treatment of prostitutes be "just" and invoked their rights as "citizens" (or bios). As Laclau (2007, 20, 22) suggested, sovereignty can be democratizing as well as totalitarian and is strung in incredibly complex relationships between the homogeneity and heterogeneity of modern politics.

One way to approach these relationships is to consider the *imbrication* of sovereign and biopowers within specific governmentalities. Thomas Lemke (2005) has argued that Agamben rightly refocuses on the power of the law, which Foucault had (in part) neglected. Yet Agamben remains (like Schmitt before him) committed to a juridico-discursive model that is insufficient for an analysis of complex governmentalities, which results in a failure to acknowledge the specificity of individual negotiations of bare and political life. Such an approach moves, methodologically, toward a different set of questions to those that animate Agamben. *What*, for instance, leads to banishment, and *why* (DeCaroli 2007)? Why is someone exiled, not punished? *How* does exceptionalism work, and *which* law is suspended (Belcher et al. 2008)?

Derek Gregory (2007) has contrasted Foucault's interest in confining outsiders in disciplinary institutions with Agamben's interest in the inclusion of outsiders through abandonment. But a third node for comparison is the mode of governmental power, not as reduced to biopolitics, but as also operating in the conceptual domain of civil society. It is this process of civil abandonment that I will address in this chapter, focusing on (inclusive) exclusion in the first half and (excluding) inclusion in the second.

### The Purge: Geographies of Exclusion

Despite the great strides forward made for the rights of women during the early twentieth century, by both social reformers and anticolonial nationalists, prostitutes found themselves in an ambiguous position. While the second section of this chapter will show that many women's reform groups worked to protect and "uplift" prostitutes, they were outnumbered by individuals and organizations that abhorred their effects on society. While Nehru had once defended the rights of prostitutes, they were rejected by Gandhi for contravening his strict moral and sexual codes (Joardar 1984, 54, 58; also see Tambe 2009b). More broadly, much of the emerging Hindu middle class had adopted sexual and gendered views of the ideal woman that were comparable to, and developed in symbiosis with, Victorian notions of the separate spheres (Whitehead 1995). Both the Brahmanical and British systems were patrilineal and demanded acts of bodily regulation regarding decorum, hygiene, dress, and sexuality. This also required the distancing of the upper castes from polluting substances such as bodily fluids, menses, and afterbirth. As Peter Stallybrass and Allon White (1986) have shown, such processes were mapped onto urban space and constituted an ethos of marginalization and expulsion. For instance, Sundara Raj (1993) has shown how the spreading of regulatory laws in Madras through the nineteenth and twentieth centuries forced prostitutes out into villages or into the fissures within disciplinary space in which client and customer could seize moments beyond the policing gaze.

Charu Gupta (2001) has focused on the spaces of the everyday to show how women were positioned as central to the nation and the community due to their reproductive and symbolic functions, yet also how they retained their ability to resist a resurgent public patriarchy. This perspective on prostitution allows one to see "how cultural values were redefined in specific geographical locations. There were attempts to undermine and expel prostitutes from municipal limits, to ensure new norms of appropriate social conduct in respectable and civilised areas. Here too there were uneasy oscillations, and women tried to rework their own spaces" (Gupta 2001, 85). Gupta showed that in Lucknow, sex workers had long been considered a means for purifying towns, providing an outlet for men's sexual drives, whether in the form of upper-class courtesans or lower-class prostitutes. These women were accepted in social rituals and resided in common urban space. However, the effects of the Contagious Diseases Acts and the other forms of colonial state regulation, along with the decline of court culture, found prostitutes becoming socially marginalized and their identities stigmatized. Economic hardship forced larger numbers of women into prostitution, making it a more competitive and public enterprise. Yet the shifts in Indian society that Whitehead suggested were also playing their part. As Gupta (2001, 112) claimed: "The prostitute became the cause of the very evil she was supposed to contain, resulting in her social condemnation. She came to be viewed, at best, as a necessary evil who had to be shown her proper place and geographical limits. Middle-class Hindus engaged in a dialect of morality and sexuality, disease and cleanliness, and a displacement of this 'other.'" In line with colonial and nationalist attempts to exert their influence over public space, municipal bazaars became unwelcoming places for the prostitute. This was no longer just in terms of venereal diseases, but in the prostitutes' role as home breaker and child corrupter, and as the cause of overcrowding and unsanitary conditions. As such, municipal acts were gradually passed to force prostitutes out of central urban spaces, despite the vociferous complaints of the women themselves. It is at the intersection of the drive by municipalities to cleanse their spaces and the drive by the military to cleanse their men that the policies of Delhi must be situated.

### Bazaar Nominalism and Placing Sexual Abnormality

Region by region throughout colonial India, the type, hierarchies, and practice of prostitution varied greatly (see Banerjee 1998; Joardar 1984; Raj 1993; Tambe 2009a). The courtesans of Mughal Delhi were notoriously influential (Dalrymple 2002, 172) and kept aloof from both common prostitutes and the soldiers they serviced; as Major McMahon, the deputy commissioner of Delhi, stated in January 1873, some prostitutes were very poor or very wealthy, yet "a very large number of women would not let a soldier come within a mile of them."[2] These hierarchies had been socially and spatially stable during the supposed "golden calm" of 1803 to 1857, yet after the "Mutiny" of 1857 the decline of court patronage and wealth in Delhi upset this stability (Oldenburg 1990; Pinch 2013). Delhi's most prestigious poet and man of letters, Ghalib, claimed that the female descendants of the last Mughal emperor, if young, were now prostitutes (16 February 1862, in Russel and Islam 1994, 269). Many more women were forced into prostitution following the mass rapes that British officers did little to stop when Delhi was retaken in September 1857 (Dalrymple 2006, 462–63). Three hundred court women, and uncounted concubines, were estimated to have been taken away by British troops.

In Delhi after 1857 an imbalance between the cantonment and municipal systems of registration created an inflow of prostitutes to the municipality from the Fort, which disrupted the existing sociosexual geographies of the city (Legg 2009a). Exacerbating these problems was the increased growth of the city after the announcement in 1911 that the capital was to be transferred to Delhi from Calcutta. As the city became overcrowded, previously autonomous social groups were forced into spatial interaction, in a cultural environment that was wedging codes of indecency and morality between them. Added to this demographic shift was the increased pace of socio-economic change brought about by technological modernization of the city. The early 1900s saw the introduction of radio stations, publications, and cinema halls that all engendered new forms of sexuality and gender. Women could now write, sing, dance, and be viewed on film in public space in ways that transgressed the boundaries of *purdah*. As the most visible and easily assailable embodiment of female sexuality, the prostitute became the target for this more general social unrest. Once it became publicly voiced in one part of the city, it soon spread throughout the walled district. The second section of this chapter will examine how the voluntary associations of civil society cooperated with various branches of the colonial state to *network* the city of Delhi into a sexually striated space. But the city was also a discursive space oppositionally defined against those who offended its civic identity. The *naming* of prostitutes as an inappropriate presence with the apparatus of the modern city marked the start of their abandonment.

The first recorded complaint came on 29 November 1912 from the residents of Egerton Road and Gandi Gali who lodged a complaint about the residence of prostitutes in their bazaars, which were in the very center of the city.[3] The Delhi Municipal Committee (DMC) responded by enacting section 152 of the Punjab Municipalities Act (PMA, III of 1911). This was the most relevant section of the legal apparatus, which could forbid the keeping of a brothel or residence of public prostitutes in any dictated area. However, the areas selected were not just those that had petitioned, but nine of the most prominent bazaars in the city, namely: Chandni Chowk, Khari Baoli, Sadar Bazar Road, Dariba, Egerton Road, Lal Kuan, Paharganj Main, Pai-Walan, and Jama Masjid Square (see map 1.1). However, such extensive action led to a feeling of marginalization among other bazaars in the city, which began their own petitioning. In response, on 27 May 1913, the ban was extended to Church Mission Road, while on 25 November 1913 it was also extended to Katra Barayan. This was after the secretary of Fatehpuri Mosque and the residents of nearby *galis* (lanes) had claimed that three to four houses were disturbing them night and day.

On 16 July 1918 the DMC acknowledged a request made by the residents of Chawri Bazar and Bazar Sita Ram for the removal of prostitutes from those areas. These two interlinked bazaars stretched southwest from the Jama Masjid through the heart of the city and had been, de facto, made into a sort of *lal bazaar* (red market, or red-light district) by the previous pronouncements. These left them as the two largest remaining intramural

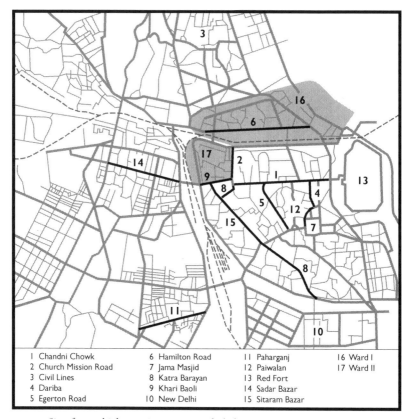

| | | | |
|---|---|---|---|
| 1 Chandni Chowk | 6 Hamilton Road | 11 Paharganj | 16 Ward I |
| 2 Church Mission Road | 7 Jama Masjid | 12 Paiwalan | 17 Ward II |
| 3 Civil Lines | 8 Katra Barayan | 13 Red Fort | |
| 4 Dariba | 9 Khari Baoli | 14 Sadar Bazar | |
| 5 Egerton Road | 10 New Delhi | 15 Sitaram Bazar | |

MAP 1.1. Sites from which prostitutes were excluded

bazaars without prostitution bans. However, the president of the DMC refused to allow the immediate ejection of the women. He indicated that a
location would have to be chosen for the women to which exception would
not be taken, as to remove women from one locality to another without
any defined policy was "not just."[4] This is just one incidence of a recurrent
trend, clearly identified elsewhere in new imperial and feminist historical
research, which belies any Manichean depiction of a solely coercive Raj.
Many deputy commissioners had embraced their positions and tried to
offer a steady hand among competing local interests. This could have disastrous effects, as in the attempts to grant all religions equal procession rights
in the 1880s which led to riots and the disruption of previously harmonious
relationships (Gupta 1981, 131). Yet on this occasion the outcome was to
present some consideration for a group that was being progressively forced
out of its residence, and possibly its occupation.

Municipal Commissioners R. R. Lal Pearey Lal, Syed Bashiruddin, and Mohammed Islamullah Khan were asked to report back to the committee with a solution to the problem, but could not agree on a recommendation. The latter two recommended leaving the prostitutes in place while Pearey Lal suggested that they remain in Bazar Sita Ram but be removed from Chawri Bazar to Burn Bastion Road. This was the first official recognition of the emergent ethos, which dictated that the women be forced out of the city and onto peripheral plots. The site was a commercially developed road, financed by the DMC, where the city wall had been demolished in the west, next to the railway line. The committee certainly had no qualms about using their developments for such purposes; in 1870 the deputy commissioner had suggested that an examination room for prostitutes as part of the Cantonment Regulations system be housed in new offices built by the DMC in Sadar Bazar.[5]

Following this indecision a further subcommittee was established on 24 August to examine where prostitutes could be moved to in the city, and to inquire as to what measures had been taken by municipal committees in Lahore, Ludhiana, and Amritsar. Their report, in line with the process of exclusion Gupta (2001) has noted across north India through the late nineteenth and early twentieth centuries, recommended that the women be excluded from the center of the city and moved to Jhandewalan, a road that was being constructed to the west of the city wall between Sadar Bazar and Paharganj. The recommendation was passed in a resolution on 28 January 1919, with the amendment protestation that Jhandewalan would eventually house three schools, such that Mondhewalan, another road being constructed that would run through Sadar Bazar, be used instead (see map 1.2). The president also added comments that laid out the future policy for the municipality.[6] It was claimed that the object was now the evacuation of prostitutes from the city within two years, apart from Mandi Pan. The only immediate action was that prostitutes from Hamilton Road should be removed. To ensure this, brothel keeping and the residence of prostitutes in wards I and III of the municipality were banned. As the secretary of the DMC explained to the chief commissioner, this area took in roughly the whole of the city north of the railway line and Khari Baoli. To understand why this area had been excluded first, it is necessary to refer to a correspondence that hinted at older links between the military cantonment and the municipality. These links were certainly not defunct by the early 1900s and also give some insight into the experience of prostitution in Delhi at this time.

| | | | |
|---|---|---|---|
| I Ajmeri Gate Bazar | 5 Garstin Bastion Road | 09 Mandi Pan | 13 Sarai Khalil |
| 2 Burn Bastion Road | 6 Jhande Walan | 10 Mondhe Wala | 14 Slaughterhouse |
| 3 Chaori Bazar | 7 Karol Bagh | 11 Motia Khan | 15 Tanda Natniyan |
| 4 Ganda Gali | 8 Malka Ganj | 12 Roshanara Road | 16 Turkman Gate |

MAP 1.2. Sites to be reserved for prostitutes

On 22 October 1918 a letter was sent to the Army Department of the government of India from the Delhi base of the Army Young Men's Christian Association (YMCA) of India, which was situated in the Kingsway Camp to the northwest of the walled city.[7] It was claimed that Delhi "offers very definite attractions to immorality in various ways to British troops" and that many men came to Delhi on leave simply to satisfy their sexual desire. Conversations had been heard among up to twenty men sleeping out of doors at night; the talk was "sheer filth and was often of things done that evening." The men proclaimed they were in for a good holiday if every night should be like the last, and that they planned to stay for three to four weeks. Such talk only confirmed a previously expressed opinion that "among the troops in India Delhi is a byeword for immorality" (on the boredom of soldiers' lives, and the links to sexual proclivity, see Peers 1998, 839).

Placing parts of the city out of bounds had had no effect on the troops, which conformed to an older pattern of military resistance to the government (including men refusing to name who had infected them during the days of the Cantonment Regulations). In particular, men had been visiting Chowri Bazar in the center of the city, and Hamilton Road, which bordered the Civil Lines to the north. Action was requested against both areas. The army member of the government of India instructed that local action be taken, and the chief commissioner was requested on 14 November 1918 to address the situation. While the subcommittee had still not reported back to the DMC by December, enough pressure was obviously put on the committee to ensure that the resolution of January 1919 explicitly targeted Hamilton Road and its environs, although the residents of Chowri Bazar would have to wait until the preparation of a space outside of the city for the ousted prostitutes.

While the residents of Bazar Sita Ram, a prominent bazaar in the south of the city, successfully petitioned for section 152 of the PMA on 27 September 1921, a year later the entire policy of the DMC was reversed. In line with the president's wishes declared in 1919, on 21 November 1922 a special meeting of the Municipal Committee resolved that the *whole* of the municipality was declared prohibited for the residence of public prostitutes except the following areas: Chawri Bazar, Ajmeri Gate Bazar, Mandi Pan, Tanda Natniyan, and all vacant municipal and nazul land next to the slaughter house, outside of Turkman Gate. The selection of the latter locality next to the slaughterhouse was a further slur on the prostitutes, as this was widely considered a polluting site, in terms of physical and social hygiene, for Hindus (Gupta 2001, 112, has shown how butchers and prostitutes were simultaneously excluded from central markets across north India at this time). However, this segregationist policy flew in the face of many other local government policies in British India. The effect of such policies had been widely criticized in Rangoon where segregated areas had supposedly drawn in local men and corrupted the neighboring environment (see chapter 2).[8] Similar protests were soon raised in Delhi, although the effect was simply to dislodge, rather than dissemble, the segregationist policies.

## Petitioning against the Lal Bazaar

In time, similar complaints were raised against the policy as those that had been articulated against segregationist policies throughout India. The problematization came in the form of a petition submitted to the DMC on 22 February 1928 by Municipal Commissioner Lala Madan Mohan Lal.[9] Mohan Lal claimed to have gathered thousands of signatures requesting the removal of the prostitutes from "Chaori Bazar." He explicitly stated that this protest was necessary because women had been expelled from several bazaars throughout the city, forcing the prostitutes into this central locality. As such, it was made clear from the beginning that these tensions were an outcome of municipal policy, yet the vocabulary of the petition drew upon much wider social stereotypes. The petition forms a remarkably concise condensation of the contemporary nominalist powers being marshaled against prostitutes in Delhi.

Mohan Lal submitted a list of fifty reasons why the prostitutes should be removed. Running throughout this justification was a process of identity stigmatization that depicted the prostitutes and the people they attracted as polluting and defiling. Throughout, the common people of the city were described as "respectable ladies and gentlemen" whereas the prostitutes and their acquaintances were variously described as "rascals," "wicked people," and "scoundrels." The points themselves sought to emphasize how incongruous it was to have a socially marginal group in such a spatially central position. The arguments can be classified around those that focused on location and economy, crime, physical hygiene, and, lastly, a form of moral hygiene.

The listing began by stressing the central *location* of Chowri Bazar. Being in the middle of the city, "every person" was compelled to pass through it in order to utilize the various services it provided, including libraries, dispensaries, pharmacies, schools, and orphanages. While the prostitutes had a clear effect on public life, they were also said to encroach upon the private life of local residents. The women and their friends were said to fly kites on the roofs of their houses, and to trespass onto other roofs which troubled local gentleman and violated the purdah of local ladies. This also prevented men from moving about the city via the series of interconnected pathways on the roofs of houses, although no mention of this activity possibly violating purdah itself was made. Intoxicated visitors to the prostitutes were also said to mistakenly enter the apartments of respectable citizens due to the shared staircases.

Beyond the domestic, the bazaar was also an *economic* center for trade in ironware, foodstuffs, and utensils, but "respectable traders" preferred not to go there anymore because of the prevalence of prostitutes. The people attracted to the area also adversely affected the remaining trade. Crowds that gathered in front of the shops below to hear the songs and jokes of the prostitutes were said to steal from the shops and affect the volume of retail in the area in general.

Indeed, the second recurrent feature in the petition referred to *crime*. Theft was said to take place from the nearby shops and residences at night due to the people who were attracted to the area. Mohan Lal's forty-fifth point claimed: "Several doors of *kothas* [apartments] open towards streets, make noises all night and theft cases are to be expected at every moment." Beyond theft, the clientele was said to have led to fights, brick throwing, and murders. The frequenters of the brothels were also said to encourage cocaine traders to ply their trade in the locality, while illegal liquor vendors were also reported. However, the practices that affected the domestic, the economic, and the personally illegal faded in comparison to the complaints regarding public, uncivil behavior.

Few of these complaints referred to the prostitutes themselves. At most, they were accused of using vulgar language while on the rooftops, gambling in public, and quarrelling with each other on the street. The real problem was with the clientele, who were even more foulmouthed, quarrelsome, and disrespectful of public and private space. They were claimed to throw lit matches at the buildings, make noise all night, and break into neighboring apartments when escaping from the police during raids.

When the prostitutes were thought to have a direct effect on the local environment, this was more in terms of hygiene, in the sense by which the term was used in Western medico-moral discourses at the time. In terms of *physical hygiene*, the women were claimed to spit and empty their *paan* refuse into the street, along with tobacco products and the leaves of sweets, which ruined the clothes of the people below. This practice was also claimed to be offensive in terms of religious practice and belief, which hints at the conflation of physical and moral hygiene to which Judy Whitehead (1995) and Gupta (2001) referred. Middle- and upper-caste Hindu concerns with the polluting nature of bodily fluids, combined with the assumption that prostitutes were lower caste, made this action socially as well as biologically threatening.

The presence of mosques and temples in the area was also claimed to make the act of prostitution unacceptable from the perspective of *moral hygiene*, because religious processions of the Hindu, Muslim, and Sikh faiths passed through the area. Prostitutes were also marginalized because of their gender as much as their sexuality; as such, the symbolic role of the virtuous woman was also mobilized against the sex workers. Gentlemen were "prevented" from allowing their ladies to see religious processions in the bazaar due to the presence of the prostitutes, and women could no longer be sent to buy goods in the area. Despite this, ladies were still said to pass through the bazaar on the way to the Jamna River for bathing, although this was held up as a reason to remove the prostitutes from the bazaar. Further religious imagery was mobilized in criticizing the Pathan (Muslims that originated from the northwest of India and Afghanistan) prostitutes. They were claimed to attract further Pathans who fought with each other, threatened local men, and attacked local shopkeepers.

In terms of the effect of the prostitutes on women, the exact nature of the municipal commissioner's fear was not articulated. However, there was a much greater, and more obvious, fear articulated around the effect of the prostitutes on boys. Girls and boys were said to pass through the bazaar on the way to school, while the sons of local shopkeepers were said to "lose their character" after sitting in their shops opposite the brothels all day. A recurrent feature in these points was the displacement of agency from the boys to the women, a common feature throughout the history of the regulation of prostitution which saw women as seducers and transmitters of disease, while men were positioned as victims of a predatory, feminine, public sexuality (Bell 1994). As such, the fact that the houses were linked together and often shared staircases, "so young boys get a chance of going to the kothas of these prostitutes," was articulated as a justification for punishing the *women* with expulsion. Religious ceremonies held in the bazaar below were said to present an opportunity for the prostitutes "and wicked persons" to entice boys into the kothas to play them songs, by which consequently the boys were said to lose their character. Perhaps most astonishingly, prostitutes were claimed to be buying for work in the brothels some girls who were well dressed and decorated, but the emphasis was on the deleterious effect this would have on the local boys, rather than on the treatment of the girls themselves.

As such, the portrayal of the prostitutes placed them as a body of the population that was too dangerous to be centrally positioned, due to their effects on the economy, on crime, on the physical hygiene of the street, and on the social and moral hygiene of the bazaar. The secretary of the Municipal Committee was, however, not so easily convinced. While agreeing that Mohan Lal would gain the support of the social reformists, and that some of his fifty points were cogent, he stressed the need for a practical and legal point of view. It was stressed that section 152 of the PMA did not allow the committee to strip people of their "citizenship," and that they must be allowed to live somewhere in peace. It was clear that the proposal would drive "these unfortunate women" out of the city, but Mandi Pan and

Tanda Natniyan were already full, and the lands around the slaughterhouse were being developed for other purposes. The other proposed territories of Mondhewalan and Jhandewalan were also claimed to be problematic as they would be very important roads one day. The Municipal Committee was thus charged again with finding a suitable place for the prostitutes to stay, while further opinion was sought on the advisability of allowing prostitutes to reside in Chawri Bazar.

Lala Sri Ram, who was in charge of the local police station, concurred with Mohan Lal and argued that "a separate area, at some distance from the populated one, be reserved for these infested women, so that there may be prevention of certain crimes." In particular, these crimes concerned cocaine smuggling, thefts, and assaults on chaste women passing by. Yet hygiene risks were also highlighted, such as the throwing of flesh onto the street, which was both physically and socially repugnant for Hindus. The deputy superintendent of police, with the support of the superintendent, agreed that the prostitutes were misplaced in the areas because "this locality is mostly populated by well to do Hindus and is also a big trade place." As a result of this support, and of complaints also received from the residents of Mandi Pan and Tanda Natniyan, a subcommittee was established to reconsider where the prostitutes could live after the resolution of 22 February 1928 announced that they would be moved from Chowri Bazar, Ajmeri Gate Bazar, "and other popular bazars."[10]

The five-member subcommittee, which included Mohal Lal and Reverend J. C. Chatterjee, undertook a "rough census" of prostitutes in the city and presented their results to the DMC on 9 January 1929.[11] The nature of this data collection was not noted, but the very existence of this exercise acknowledges the perceived need to visualize the problem in spatial terms. Indeed, the DMC policy replaced nineteenth-century attempts to make prostitutes visible through registration with a segregationist policy that only allowed, in theory, prostitutes to be seen in a certain part of the city.

The data suggested that the city contained 405 prostitutes in 245 houses, the distribution of which was listed by ward. Of the fifteen municipal wards, prostitutes were only recognized in seven, of which six were within the city walls. These wards were to the south of Chandni Chowk, with the two most populated intramural wards being divided by Chowri Bazar. The data also suggests that what was being counted was not the number of brothels but individual women, as the ratio of houses to prostitutes was only 64:84, 50:93 and 50:101 in the three most populated wards. While this data could disguise a few large brothels, the language used was, at this stage, addressed to prostitutes, not procurers or pimps. The recommendation based upon this survey was that the prostitutes be removed from the city to ever more peripheral areas. These included Malka Ganj Road in the northern suburb of Sabzi Mandi, and Motia Khan, which was next to the municipal refuse dump, although Garstin Bastion Road and Turkman Gate on the edge of the walled city were also suggested. The final recommendation was that the residence of prostitutes be prohibited from the entire municipality apart from "Karaul Bagh," in the Western Extension (see map 1.2).

However, the subcommittee announced that it had suspended its investigations because the Delhi Health and Social Services Union (DHSSU) had appointed a subcommittee to investigate the same topic. The emergence of the DHSSU (as explored further in the following section) did not mark a significant break in terms of the assumptions about the women or the means of dealing with them. Yet it did mark the beginning of the outsourcing of the regulation of prostitution and the implanting of the belief that sexual issues were perhaps more a social concern of voluntary organizations than of representative political bodies. However, the success of the DHSSU in gaining influence and patronage lies in its hygienist approach not only to the moral and social problem of illicit sexualities but also to the medical and biopolitical problem of venereal disease.

### Siting Sexual Abnormality

The DHSSU "houses of ill fame and venereal diseases" subcommittee met on 20 September 1929 and included Mohan Lal, the DMC petitioner, alongside members of the local press, such as J. N. Sahni and Lala Deshbandhu Gupta, and prominent local figures such as R. B. Mr. Sohan Lal.[12] If Mohan Lal's petition condensed the nominalist powers against the subject of the prostitute, this subcommittee marshaled the power of place naming, adjudicating which places were and were not fit dwellings for prostitutes.

The minutes of the subcommittee noted that it was felt that women of ill fame should be moved swiftly from Chowri Bazar and Ajmeri Gate Bazar but that there was difference of opinion regarding where to "segregate" such women. Seven sites were considered, five of which had been on the DMC's original list before it suspended its activities in favor of the DHSSU. A five-member site-selecting subcommittee was established but came to no agreement. One member suggested that special *mohallas* (urban walled communities) be selected throughout the city in which prostitutes could dwell, with only one gate for exit and entrance, such that any man who wanted to visit the women would be in full view. This idea was rejected by the subcommittee due to the effect such mohallas would have on surrounding communities. They reported that the DMC should be advised to expel prostitutes from the two central bazaars and confine them to smaller areas outside the city (Sarai Khalil in Sadar Bazar, plus Mandi Pan and Mohilla Natniyam), but also that more venereal disease clinics should be established and that propaganda for social hygiene should be propagated among students. Chief Commissioner Thompson commented that sufficient, unsubsidized, re-accommodation should be provided and that opposition would be met, but that expulsion should be enforceable by 1 January 1930.

Despite this, in his speech to the union in early 1930, the chief commissioner acknowledged that many were disappointed at the lack of work achieved by the DHSSU.[13] The DMC had taken time to deliberate the union's suggestions, and only accepted them in a resolution passed on 27 November 1929.[14] While the prostitutes were prohibited from Chawri Bazar and Ajmeri Gate Bazar from 1 June 1930, on 27 June the Executive Finance Subcommittee of the DMC postponed a decision on the use of section 152 of the Punjab Municipalities Act (PMA). A decision was finally made on 21 January 1931 that the whole city would be prohibited for prostitution except Tanda Natniyan, Mandi Pan, and Sarai Khalil. This was the state of affairs in which the legislation would rest for the majority of the 1930s yet, as Thompson had predicted, the prostitutes mobilized various different forms of resistance, to the consternation of another of Delhi's civil society organizations.

The Central Social Services League (CSSL) had been established in 1921 and had worked, among other things, to "sway public opinion in favour of a modern system of sanitation and medicine."[15] In 1927 it had petitioned the deputy commissioner to introduce one of four acts passed elsewhere in India to protect the children of Delhi from the risk of being drawn into prostitution. These were the Bengal Children Act (II of 1922) and the Calcutta SITA (XIII or 1923), or the Bombay Children Act (XIII of 1924) and the Bombay Prevention of Prostitution Act (II of 1923, for the broader impact of this act and the SITA, see the following chapter). But it was made clear that a Lahore High Court ruling on the case of the DMC versus Moti Jan had made it difficult for the former to take action against prostitutes dwelling in respectable areas due to the definition of a "public prostitute" and a "brothel" (defined in a Lahore High Court ruling of 1925 as a place "resorted to by persons of both sexes for the purpose of prostitution and who are strangers to the occupancy").[16] Existing laws in Delhi could not target a prostitute who was employed by another man (and hence not "public"), nor could they target "hotels" or "baths," thus leaving children vulnerable. The deputy commissioner felt the Indian Penal Code was sufficient, however.

The CSSL continued to operate in tandem with the DHSSU and on 7 December 1930 the CSSL board addressed a letter to the chief commissioner.[17] This body was dominated by members of the local legal community, and their point of concern was a suitably legalistic one. The league noted that since the DMC had started evicting prostitutes from central bazaars in the 1920s there had been challenges made in the civil court, in which women claimed they were not "public prostitutes" (see Glover 2007, for further examples of challenges to the term "public" in municipal India). This term had been used in section 152 of the PMA but was never defined. This problem of defining prostitution was an age-old, and empire-wide, one (Levine 2003, 199–229). While the sub-judge and district judge in Delhi had dismissed their case, the high court at Lahore had accepted their appeals and declared them non-amenable to section 152. While it was admitted that the women earned a living by "selling their bodies" and were, as such, prostitutes in the popular sense, they could not be called "public prostitutes" as defined by the PMA. For this, the judge felt that "it must be shown that she is available at any time to the public at large."

The CSSL showed that as long as women in Chowri Bazar could produce one man who they claimed was their partner, the DMC would have to find a respectable person to swear he had engaged in sexual intercourse with these women. An article in October 1931 by Mohammed Hussain in the CSSL journal, *Delhi Social Service*, also stressed that prostitutes were effective at enlisting the active support of their influential patrons (Hussain 1931). What these sources highlight is a different form of resistance to that displayed in the courts. As the CSSL claimed: "Each and every man of the public knows that the women living in Chaori Bazar are public prostitutes and are visited by the public without any hindrance and that they are available to all, yet these women go on residing in prohibited areas."[18] Without moving location or changing their lifestyle, prostitutes in certain areas had found themselves criminalized, and thus their very existence now marked a form of resistance (see Levine 1993, 277–78). The DMC had recently passed a resolution to define a "public prostitute" as a woman who[19]

1. is open to offers of sexual intercourse either occasionally or as a keep
2. resides in a street or exhibits herself to the public such as to give the idea she is inviting custom in sexual intercourse

This marks a classic delimitation of female mobility and independence, secluding prostitutes into the home and protecting the public sensibilities outlined in Mohan Lal's petition. Yet the CSSL wanted an even stricter definition, adding "by repute" to the beginning of the first definition above. The local administration remained skeptical regarding the utility of such an amendment so the chief commissioner wrote to the chief secretary to the governor of the Punjab on 19 January 1931, claiming that the DMC was experiencing "considerable difficulty in dealing with prostitutes in the City" and inquired as to whether there was any intention of amending the PMA. A note in the Delhi administration file from December 1930 suggested that an amendment, though under preparation, was unlikely in the near future. Because of these legal loopholes, and a general lack of funds in the DMC, very little success seems to have been met in expelling the prostitutes from the center of the city in the mid-1930s. Yet this must, in large part, also be due to the active resistance of the women themselves to the DMC's ideal geography of prostitution in the city, as the note continued: "We have seen enough of this difficult question to realise that no laws and orders will achieve the object aimed at. The Municipal machinery has failed and the women complained against have always come off best in a court of law."[20]

### Exclusionary Resistance and Rights

The resistance the prostitutes displayed to the dictates of the DMC in the early 1930s continued throughout the decade and acts as a forceful antidote to the political nihilism that a sole focus on abandonment could bring. In 1936 a petition was submitted to the man charged with establishing a Delhi Improvement Trust, pointing out the failings of existing housing policy. One of these was the failure to provide lodgings for prostitutes in a "red area" outside of the city walls, resulting in Chowri Bazar remaining full of prostitutes, who were spreading into lanes and by-lanes of the area and becoming a "real menace to the well being of society as a whole."[21]

In February 1938 a question was posed in the Legislative Assembly pointing out that Chawri Bazar was a main thoroughfare and asking why the prostitutes had not been removed.[22] The government replied that since November 1930 the area had been prohibited under the PMA section 152 and that the DMC was enforcing this prohibition. However, in April 1938 a chief commissioner's note on file regarding the more effective laws in the Punjab claimed: "The blatant way in which the prostitutes of Chawri Bazar advertise themselves suggests a defiance of authority and in any case is an eyesore to respectable citizens."[23] While the deputy commissioner noted that the Municipal Committee was backing the application of a new law in Delhi to deal with this problem (the Suppression of Immoral Traffic Act, as described in the section below), a legislative adjustment in 1939 allowed the DMC to address the sexual geography of the increasingly congested city.

On 18 February 1939 the *Gazette of India* announced that the PMA had been amended with sections taken from section 42 of the Punjab Act (III of 1933).[24] The section was very similar but increased the pressure for actions regarding the continuance of brothels or habitual prostitution.[25] The renewed attention on the section addressing "disorderly houses and prostitutes" provoked the DMC to increase its efforts given the dismal failure of its policies in the 1930s.

A five-member group that had abandoned all pretense of objectivity and renamed itself the Anti-Prostitution Sub-Committee considered the consequences for the DMC on 16 March 1939.[26] It understood that prostitutes would have to be removed from prohibited areas and issued a fresh notification under section 152. This prohibited the residence of prostitutes and the keeping of brothels except in Tanda Natniyan, as before, although Jhandewalan was supplemented for Mandipan, and Roshanara Road to the northwest of the city was substituted for Sarai Khalil. This increased the area in which prostitutes could dwell but pushed them yet further from the city center. Legal action would be taken against those who didn't comply, as announced through advertisements in the press, handbills and play cards, the beat of drum, and special publicity in the areas where prostitutes resided.

The subcommittee's decision was accepted by the DMC on 1 June 1939 and the prostitutes were given until just 15 July to vacate their homes. The *Hindustan Times* reported this on the following day under the headline "Segregation Scheme for Prostitutes."[27] It was explained that Mandi Pan had been prohibited because it contained two Muslim places of worship nearby, although others claimed that the area was so notorious that no decent man would go there. Other speakers had pointed out that previous eviction attempts had just spread the women further through the city, and that several thousand rupees had already been spent on failed attempts to eject the women from Chawri Bazar. As such, the need for re-accommodation of the prostitutes had been raised, although the locations suggested for the women were ever more peripheral, such as accommodation along the riverbank, or the separate settlement of Shahdara which was actually across the river. It had been suggested that Roshanara Road was a respectable area, but others had countered that it was frequented by persons of dubious morality and was thus, presumably, suitable for prostitutes.

Roshanara Road began at the Ridge, which was north of Old Delhi and formed the western border of the elite Civil Lines area (see map 1.2). It ran to the Ganesh Flour and Birla Cotton Mills, which were in the district of the Sabzi Mandi Fruit and Vegetable Markets. The workers and frequenters there presumably qualified the area for the location of prostitutes. However, the social geography of Delhi was rapidly changing in line with the commercial development of lands outside the congested walled city (Hosagrahar 2005, 132). Roshanara Road also formed part of a Delhi Improvement Trust scheme, the Roshanara Extension in Sabzi Mandi, to the north of the Mughal Roshanara Garden. As such, the area was being transformed by the trust from an industrial and trade zone into a suburb for the city. As Philip Hubbard (1999, 78–79) has commented, the suburbs historically stood as ordered and domestic realms, isolated from the productive space of the city. Additionally, they have been configured as feminine: a space in which to protect women from the threatening masculinity of civic space; the powerless, from the powerful. While the prostitute could destabilize male power by threatening the order of the city, she could have an even more profound effect in the suburbs. While these considerations of the suburbs were particularly Western, they informed the aesthetic and social assumptions of the Delhi Improvement Trust and were taken up by the residents of the area, despite the merchant and industrial pedigree of the district.

On 20 June the Roshanara Ward Welfare Society wrote to the secretary of the DMC promising a civil suit against the committee should prostitutes be forced onto Roshanara Road.[28] This was followed, on 30 June 1939, by about two hundred residents of Roshanara Road visiting the house of the deputy commissioner. The spokesmen consisted of two municipal commissioners, a pleader at the local courts, two members of the local administration, and a Rais (a local notable).[29] They pointed out that five hundred government servants as well as respectable businessmen lived on this road, having built their own houses after buying plots as part of Delhi Municipal Committee and Improvement Trust schemes. "Lady folk" and children were said to take strolls in Roshanara Garden and the Ridge, which proved the rhetorical crux linking the residential area to the protestations against the removal of prostitutes to that area. The spokesman had then listed eleven points against the omission of Roshanara Road from section 152 of the PMA. Although about a fifth of the length of Mohan Lal's earlier petition, many of the same stigmatizations were deployed *against* the expulsion of the prostitutes, focusing on location, crime, and physical and social hygiene.

In terms of location, the asserted respectability of the neighborhood was bolstered with claims about feminine domesticity. The husbands were said to be away from home all day, and it was claimed that the advent of prostitutes would create a sense of insecurity and nervousness in the home. Crime in general was predicted to increase, especially the abuse of cocaine and liquor; the "free use of knives" was predicted, as was general *goondaism* (hooliganism). Emphasis was also placed on the breakdown of civil order with the prediction of insults in the street, especially to the high dignitaries who visited the Roshanara Club. While no direct mention was made of physical hygiene, it was suggested that the women would "infest" the recreational gardens and the Ridge. With regards to issues of moral hygiene the area was said to be too close to the university and colleges to the north and east, posing a threat to adolescents, but also to the Civil Lines, threatening the sensibilities of the elite. Women would be insulted in the street and the prostitutes were also thought to lead to communal trouble. The president of the DMC felt the petitioners had a point, and ordered the Municipal Committee to reconsider the issue.

Before the DMC had a chance to deliberate the Roshanara case, the chief commissioner received a unique deputation. On 9 July about twenty women who resided in Chawri Bazar, and refused the title of prostitutes, formed a deputation to the chief commissioner's bungalow, in an inversive mimicry of the visit by the residents of Roshanara Road. The *Hindustan Times* reported that the women styled themselves as gramophone singers or cinema and radio artistes, and formed a "colourful procession" that marched to the commissioner's home.[30] The chief commissioner insisted, however, that it was a municipal affair and directed the deputation to the deputy commissioner, as president of the DMC. He also refused to give them a hearing, and passed them on to the secretary of the DMC. Yet, as the *Hindustan Times* reported, "the deputationists, however, did not lose heart and invaded the Town Hall."[31] Three were granted entry and put forward their case.

The secretary noted that landlords on Roshanara Road had declined to rent their houses to the women, who feared being left homeless at the deadline of 15 July. The representative stated that the women had inhabited Chawri Bazar since the reign of Her Majesty the Queen Victoria and that they were singing and dancing girls, some of whom were employed by All India Radio Artistes. The secretary was asked to save the women from future detriment, as they were not prostitutes, the residents of Chawri Bazar were happy with them, and no alternative accommodation had been provided. The secretary was impressed with these arguments and, following the Roshanara debacle, decided to launch a(nother) full review of municipal policy. The status quo was maintained in Chawri Bazar, and Roshanara Road was declared prohibited for the practice of prostitution.

However, on hearing of this news, the residents of Chawri Bazar reengaged their eleven-year-old battle to shed their residence of its red-light image. On 18 July the *Hindustan Times* reported that 130 shopkeepers from the bazaar had signed a representation to the secretary of the DMC.[32] It stressed that the presence of the prostitutes in such an important trade area was much disliked, not least because of the concentration of religious and educational buildings in the vicinity. Not only this, but a representation was also sent by an institution on Jhandewalan Road, claiming that the road hosted a temple to the Hindu goddess Durga, which thousands of women attended, and as such was inappropriate for the residence of prostitutes.

The Municipal Committee debated the issue on 20 July 1939, among what the *Hindustan Times* referred to as "recriminations, sweeping allegations and counter-allegations and emphatic denials."[33] Khan Bahadur S. M. Abdulla, who initiated the debate, insisted that protests would now be raised wherever the "dancing girls" were placed, and that a dispassionate, unsentimental, administrative, and utilitarian viewpoint should be adopted. Despite this, the representative from Karol Bagh vigorously rejected any suggestion that the women be moved there. In the face of a locked debate, the president decided to head the final subcommittee, which consisted of two vice presidents and Mr. Jugal Kishore Khanna, a prominent local Congress member.

While the subcommittee made its decision in early September, a municipal debate later in the month highlighted why the decision went against the "dancing girls." Gerry Farrell (1993, 38) has shown that by the early twentieth century traditional courtesans had been forced into the big cities in search of financial support. Here dance, music, and sensual indulgence intertwined in the kothas, while the recording industry was dominated by "unrespectable women." At a DMC meeting on 28 September 1939 Commissioner Dr. C. R. Jayna proposed that professional girls be prohibited from dancing in cinema halls, as it was detrimental to the morals of young men.[34] Unfortunately for the Chawri Bazar petitioners, the municipal counsel noted:

It is a matter of common knowledge that in this country there is a class of women known generally as "public prostitutes" but they call themselves "dancing girls" who habitually allow the use of their

persons for sexual intercourse but do also cultivate the art of singing and dancing as an adjunct as much for purposes of gains as for
additional attraction. . . . This class has from time immemorial been
in turn patronised and ignored and recognised or tolerated and condemned, but all the same it survived and till lately the art of singing
and dancing was confined to it alone.[35]

However, it was acknowledged that a new class of women in modern society was practicing singing and dancing and was without blemish, which
was more than could be said for many of the pictures at the cinema itself.
Moving on from the "ethical" to the "legal" debate, the counsel noted that
no one could be restrained from exercising a lawful profession. While the
DMC could make bylaws to control decency or order, "it should not touch
on the rights of the citizen and must not be *ultra vires* [lying beyond] of the
statute creating it." As such, while the ban itself was beyond the law, the profession of "dancing girls" was still said to be obviously linked to that of prostitution in most cases, and the petitions of Roshanara Road, Jhandewalan,
and Chawri Bazar showed that stigmatic representations of the prostitute
remained common.

As such, on 5 September, having visited various sites, the subcommittee
met and declared that the whole of the municipal area would be banned for
the residence of persons practicing prostitution and keeping brothels, except Garstin Bastion Road, Tanda Natniyan, and Jhandewalan Road.[36] The
recommendations were accepted and declared under the amended section
152 of the PMA on 22 November 1939.[37]

Garstin Bastion Road, or "GB Road," as it became widely known, rose
to infamy in Delhi's social geography as the city's main red-light district
(as it remains today). This locus for local prostitutes, established twenty-
seven years after the first petition was received seeking their expulsion
from Egerton Road, provides a fascinating example of an exceptional space.
This was a space of banishment, not of exile or exclusion. This was not
a disciplinary space, as the women were not placed there under direct or
individual surveillance, nor was this a governmental space in which their
characteristics as a population would be monitored and conducted from a
distance. Rather, it was a space created by law to embody the suspension of
the liberal freedom to choose exactly how to perform one's own profession
but not to suspend the freedom to practice that profession at all. Rather
than being an "unlocalizable" space of exception, GB Road shows exactly

how a material space can become the "threshold in which life and law, outside and inside, become indistinguishable" (Agamben 1998, 19–20, 28–29).

The road itself resulted from the westward expansion of the old city (Hosagrahar 2005, 115–52) that had begun in the 1880s and was taken up by the Delhi Improvement Trust in the 1930s (Legg 2007b, 159). Its development was facilitated by the demolition of the city wall and its replacement with commercial units and a modern thoroughfare. As such, GB Road exists on the very site that previously demarcated what was within and without the city of Delhi. It was neither a residential development, nor a clearly defined commercial project. It benefited from modern design and transportation links, but was also blighted by its location next to the noise, pollution, and hustle of New Delhi Railway Station. An Urdu short story written in the early 1940s by Saadat Hasan Manto described the life of a prostitute in Delhi and contemplated the nature of GB Road: "The houses stood side by side in a long row along the road. Each unit had two floors, with shops on the ground level and flats on the upper floors. The Municipal Committee had allotted these flats to prostitutes so that they would not set up show all over town" (from Manto 1985, 209; also see Mufti 2000, 20).

The brothels and the railway station were seen to be not just complementary, in terms of supply and demand, but also comparable, in relation to the commoditized spaces of modernity: "Sometimes it seems to her as if this world of criss-crossing tracks, of billowing clouds of smoke and steam, is itself a brothel: a crowd of numberless carriages being driven this way or that by a few bloated and self-important steam engines" (Mufti 2000, 23). But in this story the prostitute does not emerge as a mobile and transgressive *flâneuse*, but one who is lost in the anonymous modern spaces of GB Road and whose brothel is constantly under threat from outside. Despite the official sanction of this new space of abandonment, the relocated prostitutes immediately came under attack.

As Khan Bahadur S. M. Abdulla had predicted, within twelve days the first protest had been received.[38] The principal of the Anglo Arabic College wrote to the DMC on 4 December 1939. The college was located outside Ajmeri Gate, at the south end of Garstin Bastion Road, and measures were requested to stop such "undesirable women" occupying the neighborhood, especially in houses overlooking the playing field. Five days later similar complaints were received from Ajmeri Gate residents, and the superintendent of education at Delhi, the honorary secretary of the Anglo Arabic

College. However, the deputy commissioner replied that after mature consideration by the committee there would be no reconsideration in the near future. This was still the case in 1944, when a question was posed in the Legislative Assembly regarding Garstin Bastion Road.[39] The government itself described it as "one of the main roads connecting New Delhi and Old Delhi," but one on which prostitutes would remain. Tellingly, in answering a further question it became obvious that it was the women's recalcitrance that had earned them their location close to the old city. The secretary of the DMC admitted, in a letter to the deputy commissioner on 17 November 1944, that if the women had been sent further away they might have refused and taken up residence in other parts of the city instead.[40] A further question in the Legislative Assembly asked whether it was now safe to pass down the road, given the people who inhabited it, to which the government replied that "only" three people had been killed there in the last five years.

The developments outlined above give a clear sense of the governmentalities through which the prostitutes of colonial Delhi were abandoned. These processes have been analyzed using the literature that has emerged regarding Agamben's "states of exception," with particular qualifications. In terms of *geography*, the spaces of Delhi emerged here as productive, active, and identity forming. The differential levels of surveillance between the Fort and the municipality had originally forced prostitutes into the city, where increasing urban congestion forced them into new and fractious social interactions. It was particular and specific communities that petitioned for the prostitutes to be excluded from the major bazaars, and then from the municipality as a whole, apart from designated spaces of abandonment. The broader shifting geographies of Delhi's suburbs made several of these sites unsuitable, as was the city itself, resulting in the selection of a liminal site of indistinguishable location. It is in this ongoing inclusive exclusion that the intimate relation between the abandoned subject and sovereign power is laid bare. The precariously poised prostitute was exposed to the decision on her exceptional status and location being revised, reversed, and recalled for over twenty-five years before her site of abandonment was finally selected.

While the DMC and the Delhi administration were the main mediators of sovereign power here, its *imbrication* with forms of governmental power was clear. While the prostitutes were marginalized spatially, and excluded legally, this was in large part a response to growing public complaint as the prostitute became stigmatized in civil society. This was embodied in the various protests and petitions which objected to the location of the prostitutes, but they themselves have been shown to be highly effective at *resisting* decisions regarding their exceptional status. Whether through manipulating the civil courts, refusing to move out of the center of the city, or protesting directly to the chief commissioner, these women put forward their rights both as political life (challenging judgments in court) and natural life (demanding somewhere to live). This demonstrated that the precarious position engendered by abandonment was both an individual and collective position that could become a condition of mobilization (Waite 2009).

These acts of resistance occasionally found a favorable hearing within the governmental apparatus, reminding us of the *complexity* of sovereign power when put into action. Rather than stripping prostitutes down to a form of bare life, it was often the government that imbued them with political rights, questioning whether it was "just to remove the women from place to place without any defined policy" (1912) and insisting that all people deserve citizenship and to be "permitted to live somewhere in peace" (1928). Through such acts prostitutes were included in the law at the very moment of their exclusion from the city. But they would be included more forcefully within civil society by a series of voluntary associations that emerged in the 1930s and campaigned for the abolition of tolerated brothels entirely, rather than their containment and segregation at the margins of the city. It is through these bodies that a series of complex relationships will become clear, namely, between civil society and sovereign power, between the state and the institutions it co-opts to govern on its behalf, and between the powers of inclusion and harassment in the diabolical intricacies of civil abandonment.

### The Rescue: Geographies of Inclusion

"Within regimes of civil governmentality, the urban subject is simultaneously empowered and self-disciplined, civil and mobilized, displaced and compensated. Such contradictions constitute the politics of inclusion and indicate the ways in which urban struggles involve much more than 'inside' and 'outside' geographies" (Roy 2009, 161).

#### Social Apparatuses of Security

The foregoing section demonstrated how the exclusion of urban subjects such as the women and children in Delhi associated with prostitution depended on a forceful nominalist process of stigmatizing identities and places. Through these acts of naming these spaces and subjects were included within the purview of abandoning sovereign powers. These nominalist processes of exclusive inclusion were coupled with more explicitly networked processes of inclusive exclusion, whereby connections between philanthropic associations and the colonial state were used to bring women and children forcefully within the securitizing norms of the law, civil society, and the Asra Ghar rescue home. While these networks attest to the urgency with which the natural order of the city had to be constructed, they also thread through the urban with traces and impacts from beyond the city.

While venereal disease rates in Europe and India had declined from the crippling highs of the Victorian era, they were still a contentious issue, especially given eugenicist concerns about their effect on the quality of the population in both India and Britain (Hodges 2006a). In 1916 the Royal Commission on Venereal Diseases had issued its report in London, recommending free testing and treatment for the civilian population and increased efforts to educate the public regarding sexual health. In the early 1920s pressure was brought to bear on colonial governments to replicate these measures, by organizations such as the National Council for Combating Venereal Diseases and the Association for Moral and Social Hygiene.[41]

While voluntary and charitable organizations pressured the Indian government into acting against venereal diseases, they also were taken up as the agencies through which the challenge of these diseases would be met. The DHSSU has already been shown to be the most influential body in Delhi in this regard, but this agent of colonial civil society should not deflect attention from the teeming mass of associations in Delhi more broadly. A confidential survey by the Delhi police produced a list of 171 "Political, Quasi-Political and Religious Societies, Sabhas and Anjumans in the Delhi Province for the year ending 30th June 1918."[42] Their objects ranged from reviving Sanskrit as a medium of speech (the Sanskrit Ojiwui Sabha), to popularizing widow remarriage (the Vesh Bidwah Biwah Sahayak Sabha) to the Arya Samaj, which the senior superintendent of police described as having the ostensible aim of religious and social reform, but the real aim of social reform and political advancement. In the 1920s these organizations would be joined by various new bodies that sought to address the condition of women and would clash with what were seen as the conservative and state-aligned views of colonial civil society.

It was in both this international and local context that the Delhi Health and Social Services Union had emerged in 1928. The DHSSU straddled the social realm and the state, the voluntary and the governmental. While technically a voluntary association, being registered by the Societies Registration Act (XXI of 1860), it had the chief commissioner as its president, the chief medical officer of the Delhi administration as its vice president and listed among its members of the General Committee the assistant director of public health, the civil surgeon of New Delhi, and members of the DMC.[43] The actual Working Committee was headed by the deputy commissioner and contained several members of local standing. Subcommittees were formed to deal with the major issues at hand, and its concerns were divided into different jurisdictions, concerning the government; the Municipal Committee; the DHSSU, to be carried out through separate institutions; and those concerning the DHSSU, to be carried out by its own agency.[44] It was more as this fourth tier of government, than as some autonomous social body, that the DHSSU viewed itself.

The *Civil and Military Gazette* announced the birth of the union on 12 November 1928. The article commented that although Delhi already had charitable institutions, such as the CSSL and the YMCA, their work did not touch public health on a large scale and overlapped in their tasks. As such, the DHSSU was created, with some government funding, to coordinate and mobilize existing bodies in order to improve the general health of the city, while resisting affiliation to any *sabha* (council), samaj (society), or communal grouping. What we see here is not Prakash's (2002) vision of the social government being conducted through "communities," but the self-conscious attempt to create a cooperative civil society that could complement the government's policy initiatives in political society (Chatterjee 2004). The aims of the union were stated to be:

- to bring together people of all communities and organizations interested in the welfare of humanity
- to further the public health education, sanitary improvement, social advancement, and relief of suffering in Delhi
- to coordinate, stimulate, and supplement the activities of different health and social service bodies in Delhi.[45]

The chief commissioner, Mr. John P. Thompson, took an interest in the formation of the union and gave a speech at its opening meeting on 19 November 1928, which was quoted in the *Civil and Military Gazette* and also printed as a pamphlet (Dass 1929). The speech gives some insight not only into the perceived needs of the Delhi community, but also into the nature of its social realm. Mary Poovey (2002, 48) has shown that the social imaginary formed the *a priori* for civil society's representation, informing what could and could not be seen and thought. Thompson displayed the emergence of the social in terms of the objects he chose to address. While many of these objects were the outcome of discrepancies between the economy and society, such as overcrowding, there was perhaps more emphasis on discrepancies between the biopolitical and the social. Thompson claimed that the modern age had seen the birth of two ideas in the popular mind that would influence the future of the human race, namely, preventative medicine and *social* service.[46]

Preventative medicine was described as all that was associated with hygiene (in contrast to purely curative medicine, see chapter 3), with the aim of anticipating disease: "In that idea lies regeneration—the coming race everywhere 100 per cent better than the present one." This echoes Havelock Ellis (1912 [1927]) urging the regeneration of the race through personal and social hygiene in Britain, and Thompson made the comparison back to the metropole directly. He claimed that the United Kingdom was said to have slashed child mortality from 170 to 70 per thousand, raising the vitality of the nation to a higher plane, intellectually as well as physically. This was thought to be possible in India where the popular mind was instructed through leaflets, cinema, and school education.

Regarding his second topic, Thompson paid a compliment to the existing societies, which were evidence of a desire for social service. Yet their efforts had so far been beneath the city's needs, and they had not addressed a sufficient range of problems, which stretched from slum dwelling to cottage industries. The DHSSU planned to promote local action: to coordinate, stimulate, suggest, popularize, and supplement it. In his commentary that accompanied the publication of Thompson's speech, Captain Doctor Jamna Dass stressed that Delhi had to set an example to the country. His objects ranged from the apathy of the masses to preventative diseases, moral degradation, purdah, and untouchables. In conclusion, Dass stressed that government officials should recognize it was their duty to help such movements and should grant them funds, but did not suggest this should be the work of the government itself: "God helps those who help themselves. The Government is not greater than God. The people must help themselves first and prove by their thoughts and actions that they are very serious on these points. They can then not only carry Government with them, but the whole world" (Dass 1929, 18). The union went on to advise the Municipal Committee in how best to deal with the problem of prostitution, as recounted in the previous section. The policy there advocated, of segregation, had proven ineffective and was superseded in the late 1930s by a new wave of legislation that altered the terrain on which the campaign would be launched and further pushed the challenge into the realm of the social.

### Networks of Inclusive Institutions

The Suppression of Immoral Traffic Acts (see the following chapter) provided powers to provincial governments to punish pimps, procurers, and traffickers, but also brothel owners. The SITAS of the 1930s demanded that rescue homes be provided for women and children from brothels, but refused to make the government financially responsible for these homes. The implementation of the legislation therefore demanded that civil society service the state. While such laws further restrained the life world of women involved in prostitution, the major campaigners for the introduction of the SITAS were members of organizations run by women. In Delhi, these organizations were dominated by two bodies that sought to sway the opinions of subordinate bodies—namely, the Association for Moral and Social Hygiene (AMSH) and the Delhi Women's League. The former established an office in Delhi in 1932 in order to pursue its abolitionist program, as directed and funded by the AMSH headquarters in London, but increasingly by the government of India in New Delhi (see chapter 4). This intertwining with the state was very much opposed to the origins and functioning of the Delhi Women's League (DWL, as described in the introduction) which had been campaigning for the application of a SITA and the creation of a state-aided rescue home. This was, in part, a result of stimulation from the central AIWC, but the inspiration also came from farther afield. For instance, on 4 December 1934 the head of the DWL passed on a resolution to the deputy commissioner condemning the abduction of women, trafficking, and child marriage.[47] The Delhi administration was urged to take action but also to send, in reply, a copy of the League of Nations' report, *Trafficking in Women and Children in the East*. The dense networking of institutions was, therefore, interwoven into national and international debates about trafficking and prostitution, but became focused on a micro-urban demand for a particular, vital space.

On 18 July 1936 the *Hindustan Times* published an article entitled "Delhi Needs a Rescue Home." Commenting upon failed attempts by Lady Shrivastava outside of Delhi to elicit funding from the government for rescue homes, the article claimed: "All she got was lip-sympathy, with which the Government is always very lavish." As such, local philanthropists and the DWL were called upon to provide a home for rescued girls and to investigate ashrams which were selling children into the trade. Aruna Asaf Ali, secretary of the league, claimed in her printed reply of 21 July that the ashrams were the business of the police, and that lack of funds prevented the DWL from helping the victims of trafficking. The Delhi Provincial Council of Women was also campaigning in the late 1930s against trafficking and for a rescue home, although this elitist institution had less in common with the provocative DWL than with the AMSH. The institutions often worked in sync, with Meliscent Shephard joining the DPCW at its invitation in early 1933, writing back to the secretary of the AMSH in London that "these women I think I can use as a centre for spreading information. They are the wealthier and official group."[48] She also worked to penetrate the Central Social Service League, which had complained about the DMC's inability to use the law to force prostitutes out of the central city in 1930. The league had sent its reports and journal, the *Delhi Social Service*, to Alison Neilans in London, who wrote to Shephard on 15 February 1933 urging her to "put these people right."[49] Summarizing the league's perspective, she wrote of the CSSL that "it was of the opinion that out of the three methods—segregation, regulation and abolition, the abolitionist policy has failed in every part of the world and that the existence of prostitutes is found from time immemorial in every part of the world. The Sub-Committee came to the conclusion that the League should undertake the segregation policy in hand at present."[50]

The AMSH believed the CSSL to have confused the abolition of prostitution (which had always failed) with the abolition of tolerated brothels (which the AMSH was campaigning for).[51] Shephard quickly got in touch and distributed publications among the committee. By early March she was claiming that the CSSL secretary had renounced segregationism in favor of abolitionism.[52] Within the year, Shephard had produced a pamphlet under the auspices of the CSSL entitled *Methods of Dealing with Commercialised Prostitution*.[53] The pamphlet evoked sources including Josephine Butler, the League of Nations, and the All India Vigilance Association to promote abolitionism and the foundation of a Delhi branch of the AMSH.

On 28 April 1933 Shephard wrote to Neilans that she was on the verge of securing an "informed and abolitionist-minded group" in Delhi.[54] Chief Commissioner J. N. G. Johnson had given his unofficial backing, as had the secretary of the DMC and ten of the thirty-eight committee members, and (the "crux" of the matter) Mohammed Hussain, who renounced his stance on segregationism as expressed in the CSSL journal (Hussain 1931). She also converted Mohammad-u-Din Malik from segregationism to abolitionism, and convinced him to publish excerpts from the League of Nations' Far

Eastern report on brothels for public dissemination. Therefore, within five months of arriving in Delhi, Shephard had infiltrated and swayed a committed segregationist organization, which also had strong links to the DMC.

This rapid rise to prominence would not continue unhindered, however. Although Shephard had acted as a delegate for the DWL at the AIWC meetings of 1934 in Calcutta and of 1934–35 in Karachi, it was at these sessions that clear differences emerged between the approach of the AMSH and the AIWC. At the 1934–35 session Shephard suggested that moral education was the solution to the problem of prostitution in India, while prominent Congress female campaigner Kamaladevi Chattopadhyay argued forcefully that the real cause was economic (see chapter 3). The welcome address of the conference by Mrs. Homi N. R. Mehta had also criticized the persecution of prostitutes, leaving men to walk free and enact laws against them through a state that offered little protection to women or children.

These approaches, which singled out the state and its economic failures as the root cause of trafficking, were at odds with Shephard's approach, which tended to focus on failures in Indian society. These differences bubbled under the surface but would reemerge in the late 1930s as the passing of the Delhi SITA placed greater pressure on the cooperation and commitment of the voluntary sector. Until then, however, Shephard continued to work alongside the DWL, being invited by Aruna Asaf Ali to address a public meeting regarding the need for a rescue home or ashram in July 1936.[55] Asaf Ali publicly declared that, alongside the efforts of the police, "if bodies like the Delhi Women's League and the Association for the Development of Moral and Social Hygiene and the authorities concerned can evolve some method of co-operation, efforts to root out the evil may prove fruitful."[56] Shephard's report for July 1936–37 claimed that she had joined Asaf Ali in this spirit of cooperation by taking part in the investigation of ashrams and segregated vice areas.[57]

Despite this apparent bonhomie, Shephard remained acutely aware of the heightening nationalist sentiment in the city following the Government of India Act in 1935 and the prospect of local elections in 1937. In a letter to Alison Neilans, secretary of the AMSH, on 14 April 1936 Shephard stressed: "You see, the political situation is such that it is practically impossible now for any *nationalist* group of men or women to *say* that they want a society with roots in England to stay here. So we do not ask the question. Yet they remain perfectly friendly."[58] She listed among her recent visitors Asaf Ali, Mrs. Brijlal Nehru, Rajkumari Amrit Kaul, and Begam Shah Nawaz, members of Delhi's nationalist elite. She also demarcated the "waverers," like Mrs. Hannah Sen, the principal of Lady Irwin College, who would "jump with the majority," and "chaos makers," like Kamladevi Chattopadhyay, who had challenged her emphasis on education at the 1934–35 AIWC meeting.

Shephard would, however, insist on defending the actions of the government. Following the "lip-sympathy" *Hindustan Times* editorial (mentioned above), she wrote to the editor on 24 July 1936 claiming that the government sponsored a rescue home in Haldwani and was considering another in Meerut, and that a correction should be printed.[59] Despite attempts to immerse herself into the local voluntary sector, Shephard remained attached to the state, in terms of both funding and a desire to reform the legal apparatus (see the final section of chapter 3).

### Military, Municipal, and Moral Networks

In May 1935, Meliscent Shephard had returned to Delhi, having been in Simla assisting a select committee discussing the Punjab SITA.[60] In December 1935 she sent a copy of this SITA to Delhi's chief commissioner suggesting its application.[61] He remarked in a note on 24 March 1936 that it would be incongruous to apply an act to Delhi that had not been given a try in the province in which it was passed, and that Delhi would have to wait. While there was no immediate action, by 1938 pressure was mounting for change. The central government was pressing each province to display what it had been doing to tackle trafficking and the exploitation of prostitution, following pressure from the League of Nations.[62] In addition, the Home Department also wrote to the Delhi administration in February 1938 requesting the chief commissioner's position on SITAs, which he claimed to be considering.[63]

Pressure was also being applied by the military. An internal discussion in January 1938 established the need to check the spread of venereal diseases yet, rather than turning to clinics or propaganda, the emphasis had returned to the traditional ground of controlling and limiting prostitution.[64] On 17 January 1938 local army commanders were asked to suggest what powers they thought were necessary to control and limit prostitution, and thereby check the spread of venereal diseases among the troops. This was in response to prompting from the adjutant general on 5 January regarding the desirability of making prostitution in public places punishable civil offenses.

Despite the previous clashes of the army and the AMSH over military regulation of prostitution, the army recommended exactly the same powers that Shephard had been championing. The brigadier commander at Delhi Cantonment wrote to the chief commissioner on 6 March 1938 stating that it was the opinion of the military that the Punjab SITA would be of great use in preventing prostitution in Delhi, and thus reducing venereal diseases.[65] Given what the chief commissioner considered to be the drastic powers, and thus obligations, of the SITA, he tried to delay. His conviction was fortified when it transpired in May 1938 that the Punjab government itself, while retaining the ability to discontinue certain brothels in Rohtak, Gurgaon, Simla, Ambala, Amritsar, and Lahore, had not applied section 4 of the SITA, which demanded the closing of all brothels, due to "public opinion and existing conditions generally."[66]

However, the chief commissioner received prompts from the military on 19 April, 30 May, 8 June, and 24 August 1938 and from the Home Department on 15 September. He finally replied to the home secretary on 1 November 1938 following further correspondence with the Punjab on the working of its SITA. He claimed that local opinion was not yet strong enough to stand up to the vested interests that supported prostitution, but that he had no problem with the act being extended, providing section 4 *was* included. As such, the Punjab SITA was extended to Delhi on 26 November 1938, yet this only made the powers available for implementation. The chief commissioner refused to apply the act until the area to be tackled was decided and some provision was made for the treatment of rescued girls.

Before a SITA was extended to Delhi in November 1938, the government of India had made it clear that it considered the act to be situated in the contested terrain between the state and the social. In response to a question in the Legislative Assembly in October 1936 regarding whether there had been any retraining of fallen women across India, the home member Sir Henry Craik commented: "Not by Government. This appears to be more a matter for private or municipal enterprise than Government action."[67] Delhi's chief commissioner agreed, writing to the home secretary on 1 November 1938 that section 17 of the SITA, requiring the treatment of girls rescued from brothels, would be work for voluntary associations.[68] He would later claim that the main justification for funding the AMSH was not just that it advised on SITAs, but that it stimulated the DPCW and the DWL into action regarding rescue work, despite their long-standing commitment to this work themselves.[69] Shephard herself, in a statement on the history of the Asra Ghar, stressed that the DPCW had begun investigations on the topic in 1929, while Shephard only started such work in 1933.[70] Indeed, the only existing home was the Seva Sadan run by Mrs. Raj Dalari Sharma, an active member of the DWL, as recognized at their conference of 1935.[71] In addition, on 23 June 1936 Asaf Ali visited Shephard and asked her to collaborate with the DWL in its efforts to raise funds for a rescue home, rather than the initiative being the other way around.[72]

The responsibility of housing rescued girls brought with it great pressures and demands, forcing to the surface the inherent tensions between the AMSH and the DWL, which were exacerbated by the increasingly nationalistic and anticolonial political atmosphere. Shephard claimed, in a report on her work, that before her stay in England between May and October 1938, she had been asked by the DWL and DPCW to appoint three ladies to serve on an investigating committee with the chief commissioner.[73] However, while she was away, the DWL refused to cooperate in the inquiry having not been officially appointed by the chief commissioner. It was the increasing antagonism between these two bodies that would eventually undermine the rescue home that was so central to the functioning of the SITA.

In November 1938 the Delhi Provincial Council of Women had requested the application of the Punjab SITA to Delhi. On the chief commissioner's recommendation, following the introduction of the act that month, the DPCW invited Miss Shephard, of the AMSH, to explain the act to its members on 20 December. At the general meeting of the DPCW on 8 February 1939, Shephard summarized the local conditions again and took women around the brothel areas. She furthered her attempts to unify the local bodies, under the aegis of the AMSH, by requesting that the chief commissioner call a meeting of representatives from the various social service groups in Delhi to ask them to found a rescue home.[74] The institutions themselves were also penetrated and interlinked by the AMSH; Shephard served as convenor of a DPCW subcommittee on rescue work and was invited to join the DWL subcommittee on trafficking.[75] Shephard also pressed the chief commissioner himself for action, forwarding details on 7 March 1939 of the local government funds given to girls' homes in Madras.[76]

This was a critical time within the politics of prostitution in Delhi. Since April 1938 Shephard had been working with the Delhi Municipal Committee as part of their Anti-Prostitution Subcommittee.[77] On 16 March 1939 the committee submitted its report, as described above, and by 1 June prostitutes had been given their six weeks' eviction notice from the walled city. The entire geography of prostitution was in flux at this time and Shephard had cannily situated herself at the fulcrum of the purging and rescuing urges of the city. With the prostitutes unsettled and disoriented, all that was now required was the ability to intervene with the legislative powers of brothel closure and infant confiscation that a SITA could bestow to ensure the inclusive exclusion of a large body of Delhi's prostitutes.

The registrar of the Delhi administration admitted on 18 March that the SITA had still not been applied due to the lack of facilities for the care of brothel inmates and destitute women and girls, as dictated under section 17. It was agreed that a small grant of Rs 200 would be made to the AMSH in relation to this matter and the deputy commissioner argued on 31 March that section 17 of the SITA could not be framed until it was known what sort of rescue home the social works in Delhi could promise. To this end, the DCPW and National Council of Women in India met on 26 March at the town hall where Aruna Asaf Ali spoke on the need for a rescue home and public funds. A subcommittee to discuss the formation of a home was created under the auspices of the DCPW and the Delhi Women's League.[78]

Sensing that the burden of caring for the girls was being shifted from the state to the social realm, the chief commissioner wrote to a host of local voluntary associations on 6 April 1939. Rather than local communal or community-based organizations, these were elite organizations that, like the DHSSU, could serve as an unofficial level of government without being formal apparatuses of the state. The associations were the DPCW, DWL, St. Stephen's College, Children's Aid Society, Young Women's Christian Association, Central Social Service League, Minto Road Club, Women's Christian Temperance Union, and the Delhi Health Society.[79] It was stated that the SITA could not be applied until section 17 was catered to and that "in my opinion rescue work is essentially a matter for social service organisations working with or without Government aid." The DPCW and DWL were praised for their interest, and an explanation of the SITA circulated at the meeting on 17 April.

Building upon this momentum, a meeting was held at the New Delhi town hall on 18 April 1939, with all the highest members of the Delhi administration, the New Delhi Municipal Committee (NDMC), and the DMC in attendance. Representatives from the local voluntary associations were also present, as was Shephard. The DPCW had called a meeting the day before at the Delhi Women's League's residence, Saraswati Bhavan, in Daryaganj. Influential Delhi women such as Mrs. Sultan Singh mixed with nationalist figures like Sarojini Naidu and Aruna Asaf Ali and institutional figures like Shephard. The AMSH took the minutes at the meeting and noted that organizations in Madras and Lahore had been consulted in order to frame the number of staff the house would need and the nature of care required. The New Delhi town hall meeting decided that the property should be given free from rent, and that it would cost Rs 3,000 a year and Rs 6,000 in the first year.[80]

Discussion the following day turned again in favor of civil society rather than traditional communities. The argument in favor of faith-based institutions like the Salvation Army, Arya Samaj (a Hindu society), or the Islamia Orphanages (Muslim-run homes) was rejected in favor of nondenominational homes run by social workers with some public funds. While in part this was due to political fears of communal or Christian missionary conversions, it also followed police investigations prompted by a *Hindustan Times* article on 4 July 1935 entitled "Scandal of Rescue Homes in Delhi." The article reported a letter from the Katra Neel Welfare Society to the deputy commissioner which had suggested that over one hundred "widows and rescue homes" existed in Delhi, where girls were sold to the highest bidder, under the garb of marriage. The police compiled a report on rescue homes and ashrams in Delhi City for the deputy commissioner, which detailed a wide variety of organizations, many of which were suspected of illegal activity.[81] In summary the deputy superintendent of police for the city suggested that many of the homes originated in widow remarriage efforts of the Arya Samaj forty to fifty years earlier. Some had, by the 1930s, become depots for holding low-caste women from the Central and United Provinces and the Princely States who were bought for marriage, often by Punjab families. One orphanage ashram in Bazar Sita Ram Bazar was described as a "regular seat of Barda Faroshi" (an urdu term for slave trading, used to refer to trafficking in women; see the following chapter). Detailed descriptions of nine ashrams throughout the city were given. While not all were condemned, details of failed legal cases against the ashrams brought to light tales of women being tempted away from shops, the railway station and tonga stands, cinemas, *sarais*, hotels, *dharamsalas*, and Jumna ghats (bathing platforms at the river's edge), and being forcibly detained in ashrams, where many were raped by staff and patrons. These stories were revealed after some of the women escaped, while one was rescued by her brother-in-law who reportedly changed his name and worked in the ashram as a servant in order to find her out. The report concluded that these homes were in addition to the regular brothels where "unfortunate women" are brought, often by agencies of *barda faroshes* who moved women and girls between cities. In reporting to the chief commissioner in November 1935, however, the deputy commissioner insisted that the evil was "largely social and can only be eradicated by the pressure of public opinion," by changing views on widow remarriage and challenging local vested interests.

The deputy commissioner had forwarded the police report on to Meliscent Shephard in December 1935 and it had no doubt fortified her belief that a new type of rescue home would be required. Shephard went on to form the Delhi Provisional Committee for Rescue Work on 9 May 1939. She acknowledged the decade of work already done by local bodies such as the DPCW and the Central Social Services League, yet clearly marked out the AMSH as the central organizer. The meeting contained a dazzling array of voluntary associations, adding to those already mentioned the representatives of Lady Hardinge Hospital, the Bengali Club, the Teacher's Hostel, and the Baptist Mission of Daryaganj.[82] The committee produced a pamphlet for popular circulation in Hindu, English, and Urdu, advocating the formation of the Asra Ghar.

### The Rescue Home

It was decided that the Delhi Women's Rescue Home would be located on Rajpore Road, in the Civil Lines, as a shelter for girls and women who had sought or needed help and who wished to earn an honorable living. It was a stark materialization of the inclusionary urge at the dialectical heart of Delhi's civil abandonment of its prostitutes, testifying to the ever-present disciplinary institutions that track and augment security apparatuses. The home was to be run on "strict disciplinary lines" and would not be like other ashrams of the past, such as the one on Chawri Bazar from which boys had been rescued in July 1939. The home was said to need Rs 10,000 a year, against the Delhi administration's initial offer of Rs 200, and donations were requested. However, as the home took shape, certain questions arose for the local government, which harked back to nineteenth-century debates on the coercion and confinement of prostitutes. On 10 May the chief commissioner had written to the home member for legal advice.[83] He claimed that the SITA nowhere expressly provided that the girls could be *detained* in rescue homes or the like, and that detention was essential if the girls were to be protected. The Legislative Department noted that the Punjab SITA was deficient in terms of allowing the custody of a girl and that any powers to "curtail personal liberty" would have to be clearly written in law and that the chief commissioner's suggested draft rules would stand up in court.[84]

With her usual perspicacity with regard to the chief commissioner's affairs, Miss Shephard wrote to him on 6 July following a recent scandal in the *Hindustan Times* regarding the prosecution of an underage prostitute.[85] Addressing the safe custody of girls, Shephard warned the commissioner against introducing clauses that would mean that the victim was compulsorily confined in a named institution for a number of years against her consent. As such, on 21 July a note on file recorded that Shephard had suggested the United Province SITA (VIII of 1933) for use in Delhi.[86]

Despite this, on 2 August the chief commissioner wrote to the home secretary having looked through the United Provinces and Bengal SITAS, both of which allowed the detention of girls. The chief commissioner decided on the latter, with the Punjab SITA having fallen off the schedule in May 1939 because its implementation had been delayed for so long.[87] As the necessary amendments were worked on, Shephard wrote to the chief commissioner with her own suggested amendments on 16 November 1939, and again to the secretary of the Legislative Department on 15 December.[88] However, these changes were considered too radical. As the chief commissioner wrote to the home secretary on February 1940: "No attempt has been made in the past in Delhi to control brothels or to deal with prostitution, and it is evident to me, but perhaps not to Miss Shephard, that the effect of the act must be gradual."[89]

The Bengal SITA was notified in Delhi on 28 December 1939 and applied on 26 March 1940. The act punished the keeping of a brothel as defined by the superintendent of police, whose decision would be final and unquestionable.[90] The SITA also punished solicitation, living on the earnings of prostitution, procurement, importing women for prostitution, and detention of prostitutes. In the case of the latter, girls aged under sixteen could be removed and placed in the custody of a suitable agency who would have the powers of a parent over her. The chief commissioner placed extra rules in the schedule of the Delhi SITA to clarify the conduct of such approved institutions. When someone was removed from a brothel, the first action was to test the girl for venereal diseases in the nearest women's hospital, and to register her as an outpatient for treatment if necessary. The girls were to be protected from "evil influences" and be provided with a separate bed, clothes, wholesome food, and suitable education and employment such as housework or sewing. No girl would be allowed visitors or letters without the permission of the head of the institution and any necessary visits to the police or a court would require accompaniement by a member of staff. The only approved institution was the Rajpore Road Asra Ghar.

The Delhi Provisional Committee for Rescue Work's wish that the home be run on "strict disciplinary lines" had certainly been granted. It would be a mistake to portray the home as unnecessarily punitive as there *had* been terrible abuses of children in brothels throughout India and the rules were as much to protect the children as to prevent them leaving. The home itself was designed as an amalgam of a workhouse, a lock hospital, and the reformatory Magdalene Homes of the pre-1900s (Ogborn 1998; Bartley 2000; Mahood 1990). In line with the shift from solely medical notions of physical hygiene to moral and social hygiene discourses, the women were also trained in self-conduct as with the reformatory homes of Victorian Britain, while the senior superintendent of police vetted any visitors. However, women and girls always had the option of leaving these homes in the United Kingdom, although they would be passed on to the more disciplinary lock asylums should they be infected (Mahood 1990, 76). Yet, in the Delhi home, as in the lock hospitals of the Cantonment Regulations, girls were incarcerated and cured of disease. Rather than being an anomaly, this example fits into a long tradition of colonial disciplinary institutions being more carceral and segregated than their European equivalents, even if the colonies were what Prakash (1999, 13) termed overextended and underfunded laboratories of modernity.

As with many such carceral yet poor institutions, the Asra Ghar was declared a failure just a year after its official sanction and closed down in May 1942.[91] Many homes had met a similar fate in the United Kingdom, with reform penitentiaries and preventative strategies giving way to social purist attempts at suppression in the twentieth century, as embodied in India by the SITAs. Mrs. Chatterjee, the nominated visitor, claimed that the home had failed to achieve its purpose and was wasting its public funds, that is, the NDMC grant of Rs 600, the DMC grant of Rs 10 per month per girl and the central grant of Rs 200. The chief commissioner, due to the home having so few "inmates," suspended his grant in June 1941. This was despite the claims of those who ran the home that the police and magistrates had not been making enough detention orders. The DPCW issued to the chief commissioner a plea for more funds in November but received a curt reply on 3 December claiming that few people thought the home justified its existence so far as it was. Shephard replied on 8 December, on behalf of the renamed Delhi Asra Ghar Association, claiming that a school for fifty children had been organized in the last year and twenty-eight girls had been helped in the home in the past two years. Paula Bartley (2000, 29) has shown that this was not inconsiderable for a new home, with most homes having around twenty women in the United Kingdom. Shephard (1948) later publicly commented that unspecified "political unrest" had doomed the home.

In private correspondence Shephard was less discreet and more bitter. A letter from August 1945 to Sir Francis Mudie, the secretary of the Home

Department, claimed: "We organised with full representation from every community and wholly Indian management, a well-run Rescue Home called the Delhi Ashra Ghar. This was closed in 1942 largely owing to the propaganda against it, inspired by Mrs Asaf Ali, Mrs Hannah Sen, and their politically-minded friends. Lady Glancy and I did our best to keep the Home going."[92] By 1941 Asaf Ali had thrown herself into the Congress protest against Britain's decision to enroll India into the war, and in 1942 would distinguish herself as one of India's most controversial and elusive freedom fighters in the Quit India movement. Hannah Sen was a more conservative figure, but still a committed nationalist.[93] As the principal of Lady Irwin College she was the head of Delhi's flagship female educative institution, but promoted Congress values to her girls and kept in contact with Asaf Ali when she went underground during the Quit Indian movement. Although earlier categorized by Shephard as a "waverer," Sen had a history of speaking out against "imperial feminists" who saw fit to proclaim their views on Indian sexuality (see Woollacott 1999, for Sen's comments in 1930 on the "Mother India" controversy). Left with only Lady Glancy of the DPCW, Shephard found the voluntary work in Delhi split not only along lines of class but also of race, which condemned the rescue home to closure.

On 18 May 1942 an emergency meeting of the association was prompted by a letter from the Marchioness Linlithgow, the vicereine. The remaining Rs 400 of the vicereine's donation was given to the AMSH to benefit distressed and destitute women and girls in Delhi, and the Asra Ghar disbanded. The AMSH later reported that many women who needed assistance would be left without help, but that the General Committee would budget financial help for those desperately in need.[94] The financial stringency and political unrest associated with the closure of the home must be associated with the wartime conditions. Yet these conditions also led to a rise in the number of prostitutes as Indian, British, and American troops gathered in Delhi. This increased the need for SITA-level action, yet the policies of the DMC and Delhi administration remained paralyzed until independence in 1947.[95]

This condition of stasis did not go unnoticed, and a series of questions in the Legislative Assembly was posed regarding trafficking and prostitution in Delhi by Shrimati K. RadhaBai Subbarayan of Madras in February 1945.[96] Subbarayan was a conservative suffrage campaigner, who became an elected minister in 1937 and was a central figure in Indian National Congress circles in the 1940s (Candy 2000). The questions she posed asked whether the government was aware of the increase in brothels and trafficking in the capital and the threat this posed to the local female population and whether the government maintained a rescue home. The government had to admit that there had been an increase in the number of brothels and prostitutes in Delhi and that there was no specially designed home for reclaimed prostitutes. Mrs. Subbarayan was in contact with Shephard and wrote to her on 3 June 1945 exclaiming her surprise that such a state of affairs existed next to the office of the AMSH in India. The responses of the Delhi administration and of Shephard herself illustrate the legislative, personal, and policy deadlock that had been reached.

The closure of the Asra Ghar and Shephard's laying of the blame for this on the shoulders of Delhi's female anticolonialists seems to have attached her more than ever to the state. She forwarded Subbarayan's letter to Sir Francis Mudie of the Home Department under the pretext that "since fore-warned is fore-armed" his colleagues should be braced for further criticism. She defended the activities of the AMSH in Delhi, insisting that the closure of the Asra Ghar had been politically motivated, and wrote: "There has been nothing done to stop any Indian social workers from starting a Reclamation Home for Prostitutes. There is one place in Rajpur Road which a dentist helps to run, but it is *not* satisfactory and should be *closed*." She went on to comment that Mrs. Subbarayan was not listed as an active welfare worker in her own district nor had she visited any of the reclamation homes there.

While nationalist opinion appears to have swung against Shephard in Delhi, there also seems to have been a policy shift against her abolitionist vision in the Delhi administration. In response to Subbarayan's question, the Home Department of the central government recognized the need for action against brothels and seemed willing, in June 1945, to consider a grant to Shephard to reestablish a home, and sought the advice of the chief commissioner.[97] He passed on a letter from the deputy commissioner, communicating the views of the Delhi Municipal Committee, speaking as its president. What he stressed, in a letter of 16 May 1945, was that there was a clear lack of central policy regarding the treatment of brothels and prostitution. While the wider view supposedly suggested the "total elimination" of prostitution as policy (a still common misreading of the attempt to abolish tolerate brothels), this only drove the practice underground. In contrast "the policy adopted by the Delhi Municipal Committee, which may be considered representative of public opinion in this respect, in [*sic*, is] segregation of prostitutes to certain areas, but this policy has only been enforced with very limited success and the staff employed for this purpose is totally inadequate. Nevertheless the policy of segregation and consequent limitation of the vice seems to me to be a practical step in the right direction."[98]

The deputy commissioner went on that if the government followed the DMC in recognizing the existence of brothel areas for caste prostitutes, it could do some useful welfare and propaganda work (his suggestion was to limit prostitution to "low-caste" women who had habitually practiced it and forbid it to other "strata" of society).[99] If these steps seemed regressive in terms of the AMSH's vision, even more radical steps were proposed with regards to sexual health. Wartime conditions had led to a steep increase in military personnel in Delhi, and a proportionate increase in concern about venereal diseases. While the British seemed relatively content with the situation in Delhi, the presence of the U.S. Air Force in 1944 shone a light on some of Delhi's more extraordinary prostitution geographies. Tongawallas had been taking women to "unfrequented" areas, then picking up members of the armed forces, taking them to the spot for forty-five minutes, then returning and collecting more men while the women moved on to another prearranged spot.[100] American soldiers reported to their military police that they had been solicited in the very heart of the capital, in a park at the intersection of Kingsway and Queensway (today's Raj Path and Jan Path, next to the National Archives). The U.S. military police raided the park on 8 February and handed over three tongas and nine women (Rozi, Sultana, Shanti, Maya, Waziro, Shankuntla, Ganga, Katoria, and Lila) to the New Delhi police station. The reporting officer claimed that several American soldiers made their getaways in tongas, while he had personally seen one "girl" having intercourse with a soldier. The following day three American soldiers and five additional "prostitutes" were arrested at the same spot, in what was referred to as a "routine check of suspected out-door brothels." The deputy commissioner noted that the Bengal SITA provided powers against solicitation in Delhi, yet the age-old problem of the "clandestine prostitute" seemed to be as evasive as ever. But if the problems seemed to be unchanging, so did some of the planned responses.

Lieutenant Colonel A. N. Chopra was appointed as officer on special duty with regard to medical relief and public health in Delhi Province, and produced his *Delhi Health Development Plan* in 1945.[101] In terms of venereal diseases, three points of action were noted. Two regarded regulative actions for the population, namely free diagnosis, treatment, and education. However, the third proposal regarded much stricter measures for the notification of disease, and special disciplinary measures for prostitutes in line with Lieutenant Chopra's military background. These measures harked back eighty years to the language of the Contagious Diseases Acts, and suggested that "all the prostitutes should be required to get themselves registered and medically examined. They should keep with them the medical certificate which should be open to inspection by authorised persons. They should keep a prophylactic kit for their use. They should be examined at regular intervals at the brothels and treatment afforded."[102]

It has, therefore, clearly been shown that the interwar years saw the prostitutes of Delhi systematically excluded as their collective *name* became increasingly stigmatized. They were excluded from the city, their sites of occupation (such as the street or the brothel), from self-definition (as artistes or dancers), from economic self-sufficiency, and, most fundamentally, from equal moral standards between men and women. Yet, as a constituent feature of this exclusion, they were simultaneously included within *networks* of the state and civil society. The local government stepped in to defend their rights as citizens, while they themselves used the legal apparatus to negotiate the degree and location of their abandonment. In terms of civil society, it was exactly at the moment that prostitutes were forced out of urban space that they became central to the discursive space of the emergent middle classes. The prostitute embodied the problem of hygiene, of self-conduct, and of disease which Delhi's voluntary associations debated at length. But the re-inclusion of the prostitute in the city was not just discursive; "rescued" girls were also physically reclaimed from the fearful site of the brothel.

The processes of petitioning, resistance, siting, and sexuality have been shown to be thoroughly dependent on Delhi's local geographies. But it is also clear that people, ideas, technologies, laws, and materials were at work in the ~~city~~ that had traveled along networks of varying lengths. The SITAs had been evolving elsewhere in India for over fifteen years and bore within their clauses and powers the traces of other places and battles that had been fought over the competing urges to segregate or abolish brothels. Meliscent Shephard, who insinuated her way into the key governmental mechanisms for excluding prostitutes from the city while including them within civil society, arrived in India in 1928, bringing with her a series of beliefs and approaches from England that she would tirelessly pursue. In so doing, she often invoked the League of Nations, which represented a new scale of political organization that took up the issue of trafficking in women and children in the East. Its impact on the terminology and technologies of reform, as well as on the requirements placed upon the central government, had a direct impact on Delhi. It is to these broader spatial genealogies that we shall now turn.

# Two

# ASSEMBLING INDIA

———·•·———

## THE BIRTH OF SITA

### Natural Orders

In 1923 the Bengal Legislative Council passed the Calcutta Suppression of Immoral Traffic Act. The act drew upon legal precedents recently established in Bombay and Burma, but was also inspired by fears, rumors, international anti-trafficking laws, and myths regarding the abduction of women and their forcible entrapment into sexual service. The Calcutta law became a model for other provinces that, under the legislative systems of dyarchy (1919–35) and of provincial self-government (1935–47), set their own agendas regarding health and social services. By 1940 six provinces had their own SITAs, while others adopted clauses and sentiments from these acts. They provided powers to target those involved in importing, detaining, and procuring women. But they also punished solicitation, keeping a brothel, and living off the earnings of women involved in prostitution, ushering in an abolitionist program of brothel closures and the outlawing of certain public displays of female sexuality. Swathed in the patriarchal language of protection and guardianship, the acts reinforced the state's powers over women who chose to satisfy the sexual desires of men and to craft their own space within a masculine, colonial political economy.

While the title, Suppression of Immoral Traffic Act, drew upon the international discourses regarding trafficking and immorality of the time, the acronym "SITA" also presented a gift to legislators and campaigners. Sita is one of the most revered Hindu goddesses, abducted by the demon king Ravan, and rescued by Ram, an incarnation of Vishnu. Her rescue thus represents the ideal of the anti-traffickers: the passive and victimized woman, returned to the safely of male trusteeship. However, as Veena Oldenburg (2007) has made clear, there are competing and ambiguous narratives of sexual violence within the various tellings of the *Ramayana* story. After her rescue, doubts remained among the common people about the sexual loyalty of the pregnant Sita, which led Ram to insist on a public trial by fire to prove his wife's sexual purity. Although she passed, she was then abandoned in the forest. This exile mirrors the civil abandonment of prostitutes to an urban existence beyond the center of towns, beyond medical care, and beyond social understanding on the basis of a normative judgment regarding their sexuality. After Sita had raised her children alone, she encountered Ram again, with two divergent results depending on which telling one hears. In one version, Sita refuses to forgive Ram and wills the Earth, her mother, to open up and consume her. A model of female agency and independence, Sita would rather perish than resubmit to the doubting will of Ram. In the other telling, however, Sita faces another trial, proves her purity, and institutes a divine reign of the reunited couple. In this telling, Sita represents the perfect wife: knowledgeable, wise, rescued, tried, and controlled. The twentieth century would see the model of the perfect, complementary wife venerated and politicized, a figure in many ways dialectically constructed against the image of the denounced and apolitical prostitute (Chatterjee 2010, 128).

In this sense, the SITAs fit into a long line of legislative interventions that sought to delimit and define the sexual and gendered position of Indian women. In terms of scalar domains, the Raj assemblage was, for many, a force of *nature*, bringing with it art, science, civilization, and the rule of law. With this belief came understandings of human natures: of what it was to be a woman; of what role sex should play in that being; and of what it meant to think about, and attempt to govern, Indian female sexuality. The opening section of this chapter will show how people at the time, and the theories we use today, did and can expose the myth of these semiautonomous natures. Current theory, just as interwar politics did, exposes colonial law as saturated with power relations, violence, and racially inflected normativity. Contemporary sexology literature was also emphasizing the significance of context and environment in sexual behavior, naming and

defaming the brothel as an especially corrupting site that colonial governments and economies were implicitly supporting. This process was driven
not by the civilizing urges of the Raj, but by a series of scandals that exposed
the "social evil," "horrors of enforced prostitution," and "open toleration
of vice" that the Indian government was harboring in its busiest port cities.
Attempts to sustain the impression of the Raj, of law and order, and of
sexual propriety involved dense and intricate forms of *networking*. Through
this strategy the states of British India sought successful experiments to
implement in their own brothel quarters, and they often drew on examples
from the empire and beyond.

This chapter will simultaneously try to represent the geographical difference of India while also working against the methodological nationalism that has dominated much writing on prostitution. Philippa Levine's
(2003) magisterial overview of regulating prostitution in the Victorian empire, for instance, speaks of "India." While she details the heterogeneous
spaces of prostitution regulation, the impression of subcontinental coherence endures. This was an impression that was easier to project, and the
government willingly did so, in the nineteenth century when the will and
capacity existed to pass All India Acts (i.e., applying to all of British India)
regarding sexuality. This was much more difficult in the twentieth century,
with health legislation devolved to provincial administration and the central state, which was fearful of a politically damaging incursion into the
domestic realm. The task for campaigners, therefore, became one of stitching together a network of provincial legislation that would eventually encompass the space of "India." This should not, however, be taken as a sign
of central inaction over prostitution. Venereal disease remained a concern
for the government, which was increasingly forced to consider the health of
the Indian population, rather than just that of the colonial elite. Its solution
was a scalar one. Rather than legislate *nationally*, it formally insisted that
prostitution was a *local* problem, while informally hinting, suggesting, and
pressuring provincial governments into action (for a prehistory of these
central-local relations, see Legg 2012b). The provincial politics of passing
the sitas forms the centerpiece of this chapter's investigation of the turn
from segregation to suppression in interwar India, which will draw on the
phenomenally rich literature on colonial law, gender politics, and sexology.

### Colonial Law and Ordering Indian Women

The idea that law should be discarded from Foucauldian analysis along
with the sovereign's head, in terms of power relations, has now been fairly

comprehensively dismissed. In my previous work I sought to demonstrate how the law was taken up by colonial governmentalities and used to structure space not just through jurisprudence, but through coding behavior, banning practices in certain places and periods, and withdrawing its protections in states of exception (Legg 2007b, 97). However, such an analysis, while addressing the uptake and production of forms of *knowledge* and the circulation of techniques of *power*, fails to acknowledge Foucault's third concern of *ethics*. It also risks emptying the legal domain of any particular *characteristics* that it may consistently possess regardless of its governmental formation.

Ben Golder and Peter Fitzpatrick (2008) have explored the latter lacuna and hinted at the centrality of the former, in stressing the radically uncontainable nature of "Foucault's law." While the law, for Foucault, *did* become the instrument or accessory of external powers, it also remained illimitable and responsive to its outsides, acknowledging both its contingent nature and the ongoing ethical self-formation of the subjects of law. This is not, however, to apologize for Foucault's inconsistencies on governmentality and law; where are the tensions between administration and legality (Golder and Fitzpatrick 2008, 35)? What are the specificities of law in these new power formations? How does law shift from being juridical (focused on command and sanction) to being normative? When we draw upon Foucault's writings on Maurice Blanchot and Georges Batailles, a more relational view of law emerges that is forever evolving out of being determined (Golder and Fitzpatrick 2008, 54). The many theoretical interpretations of Foucault's law that seek out abstract totalities in his work run against the anti-positivism with which he insisted upon the non-autonomy of law. While enveloped and put to work by disciplinary and governmental apparatuses, laws were also parts of assemblages that confronted these apparatuses with their outsides, with recalcitrant subjects, with terrains that forced their mutation, and with limits that constituted the law by insisting upon their transgression (Golder and Fitzpatrick 2008, 76). The brothel provided a space, and the prostitute a subject, that forced endless experimentation and renewal: a space that cloaked itself in domesticity to evade the gaze of the law, but which proved itself to be a site subject to national, imperial, and international legal imperatives to intervention; and a subject whose liberty to use her body as she wished could not be infringed, but whose biological and social risk had to be managed.

These realizations in Foucauldian theory mirror those in diverse strands of broader literatures. Nicolas Blomley (2008) has long stressed the importance of legal geographies, whether in state initiatives, territorial formations, political conflicts, interactions between citizens, or debates over rights. Matthew Cook (2006) has outlined the centrality of legal frameworks to the analysis and regulation of sexual practices ranging from homosexuality to sexual violence, marriage, and abortion, but also the difference between abstract "justice" and administered "law." The establishment of "law and order" was obviously central to the "civilizing mission" in India, one which ingrained white violence at its heart (Kolsky 2010). At the intersection of these interests lies a substantial body of work by Indian feminists that has dissected the role of the law in crafting the lifeworlds of women under colonial and nationalist rule.

As Tambe (2009a, 1–25) has demonstrated in her survey of literature on sexuality, law, and the colonial state, in the nineteenth century women in India became the objects of colonial legal reforms. The ban on sati (widow immolation) in 1829, the defense of widow remarriage in 1856, the penalization of female infanticide in 1870, and the raising of the age of consent to twelve in 1892 instituted attempts to regulate female sexuality. This lofty goal, most confidently imagined during the high imperialism of the late nineteenth century, was soon compromised by interwar power broking with nationalist, reformist, and orthodox social and political movements.

To view this legislation as regulative in a purely negative sense would be to misinterpret its power, and the intentions of many of its authors and campaigners. The laws were also intended to empower and include women within the protections of civil society. But this inclusion positioned women within Western sexual subjectivities, overcoming yet entrenching in law the difference, backwardness, or danger of Indian sexuality. As Ratna Kapur (2005, 2) has argued: "These inclusions and exclusions have been produced in and through law, either by emphasising the difference of the subaltern subject as incapable of choosing or consenting, and thus incapable of exercising rights, or as backward and uncivilised, to be redeemed and incorporated into the liberal project through the process of assimilation. A third approach is to regard the Other as dangerous and a threat to the security of nation-states, to be either incarcerated or annihilated."

Against this, the challenge for postcolonial feminist legal theory is not to recuperate an authentic primordial identity from within the archive, but to analyze who is speaking for whom, how, and when, as well as who is listening and why (Kapur 2005, 4). Yet, vitally, Kapur also points out that much work remains to be done on investigating the trappings of the colonial system and the first-world formations this law was based on, working *along* the grain of the colonial legal archive (Stoler 2009). If this encouraged us to consider the power/knowledge formations of colonial law, Kapur and Brenda Cossman (1996) also urged us to consider the ethical possibility of legal self-formation by questioning the extent to which law was a "subversive site." They approached this question pessimistically, noting the conservative and power-saturated nature of the law, as traditionally viewed. Yet while rejecting perspectives that women needed the protection of the law, or that liberal feminist equality could be achieved through the law, they also rejected the radical view of law as a site of total and patriarchal oppression. Rather, the law is a complex and diverse discourse with variable, and thus potentially subversive, effects and meanings. Recognizing this heterogeneity, the challenge becomes reenvisioning the subject of colonial law outside of discourses of protection (the precarious), equality (the global sisterhood), or patriarchy (the victim), and within those of diverse subalternism (including the desiring or erotic subject). Kapur (2005) insists that the subaltern can not only speak, but can *feel*, and that this must be the presumed subject of the laws that we investigate historically.

These colonial laws increasingly spread into those areas initially reserved for Hindu or Muslim "personal laws." Such incursions were justified as unquestionably beneficial to women, but Flavia Agnes (1999, 47) has highlighted how they also extended men's property rights through codifying inheritance and matrimonial rights (also see Nair 1996). Likewise, child sexuality was later defined as acceptable within marriage, and thus controlled by the husband, but dangerous and unacceptable outside of it (Tambe 2009c). Such cases were often addressed through case law not codified law, such that precedents could be surreptitiously established, and colonial sexual and gender norms extended, in Hindu and Muslim personal law. When lawmakers attempted more unabashed legal interventions, such as raising of the age of consent from ten to twelve in 1891, this sparked pitched battles over Hindu conjugality, with social reformers reluctantly siding with the state against upper-caste Hindu orthodoxy.

Sinha's (1995) groundbreaking work insists that these legal shifts were both trans-colonial, situated in "imperial social formations," and as much about masculinities as femininities, providing evidence that Indian men could de-orientalize, and protect their women, just as well as colonial men could. The controversial debates accompanying the act of 1891 forestalled the colonial government from legislating on such matters until the Child Marriage Restraint (or Sarda) Act of 1929 (Sinha 2006, 6). By this point Indian social reformers had become so active that the state was effectively posed as the obstacle to reform, not the engine of it. These conditions heightened the need for Britain to prove its role as "trustee" of India, and to distance itself from the views of authors like Katherine Mayo, whose book *Mother India* (1927) had castigated Indians for the treatment of their womenfolk.

The Sarda Act of 1929 was supported by men and women across the communities of India who came together to reform the legislative frame of sexuality *within* the family (sexuality outside the family was not included) by raising the age of consent to fourteen for girls. This represented one of the first major appropriations of the state domain by nationalists, aligning the "political" and "social" spheres in India (Sinha 2006, 163). It was on these forged alignments that women would continue to campaign in the 1930s, continually re-smelting the link between the social need for action regarding prostitution and the political imperative for doing so, even as political divisions in the religious community or on the political spectrum split the nationalist consensus. Although Gandhi called forth women into the public realm and helped them politicize the domestic world, female nationalists failed to secure more favorable legislation to regulate marriage, divorce, or inheritance after provincial autonomy was devolved in 1935 (Agnes 1999, 64). Prostitutes fared even worse under the Indian National Congress. Calls to end the registration of prostitutes at the 1888 Congress were actually some of the first motions passed regarding women, but under Gandhi's strict regimen of personal discipline and sexual abstinence, prostitutes were rejected entirely from the new national vision (Kumar 1993, 34, 84; Tambe 2009a, 105; 2009b). Bodies like the All India Women's Congress would campaign for the reform of the devadasi and trafficking systems (Basu and Ray 1990, 77–81), but with prostitutes as objects, not subjects, of reform. The SITAS were able to spread gradually because they combined both sociopolitical needs with those of an evolving medico-moral discourse (Mort 1987) in which public and international health institutions were increasingly demanding action.

### Sexology and the Nature of the Brothel

But beyond these troubled pleasures, [*scientia sexualis*] assumed other powers; it set itself up as the supreme authority in matters of hygienic necessity, taking up the old fears of venereal affliction and combining them with the new themes of asepsis, and the great evolutionist myths with the recent institutions of public health; it claimed to ensure the physical vigor and the moral cleanliness of the social body; it promised to eliminate defective individuals, degenerate and bastardized populations." (Foucault 1979, 54)

Venereal disease had never fitted into the miasma episteme of disease; its genital manifestations made its origins clear. Thus while not exposed to the extreme sovereign and disciplinary spaces of quarantine, prostitutes have throughout history been segregated, not just to cast them out, but to make them visible (see Hubbard 1999). Ballhatchet's (1980) classic text detailed the military registration of prostitutes through the Indian Contagious Diseases Acts (CDAS, 1868–88) and the Cantonment Regulations that survived them. Concern had been growing about the ability to safeguard British soldiers from infection, a question that seemed increasingly inseparable from native sanitary conditions (Mann 2007, 2). This had been impressed upon the government of India by the Royal Commission on the Sanitary State of the Army in India of 1863, which linked that state to the conditions of the civilian population and instilled the need to progress from curative to preventative medicine (Hoops 1928, 12).

The solution posed by the Indian CDAS to venereal disease was, however, that of segregation, a solution more common in the colonies where the desire to bring prostitutes into view, rather than banish them from respectable public space, was dominant (Levine 2003, chapter 11). Yet prostitution proved, more clearly than any other form of contagion, that interaction between British and Indian populations was impossible to stymie by spatial segregation (Cell 1986, 315). The transition from miasmatic to germ theory in the 1890s further cemented the belief in the inseparable nature of troop and native health and sanitation. This set the government of India on the path to eventual recognition of its duty to improve the health of the whole population, not only of a segregated civil and military elite, and that the way to do this was through both grand sanitation infrastructural works, and through attention to individual hygiene. In 1909 the sanitary commissioner remarked on the success of "personal or individual hygiene" over public hygiene alone in dealing with troop health (cited in Guha 1993, 397); between 1899–1904 and 1909–14, when hygiene methods started to be introduced into the military, venereal disease rates decreased by 79 percent. Ballhatchet and Levine, however, barely extended their studies into the interwar years when the threat of venereal disease was presumed to have subsided. It was, in fact, a threat that periodically erupted and caused the military no little anxiety, while the challenge of extending hygiene, both social and moral, to the military and Indian population remained unfulfilled (see chapter 3).

The link between venereal disease and personal hygiene was supported by health institutions in part due to the evidence provided by the emergent "science" of sexology. The study of sex and the relationship between the sexes emerged in late nineteenth-century Europe, and by the First World War was established in journals, books, conferences, therapy, and popular culture (Waters 2006). It emerged from the broader realization that a nation's health depended upon the well-being of its population. While at one biopolitical extreme this could lead to the selective breeding associated with extreme eugenics, at the other it encouraged new practices of self-conduct, sexual reform (through the law and civil society), and sex education. The moral laxity of cities was central to sexological understanding, but this did not lead to an urban environmental determinism in explaining sexual behavior. Rather, the concept of sexual identity took shape, which was essentially entwined with reproduction, and its associated perversions which were named and classified between the 1870s and 1890s (Foucault 1979). While socially constructed, what emerged was a "medico-biologico-*naturalist* notion of sexuality" (Foucault et al. 2011, 387–88, emphasis added) that suggested a sexual domain of processes and urges common to all, though with reservations regarding race, gender, and age. Chris Waters (2006, 46) stressed how the type of sexology differed by nation and period, being relatively marginal in Britain, but reached its peak reformatory power in the interwar period. Its reinterpretation in India has been studied (Ahluwalia 2012), especially through debates about eugenics and neo-Malthusian birth control (Hodges 2006a, 2008).

What is less often acknowledged is the effect of new sexology writings on colonial officials. These writings gradually began to erode ingrained Victorian notions about sexuality and prostitution, with the *name* of the brothel as a site of safety and visibility being overturned. This shift can be demonstrated in the writings of Iwan Bloch, August Forel, Havelock Ellis, and others which were read in administrative circles, as will be demonstrated in the discussion of the Burma Bill of 1921. This should not be taken, however, to suggest a total break between earlier moralistic writings on prostitution and those of the new sex science. Bloch's (1908) influential *The Sexual Life of Our Time in Its Relations to Modern Civilization* openly declared its dream of abolishing both prostitution and venereal disease which would, for Bloch, have solved the sexual problem. He continued the well-known metaphorical association of prostitutes with infection, likening them to an ulcer in the body of society. Their study had to involve "local" conditions (in terms of medicine and hygiene) as well as "internal" conditions (in terms of ethics, pedagogy, and social sciences): causes of prostitution were thus named as insufficient education, premature exposure to sexual depravation, and miserable housing. But he also acknowledged the international assemblage which had formed to tackle prostitution and trafficking: "Today medicine, social science, pedagogy, jurisprudence, and ethics have combined in a common campaign; and this is not national merely, but unites all civilized nations in a common cause" (Bloch 1908, 307).

Such a trans-scalar understanding allowed Bloch to establish a clear relationship between trafficking in women and children, and brothels. Prostitutes' growing dislike of brothels, he claimed, was leading to the demand to refill these houses, mostly with girls from eastern Europe. In a replication of the widespread anti-Semitism that characterized anti-trafficking discourses, Polish Jews were blamed for the trafficking, five-sixths of whom were described as *luftmenschen* (men of air) with no livelihood or location. Where brothels existed they were denounced as "evil" due to their shameless display of sex and solicitation, which poisoned public life and obliterated the boundary between cleanliness and contamination. "And yet brothels are a still greater evil! They constitute an incomparably more dangerous centre of sexual corruption, a worse breeding-ground of sexual aberrations of every kind, and last, not least, the greatest focus of sexual infection" (Bloch 1908, 339). Brothels were said to function as "the high-school of refined sexual lust and perversity.... *Here, in the brothel, psychopathia sexualis is systematically taught*" (Bloch 1908, 340, emphasis in original).

Forel's (1908) *The Sexual Question: A Scientific, Psychological, Hygienic and Sociological Study for the Cultured Classes* was more critical of the medical regulation of tolerated brothels as widely practiced on the Continent, and temporarily used in the British Empire through the CDAs and Cantonment Regulations: "To tolerate, to license, to organize, to recognize and favour, to protect and recommend are notions which merge into one another insensibly. As soon as the State tolerates prostitution and brothels, it is obliged to enter into official contracts with prostitutes and proxenetism [making a business out of prostitution]; therefore it recognizes them" (Forel 1908, 300). Medical examinations were denounced for giving a false sense of security, while brothels were shown to lead to rapid infection of prostitutes, as brothel keepers would not allow prostitutes full treatment for venereal diseases due to the cost and their time out of profitable employment with clients. Prostitutes were slaves, shackled by the "gifts" of clothes and food, police corruption, and the threat of bring trafficked abroad, while their effect on the public was to induce an "arithmetical progression of mutations of sexual intercourse." Rather than inspiring anti-trafficking and abolitionist campaigns, Forel was inspired *by* the campaigns of Josephine Butler and others against tolerated brothels, but also against the "masculine autocracy" which supported the system, and the lack of education, cleanliness, and disease treatment in the general population.

The most thorough exegesis of prostitution, and the most controversial in Britain, was Ellis's (1910 [1925]) *Studies in the Psychology of Sex, vol. VI: Sex in Relation to Society*, the first volume of which had been banned on charges of obscenity. Ellis's object was to link individual psychology and social hygiene when considering sexual questions. The largest chapter in the book addressed prostitution and was situated incredibly broadly: most generally through the historical suppression of primitive and muscular forms of orgy which had led to the emergence of prostitution and attempts to stamp it out. Regulation was condemned as a thing of the past, yet was justified in certain circumstances, including that of the British Army in India (Ellis 1910 [1925], 252). In general, however, regulation was dismissed on the grounds of pragmatism (it was impossible to register all women), morality (it punished only women), and practicality (it was ineffective).

Ellis went further in his examination of the causes of prostitution, however, evoking similar arguments to those made by postcolonial legal feminists. Just as Waters (2006, 51) suggested that sexologists were the first people to attempt "histories of sexuality," so they may also have been the first to construct critical legal and economic analyses of sexual relations. Ellis (1910 [1925], 255) suggested that the rise of the patriarchal family and regulated marriage made it more difficult for a woman to dispose of her own person, being owned by her father and effectively bought by her future husband. The creation of a market value of virginity led to a population of men without wives, and women without prospects of marriage, making prostitution "inevitable." Superfluous women utilized their money value and revived earlier traditions of sexual freedom to satisfy the demands of men. But this decision was also conditioned by four other factors. Arguments regarding economic necessity, including the work of Parent-Duchâtelet and William Acton, were questioned, as were those in general who sought to explain all social phenomena by economic causes. Wages alone could not solve or explain prostitution. The biological element was considered, accepting the prostitute as what Kapur (2005) termed an "erotic subject" and acknowledging that she herself would have sexual drives. Ellis refused to accept that prostitutes' sexuality was the equivalent of male criminality, but did provide what were believed to be a series of common bodily features of such women. Morally, Ellis reviewed those arguments that justified prostitutes as a necessary evil, of benefit to society at large, functioning, as William E. H. Lecky (1926 [2004]) termed them in 1869, as the "guardian[s] of virtue." This view that prostitution buttressed marriage was contrasted to the less widely accepted civilizational value of the prostitute, namely, that she added gaiety to monotonous urban life and relief from mechanical, industrial routine (Ellis 1910 [1925], 287). This appeal was said, more than any other motive, to draw women into prostitution, and to create male demand for it: "It is the prostitute who incarnates this fascination of the city, far better than the virginal woman, even if intimacy with her were within reach" (Ellis 1910 [1925], 299).

While Ellis seemed to underplay arguments regarding the economic necessity of prostitution, and even suggested that women enjoyed prostitution (sensorially, if not sexually), when he discussed the brothel his views were less ambiguous. As the target of growing international repugnance, the brothel was denounced as the home of only the most "helpless or the most stupid prostitutes." Moral force in contemporary society was encouraging women from "cloistered prostitution" to "free prostitution" and the resulting decline in supply was thought to link the brothel to the white slave trade. Also suggesting links with the philosophy of Josephine Butler, Ellis ended with a denouncement of the idea that some women (wives) could be protected by selling others (prostitutes), and of the cruel denial of the realization that prostitutes were also women.

The concepts emerging from the sexology literature had wide-reaching effects in terms of altering understanding of the causes, manifestations, and solutions to the problems of prostitution. Abraham Flexner's (1914) Rockefeller-funded *Prostitution in Europe* was influential in India and drew upon the sciences of sex emerging in Europe when he had visited in 1911. He spent a year visiting twenty-eight cities in twelve countries in western Europe (Bonner 2002), but also contacted Bloch and was given access to drafts of his forthcoming works (Flexner 1914, 4). Like much of the foregoing work, he linked the problem of prostitution to the anonymity of urban space, which made regulation increasingly ineffective while targeting women only. Setting a model for later League of Nations work (Legg 2012a), Flexner emphasized the need to *define* "prostitution" (promiscuous bartering with "emotional indifference") and to outlaw "regulation" (Flexner 1914, 122, i.e., handling prostitution by making it submit to certain rules). Segregation was condemned for promoting vice, moral contagion, police corruption, and, most significantly, trafficking. Abolitionism was promoted, as it targeted regulations, not prostitutes, and replaced the negative targeting of the women involved with what Flexner (1914, 287) termed "constructive social action." This involved giving prostitutes the same rights as other women, not a set of laws specific to them, although the prostitute should be prosecuted using these laws should she make herself "obnoxious" through her practicing of prostitution. The task thus went beyond that of the law and of disciplining a minority to actually constituting society more broadly by circulating knowledge about prostitutes and trafficking; by rationalizing social life to forestall "natural impulses"; and by using education, sanitation, and statesmanship to overcome the nature of the problem (Flexner 1914, 401), that is, to a thoroughgoing governmentality.

While these new literatures contributed to anti-trafficking movements, they also drew upon the conclusions of suppressionist campaigns against trafficking and regulated brothels themselves. For instance, James Marchant's (1917, xi) *The Master Problem* investigated how to challenge the dire physical and racial consequences for troops and civilians of prostitution and trafficking *without* resorting to the "false and revolting European solutions" that Britain experimented with in the 1860s. Marchant's analysis repeated much of that from the canonical sexology texts: the mixture of causes from poor housing to lack of education, unmarried workers, and poor women. Segregation and regulation were discounted but recent suppressionist conventions on trafficking were applauded, as were anti-procuration and souteneur powers included in the British Criminal Law Amendment Act of 1912. The solution to the problem was a suppressionist variant of abolitionism that combined an increased age of consent with measures to suppress brothels, banish regulation, and impede traffickers wherever possible.

While Marchant focused on America and Europe, Mrs. Archibold MacKirdy and W. N. Willis's (1912) *The White Slave Market* extended their sensationalist exposé to the East. The government of India's measures against pimps and British prostitutes were condemned as imperiling not just the lives of white women, but also the chances of converting "heathens," who would not consider Christianity when they saw that Christian women could be bought. These "imperial" concerns would resurface during the debate on the sitas and their precursors in India, but the more lasting effect of the sexological and hygienist literature was the condemnation of the brothel. From the regulationist belief that the brothel made women visible and disease detectable, it was reenvisioned as a site of occluded sexual practices, infection, sexual deviancy and mutation, slavery and trafficking. This literature thus provided the medico-moral justification for the arguments made by Indian social reformers for action against brothels, although these campaigns were more often focused on the effects of brothels on their localities than the presumed slavery they entailed. By the 1930s this sexological literature was increasingly out of date and had to be updated with more contemporary hygiene literature, as will be demonstrated in chapter 3 by Meliscent Shephard's circulated reading lists from 1930 (as she wrote to her colleagues in London: "I am trying to get the funds to print something. Men are still being brought up here on Havelock Ellis!").[1]

The SITAS introduced the suppressionist brand of abolitionism to India, including the belief, shared by sexologists, hygienists, and many Indian social reformers and anti-traffickers, that brothels were both the cause and locus of the major problems associated with prostitution: venereal disease, social exploitation, and transnational trafficking. They supplemented previous abolitionist movements against registration with powers against segregated and tolerated brothels. Segregation was not just a social phenomenon (as often claimed, see Edwardes 1924, 90), but a conscious tactic by governors that allowed them some sort of control over the interactions in brothels after the removal of CDA and Cantonment Regulations. One of the responses that was encouraged by the central government was for municipal or local police powers to be used to segregate prostitutes into one segment of cities. They could then be surveyed, from a distance, and the military police could be used to prevent soldiers entering the area (Legg 2012b). This often mutated into the military police insisting that soldiers use medically inspected brothels, despite central orders, as exposed by Shephard's investigations (see next chapter).

### Defaming the Brothel: Scandalous Sites, 1917–1922

In 1917 two scandals finally demolished the legitimacy of segregated brothel zones in India. These scandals illustrate the nominalist force of having two of India's busiest and most significant ports defamed on account of the way their prostitutes were being treated. As with Delhi, place naming and subjectification were indissociable and uncontainable. Scandals thrive on heterogeneous assemblages; they place the scientific and fantastical, the criminal and legal, the immoral and the ethical, the near and far, side by side and thrive off their contradictions. Their problematizations have the capacity to unnerve and smooth out the striations of state apparatuses, which are forced to re-cartographize their spaces, states, and subjects. The *unnatural* barbarity of the brothels called forth the apparatuses of civil society and the legislative state to purify the reputation of their cities, and of the Raj itself. The scandals of Rangoon and Bombay will be presented as the precedent to the onset of suppressionist legislation in 1921, culminating in the *networking* of the SITAS across India in the 1930s.

*Rangoon: The Morality of the Municipality*

"The chief object perhaps is not the morality of the municipality but the health of troops."[2] This was how F. Cowie of the Home Department dismissed concerns about the powers of segregation in Rangoon in September 1901, which were granted through the amendment of the Rangoon Police Act in 1902 (Legg 2012b). This act had cleared public prostitutes and brothels from the port-side grid of colonial offices and businesses, but had allowed a three-street red-light district to remain, in the center of the city. While anticipation of the effects of such a spatialization of commercial sexuality had been hindered by the phrasing of the act, Cowie's comments proved particularly shortsighted. While the troops were kept to the northwest of the city at a distance from the segregated prostitutes, it was the morality of the municipality that was soon affronted by the creation of segregated prostitution zones in the heart of Rangoon's civil center.

There had been some commentary on the effects of segregation in Rangoon in the prewar years. These included a report by T. F. Pedley entitled *The Evolution of the Social Evil in Rangoon* and Charles Tarring's paper on the prevalence of venereal disease in Rangoon, both from 1908.[3] Protests had been raised by representatives of the Women's Christian Temperance Union, the YMCA, and the American Baptist mission.[4] But the institutions of civil society only found their collective voice under the campaigning crusade of John Cowan, who arrived in Rangoon from Ceylon during Easter 1914 under invitation from Bishop Fyffe, president of the Rangoon Vigilance Association. He stayed in Rangoon from April 1914 to May 1915, and October to November 1915.

On 20 January 1915 Cowan gave an interview to the Association of Moral and Social Hygiene (AMSH), advising them on how to do work in the East.[5] While he was downbeat about the potential of addressing the prostitutes themselves or working with the police, he was enthusiastic about the potential for "public opinion" in India, which he claimed was more easily influenced by new ideas, and to which the government was sensitive. Cowan worked effectively both with the institutions of civil society in Rangoon and with the AMSH in London to create an international movement to rid the town of its segregated zone.

In June 1914 a memorial was submitted to the lieutenant governor of Burma from an impressive array of society and government figures, namely, the Right Reverend Bishop Fyffe, Right Reverend Bishop Cardot, the officer commanding Rangoon Brigade, the inspector general of hospitals, the officiating director of public instruction, the principals of six leading schools, and the representatives of various different religious communities. The aim of the memorial was clearly stated: to secure the local governments' cooperation in the *suppression* of brothels. This was in response to a "disastrous" state of affairs that went beyond the nine thousand cases of venereal disease treated at the General Hospital in 1912–13. The disaster was related solely to the policy of segregation, which had permitted brothels in central parts of the city. Other cases and medical opinion were said to be united in highlighting the failures of this policy, which had not only failed to contain disease, but advertised evil, lowered the tone of the whole community, and blunted the keenness of the police by leading them to believe that this "evil" was supported by government. Rangoon was also said to actually create demand, leading to the procurement of girls into the trade. The memorialists then expanded the scope of their appeal. The first claim was transgenerational. Children were said to be missing out on school, as parents would not send them out near the segregated zones. But an appeal was also made in the name of "religion and science to safeguard the interests of all citizens of Rangoon, of the children of this land and of the millions yet unborn, who will be the unconscious and helpless victims of this pernicious trade if it be allowed to continue."[6]

The science being represented here was the emergent field of eugenics, which featured as much in the pages of the *Shield* journal published by the AMSH as it did in scientific periodicals. Religion was also represented by a co-submitted "purely Christian memorial" which stressed that the laws of Jesus Christ were also being transgressed, including abstinence from fornication and fulfilling the lusts of the flesh. The memorial seemed to have an astonishingly quick effect; on 28 October 1914 the central government issued its opinions on the memorial and on 17 November the segregated zones were placed on the same footing as the rest of the town. While this technically ended the system of segregation in Rangoon, the ongoing campaign highlighted why the town was not just the site for a failed experiment with segregationism, but a site in which the abolitionist campaign moved seamlessly from that of antisegregation to that of pro-suppression.

The reason for the continued agitation was that section 43B of the Police Act of 1902, which now applied to the entire town, meant that a brothel within this area *could* be forced to close, but that well-behaved brothels could also be tolerated. It was toleration, rather than segregation, that became the new object of ire for the abolitionist campaigners. Shortly after the extension of 43B to the whole city, in December 1914, Cowen published a pamphlet entitled *Welcome to the Territorials* through the American Missionary Press in Rangoon.[7] He suggested that brothels were being maintained for what the secretary of state for India referred to in a telegram to the viceroy on this matter on 20 April 1915 as "raw and inexperienced men" mobilized for the war. On Viceroy Hardinge's orders inquiries were sent to the governor of Burma, who insisted on 13 June 1915 that segregation had been abolished before the pamphlet had been written, and that the police were suppressing brothels in undesirable localities and prohibiting the open advertisement of vice. It was, however, the division of Rangoon into desirable and undesirable localities for brothels that Cowan would continue to campaign against.

The nature of the action taken by the local police was contested more comprehensively by the AMSH in 1916 after Cowen submitted a substantial, concluding report on the conditions in the town. The official view was that the "permissive area" had been cleansed. The Rangoon police report for 1915 argued that, contra Cowie's statement in 1901, the police had undertaken sustained activity to improve the "morality of the town." All blatant advertisements to vice had apparently ceased although the powers of Rangoon's reputation was admitted: "A very long time must elapse before the unsavoury reputation of this area can entirely die and respectable people be induced to live in it."[8] From November 1914, under sections 43A and 43B, 4 house owners, 219 brothel keepers, and 464 prostitutes had been dealt with.

In line with the comments of the inspector general of police of Colombo regarding the end of segregation in Ceylon two years earlier (Legg 2012b), it was claimed that the police action had driven brothels and prostitutes beyond the zone covered by 43B. Only one complaint had been submitted by inhabitants of this zone under section 43A, which was taken as evidence of the general apathy of the public on this topic. Predicting the common criticism of suppressionist legislation, the commissioner of police concluded his report as follows: "I have no reason to believe that prostitution has diminished in consequence of such action, but its open advertisement and allurement have been reduced in a most marked degree." Those women who had moved outside the zone of 43B were further disturbed when its remit was extended in April 1916 to include the cantonment and Ahlon Police Station.

John Cowen, however, had uncovered a very different life in the former segregated district, which his employers, the AMSH, submitted as a sixteen-page printed report to the secretary of state for India on 13 July 1916. In the accompanying letter from the AMSH, the system in operation was referred to as one of segregating and controlling brothels, which the Burmese government itself had declared a failure in 1914. Their comment on Cowen's report utilized the full *nominalist* force of both empire (civilizing mission) and Eastern city (vice): "He described in Rangoon a state of things which, we hope, is unparalleled in the British Empire. The open toleration of sexual vice under official sanction amounts to official encouragement, and the resulting conditions must be disastrous to the health and the morals both of the European and Indian population, demoralising to the police and other officials, and dangerous to British prestige."[9]

Although the government's reply, on 25 August 1916, commented that section 43B allowed the closure of brothels under complaint, it did not mention that the police could also do this of their own volition, and that their failure to do so marked a system of open toleration. But Cowen's report revealed more than this. The edited version of the report was still sixteen pages long and combined a journalistic turn of phrase with a statistician's analytical eye and an abolitionist's zeal for social purity. The report excelled at combining general comments about the evil of prostitution with comments on its specific and remediable context. As the opening paragraph stated, the immorality that continued in Rangoon was "due not so much to the depravity of British regiments as to local conditions, fostered by the policy of the Administration."

Like many critical accounts of Raj policy, Cowen's began by adopting the form and statistics of colonial reportage (see Legg 2006). The legislative status of the province was followed by census data that highlighted Rangoon's distorted sex ratio (male to female of 208,111 to 85,205) and provided a platform for a fascinating and effective form of counter-networking and colonial comparison (McFarlane 2008, 420). Madras, Rangoon, and Colombo were compared as capital cities, ports, and garrison towns, with populations of 520,000, 300,000, and 251,000, respectively. They were actively connected by steamer through the Bay of Bengal and served many similar functions. However, "in spite of these resemblances of circumstance and population, climate and position, the singular fact stands out that while Madras and Colombo are generally free from segregation, and from known public brothels of any sort, Rangoon has the largest segregation area of public brothels in India, besides the largest number of brothels outside the segregation area."[10]

Not only did the other ports lack segregation, they also were free of "'scattering,' which is sometimes suggested as the inevitable alternative to segregation and of suppression of licensed houses. There is no toleration of brothels at all, segregated or isolated. . . . What makes the difference?"[11] The unacceptability of the segregated zone was then established by noting its location, and the activities of the people within it (much as Mohan Lal's petition would do twelve years later in Delhi). The segregated streets were shown to be close to government offices, churches, colleges, and several main thoroughfares, as if they had been "designed to spread vice and disease throughout the city."

The segregated streets were then taxonomized by the race of the prostitute working there. The European quarter was on one side of Twenty-Ninth Street, with fifty women of east or south European origin in residence. Cowen met a "particularly villainous" German Jewess whom he had known, and campaigned against, in Colombo, who welcomed him as if an "old friend." The other side of the street was occupied by Japanese, Chinese, Arab, and other prostitutes and included a resort most popular with British soldiers, in spite of efforts by the military police to prevent soldiers from using such brothels (the military police also attempted to move on Cowen and his campaigners, who preached and sang hymns outside the brothels). It was not until 1915 that the brothels were officially placed out of bounds for soldiers. Streets twenty-seven and twenty-eight were for Indian prostitutes, while the brothels on Thirty-Third and Thirty-Fourth Streets, populated by Indian, Burmese, and Japanese women, were the busiest with local clients.

The government's efforts to date were damned, such as the insistence that brothels have curtains in their windows, should not use balconies to entice customers, and should regulate the dress of their occupants in public. The suggestion that brothels protected local girls from predation was dismissed, as the brothels "stimulated the seduction of young village girls." Girls could also be hired for a few days, with the segregated zone functioning as a "general market of prostitution. So far from its limiting vice to a particular area, vice radiated from it in all directions."[12] This was also demonstrated through the preponderance of brothels outside the segregated zone, and also in towns beyond Rangoon such as Mandalay and Maymyo.

Moving toward an explanation of this situation, Cowen addressed the relationship between law and police power, showing that the law was adequate but that the police were restricted from enforcing it by the executive powers. Section 45B, which should have led to the eradication of brothels, had been suspended from five streets. This was not part of the law, but the suspension of it: "Thus it is not by Act, but by an administrative order appended to an Act, that the Local Government authorises the terrible congeries of public brothels in the heart of the city, which is the cause of so much complaint, disease and widespread corruption."[13] Police control was, therefore, at the heart of the system, and had been condemned by Sir H. Adamson, the previous lieutenant governor of Burma, who had ordered its cancellation in 1914, after receiving the Rangoon memorial and reading Abraham Flexner's (1914) abolitionist *Prostitution in Europe*.

The report and the correspondence predating and resulting from it were summarized in an article in the *Shield* in 1919.[14] The opinion expressed by the commissioner of police that "open advertisement and allurement [of prostitution] have been reduced in a most marked degree" was dismissed, the segregated area was shown to be as alive as it ever had been, and the toleration of brothels was blamed for having created a system reliant upon the discretionary action of a police commissioner who seemed to favor segregation: "Obviously what is required is one consistent law vigorously applied to the whole of Rangoon. It is perfectly useless to have brothels allowed in one street and forbidden in the next. Of course the whole place becomes contaminated. With laws applied in so 'spotty' a fashion . . . it is little wonder prostitution spreads." As such, in the face of growing criticism, the Burmese government found themselves considering two options in 1916: either to clear all brothels from the city center, and thus increase them at the periphery, or to apply 43B to the whole municipal area, and thus to grant the powers to eliminate brothels entirely. In the face of police opposition to both options, the Burmese government took the highly unusual step of announcing, in January 1917, that they were sending Deputy Inspector of Police E. Shuttleworth on a tour of Calcutta, Bombay, Madras, and Colombo to analyze the working of laws there in relation to prostitution. His findings, like the suggestions of the Madge Bill in 1912 (see Legg 2012b), represent a tipping point between segregation/toleration and abolition/suppression. The report itself foreshadowed the League of Nations' traveling inquiries into the trafficking of women and children in the 1930s, although they would criticize tolerated brothels in a way that Shuttleworth found himself unable.

Shuttleworth performed his investigations in the summer of 1917 and that October submitted his report, entitled MEMORANDUM: Extent, Distribution, and Regulation of the "Social Evil" in the Cities of Calcutta, Madras and Bombay and in Rangoon Town. In Colombo Shuttleworth found the abolitionist policy to have been effective in clearing the streets, although he was assured that prostitution had been driven underground and not decreased, while soliciting and "homo-sexualism" had increased.[15]

The reports on the port cities provide a fascinating insight into the social geographies of prostitution during the years of the First World War. As in Cowen's report, but more systematically, criteria were addressed to all four cities, moving from questions of population and classification to public presence, laws, and associated crimes. Two of the cities had performed specific censuses of their prostitute populations: Rangoon found 478 women, in a city of 300,000; Calcutta found 15,000 prostitutes in a city of 1,043,307 at the 1911 census, although four times as many clandestine prostitutes were assumed to be at work. Only 1,000 prostitutes were estimated to service Madras's population of 518,660, while Bombay was assumed (without much reasoning) to also have 15,000 prostitutes based on its population of about 100,000.

In terms of "classification, nationality, recruitment and distribution of prostitutes" the concept of the white slave trade was dismissed in the discussion of foreign prostitution. Calcutta had seventy European prostitutes in twenty-one houses, nineteen of which were in Karaya Road in the suburb of Ballygunge (as Meliscent Shephard would find in the late 1920s to still be the case). These houses were registered by the police and strictly run by madams who cooperated with the police. Japanese brothels numbered eighteen, containing sixty women in Watgunge Street in Kidderpore, which were less tightly regulated. These women were "allocated" (segregated) near the docks. Bombay was said to divide its foreign prostitutes into classes, using the powers of segregation initiated under the amendments to the Bombay Police Act in 1902. The first class, with twenty-four women in four houses, was well conducted and left to its own devices. The second and third classes contained eleven houses and forty-three women, who were deemed less responsible and were "herded together with Japanese and Indian prostitutes in a quarter of the native town known as Kamatipura."[16] Across all three classes the majority were Russian (35), Roumanian ([sic], 11), or Italian (6). Bombay's Asiatic prostitutes were also more eclectic: 103 Japanese women were joined by 26 girls from Mauritius, 50 "Asiatic Jewesses," and 15 Muslim women from Baghdad. These were ranked with third-class European prostitutes and were localized with them in Suklaji Street, Duncan Road, Falkland Road, and Grant Road (Kamathipura).

Indigenous women were said to represent almost the whole volume of prostitution in India. Shuttleworth's descriptions of the habitations of these women were almost wholly negative and reverted to the common animalistic metaphors that were regularly deployed in the *naturalistic* tropes of orientalist stereotyping (Spurr 1993). In Madras there was no segregation and very few brothels, with mostly clandestine prostitutes who did not widely solicit. They were said to live throughout Calcutta, having been recruited from rural areas and other parts of India such as the United Provinces and Bihar, but especially dwelt in the northern portion, along Chuitpur Road, Beadon Square, and in the Sonagachi district. Of the latter Shuttleworth commented that "this part of town is a seething mass of Indian prostitutes," with the small lanes forming "a veritable ant-hill of these unfortunates." The main regulation of women in the segregated district of Bombay was said to be the attempt to keep them behind barred doors to reduce molestation of passersby. He continued: "A most weird impression is made on a stranger like myself passing down whole streets flanked on both sides with houses with barred doors and windows crowded with women looking out like caged animals in a zoo. The whole quarter is a festering mass of prostitution under its most repellent forms and it throws up localisation in its very worst aspect."[17]

Relatively little attention was given to pimps, who were said to have had war waged against them through the Foreigners Act (III of 1864) in Bombay to great success. There was little evidence found of kidnapping or abduction for the purposes of prostitution, with only 120 cases in Bengal in a year, and 151 cases in Madras for 1915 (the difficulty of the term "kidnapping" in these cases will be further explored through provincial police reports below).

Having adopted this statistical-forensic approach, Shuttleworth then concluded with two extraordinary passages that must have influenced the skeptical reception that his report received by the government of Burma. While an agent of the Burmese state apparatus, the breadth of his commission necessitated a combination of observations, data, and surveys. But Shuttleworth went much further than his formal remit and produced an assemblage that exceeded, by far, the gendered and sexed politics of the Raj.

In a section entitled "Causes of Prostitution," Shuttleworth summarized contemporary scholarship on the topic. Although briefly referencing the work of Parent-Duchâtelet on the economic conditions of prostitutes in France, and the comments of the ex-commissioner of police in Bombay, Mr. S. M. Edwardes, on the relation between wages and prostitution, the majority of this section was plagiarized from Ellis's (1910 [1925], 203–4) *Sex in Relation to Society*. Whole sections were reproduced, unattributed, regarding "civilisational value" and the "special condition of urban life." The dull routines of urban life and the stress of competition made men and women more enamored by excitement, while the illegitimate intercourse this could lead to was harder to detect within the anonymous landscape. Shuttleworth even quoted "a student of the urban," whom Ellis (1910 [1925], 289) himself had quoted (citing this student as Sherwell 1897), arguing that "the problem of prostitution is at bottom a mad and irresistible craving for excitement, a serious and wilful revolt against the monotony of common place ideas and the uninspired drudgery of everyday life."

While the sexology literature, as will be seen in the discussion of suppression, was increasingly being read in government circles, Shuttleworth appealed to even more radical sources in his conclusion. He argued that the feminist movement throughout the world was attacking the question from the right direction, targeting the economic dimensions of women's wages and trying to equalize the laws regarding men and women. This would entail "the sweeping away of the purely artificial conventions whereby the male is permitted to be a polygamist, whereas the female under all sorts of social pains and penalties is regarded as a monogamist." He ended by invoking "Lecky's dictum" against anyone who had nothing but condemnation for prostitutes.

The passage was taken from W. E. H. Lecky's comments from 1869 (reprinted in Lecky 1926 [2004], 103–4) on the "position of women" in his volume on the history of European morals. The prostitute was here referred to as the most mournful upon which a moralist could dwell; one who counterfeits with a cold heart the transports of affection and submits herself as a passive instrument of lust, being doomed to disease and abject wretchedness; and the "eternal priestess of humanity, blasted for the sins of the people." Yet Shuttleworth chose to focus on Lecky's comment that the prostitute was an efficient guardian of virtue, without whom the purity of countless happy homes would be polluted. This idea of the prostitute as conduit for the release of excess male virility was a Victorian notion that was quickly dying out, but one that seemed to have swayed Shuttleworth. This was despite his invocation of Havelock Ellis, whose advocacy of social hygiene (Ellis 1912 [1927]) would be so influential, and who had condemned the brothel as a decaying artifact of a less moral age (Ellis 1910 [1925], 303). Despite this, Shuttleworth seemed more convinced by the advice of Edwardes, who had experienced and enforced segregation in Bombay. In a review published seven years later, Edwardes (1924, 90) admitted that there was pressure to overturn segregation, but fell back on arguments similar to those made in Colombo: that suppression simply spread prostitution through the city and that it was an Indian tradition to have particular trades residing in particular areas. Edwardes did, however, stress the need to tackle immoral trade and the condition of low-class prostitutes who were often kept "like caged animals" in native brothels. The influence of Edwardes seems self-evident in the three recommendations Shuttleworth put forth as a result of his investigations:

1. The total abolition of European prostitutes
2. The granting of discretionary powers to the commissioner of police for dealing with pimps and brothel keepers
3. The restriction of foreign, Asiatic, and indigenous prostitutes to an area where they would be least in evidence

The first issue was an imperial one regarding whiteness and race, while the second hinted at the coming powers of the suppressionists against the most abusive brothels and bullies. The third, however, clung tenaciously to the segregationist system. Acknowledging that he was, with increasing obviousness, swimming against the tide of local opinion, Shuttleworth attempted to anticipate criticisms of his tacit condoning of prostitution by insisting: "To me this appears to be an entirely erroneous view-point, and the answer to it would be that Government, recognizing its inability to suppress prostitution entirely, does the next best thing in its power, which is to 'crib, cabin and confine' to the least prominent localities."

The report itself was subject to vetting by a committee established by the local government, which submitted its report in November 1917.[18] The committee was composed of two British members of government; three barristers representing the Chinese, Burmese, and Indian "communities"; Dr. G. R. T. Ross, representing the Rangoon Vigilance Society; and Shuttleworth himself. Ross's displeasure with Shuttleworth's conclusions comes out clearly in the committee report, in which he pleaded for the ceaseless harrying of prostitutes, whom he wanted to "diminish totally." While he secured some shifts in the streets proposed for segregation (all numbered streets between Judah Ezekiel Street and Thompson Street), he displayed a completely different mental attitude to the members of the committee, insisting prostitution was evil, while the report stressed that the other members of the committee would "refuse to simplify like that."

The report went on to state a few "commonplace" facts, namely, that nature makes males want to mate between the ages of sixteen and eighteen, and the females between the ages of thirteen and fifteen; that civilization and economic developments had led to an unnatural inability of natural satisfaction; that while women have been forced by social sentiment into chastity, men have not felt this pressure, thus prostitution had emerged as "[a] safety valve[] through which ebullient sexual energies of celibate adult males are diverted into harmless channels without damage to the purity of the more respectable female population."[19] Compounding these gross sexual and gendered essentialisms, the committee added some comments on race and class. The distortion of the gender ratio in Rangoon was said to be by laboring men in the prime of their life: "They belong to races and classes in whom the idea of self-restraint of any kind is feeble and that of sexual self-restraint almost unknown." In the face of such "great natural forces" the "petty persecutions" proposed by Dr. Ross were dismissed.

Raising fears of "homo-sexualism" and disease, the committee therefore accepted the recommendation of segregation: "Put them, therefore, like slaughterhouses and cemeteries and other necessary evils, in some place out of the way but not so far out of the way as not to be readily accessible to those persons who require their services." It was even suggested that regular inspections for venereal disease be introduced. As will be shown, the government of Burma seemed horrified by the reactionary nature of the committee's comments. It did, however, use the wartime conditions to argue that immediate action would be inappropriate. It was only under international pressure after the war, in conjunction with national revulsion over the murder of a young prostitute in Bombay, that the segregation system would finally lose its sanction from central government.

### Bombay: Civil Abandonment and the Violent End of Segregation

On 6 April 1917 the *Times of India* carried an article that sounded the death knell for centrally sanctioned segregation across the subcontinent. Unlike former problematizations of governmental policy, the immediate object of concern was not the syphilitic state of the soldiery, nor the mobilization of civil society around the sexualization of civic space, although both these scandalous discourses would later be invoked. This scandal concerned a young woman, who in the court cases, government documents, and press articles that followed, was named as Taibai, alias Akootai. But it was not the girl's life that garnered so much attention; she very much remains a mostly silent subaltern in these documents. Rather, it was her death, and the world upon which her passing shed light that fascinated governmental and popular opinion alike. This was not an underworld; a flitting, nefarious, unlocalizable space. Rather, it was an otherworld, *abandoned* through segregation by governmental policy and watched over under the ordinances of the Bombay Police Act powers amended in 1902. The debate very much reflects this ambivalence: the belated mourning for a woman little cared for in life, and a belated concern for the city's prostitutes, fifteen years after they had been civilly abandoned around Grant Road.

The Bombay edition of the *Times of India* reported that a man, a "wife," and a "child" had been charged with the murder of a prostitute who had been forcefully detained in their brothel. She tried to escape but had been captured, brought back, and beaten to death with an iron rod and stone, having been branded with lit matches, forced to drink her supervisor's urine, and made to bathe in scalding water (for a sensitive exploration of this case, see Tambe 2009a, chapter 4). The man was named as Miroza Syedkhan, alias Mir Afzalkhan Syedkhan (known most commonly as Mirza Syed Khan), and his accomplices as Gangabai, alias Mariambai, and Gomtibai, alias Sakinabai.

Within a week the Bombay Humanitarian Fund had submitted a petition to the government regarding the "horrors of enforced prostitution in India" and demanding an inquiry.[20] The central government ordered a report, which the government of Bombay set about compiling. The commissioner of police in Bombay, F. A. M. H. Vincent, set out his position in a letter to the Judicial Department of the government of Bombay on 11 August 1917. He showed that this was not an isolated incident, but that without extra powers the police could not tackle the bullies or pimps who took all the earnings of prostitutes and fed them in return. Such powers, along the lines of the English Criminal Law Amendment Act (CLAA) of 1912, would be justified by an appeal to the "coastal cosmopolitanism" (see Legg 2012b) of Bombay: "The problem in a large cosmopolitan city like Bombay is very different to the form of rural or even smaller towns like Ahmedabad or Poona, if only for sheer number of people involved."[21] Within this geographically exceptional space, Bombay's prostitutes were taxonomized in the grand colonial tradition. Vincent insisted there were three degrees of prostitution that could be understood clearly by their location:

1. Better class Indian houses: serviced by various women, from the clandestine prostitute, to the singing or dancing girls of repute, to the kept mistress

2. Indian houses run along the lines of third-class European, or Japanese, brothels in well-known areas, operated under supervision from the police

3. Evil dens: the type of brothel run by Mirza Syed Khan, run for poorer customers, also used by low-caste clandestine prostitutes

Vincent recommended that no interference was required for the first class, while the second was already under surveillance. In considering the third class, however, he reminded the government that they were dealing with "a class steeped in abysmal ignorance, people whose social and moral fabric is elemental not to say barbaric." Court cases involving the lower classes were invoked to communicate their "low degree of civilisation" and "evolution" (that is, their *unnaturalness*). However, these comments were not deployed in favor of overturning segregation, but to assert the impossibility of such a class surviving without it. As Vincent continued: "It is because I appreciate this fact, because I know that it is impossible to restrict, far less abolish, prostitution, and because I am aware of the dangers of too strict an executive system of control that I suggest limiting Police activity to the procurer, the pimp or the bully and recommend that action against him, either executive or judicial, be undertaken only at the instance of the Commissioner of Police."

Alongside previous attempts to introduce the regulation of trafficking by Shuttleworth, Vincent was advocating the legislative governmentality that would be used to target trafficking and the suppression of prostitution, while also maintaining a commitment to segregation. While conceding that the United Kingdom's CLAA of 1912 had been intended to abolish brothels, such powers were claimed to be too rigorous for the East. Therefore, the recommended course of action was to amend the City Police Act to provide greater powers against the orchestrators of prostitute exploitation.

While the Mirza Syed Khan case was obviously highly specific to Bombay, the jury in the Bombay High Court case expressed its horror that such an event could take place (anywhere), and requested that immediate steps be taken to see that similar dens of horror did and could not exist elsewhere. This effectively forced the central government to become involved in expanding this from a local to an all-India inquiry. On 14 December 1917 the Home Department forwarded details of the court case to the provinces of British India and inquired as to the extent of similar evils. The debate prompted by the Bombay scandal allowed moral pressure to be placed on the central government to act. Commissioner F. Booth Tucker, of the Salvation

Army, wrote to Home Secretary Sir William Vincent on 16 September 1918 claiming that girls were practically being sold into slavery in the brothels of Calcutta, Bombay, and other cities: "It seems quite on a par with the evils of Sati, girl infanticide, and of burying lepers alive, referred to by Mr Oldrieve in his lecture last Wednesday[22]; and surely the time has come for the Indian government to put down its foot and say it shall not be, and that we will hunt down and give the heaviest sentences possible to people who are engaged in this iniquitous traffic."[23]

It was felt that with government support, there were mechanisms already in place to deal with the "human harpies" carrying out this business, whether through the police or through a question in Parliament. Vincent agreed that both of the latter would be useful and was thus presented with a further opportunity to outsource what could have been a burdensome load for the central government when the replies to his circular memorandum of December 1917 were collated and discussed in October 1918. By this time, however, Bombay had amended its police act to provide greater powers against those like Syed Khan.

The City of Bombay Police (Amendment) Bill was sent by the government of Bombay to the Home Department of the government of India on 23 September 1918.[24] It was stated to be a direct response to Commissioner Vincent's letter as described above, targeting the revolting conditions of the lowest class of brothels in Bombay, where women were kept in a state of slavery and cruelty. This was often achieved through withholding the clothes or property of the women and keeping them indebted through loans of money or clothes. The amendments provided powers to require the removal of owners or managers of brothels outside the city, taken from the Foreigners Act (1864), and through applying a section taken from the British CLAA (1885, which made it an offense to detain a woman in a brothel against her will, whether physically or through financial obligation). The amendments were approved by the Home Department, despite some fears that the police would abuse their powers and blackmail the newly liberated brothel girls, and were signed by the viceroy on 18 January 1919.

The powers of the act would be of great interest to other provinces throughout India, although the discussion in 1918 of the replies to the memorandum of 1917 on Syed Khan showed that Bombay was seen to be a unique case. No other province claimed to have anything like the problem indicated in Bombay; only the Punjab and the North-West Frontier Provinces had evidence of similar cases. Most provinces opposed police intervention, but Bengal and Burma replied that they were considering the situation in Calcutta and Rangoon respectively and would watch to see what happened in Bombay after the amendments of the Police Act with interest. Commenting on these replies on 13 February 1919, T. Slogan within the Home Department raised the key issue of scale to which these replies had been gesturing. There were, he summarized, local conditions of such paramount importance that they should be left to local governments. However, there were also features of prostitution confined to no one city or province that should be dealt with on uniform lines. The best policy was concluded to be that of local innovation, with the central government keeping a close watch. J. H. DuBoulay commented on this note on 13 April 1919 that, while all-India legislation should not be proposed, many women in brothels seemed to be kept in a state of financial servitude due to the debts they were made to owe to their pimp or madam. Yet, short of absolute suppression of brothels and procurers, deemed to be a proposal for which India was not yet ripe, he could not offer further suggestions. Concluding this debate on the future nominalist scalar politics of prostitution in India, Vincent commented on file on 14 April 1919: "The matter is one for Provincial Government and there is no ground for any All-India Act at present rate. I approve of action on the lines suggested by the Secretary and would ask that we leave it to local Governments to indicate such legislations as they see fit."[25]

This cemented the scalar division that the government of India had been working toward since the repeal of the Indian Contagious Diseases Acts and the expulsion of prostitutes from military bazaars in the late nineteenth century. Through powers of suggestion and stimulation, local governments had increasingly come to pass laws that catered to the will of central government. This had followed a path toward segregation at the turn of the century, creating spaces from which the military could supposedly be forbidden, to a consideration during the war years of how to tackle trafficking and procuration while refusing to relinquish a belief in segregation as a successful mechanism for, as the Bombay amendment act put it, "the more effectual control of prostitution in the city." Throughout this process prostitution had been *named* a local affair, not one for central government (as Howell 2009, 234, has argued, "The isolation and autonomy of regulated places was always a convenient imperial fiction"). The scandals of Rangoon and Bombay precipitated the end, however, of segregation as a centrally sanctioned policy, by highlighting the negative impacts of segregation on both the area which surrounded it and the captives often held within it. These two scandalous Indian sites helped usher in an age of suppression, in line with developments across the globe. While the amendment of existing powers in Bombay and Burma aimed to remedy the worst abuses of the system, Shuttleworth and Vincent sought to defend segregation. In the 1920s, however, the emphasis shifted decisively from toleration and segregation to abolition and suppression.

*Discrediting Segregation: 1918–1922*

The immediate postwar period in India saw the final jettisoning of segregation and the search for legislative powers that would enable the targeting of the brothel, which was re-envisaged as a site of invisibility and disease, no longer a site that made prostitutes visible and healthy. While this marked a significant shift from the earlier segregation policies, the greatest disjuncture would come when the brothel was focused on as a node in trafficking networks, not for its effect on its inhabitants or locality. This would see a more fundamental shift in the geographical imagination informing suppression campaigners, from a focus on the absolute and inherent characteristics of the brothel to its relational function within wider networks. This would also entail a shift in statistical thinking, from the supposed sureties of facts, such as venereal disease per thousand troops of the nineteenth century, to an acknowledgment that governmental statistics were neither subtle nor dynamic enough to represent the realities of prostitution in twentieth-century colonial India. The central-local dilemma here involved would also be resolved through a series of provincial laws that conformed to the wishes of the central state.

While these developments would only really accelerate after 1923, they were dependent for their inspiration on the Burma-Bombay axis which had proven itself to be the progenitor of segregation at the turn of the century and had provided the scandalous sites by which it had been discredited during the war (see Pivar 2002, chapter 5, for evidence of the competition among New York, Chicago, and San Francisco for national prominence in tacking prostitution in the United States). The civil administrations of the presidencies of Burma and Bombay would provide the templates for later suppressionist legislation, but this should not be taken as evidence that the military, and its concern with venereal disease rates, was no longer influential. It was their admonishment of segregation at the end of the war that made it clear to central authorities that a new governmentality was required, and that provincial experimentation with suppressionist legislation should provide it.

The military had played a key role in encouraging the segregation of prostitutes at a distance from cantonments in an attempt to decrease venereal diseases among its troops. However, the revised Cantonment Regulations, while banning registration and inspection of prostitutes, had tolerated their existence, if healthy, within the civil lines, which continued to attract the attention of campaigners. In 1903 Maurice Gregory visited India and widely publicized what he viewed as neo-regulationism, through government-maintained houses and inspections of infected women (Pivar 2002, 8). Mrs. K. Dixon, the wife of an English chaplain in India, only discovered this system in 1913 on her return to England but set out, like anti-regulation campaigners Elizabeth Andrew and Katharine Bushnell in the 1890s, to expose it to civil society in the United Kingdom and abroad. From 1917 to 1919 she toured India, under the auspices of the AMSH, campaigning against tolerated brothels within both cantonments and municipalities.[26] Dixon worked and published tirelessly, and eventually secured an interview with the commander in chief. Shortly afterward a significant shift in military policy was announced, which the *Shield* claimed on Dixon's behalf as a "Victory in India."[27]

On 20 July 1918 Regulation 12C was passed under the Defence of India Act (1915) sanctioning the closure of brothels in or nearby cantonments, although it was noted by the editorial in the *Shield* that these powers already existed in many parts of India anyway. What was significant was that on 2 August the adjutant general circulated a memorandum on behalf of the commander in chief to all general officers commanding, instructing them to ban soldiers from visiting brothels, even if they were believed to be under military control.[28] Science had now shown, it was claimed, that no examination could prove that a woman was disease free, and that the only protection was the cultivation of opinions against sexual incontinence and to protect soldiers from temptation. As with earlier cases by which municipalities had been stimulated into action, it was suggested that military authorities should use these powers rigorously within cantonments, but with discretion and in consultation with civil authorities outside of them. As the *Shield* article commented: "This is a good sign; it has for some time been evident that the military problem in India cannot be finally or satisfactorily dealt with while tolerated vice flourishes unchecked in the cities."

This coalition between the old enemies of the AMSH and the armed forces in India marked the beginning of a new suppressionist campaign that would operate on both military and civil space. The *Shield* also singled out the memorandum's provision of financial support for the Salvation Army to help women who had been expelled from cantonments: "Here is, indeed, a new note for the military order. The women are to be cared for." While one may assume that the motive behind this gesture was to have the women take up an alternative life, rather than settling outside the cantonment in the 1880s, it set an interesting precedent with which local governments would grapple when they implemented their suppressionist legislation in the 1920s.

The AMSH was not, however, totally uncritical. The Defence of India Act was an emergency criminal law passed in the state of exception that the war had created. As such, the regulations were temporary and needed to be embodied in ordinary law.[29] There were also doubts within government that the law could be so used. On 29 July 1916 the general officer commanding the Burma Division requested that the government of Burma propose the use of the Defence of India Rules to deport women from military stations who were believed to be suffering from venereal diseases, as this decision could not be challenged in a court of law.[30] The chief secretary who forwarded the proposal expressed his doubts, and the Home Department was quick to stress that it would be straining the legitimacy of the rules to suggest that infected prostitutes were acting in a manner prejudicial to public safety. The *Shield* also pointed out that the law was permissive, encouraging action, rather than compulsory, in requiring it.

It was clear, however, that if such powers were to be used, the way in which prostitutes were to be treated would have to be stipulated. On 25 November 1918 H. R. V. Dobbs, agent to the governor general in Baluchistan, wrote to the Foreign and Political Department, informing it of the planned response to the adjutant general's memorandum with regards to troops stationed in the town of Quetta.[31] The general officer commanding proposed that the Defence of India Rule be used to close all brothels in the municipality and then to confine the women to a locality that could be closed off to the troops. Their current location in the bazaar meant that it was impractical to place it out of bounds, while expelling the women from the town entirely was predicted to lead to an increase in crime and disease. The legislative model would be section 152 of the Punjab Municipal Act (III of 1911) which could be used to confine prostitutes to quarters of the city. Dobbs admitted some concerns over the proposals. Firstly, that if the soldiers were deprived of their "formed normal and recognised opportunities for the indulgence of their passions," they might turn to the women in the surrounding villages or to "unnatural vice," exciting the animosity of local tribesmen and spreading venereal disease in a manner more difficult to cope with than in existing circumstances. The secretary of the Foreign and Political Department, Denys Bray, expressed his concerns regarding the proposals on 28 December 1918. To "pen prostitutes up in one quarter" seemed very much like the state regulation of vice, and it seemed doubtful that the Punjab Municipal Act had been drawn up with that intention in mind. Bray requested the comments of the Home Department, which were provided on 10 March 1919. It was stressed from the outset that this was a municipal, not central, issue. Immediately overriding this scalar distinction, however, it was pointed out that Calcutta had refused to implement segregation in 1903, despite the suggestions of the secretary of state. The scandal in Rangoon was also recounted, although action had stopped at abolishing the segregated zone, but not the tolerated brothels.

Despite this, G. M. Young's comments on 13 March within the Home Department still stressed that segregation could be considered as a local initiative: "There is[, however,] a considerable difference when such measures are carried out by an elected or semi-elected body such as a Municipal Committee, as compared with a police officer acting directly under Govnt."[32] However, J. H. DuBoulay commented on 22 March that the Home Department should be greatly interested in the Baluchistan case, as it did not have a definite policy on the matter and had carefully abstained from providing one in Rangoon. He agreed with the comments of the chief secretary of Burma, W. F. Rice, in 1914 that segregation should be opposed. He was joined in agreement on 24 March by Sir William Vincent, the Home Secretary who also had to deal with the fallout from the Mirza Syed Khan case, and on 29 April by a representative of the Army Department who insisted that any form of segregation be condemned. As such, on 26 July 1919 Denys Bray replied to the proposal to use the Defence of India Rules to instigate a new system of segregation by pointing out that such a policy had proved a failure in large cities and had enhanced the evils arising out of prostitution: "The result of such segregation has been to advertise vice and to give to school boys and students and to the vicious an easy way to fall into temptation. Another of its lamentable consequences is that in the segregated area public decency does not exist. These facts have been recognised elsewhere and segregation has been in consequence abandoned as a policy in the greater part of Europe except in a very few towns on the Continent, and appears to be generally discredited."[33]

These official notes therefore established what the Home Department claimed never to have had, despite its stimulation and suggestion of segregation at the turn of the century. The definite policy of the central government was now to oppose segregation, in agreement with the Army Department, the AMSH, and international opinion. There was, however, a need for a policy, rather than just a denouncement. DeBoulay's suggestion that the government would be greatly interested in local experiments held true, as did Young's prediction that semi-elected bodies would be able to achieve more than a police officer, like Shuttleworth, or Vincent, working directly under the government.

Although in the early years of the twentieth century Burma, and Rangoon especially, came to be associated with segregation, the archives also record a failed genealogy in which proposed suppressionist legislation that would have specifically targeted trafficking was rejected in 1902. The stimulus for this legislation came from civil society, in response to government statistics consistently indicating that the rate of venereal diseases in Rangoon in the 1890s was among the highest in the country.[34] The Burma branch of the British Medical Association made four suggestions in the summer of 1901 for tackling the problem of prostitution and venereal diseases: compulsory examinations, a special hospital for venereal diseases, a Magdalene hospital for reclamation, and a version of the British Vagrancy Act. The first was stated, by F. Cowie of the Home Department on 11 September 1901, to be against government policy, the second to be addressed by a special ward at Rangoon General Hospital, the third to be something better left to private philanthropy, while the fourth would be addressed by the fact that government was already "stimulating municipal legislation" to deal with solicitation and brothels. Other members of the Home Department, however, pointed out that the Vagrancy Act was concerned with a whole other dimension of the problem, tackling those who "lived on the earnings of prostitutes, or who publically solicits for immoral purposes."

Various clauses of the Indian Penal Code were quoted as suitable for dealing with such problems. These clauses included sections 361, for kidnapping from lawful guardianship; 362, for abduction by force; and 498, for enticing or taking away and detaining a married woman. But it was pointed out that these powers ended at the removal of a person from their home or guardianship, without extending to traffickers themselves. The case for legislation was pressed for by A. Williams of the Home Department, who insisted on 21 December 1901 that existing police acts throughout the country were insufficient because they only related to brothels and soliciting, not men who procure women or who live on the wages of prostitutes. Viceroy Curzon was thus convinced to cautiously refer to local governments for their opinion, but felt their answers to be inconclusive and thus ordered the government to "drop the matter" on 22 May 1902. It would be another seventeen years until, after the scandals and exceptional circumstances of the First World War, these suppressionist powers would be considered again.

Just as before and during the war, the local and central governments in India were once again forced into action over Burma by the campaigning of the Association for Moral and Social Hygiene in the imperial capital of London. On 6 June 1919 the AMSH wrote to the secretary of state for India requesting a copy of Shuttleworth's report, having initially requested it in January 1918, almost immediately after it had passed through the vetting committee in Rangoon.[35] The secretary of state had replied, passing on relevant correspondence with the chief secretary to the government of Burma which confirmed that fuller legislation had been avoided for fear of causing a disturbance during the war.[36]

The AMSH continued to pressure him when the report was not forthcoming, threatening an exposé of what they termed the "continued atrocities" in Burma. The secretary of state requested that the government of India send him a copy of the report on 17 July 1919, although this was too late to prevent the AMSH from publishing an account of Rangoon in the August–September 1919 edition of the *Shield*. It was penned by Mr. Conyers Baker, general secretary of the Rangoon YMCA, and clearly showed that the segregated area had in no way been abolished.[37]

On 22 November 1919 Shuttleworth's report was submitted by C. M. Webb, the chief secretary to the government of Burma, to the Home Secretary in Delhi, summarizing its three recommendations that living on "immoral earnings" be criminalized, that foreign prostitutes be deported, and that the area in which prostitutes could live in Rangoon be delimited.[38] The lieutenant governor of Burma agreed with the first two recommendations, proposing local legislation to ban the keeping of a brothel, though not infringing upon the liberty of a woman or a small group of women living together to practice prostitution should they not affect public decency or advertise their trade outwardly. However, the third recommendation was rejected, despite the support of Shuttleworth and the committee. As Webb put it: "This proposal amounts in effect to a reversion to the old system of segregation which previous experience has proved to be a failure." The existing Police Act embodied principles of toleration and regulation of prostitution in certain parts of the town that were now felt to be opposed to public policy.

The new legislation that would target those who profited from prostitution while abolishing segregation was entitled the Burma Suppression of Brothels Bill and was submitted to the central government for approval on

5 November 1920.[39] The principles underlying the bill had, however, been drafted by the then lieutenant governor of Burma, R. H. Craddock, a year earlier. He admitted that, outside of cantonments, the British government in India had tended to adopt slight control rather than abolition or suppression. However, in larger towns the need to remove objectionable brothels from certain areas had led to their "swarming" into others. Craddock was completely unwilling to accept segregation, terming it the home of licensed vice and claiming that the committee's review of Shuttleworth's report had not been particularly illuminating as it had failed to consider developments in thought in Europe, or spend its time proving why such developments should not apply to conditions in Rangoon.

Craddock's preference was for suppressing prostitution on the English model by legislating against the pimp, procurer, and brothel keeper, citing the horrors of the Bombay murder case as a motivation. Craddock was entirely dismissive of Edwardes "so called classic" about prostitution, calling it nothing less than an apologia of prostitution on a par with Lecky. He stressed that the world had moved on since the time of the latter, who wrote only of prostitutes, not of brothels. Making a plea both for a solution to a local problem and naming Burma as an experimental site in an imperial network that stretched over India and beyond, Craddock concluded: "In fact, it may be urged that Rangoon offers a very valuable field for an experiment of this kind, and that it is particularly important that such legislation should first be introduced, not over the country at large, but in those particular cities in which the evil is particularly rampant."[40]

These points were obviously influential over the bill that was submitted a year later. In the covering letter submitted on 5 November 1920 to the Home Department, F. Lewisohn, the chief secretary, depicted the segregation system as something that had now been abandoned in much of Europe. The failings of segregation in Rangoon were listed in a slamming indictment of previous policy, showing that it had not prevented brothels becoming scattered over the whole town, advertised vice, offered a semipublic temptation, not prevented the spread of disease, not protected women, and led to a flaunting of temptation and a complete absence of regard for public decency "which was a scandal and a reproach to Rangoon." Abraham Flexner's *Prostitution in Europe* (1914) was cited as evidence that segregation never leads to abolition of brothels outside the demarcated zone.

The object of the bill was not to end vice, but to end the commercialization of vice, the core of which was the brothel. Founding a link that would be a leitmotif of the coming suppression campaign, the bill posed the brothel as the source of demand that the "white slave traffic" supplied. Only a "frontal attack" on the brothel keeper and procurer could be effective. While the majority of public opinion may have been in favor of toleration, Lewisohn insisted that there "is no more reason why Government should defer to this *laissez-faire* attitude in dealing with this particular evil, than it does in dealing with such other evils as murder, leprosy or small-pox."

Since this was such an obviously stark departure from precedent, U. C. Stuart in the Home Department was asked to comment on the case. Remarking upon Craddock's insistence that developments in European thought be attended to, Stuart alluded to what he felt were the "weightiest contributions to the literature on the subject in recent times," namely, Bloch's *The Sexual Life of Our Time* (1908), Forel's *The Sexual Question* (1908), and Havelock Ellis's *Sex in Relation to Society* (1910 [1925]). Other mention was also given to the campaigning literature of Mrs. Olive MacKirdy and Mr. W. N. Willis on the *White Slave Market* (1912), Reginald Kaufman's *Daughters of Ishmael* (1911) and *Broken Pitchers* (1912), and James Marchant's *The Master Problem* (1917). As shown in the introduction to this chapter, this literature was unanimous in condemning the brothel as a site of occlusion, disease, sexual deviance, slavery, and as a site of demand and supply for the trafficking of women and children. The *use* of this literature was vital, however. The review of the Burma Bill by members of the Indian Civil Service made use of the sexology literature and Flexner's work to strengthen their case. Shuttleworth, however, had quoted some of the most radical parts of Ellis and Lecky which discredited his report in the eyes of his conservative appraisers in New Delhi. The review of the literature was, therefore, used to justify the Burmese legislation, which did not try to stamp out prostitution. Rather, Stuart claimed: "It realises that men and women cannot be made moral by legislation, but rather than adopt a *laissez faire* policy it proposes to attack the vulnerable points in the citadel of prostitution."[41] These were said to be:

1. The brothel
2. The pimp, "bully" or "fancy man"; who lives on the earnings of prostitution
3. The procurer: purveyor of women for brothels and chief figure in vice commercialization

While less explicitly geographical in that it did not tolerate a zone of prostitution over others, the proposed bill had an explicit spatiality in the way in which it targeted the brothel, which was said to be a focus of venereal disease and a "hot-bed of various forms of sexual perversion, e.g. sadism, masochism, homosexualism." The reverberations of the Bombay murder case were also still apparent. In debating whether the punishment of whipping should be including in the bill, Stuart argued: "Most people would, I think, hold that the scoundrel *par excellence*, the principal actor in the Bombay tragedy (assuming that his victim had not died) could not be punished severely enough by whipping, imprisonment or fine, or a triple dose of all three."

Stuart obviously found Craddock's comments on the usefulness of the legislation to the rest of India convincing. Stuart argued that the bill was not a novelty, but was based in legislation in England and Ceylon, while India itself was composed of various conflicting local laws. Bombay had amended its Police Act, Bengal had its Disorderly Houses Law which had fortified the process of segregation taking place in Calcutta, while various municipal acts dealt with public solicitation in a host of ways. As such, it was argued that there should be no hesitation: "The experience of the working of the proposed law in Burma will be of great use in approaching the problem of prostitution in other parts of India." While acknowledging the drawbacks, such as the expected increase in street walking and clandestine prostitution, or the refusal of prostitutes to testify against their pimps, Stuart pragmatically concluded: "Prostitution is a hydra-headed monster which we can only hope to scotch and not kill." On this recommendation the Home and Legislative Departments recommended the bill be passed, leading to the Burma Suppression of Brothels Act (1921). The bill was presented to the Council of the lieutenant governor of Burma on 26 February 1921 by Lewisohn and had four objects:

1. To make brothel keeping and the detention of women in brothels against their will illegal
2. To make it illegal for a man to live on the earnings of prostitution
3. To penalize the procuring of women for immoral purposes
4. To extend the definition of soliciting to protect passersby from allurements and indecent gestures made from within their houses

Lewisohn opened his introduction with an admission regarding the bill's deficiencies in defining a "brothel" (see Levine 2003, 188, on imperial inabilities to define prostitution and its associated sites and vices).[42] Attempts at this definition had always been abandoned by the Burmese government before, and Lewisohn requested the reviewing Select Committee to provide a definition. The Bombay case was mentioned, and it was suggested that it was the "first duty" of government to save such women. But it was

CHAPTER 2

the brothel, again, which was brought into central focus: "It is the brothel which is the core of the whole problem. It is the brothel which created a demand, for which the procurer and the seducer act as a supply." Flexner was cited, as the highest authority on the subject, in repeating the now well-rehearsed condemnation of segregation.

On 17 March the Select Committee provided its definition of a brothel, being any house, room, or place which the occupier or person in charge thereof habitually allows to be used by any other person for the purposes of prostitution. Otherwise, the bill was passed without major alteration and received the viceroy's assent on 16 June 1921. The majority of the clauses had been taken from English legislation, along with a few from Ceylon. Only one had been directly inspired from Indian legislation, and this was the Bombay City Police Act. Though useful in tackling the segregated zone, the Bombay Act had been proven insufficient for tackling the diversity and number of prostitutes in the city, leading to another influential experiment that, more ambitiously, termed itself preventative, rather than merely suppressive.

### THE BOMBAY PREVENTION OF PROSTITUTION ACT (XI OF 1923)

While the Police Act amendments of 1920 provided powers to dissolve the segregated area and to rescue detained women from brothels, the Syed Khan scandal had damaged the city beyond the repair of a few amendments to the City Police Act. An editorial in the *Shield* (Neilans 1921) had shown that the Bombay Presidency Women's Council and the YMCA had produced a pamphlet that highlighted the plight of girls in the city who were "practically bought slaves." This was blamed solely on deficiencies in the law, which permitted the police to close down brothels, but did not mandatorily bind them to do so.

While the Shuttleworth report had estimated that Bombay contained 15,000 prostitutes, later estimates would put this much higher. At the Imperial Social Hygiene Congress, held in London during October 1925, a paper was presented by Herbert Bryant, then general secretary of the Bombay branch of the YMCA (published as Crowdy 1925). Although he cited police figures from 1921, listing the total number of prostitutes in Bombay at 5,164 and the number of brothels as 885, he insisted that the actual total may have been up to 50,000, but not less than 25,000. He also, however, mentioned the appointment of a committee in 1921 to investigate prostitution in the city that would produce the second significant form of suppressionist legislation in India within two years.

In September 1921 Mr. Kanji Dwarkadas, a member of the Bombay Legislative Council, moved a resolution asking the government to make brothels illegal. This resulted in a Prostitution Committee being established to consider the means for "remedying the evils of prostitution in Bombay," which submitted its report on 19 April 1922.[43] It had been chaired by Sir Jamsetji Jejeebhoy, a prominent member of the Parsi community, and also included the bishop and archbishop of Bombay, the commissioner of police, municipal commissioners, doctors, lawyers, and the secretary of the Salvation Army. The report recounted the history of the present condition of affairs, including the two thousand women registered during the CDA years. After repeal in 1888, thirty years of "laissez-faire" policy were blamed for the worst evils of prostitution emerging. The Syed Khan case had prompted attempts to protect prostitutes from illegal detention, although the segregated area was admitted to still be in existence, despite the widespread practice of prostitution outside of it.

As regards segregation, the Jejeebhoy Committee was not as condemnatory as the government of Burma. It suggested that dispersed prostitution would have spread the problems further afield, and that segregation encouraged the public at large to hold themselves aloof: "We doubt if any citizen of Bombay can entirely eliminate from his mind the horror and disgust inspired by the contempt of morality which 'Grant Road' implies and the misery of the unfortunate women which it displays." (Jejeebhoy may have felt particularly strongly about this as his forefathers had established the Sir Jamsetjee Jejeebhoy Hospital at the end of Grant Road in the 1840s.) The brothels were said to be supplied with girls from all over India, keeping virtual slaves in insanitary conditions with no medical care.

Future policy would have to choose between two rival systems upon which there was said to be worldwide division of opinion: regulation (the registration and licensing of prostitution and brothels, with compulsory medical examination and treatment) or abolition (the destruction of brothels by making it an offense to live wholly or in part on the immoral earnings of a woman). Jejeebhoy found in favor of abolition, condemning regulation for being directed at only one sex and for indirectly encouraging vice by tolerating it. As such, the committee recommended that the government of Bombay should make illegal the following:

1. The keeping of brothels
2. The procurement of women
3. The letting of houses for prostitution

Unlike the Burma Act of 1921, by which it was directly inspired, the act would be applied over a longer period than three months so the women could have a chance to find alternative accommodation. Abolition was also stated to need more social work from the YMCA, Salvation Army, and community institutions, as well as the provision of rescue homes for girls and women taken from brothels.

Despite the protestations of representatives from the municipal committee, the military, and the police, the committee's recommendations were taken straight forward into a bill, which was approved by the central government in July 1923.[44] It stated that the prime target would be the procurer, of the committee's three recommendations, as inspired by the Burma Act of 1921. However, the Bombay Prevention of Prostitution Act as passed included clauses so substantial that they could potentially justify its claim to actively prevent women being drawn into prostitution. The act carried forward developments made in amending the Police Act, such as sections that barred proceedings against women or girls unlawfully detained in any premises for sexual intercourse for repayment of loaned items. But the act also provided punishment through the following sections:

1. Soliciting or molesting any person or loitering for the purpose of prostitution or carnal intercourse, whether in or in sight of a public place or street
2. Allowing prostitution in a place of public amusement
3. Living on the earnings of prostitution
4. Procuration, or attempt at procuration, for the purposes of prostitution
5. Importing or attempting to import women or girls for prostitution
6. Unlawful detention for prostitution
7. Segregation of brothels by notifying prostitutes or those managing such women to not reside in or frequent specified areas, or to take up residence in a place within or beyond the City of Bombay

However, as an article in the *Shield* pointed out, the act did not make brothels illegal, nor did it attack the segregated area.[45] On the contrary, the opening sections, which proposed an abolitionist rash of measures, were joined by section 9 which suggested there were areas more or less appropriate for the act of prostitution, the inner geographical assumption of segregation. The main power bestowed by the act was to make it an offense for a male to manage a brothel, leaving the vice area "unaffected" (Bryant 1931), being under discretional, not compulsory, powers of censure.

These deficiencies in the act were compounded by the resources made available to enforce it. The annual reports on the police of Bombay City make it clear that between 1923 and 1927 there were no staff sanctioned to enforce the Bombay Prevention of Prostitution Act (BPPA), or the Bombay Children Act (XIII of 1924), which allowed children under the age of fifteen living in brothels to be removed.[46] During this time police reports detailed circumstances and lives that seemed worryingly unchanged from the dark days of 1917. For instance, the report from 1926 told of a sixteen-year-old girl named Kesarbai from Kashmir who had been kept as an inmate in Kamathipura, near Grant Road. When she ran away, the prostitute and her "paramour" who had been running the brothel strewed their possessions on the floor and accused Kesarbai of theft, although she proved her innocence to the police. The continuation of the segregated district was criticized both within and beyond India. In 1926 the *Shield* published an article correcting a report from the Glasgow socialist newspaper *Forward*, which had told of nine hundred women kept in cages, on full display (see figure 2.1: the captions read "Photograph of iron cages for prostitutes in Bombay"; "A man entering. Observe proximity to the tram lines"; "Women out for an airing"). While the cages were to keep men out, as much as women in, the AMSH agreed that the women would remain little more than slaves until the segregated area was clearer.

From May 1927 one detective inspector, two superintendents, and four head constables were deputed to enforce the acts. The most immediate effects were actually delivered through the Children's Act, with 119 notices being served on prostitutes or brothel keepers in 1927, 50 in 1928, but only 18 in 1929. While some of the children were sent to schools by the juvenile courts, most were sent "up country" to their "native places" or "respectable localities," far away from the corrupting influence of the coastal cosmopolitanism of the port town. In contrast, 1927 saw only seven cases under the BPPA: two for living on the earnings of prostitution (section 5); two for procuration (section 6); and three for importing (section 7). Over the next two years, work was transferred from the Children's Act, with cases falling to fifty then seventeen, to the BPPA, which the commissioner of police claimed was due to brothel owners learning of the law and removing minors to other locations; a "well-to-do" class of prostitutes even established and ran their own boarding house for children no longer allowed in brothels.[47] The act was used in sixty-one cases regarding soliciting between 1928

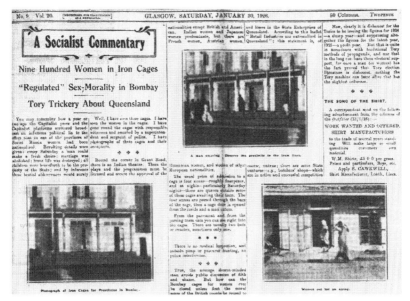

FIGURE 2.1. Article from the *Forward* newspaper. © The British Library Board, system number 013928230.

and 1929, twenty-five cases of living off the earnings of prostitution, twenty cases of procuration, and five cases of importation. However, the provisions to target the segregated area were not systematically enforced.

As such, the Bombay Vigilance Association and other social organizations continued to campaign against the vice area, supporting amendments to the act to provide greater punishment for solicitation.[48] In 1928 a petition requesting that the government amend the act further to include the suppression of brothels attracted three thousand signatures (Gedge 1931). As a result of the campaigning and consultation, a further amendment act was passed on 3 September 1930 that raised the punishment for pimps and procurers from two to three years' imprisonment, allowed the prosecution of female brothel owners, and allowed a landlord to be prosecuted for permitting his premises to be used for the purposes of prostitution. The amendment was not without its critics; Mr. A. Greville Bullocke, a member of the Legislative Council, pointed out in a minute of dissent from 16 June 1930 that it threatened to displace three thousand women from the segregated area "without, apparently, attempting, or desiring, to do more than rely on the exceedingly vague statements made by various representatives of the Bombay Vigilance Association as to the need of Rescue Homes."[49] This would become a key issue in the debate on the SITAS in the 1930s but was overlooked at this time. The key features, as Meliscent Shephard (1931) pointed out, was that it made brothels illegal and thus abolished the "great vice area" in which it was now estimated that nine hundred brothels and five thousand women resided. Bullocke's concerns were addressed by the home members of the Bombay Legislative Council who stressed that brothels would be cleared up one by one. This began a year after the act was passed and the brothels given notice, in August 1931, when the European madams were given just a week to close down their brothels or be imprisoned. A special correspondent for the *Evening News of India* toured the most famous houses in their last week and reported: "The girls were depressed but showed plenty of pluck. All were determined to earn their living without sinking to night-clubs or the streets" (cited in Shephard 1931, 75). Some planned to head to Calcutta, or farther East, while others had taken apartments in Bombay and planned to work alone.

This gradual application of the amended act was as much due to the impossibility of enforcement as it was concern for the welfare of the women. As the commissioner of police stressed in his annual report of 1930, the minimal staff at his disposal could barely enforce the previous provisions; abolishing the estimated six hundred brothels would be "impossible to enforce with any success" in the short term. As such, two test cases were attempted, but it was found to be incredibly difficult to prove that a landlord knew that a building was being used as a brothel, due to the chain of agents and rent collectors that mediated the lodgings and the owner. There were also several loopholes that pimps immediately exploited, including subletting rooms to individual prostitutes and the creation of "Turkish baths." Case numbers remained relatively constant for 1930, but cases for soliciting and living on the earnings of prostitution doubled in 1931 to forty-one and fifty cases respectively. The commissioner still complained that Turkish baths and the new massage parlors were simply brothels in disguise but also stressed that most of the brothels in the old tolerated area had closed down, although the number of women renting rooms individually had increased.[50]

This evidently made an impression on Shephard, who commented on the effect of the amendment. Writing to the London headquarters of the AMSH on 11 July 1931, she remarked on a most distinctive change in the district.[51] While the cheapest areas were said to still contain women and girls selling themselves for four to five annas, they were now in their own rooms and ran their own affairs. The major tram roads had been cleared of the gaudily lit balconies of previous years. In the richer men's areas, where women charged between Rs 150 and Rs 500, almost everything was reported to be closed. While not discounting the effects of economic depression making the business harder to carry out, Shephard was sure the law was having a great effect.

While there were occasional cases for procuring or importing prostitutes, and about 20 cases a year of living on the earnings of prostitutes, the early 1930s saw a massive increase in cases for soliciting. From 41 cases in 1931, the figure rose to around 190 for 1932–33 and around 210 for 1934–35, with high conviction rates. However, while the early effects of the provisions against public solicitation may have been impressive, the loopholes regarding brothel owners continued to be exploited, as a Bombay Legislative Council debate from 24 August 1934 illustrated.[52] Mr. Syed Munawar asked a question regarding the number of landlords that had been persecuted under the act of 1923 between 1932 and 1934, to which the answer was "none." On being asked the reasons for this, the Hon. Mr. R. D. Bell replied that the amended definition of a brothel in 1930 had allowed previous residences to be converted into one-room tenements, which were outside the law. When asked whether the government would be amending the act, Bell admitted that the government had not yet found the money for a full-time police staff to implement the existing laws, and thus the amendments would not be made until the provisions of the existing law had been fully tested. This testing continued into the 1940s and no further significant amendment took place. Annual cases for solicitation varied between 160 and 200, and those for living on the earnings of prostitution between 15 and 20. A push was made to use section 9 to move prostitutes out of "respectable neighbourhoods," with notices being served on 101 women in 1937, and on between 74 and 136 women each year until 1941 when the act was suspended as a "war measure."

While the BPPA was effective in many of its clauses, despite the loopholes which prevented the easy conviction of brothel owners, it must be seen as part of a broader legal mechanism. The Children's Act continued to be used throughout the 1930s, with cases against children in brothels increasing to about 70 a year. And while the police reports rarely gave commentary on cases tried under the Indian Penal Code (IPC), relevant cases rose from 83 a year in the 1920s to 105 per year in the 1930s. These cases referred to kidnapping, abducting, or inducing women into marriage or illicit intercourse, procuration, importation, selling girls into prostitution, or buying minor girls. While the BPPA duplicated some of these functions, the IPC was focused on the movement of women and girls around the country for the purposes of prostitution. As such, it provided the government with a degree of defense in the face of charges that it was not protecting the women and children of India against trafficking. This defense would, however, become weaker as the abolitionist institutions grew stronger both within India and abroad. They would demand legal provisions that would effectively target tolerated zones and provide protection against the (often-imagined) threat of the trafficker. It was in response to this need, and as an amalgam of the BPPA and the Burma Suppression of Brothels Act, that the SITAs were born.

### Provincial Networking: The SITAs, 1923–1947

By 1918 the brothel was increasingly discredited as a site of biological security, but the exigencies of war had sheltered its existence in India. The damage done to the reputations of Rangoon and Bombay by their brothel outrages had transformed them from scandalous to experimental sites. Drawing upon worldwide examples, they had networked together a legislative apparatus that proffered a solution to the social and biopolitical problem of the prostitute and of trafficking. The acts would be networked themselves, forming part of the central state's attempts to order the new legal geographies of dyarchy. This was itself a deeply nominalist project, insisting on the "local" nature of prostitution regulation while surveying and stimulating it from the center. But the natural ordering capacity of the Raj appears here at its most frantically networked, between the league in Geneva, the British in London, and the various Indian women's groups in cities up and down the country. The specificities of each network will be used below to portray the spread of suppressionism through British India.

### *The Liberty of the Subject: Calcutta, 1923*

In his report of 1917, Shuttleworth had estimated the total population of prostitutes in Calcutta, both "open" and "clandestine," to be fifty thousand. Although the city lost its status as capital of British India to Delhi in 1911, it continued to flourish as a colonial metropolis. As Banerjee (1998) has demonstrated, urbanization and modernization had *created* and mediated prostitution in the nineteenth-century city, and the failure of the city authorities to generate a means of regulating the prostitutes of one of India's main port cities came to be seen as a disgrace. While the AMSH had been prominent in forcing the hands of local governments in Bombay and Burma, the pressure in Calcutta came from the city's own formidable intellectual community and civil society. While there had been some individual Brahmo efforts in the 1870s and 1880s to help individual girls, prostitution only became a major issue after a scandal in the 1890s (Southard 1995, 218). Following two dramatic abductions, police raided a series of brothels and arrested the procurers for kidnapping. The public interest in the matter inspired Christian missionaries to work alongside Hindus and Muslims to call for action against brothels, although the police insisted they had sufficient powers.

The Calcutta Vigilance Association (CVA), a social purity organization operating through rescue work, public education, and amending government regulations, soon became involved.[53] It made appeals for funds toward a rescue home, claiming that between sixteen hundred and two thousand young girls were detained in the city's brothels (the nature of this campaign will be analyzed in the following chapter). In the CVA's annual report for 1925–26 it claimed that its response to the lack of police intervention led directly to the Calcutta SITA, the first of its kind.

Despite this, the origin of the SITA in the experimental sites of the early 1920s is clear. A subcommittee of the CVA, established to consider the situation, was directly charged with drafting local legislation along the lines of the Burma Act of 1921. As such, a bill was drawn up to target brothels and immoral traffic and was presented for comment to Mr. H. L. Stephenson, who later became governor of Bengal. He reiterated the now-entrenched view of the government that it could not introduce the bill directly, but that it would adopt an attitude of "benevolent sympathy" if the bill were introduced by a private member. As such on 12 January 1923 Professor S. C. Mukerji introduced the bill into the Bengal Legislative Council. A Select Committee was formed and its reports were presented to the Bengal Legislative Council for discussion on 17 August 1923 by Stephenson himself.[54]

He stressed that although the committee was fully in support of suppressing immoral traffic, it was also wary of progressing too far in advance of public sentiment, especially with regards to a topic that it felt should be addressed by societies and other bodies. The committee had struggled with the issue of solicitation and it was this proposed clause that provoked the greatest level of debate. Mr. F. E. E. Villiers proposed that the section regarding solicitation be dropped because its prevalence had been overemphasized, the existing laws were sufficient, and the clause would have "pernicious effects which will jeopardise the liberty of the subject." In defense of his line of reasoning, Villiers pursued several arguments that drew on recurrent tropes in the broader debate about prostitution. The liberty of women was the linchpin of his argument, but these women were respectable ladies of the city who would be at risk of misidentification, not prostitutes themselves.

The respondents in the council were more willing to acknowledge the rights of prostitutes themselves, however. Rai Jogendra Chunder Ghose

Bahadur stressed that, while he agreed with Villiers's amendment, "I cannot kick at a helpless poor woman, not even for the sake of morality." It was stressed that most prostitutes were poor and often deserted by their clients, presenting the saddest spectacle imaginable. As with Lecky's vision, the prostitute was the eternal figure here, blasted for the sins of mankind. Villiers himself admitted that prostitutes only existed to serve the desires of man, while Rai Nibaran Chandra Das Gupta Bahadur argued that there was no reason women should be punished for satisfying this demand while men walked free. His main argument was, however, that the powers to arrest without warrant were an offense to the liberty of the "people." The proposer of the bill, Professor Mukerji, stressed that such a provision had been part of the Burma Act of 1921 and had just been passed in the Bombay Prevention of Prostitution Act, and that solicitation was growing in the city. Villiers's amendment was carried, however, by fifty-four to thirty-one votes, so the Calcutta SITA was passed without powers to arrest for solicitation. Its powers were to:

- Empower police to order discontinuance of the use of a house or place as a brothel
- Empower police to remove underage girls in brothels and place in separate custody
- Penalize men living on earnings of prostitution
- Penalize procuration, importation, detention of a woman or girl for immoral purposes

The international origins of this new concern with trafficking were welded to a more traditional concern with the "immorality" of prostitution, just as the next chapter will examine how Meliscent Shephard was called out to Calcutta by the CVA to help implement and amend the Calcutta SITA. It is worth noting here, however, that like the Bombay and Burma acts, the SITA had two interlinked but separate concerns. The first concern was with immorality and brothels: their impact on the neighborhood, the detention of women or girls, and the activities of pimps or madams who profited from prostitution. The second concern was with trafficking and the entrapment of women: the procuration, importation, and detention of women or girls.

Over the following sixteen years, the SITAs would spread through the legislative provinces of India, profiting directly by association with the international concern for trafficking in women and children, as addressed by the League of Nations. However, while measures to tackle trafficking were prominent in the clauses and debates about the SITAS, in *practice* they retained the function of the Burma and Bombay acts: to both prevent and suppress prostitution by targeting the brothel. While it would be seven years until the next SITA was passed, the 1920s saw continued debates about the military, the role of central government, and the feasibility of tolerating brothels in a period of growing abolitionist influence.

Following the commander in chief's declaration against brothels in 1918, the Cantonment Act (II of 1924) provided the legal mechanisms by which the military and civil sections of cantonments could be, supposedly, cleared of prostitution. This would make permanent the orders that had been issued in 1918 as a result of Katherine Dixon's campaign. Dixon's supporters, the Association for Moral and Social Hygiene, had written to the governor general of India on 29 July 1920, requesting that he make permanent the policy of closing all brothels in or near cantonments.[55] To make clear the widespread support for these measures in the United Kingdom, the AMSH had passed on resolutions that had been made at meetings addressed by Dixon in her UK tour; between November 1919 and June 1920 twenty-four resolutions were passed to the India Office from voluntary organizations based all over the United Kingdom.

The Cantonment Act, when passed, gave powers to force the discontinuance of a brothel, to penalize anyone loitering for the purposes of prostitution or importuning, and to remove lewd persons from the cantonment. Meliscent Shephard's campaigning in India from the late 1920s to the early 1940s (see next chapter) would illustrate the extent to which these provisions were not enforced, or else were maneuvered around by the use, and at times provision, of brothels in municipal areas. The Cantonment Act applied to the whole of British India, but it was only with regards to prostitution and the military that the government of India was willing to legislate at this scale. For instance, in the Legislative Assembly on 27 January 1926, Khan Bahadur Sarfaraz Hussain Khan asked whether the central government was aware of legislative developments in Great Britain in line with the recommendations of the National Council for Combating Venereal Diseases, and whether the government was willing to legislate to penalize prostitution in India.[56] J. W. Bhore responded: "The Government of India do[es] not propose to introduce legislation on this subject in the Central Legislature. They consider it essentially a matter which should be dealt with by provincial legislation." Again, a similar response was given in answer to a question by Khan Bahadur Sarfaraz Hussain Khan on 4 September 1928.[57] His question regarded legislation rumored to be under consideration in London that would tackle trafficking in women. J. Crerar replied for the government that the Indian Penal Code was sufficient at an all-India level, while Bombay, Burma, and Calcutta had useful local enactments. Sanctioning further experimentation upon these lines, Crerar continued: "It is obviously for the local Governments to consider whether the special conditions existing in any area within their jurisdiction call for any special measures on the lines of the enactments referred to."

However, having not specified what these special measures might be, the central government could not dictate the nature of these laws. While it always had the power, via the vetting capacities of the central departments consulted during lawmaking, to censure such measures, in the dyarchy years of the 1920s when the government repeatedly stressed that prostitution was a local issue the influence of central government was sometimes in question. So, despite its official backing of abolitionist legislation, this did not stop segregationist laws from being passed and maintained. The previous chapter showed that Delhi continued to use the Punjab Municipal Act to segregate prostitutes into the 1930s. Similarly, the Assam Municipal Act (I of 1923) authorized the prohibition of brothels or public prostitutes in any specific area, introducing the sort of "spotty" legislation that the AMSH had campaigned against in Rangoon and Bombay. Also the government adopted clauses from the Bengal Disorderly Houses Acts of 1906–7 to ban brothels if they were next to cantonments, educational institutions, hostels, or places of worship. Similar sections were inserted into the Ajmer-Merwana Municipalities Regulation (VI of 1925).

On 20 February 1930 a United Provinces Prevention of Prostitution Bill was presented to the provincial Legislative Council by Saiyad Tufail Ahmad.[58] It was a transcript of the Bombay Prevention of Prostitution Act of 1923, but was proposed for extension to the whole province, not just particular cities. This included section 9 with its powers of segregation, which the bill proposed to extend to the lower levels of the magistry. While both the central and provincial governments disapproved of the proposals, they were bound by the principles of sanction established under the dyarchy system to allow the bill to be presented. The bill did not pass, however, as two other acts were successfully proposed that year that targeted aspects of prostitution. The Naik Girls' Protection Act (II of 1929) and the United Provinces Minor Girls' Protection Act (VIII of 1929) aimed to protect girls of the Naik caste, which was associated with providing "temple dancing" girls, while the second act allowed these provisions to be extended to any chosen community, class, or group. Four years later the province would decide that greater powers would be required. But by this time the SITA model, rather than that of Bombay, was becoming established as the unequivocally anti-segregationist model on which such legislation would be based.

### A Social Act or Civil Abandonment? Madras, 1930

In Shuttleworth's comparison of Indian cities in 1917, Madras had fared well compared to the other presidency cities. Its number of registered prostitutes was said to be negligible, although the clandestine rate was thought to be higher. Police regulation was sparse, as was solicitation or obvious brothels. Yet this appraisal is in stark contrast to the work of S. M. Raj (1993), who has charted the ongoing discontent within Madras over the government's capacity to regulate prostitution, and its effect on local women and children, in the city. Influenced by international conventions on trafficking, local societies for the protection of children campaigned for powers to remove minor children from brothels, although such requests were denied on the grounds that there were no rescue homes for the children to go to. The Madras Children Act (IV of 1920) was eventually passed, which gave courts the right to commit children under fourteen who were found to be living in brothels into school or suitable custody.

As with Calcutta, developments in the city had a significant impact upon the nature of prostitution in twentieth-century Madras. Raj (1993, 69) has shown how prostitutes worked near temples, education institutions, thoroughfares, residential areas, and railway stations. Many occupied brothels, which were a new and threatening phenomenon within the urban landscape and became the target for campaigning within civil society. This was especially the case with the Women's Indian Association (WIA, founded in 1917) which, despite its title, remained focused on Madras although its journal, *Stri Dharma*, was widely read, and has been described by Tusan (2003, 624) as an anticolonial, pro-nationalist, international publication. An article from October 1925 criticized brothels as "a new menace to our social life" that were as dangerous for the public as they were for their inmates.[59] Appeals were made to the journal's readers to cooperate across grades and positions of society and to consider the welfare of "our sisters" ministering to the passions of men. The article reported the establishment of a Madras Vigilance Society (MVA) that year to challenge the spread of brothels.

This society had quickly established that the Madras City Police Act of 1888 was incapable of dealing with the rapidly increasing urban population.

In comparison, Calcutta, Bombay, Rangoon, and Colombo were shown to have new acts that targeted both trafficking and brothels. It was said to be the duty of the "enlightened and self-respecting public" of Madras to push for such legislation, and for rescue homes to care for girls that were released from the brothels. A year and a half later the journal could report that Lord Lytton, the ex-governor of Bengal, was supporting the funding drive for a rescue home at Cossipore and had recommended the Calcutta SITA after his time as governor of Bengal.[60] The journal also provided a brief review, in June 1927, of the League of Nations' report on traffic in women and children, which had stressed that the brothel provided the market for the trade.[61] Finally, in July 1927 *Stri Dharma* reported that a Madras Suppression of Immoral Traffic Bill was to be put to the local government, as the result of intense local campaigning.[62] This had brought to light tales of girls trapped in "lives of immorality: locked away, beaten, sold, robbed" that made it clear that brothels must be made illegal. Campaigning directly for a favorable reading of the bill in November 1928, the journal stressed that mothers should not tolerate in towns and cities places that were centers of moral and physical disease and were supplied by girls that had been kidnapped, enticed, and seduced by men.[63]

The bill had been drafted by E. H. M. Waller, Lord Bishop of Madras, who had been studying brothels in the city since 1924 (Reddy 1930, 193). It was drafted along the lines of legislation from Bombay, Calcutta, Burma, and Britain and was put forward by the MVA and the WIA together. The bill was submitted on 23 October 1927 by K. R. Venkatarama Ayyar who stated that it had been made necessary by the growth of the urban population, and especially of single young men, over the last forty years.[64] New powers were required to match the changing nature of brothels, which were a growing public nuisance and "becoming paying business propositions, able to maintain a regular staff of importers, procurers, managers and landlords." The proposed powers would suppress brothels, rescue and protect young girls, and punish men and women who profited from prostitution.

The bill did not pass smoothly through the legislature, coming up for debate after the Select Committee's second report on 31 January 1930. Their previous suggestion that the local government should be obliged to provide rescue homes was refused sanction by the governor of Madras, so the bill had to be redrafted to exclude such obligations. The debate in council was wide ranging and clearly exposed the range of inspirations behind the bill. Mr. F. E. James commented on the League of Nations' publications encouraging action against *souteneurs*, which Dr. S. Muthulakshmi Reddy had circulated to her fellow members (Reddy 1930, 196). Others commented on the inspirational and practical role the Bombay and Burma acts had played in the constitution of the Madras bill. This was not entirely positive and resurrected the geographical quandary (as debated in reference to the Cantonment Acts in 1899, see Legg 2012b) regarding the specificities of context versus the generalities of an all-India, and international, phenomenon. Rao Bahadur Sir AP Patro argued against drawing analogies from conditions existing in Madras to those in other countries. Even within India, Bombay and Calcutta were said to have much more diverse classes of people, and their Grant Roads and Lower Chitpur Roads were notorious centers of vice. But drawing analogies was exactly what proponents of the bill did, reflecting on the experiences of Bombay and Rangoon in an attempt to craft a finer bill which Reddy, one of the main proponents, felt she had helped achieve.

She also made it clear, in her concluding address, why the act was significantly different from those that had gone before. By having governmental provision of rescue homes clearly rejected, the bill would have to be carried out in a "humanitarian" spirit, not one of police or discipline. This would be a "social Act" which would seek to preserve what Reddy termed the "sanctity of the human soul," the personal right of the individual to be protected, and the un-trespassed-upon liberty of the individual. As an example of the sort of worker that would be required, Reddy mentioned only one person, Meliscent Shephard, who was working for the Calcutta Vigilance Association at this time. The proposer, K. R. Venkatarama Ayyar, thanked the Madras Vigilance Association, for drafting the bill, and stressed that without social workers and rescue homes, the law would remain a dead letter. The Madras SITA (V of 1930) as passed allowed the removal from a brothel of a girl under the age of eighteen and her placement in a rescue home until the age of twenty-one, or some shorter period, but Reddy's attempts to include powers to penalize living off the profits of prostitutes had failed. The SITA allowed for punishment, under the following sections, of:

- Keeping a brothel or allowing a premises to be used as a brothel
- Importing a woman or girl for prostitution
- Detention for prostitution
- Procuration
- Soliciting

As was anticipated in the closing debate, the SITA did not make an easy transition to enforcement. In May 1930 an article in *Stri Dharma* cautiously welcomed the SITA but stressed that funds would now be required to build a rescue home such that the act could be applied.[65] A year later the WIA resorted to a deputation to the home member to the government of Madras to press for the enforcement of the SITA, and to submitting a memorandum that detailed the continued abuses of children in brothels.[66] The main problem was that the act could only be applied to the whole province at the same time and that there were not enough rescue homes to do this (Raj 1993, 98). As such, the SITA had to be amended within a year of its passing to allow its application in particular areas, and to apply those provisions as are practicable in those particular areas.[67] The WIA was opposed to this, predicting that brothels would simply move beyond the jurisdiction of the act and that the number of girls that would be taken into homes would be less than anticipated by the government.[68]

When the act was finally implemented in 1932, it was done in something less than the humanitarian spirit Reddy had been hoping for.[69] Operating more as a police than a social act, the closure of brothels resulted in prostitutes being abandoned on the street or in their leaving Madras in a state of "panic and helplessness." No notice was given to the institutions of the city that could have provided custody of minor girls, not that the police seemed to be interested in this aspect of the SITA. As a *Stri Dharma* editorial claimed in May 1932: "We wanted legislation not only to suppress the vice-areas, but also to save the minor girls from a life of shame and misery." The blame for this situation was laid firmly at the door of the local government, which had refused any type of grant for the girls due to the economic climate (the depression years). The annual police report referred to the "Brothels Act," rather than the SITA, and showed that from 1 April 1932, ten brothels were raided and eleven persons convicted.[70]

Shephard visited Madras in November 1933 as the Indian representative of the AMSH and found the SITA to be badly defective.[71] She reported that the police had been ordered to put the punitive clauses of the act into operation in four outlying areas, leading to the "gravest scandals" because women were being turned out "neck and crop," while there were no social workers on hand to "handle the police," challenge public conscience, found rescue work, or collect funds to help.

By January 1934 *Stri Dharma* could still report a failure to find the money or workers to establish a rescue home, just as the tolerance of brothels was continuing.[72] While the public had come to recognize the presumed benefit of one aim of the SITA, to close down brothels, they were said to be unwilling to accept that tackling trafficking and the reclamation of girls was an equally important task. It was only by March 1934 that the WIA opened its Home for Women, which would help to house girls from some of the 150 houses of ill fame that had been closed to date.[73] Despite this, the facilities remained woefully deficient. In an article of February 1935, *Stri Dharma* asked what was happening to the women who were being dispossessed of their shelter and earnings when brothels were being closed down?[74] Data provided to the League of Nations Traffic in Women and Children Committee showed that of 448 women turned out of brothels, only 7 had been taken into rescue homes. The rest were suspected to be fueling the rise in prostitution in neighboring cities.

That the SITA had ended up focusing solely on brothels and not on trafficking would have come as no surprise to Reddy. Her original plan to include a clause penalizing living off the profits of prostitution had been dropped during the bill's long journey through the Select Committees and Reddy had failed to get it reinserted during the final reading (Reddy 1930, 198). These clauses were those that were more successful for targeting procurement and importation, as well as brothel keeping. The police report from 1936 admitted that, in spite of closing down ten brothels that year and rescuing forty-six females, thirteen of whom were minors, it was proving impossible to tackle the orchestrators of the trade.[75] Prostitutes had proven unwilling to testify against their souteneurs and had usually preferred perjury. Something along the lines of the Bombay Act, which shifted the burden of proof onto the accused, was desired by the police.

Yet it was only in 1938 that these amendments were made to the SITA. The bill was proposed by K. Raman Menon on 22 March 1938 and was passed, although it was also limited to urban areas. However, despite this leveling up of the provisions that targeted brothels and traffickers more specifically, the effect of the SITA in practice remained very much against soliciting and brothels than it did the orchestrators of trafficking. The police report of 1938 noted a vigorous campaign against brothels with twenty-three raided, following twenty-five the year before.[76] Tellingly, the report stated that sixty-six women had been arrested or rescued, making no distinction between the two, and sent to houses administered by the MVA. In 1939 forty-seven brothels were targeted, although even the amended act was proving difficult to enforce due to magistrates insisting on evidence that a building was being used as a brothel. Yet forty-three girls were rescued and sent to the MVA rescue home.

Statistics supplied by the government of India to the League of Nations as evidence of its efforts against trafficking show that this trend continued

TABLE 2.1  Cases under the Madras SITA between 1937–38 and 1942–43

| | 1937–38 | 1938–39 | 1939–40 | 1940–41 | 1941–42 | 1942–43 |
|---|---|---|---|---|---|---|
| Pimping | 0 | 3 | 8 | 4 | 5 | 1 |
| Importing | 3 | 8 | 4 | 7 | 1 | 6 |
| Soliciting | 1 | 180 | 183 | 235 | 127 | 139 |
| Brothels | 19 | 71 | 49 | 54 | 23 | 41 |

into the 1940s (see table 2.1).[77] Cases under section 9 (importing girls for prostitution) and 3 (pimping), which would target key individuals in trafficking, totaled 50 cases between 1937–38 and 1942–43. However, cases under sections 5 and 8 (keeping a brothel, letting premises be used as a brothel, or living off the earnings of prostitution) and section 12 (soliciting) totaled 1,122.

By 1945 the police had scaled back their efforts under the pressure of war conditions.[78] Only two brothels were raided, as against eleven in 1944. However, the high number of Fighting Services in the city, and the street prostitutes that had emerged to service them, had necessitated the use of the military police, who had rounded up 408 prostitutes, leading to 404 convictions, following 203 arrests and 199 convictions in 1944. Of the 404 convictions, only three women were sent to the MVA home, following the eighteen women and girls that had been sent there the previous year.

What the experiment in Madras showed was that the SITA model could be deployed outside of its home city of Calcutta, although with substantial revisions and subsequent amendments. But what it had also illustrated was that the state viewed caring for children that were rescued from brothels as the duty of civil society and charitable institutions, but also insisted that it was the linchpin of the SITA system. The latter insistence made it easier to claim compliance with the League of Nations' stipulations on combating trafficking in women and children, but the former claim meant that this duty would effectively be outsourced to civil society. Yet, despite their naming and billing, the SITAs in practice focused most intensely on only one side of their double aims. While the SITAs had relatively little success in tackling importation, procurement, and living off the profits of prostitution, brothels and soliciting were effectively targeted. In effect, this removed prostitutes from their locations of income and, in many cases, security, and forced them beyond the jurisdiction of the SITAs where they could be, ironically, more vulnerable to the "immorality" and "trafficking" that the acts in action did little to suppress.

However, just as a misapplication of the governmentality literature can lead to over-attentiveness to the writings *about* government, rather than the *application* of governmental rationalities, the passing of the Madras SITA was taken as evidence at the time of a new and effective model. In 1931 a Suppression of Immoral Traffic Bill was considered in the princely state of Travancore,[79] although *Stri Dharma* reported with regret in 1932 that the bill had been rejected by the state of Mysore (it was eventually passed in 1937, see Nair 2008, 218).[80] Yet the idea of SITA legislation spreading organically from state to state was not only preferred by government but had been accepted by social campaigners across the country. Provincial groups were pushing for their own SITAS throughout the 1930s, and by 1933 the AMSH abandoned its hopes of an All India SITA. Writing to Alison Neilans in London on 31 May 1933, Meliscent Shephard argued that such a bill would be in advance of public opinion and would be worked differently under the new constitution, which would result from the Government of India Act of 1935.[81] Shephard found herself in agreement with the home member, with whom she had discussed the issue, who argued that the present policy of advancing province by province was the right one. While the All India Bill would never arrive, other provinces (including Bengal) would continue to follow the SITA route. Articulating how the political geography of dyarchy would alter after 1935, Shephard claimed:

> If we press now for an All-India Bill, we have only seven provinces and four States where there is anything like an Abolitionist Bill operating (Bengal is only now receiving the Viceroy's Assent). The Provinces are to be autonomous in matters relating to Crime, and will be jealous of any imposition from the Centre of an All-India Bill UNLESS there are so many Provinces with good bills, that they, of themselves, wish to be linked up and so stop the gaps through which traffickers can jump. On the whole—therefore, I feel that my best policy is to go on educating leaders in the Abolitionist principles, starting groups where possible, and leave the All-India Bill to come naturally, after education and not before.

### Beyond Calcutta: Bengal, 1933

As with the Burma Bill of 1921, the Bengal SITA was not a new act, but the revival of a bid that had previously been blocked. A bill had been proposed by Shah Syed Imdadul Haq, a member of the Bengal Legislative Council, and was debated by the central Legislative Council in early 1923.[82] The Bengal Suppression of Brothels Bill was a close reproduction of the Burma Suppression of Brothels Act, passed two years previously. S. W. Gwynne of the Home Department noted on 10 February 1923 that although the Indian Penal Code would overlap with the provisions of the proposed bill, the experience in Rangoon had shown that "experimental legislation in the matter of social abuse" could be sanctioned. However, the Calcutta SITA was proposed on 12 January and so this bill was deemed both too coincident and also applicable to too large an area. As such it was proposed to try Calcutta first.

Six years later the Calcutta SITA was found to be lacking, just as other legislation elsewhere in India was found to be more effective. Meliscent Shephard wrote to Alison Neilans on 9 April 1929, while she was working for the Calcutta Vigilance Association (CVA), that the Bombay Prevention of Prostitution Act of 1923 was proving so effective that five "girls" had come to Calcutta from Bombay within the last ten days in order, as she paraphrased, "to catch the trade before the rush begins."[83] (This outwitting of provincial legal geographies was common; in 1934 a trade of Naik caste girls from the Kumaun division of the United Provinces to Delhi was reported as the latter had not extended the Naik Girls' Protection Act [United Provinces, II of 1929] leading to "so called 'white slave trade'" of girls into Delhi.)[84] While brothels in Bombay were anticipated to close in three years, there were no such fears in Calcutta, and this impression was keenly felt within the city.

While the CVA had been important in pressing for the Calcutta SITA, it was the All Bengal Women's Union that rose to prominence in the fraught political context of the early 1930s. It was formed in May 1932 to push for new legislation, and its contribution has been recalled in detail by Southard (1995, 226–56). It was itself an amalgam of people and ideologies from the Bengal Presidency Council of Women and the All India Women's Congress. The union's objectives were to rouse public opinion, to press for a new SITA, to cooperate with government and approved societies, and to provide an aftercare home for girls. Between its formation and the discussion of the new Bengal Suppression of Immoral Traffic Bill, the All Bengal Women's Union campaigned intensively, submitting a petition with seventeen thousand signatures from all over Bengal (Southard 1995, 236). The same mistakes were not made as in Madras, and the bill did not suggest that the Bengal government would have to fund a rescue home. Herbert Anderson (1933), of the All India Vigilance Association, wrote that the Bengal Act had self-consciously been drafted following the lead of the acts in Ceylon, Burma, Bombay, and Madras.

The bill stated its objects to be the repealing of the Calcutta SITA and certain sections of other relevant acts in order to better check the evils of commercialized vice, which would lead to the gradual suppression of brothels and immoral traffic. This would be done by granting the police greater powers to order the discontinuance of a brothel, giving the authorities more powers to take charge of minor girls in brothels or places used for prostitution, and to enable landlords to get rid of objectionable tenants. All of the new sections were taken from either the Burma Act of 1921 or the Bombay Act of 1923. As Southard (1995, 252) has described, the bill went through various modifications via the Select Committee and Legislative Council, but survived the dynamics of Hindu-Muslim and nationalist politics and was passed in the spring of 1933.

During the Select Committee's discussion, Mr. J. N. Gupta argued that recent League of Nations investigations had examined the question at hand in detail, from biological, social, and medical perspectives, and had been unanimous in recommending that recognized brothels were not medically sound.[85] The success of the actions in Bombay were cited, as was the increased participation of women in Bengal's civil society. When passed, the Bengal SITA (IV of 1933) provided detailed sections to allow the closure of brothels, to place landlords under closer scrutiny, but also for the commissioner of police to order the discontinuance of a brothel if it was annoying local residents or institutions. Additional penalties were provided for soliciting, living on the earnings of prostitution, procuration, importation, detention, and seduction of prostitution of girls under the age of eighteen. The main change, as noted by the League of Nations, was that brothel keepers, managers, and landlords would be liable to prosecution for letting houses and using them for "immoral purposes," while women could also be charged for living off the earnings of prostitution.[86] Repeating the phrase used in relation to the Calcutta SITA, the home member, as Shephard commented, "said that the Government 'regarded such Bills with benevolence.'"

While the Bengal SITA would stimulate other provinces seeking abolitionist legislation, its working in practice provided further evidence of the imbalance between suppressing brothels and protecting the victims of the brothels themselves. Despite the amended powers, the Bengal SITA did not have an immediate or dramatic impact upon police activity in Calcutta and its suburbs. The annual grand total of true cases passed under the SITA actually declined, from 58 in 1933 to 24 and 25 in 1935 and 1936, respectively. The figures then rose, to hit 65 in 1939 and 144 after the first full year of war conditions in 1940. This pattern was reflected in brothel closures, which remained at between 40 and 52 per year between 1933 and 1936.[87] Over this period the number of girls in court ranged from 43 to 56, which resulted in between 14 and 18 girls per year being sent to various reformatory schools or institutions. However, from 1937 the numbers of brothels being closed started to escalate, to 70 and 78 in 1937 and 1938, then to 135 in 1939 and 134 in 1940. But it was at exactly this time that the number of girls in court and those being sent to homes went into decline. The numbers of girls in court dropped from 47 and 41 a year in 1937 and 1938, to 19 in 1939 and 12 in 1940; the figures for girls being passed into care dropped from 18 and 14 in 1937 and 1938, to four in 1939 and just two in 1940. For comparison, in 1930 under the old Calcutta SITA, 14 cases were dealt with that involved 79 girls being rescued from brothels; 12 were sent to guardians while 30 went to a rescue home.[88] In 1931 the figures were: 86 girls rescued, 35 into suitable custody, 22 to rescue homes.[89]

This was part of a wider trend in juvenile crime in Calcutta and the suburbs. There had been an increase in the total number of children "sent up," from 1,061 in 1933 to 6,168 in 1939, but an increasing number of these were simply warned and discharged, from 581 (55 percent) in 1933 to 4,789 (78 percent) in 1939. This year also saw a record number of children fined, rising to 1,001 from an average of 286 between 1931 and 1938. At the same time, the number of children sent to schools or institutions declined from around 90 a year (between 6 percent and 9 percent of all arrests) in the early 1930s to around 80 a year (between 1 percent and 2 percent) in the late 1930s.[90]

As with Madras, under the wartime conditions when women and children were more vulnerable to exploitation, the police focused less on tackling trafficking or unlawful detainment of women and children directly, and attended to the closure of brothels that could have infected military and civilian workforces. It is perhaps telling that in the police reports the closure of "disorderly houses" was listed alongside other offenses such as begging, suicide, street accidents, cattle, horse and dog pounds, and kennels for lost dogs. With the passing of the Bengal SITA in 1933, India's four major port cities now had suppressionist legislation to counter their coastal cosmopolitanism. But this still left a great swathe of inland territory yet to be legislated for. In these areas "trafficking" referred to internal trade between provinces, such that the applicability of the very term itself would be thrown into doubt by the government's own statistics.

The United Provinces and the Punjab have very different historical geographies to the three oldest presidency provinces. Madras was drawn into the East India Company sphere of influence in the 1640s, Bombay in the 1660s, while Calcutta was forcibly assimilated in the early 1700s. The United Provinces and the Punjab have more in common, however, with Burma, which was aggressively conquered by the company in the nineteenth century, finally being incorporated into the Raj in 1886.

As the authority of the Mughal Empire waned in the eighteenth century, vying forces carved up the territories beyond the immediate reach of Delhi. From the 1740s a Sikh Empire emerged in north India, which was divided into thirty-six areas. Of these, twenty-two were allied to Maharaja Ranjit Singh, and fourteen to the British. On the death of Singh in 1839 the British moved to annex the remaining territories, leading to the creation of the Punjab in March 1849, which was bordered to the north by Kashmir and the Northwest Frontier Province, the princely state of Rajputana to the south and, eventually, the United Provinces to the east. This latter area was similarly disputed during the decline of Mughal power, but had no emergent unifying force to challenge the British, who gradually spread through the region in the nineteenth century. The existing acquisitions were unified into the presidency of Agra in 1834, which was partly reorganized into the Northwestern Provinces in 1836. Further acquisitions included Oudh in 1858 and the establishment of Ajmer, Merwana, and Kekri as commissionerships in 1871. These territories were unified into the United Provinces of Agra and Oudh in 1902, which were renamed the United Provinces of British India in 1921, and the United Provinces in 1937. This province bordered Kashmir to the north, Bihar to the west, princely states to the south and west, and the Punjab to the northwest. While covering vast terrains, from the Simla hills to the Gangetic plains, both the United Provinces and Punjab were landlocked provinces with interactive flows of migration, trade, and culture. What unites them in this context are the problematic considerations that their traditions provoked on the "problem" of "trafficking" in relation to the internationalist discourse of immorality and exploitation, although SITAS were eventually passed in the United Provinces in 1933 and the Punjab in 1935.

### TRAFFICKED SLAVES OR WILLING WIVES?

The annual police reports for the Punjab present a remarkably complete set of reflections on what was explicitly referred to as "Traffic in Women" from

1920 through the entire interwar period.[91] During this time convictions were conducted through the Indian Penal Code, including the following sections: 363 for kidnapping, abducting, or inducing women to marriage or intercourse; 366A for procuration of a minor girl under eighteen years of age for illicit intercourse; 366B for importation of a girl from a foreign country; 367 for kidnapping or abduction to subject a person to unnatural lust; 372 for selling minors under eighteen years old for prostitution or illicit intercourse; and 373 for buying minors for prostitution or illicit intercourse. The total true cases per year were exceptionally stable in the interwar years, ranging between 600 and 1,000 a year, with a peak in the mid-1920s and a steady decline to an average of 704 between 1935 and 1940.

In terms of the nature of the crimes, the inspector general of police, who compiled the Punjab reports, was eager to stress in his digest of 1920 that the main point of concern was the kidnapping of children to be sold as prostitutes, but he insisted it was uncommon. Despite this, the reports include clear evidence of women being moved around the country in return for payment, which often resulted in their being exposed to gross maltreatment. The report of 1924 told of an imported woman who was murdered in a village near Amritsar, which was found to be "stocked" with imported southerners. These investigations also unearthed bad cases of swindling, seduction, and coercion, including the discovery of two gangs from Hoshiapur who carried young women off by force during their "reign of terror."

The report of 1926 detailed two "brutal outrages" from the central Punjab. The first, against Bishen Kaur and her young daughter, took place at Narwar Railway Station between Lahore and Amritsar. Kaur was feeling unwell and accepted medical aid from two local men. She subsequently lost consciousness and woke to find herself a prisoner in Narwar, where she was "frequently outraged." She managed to escape after a few days to the railway station, after which her captors attempted to raid the station to retake her, but were repulsed by the stationmaster. The second case, against Must. [Mussumat] Parbati from Amritsar, occurred after a woman had offered to drive her to the canal for "a bathe."[92] She was joined there by two additional men who took her to a village, where she was "subjected to brutal maltreatment by four Sikhs." She also escaped to a police station, but was recaptured and toured around local villages in an attempt to sell her to a local buyer. The report of 1930 even told of a cart that had apparently been discovered in Ludhiana with a deep well in the middle into which children could be seized from the street, dropped through an upper compartment, and concealed within while they were driven away.

These cases, which conform to the myths and fears associated with broader discussions of trafficking in women and children and the (non-) white slave trade, only represent a minority of the seven hundred to nine hundred annual cases, however. As the report of 1920 claimed, "A good many willing wives are abducted and sold to men wanting a wife and some low caste women are sold as being of high caste." Referring to the village "stocked" with imported women, the report of 1924 insisted that the women were generally content with their lot, and that police inquiry usually led to distressing results in the "less reprehensible cases." A controversy in 1927 led to a thorough investigation of the Nepali community in Benares, after the murder of a Hira Lal Agarwalla by a fellow Gurkha following allegations of the mistreatment of a young girl, Mst. [Mussumat] RajKumari.[93] The investigation found no evidence of kidnapping of Nepali girls for sale into public prostitution, despite clear evidence that girls were being bought and sold for marriage in the Punjab by "brokers." The home secretary, Harry Haig, felt the police took a rather casual view, but it was concluded that a decision made in 1925 not to legislate against the "nefarious class of persons" known as bardafarosh (slave traders) was not open to criticism.

As further evidence of the active consent of women in this trade, the report of 1930 told of women being sold on, then disappearing from their new partner and rejoining their "protectors" for resale. Most men would be unwilling to report having attempted to buy a wife, while if a woman offered her consent, the police could not intervene. As the report of 1935 put it: "The kidnapper is frequently no more than a dealer, and kidnapping does not enter into the matter. The women leave poor hard-worked homes for comparative affluence where they are given the status of wives; and they willingly go with the dealer."

These suggestions raise a variety of complex questions regarding their representations of women, with many parallels to the debate about sati and the colonial archive (see Mani 1998). In one light, women are presented as making rational decisions about their lifestyles based on increased economic prosperity and, in many cases, elevated caste status. They were also shown to be willing conspirators in plans to swindle men who purchased their spouses. Yet, given the cases of violence that have been shown to exist, the wishing away of the problem as one of "willing wives" adhering to some invisible hand of demographics allowed the government to abnegate its responsibility to investigate what could well have been an internal form of human trafficking and slavery. Attempts to tackle this slavery did, however, founder on the issue of consent, which threw into doubt the police's ability to comprehend the nature of the problem.

The examples proffered above were part of a systematic attempt to discount the police's own statistics. The report of 1929 claimed: "Statistics regarding this form of crime are as unreliable as those in connection with cattle theft." Because the people trafficked did not put themselves "within the reach of the law" they blurred the line between criminality and disreputability. The report of 1931 explicitly urged the reader not to believe its own statistics, because neither the consenting woman nor the deserted or deceived husband would report the crime.

If the issue of consent threw the statistics into doubt, it also destabilized the very concept of trafficking itself. The reports persistently returned to the free trade language of political economy, marking the movement as a sexualized and gendered form of migration and sex-ratio equilibration. The report of 1921 claimed that "a regular sale depot was discovered in the Hissar District and a large number of women were found in the wrongful confinement of the accused," depicting the brothel not as a site of inversion or immorality but of storage and trade. Continuing this interpretation, the report of 1924 claimed that "the traffic arises out of the laws of supply and demand, and is very lucrative and flourishing," arguing that it was cheaper for men to buy women than to engage in the protracted and costly regulations of marriage. In 1926 it was claimed that the demand by a peasant for a wife was usually met by the supply of a contented woman who found a comfortable home.

This supply and demand was linked to particular population geographies in the report of 1928. It was claimed that a dearth of women in the plains of the Punjab meant that girls were "tempted" away from the Simla hills by gangs based in Lahore and Amritsar, renamed, and then sold on to wealthy zamindars as part of the barda faroshi (slave trade).[94] It was even claimed that in Simla a system of Rit (custom) existed whereby compensation was paid to the husband or father from whom the girl was taken. Census data confirm a disparity between the two states. In 1921 the population of British India was put at 244 million, with an extra 70 million in the princely states.[95] In British territory the population was enumerated as 51 percent male and 49 percent female. However, both the Punjab and United Provinces had lower proportions of women in their territories. The United Provinces' population was 48 percent female, but the Punjab's was only 45 percent. The differences in overall population (Punjab of 19 million, United Provinces of 47 million) meant that in terms of the number of individuals, the Punjab had just under 9 million women, while the United Provinces had 22 million. This gendered difference was more likely to be equalized due to the widely noted-upon connections between the two provinces, with the report of 1924 claiming that the United Provinces were the main source of supply for the Punjab. The summary of 1930 showed that the eastern border of the Punjab with the United Provinces was the most active zone for movement of women and girls, while the report of 1934 claimed that the majority of movement was of low-caste women from the United Provinces who would be sold to Jat Sikh zamindars.

However, these stable IPC statistics and recurring rhetorical tropes did not indicate a static system. The 1920s *did* seem to be a period in which the movement, whether it be trafficking or migration, increased. The report of 1929 insisted that the trade in women was increasing and becoming more organized and developed, and that "bad characters" were adapting to trafficking as it became a more profitable and less dangerous alternative to *dacoity* (gang robbery). The system was not simply, as in the past, one of unmarried girls moving for better life chances, as Kashmiri girls were being fed into prostitution in Lahore or other big cities. The reports for 1930 and 1931 also reflect a growing concern that the trafficking in women and girls for prostitution was on the increase. Yet this was combined, as elsewhere in India, with the belief that this was not a solely police or governmental problem. The reports had long complained that public opinion was not sufficiently against the trade in women, and that many influential figures had an active interest in it. The report of 1927 labeled the trade a "social evil" that the police could not remedy because the public did not demand it, to the extent that the police were often assaulted when they attempted to intervene. It was suggested, in the report of 1928, that women coming from the United Provinces achieved an increase in life standards so would not complain, and that this view could only be tackled by education and social reform. It was at this juncture in the early 1930s that pressure for both Punjab and United Provinces SITAs emerged. The dual interest in closing down brothels as sites of both abuse and trade, and in preventing the abuses of trafficking were present, as was the suggestion that "society" should bear some of the burden of dealing with this problem.

### THE SITAS

The Punjab Suppression of Immoral Traffic Bill was introduced to the Punjab Legislative Council on 25 October 1934. The stated objects were more implicit in their acknowledgment of the brothel as a target: the first object was to give the authorities greater powers to tackle trafficking in women and children; the second was to protect those in danger from procurers, traffickers, and others engaged in commercial vice.[96] The means to achieve these objects were more explicit, however. The Punjab Municipal Act (III of 1911, as used in Delhi) would be amended, as would other laws so as to enable authorities to order the discontinuance of a brothel, while penalties for the standard offenses targeted by SITAS would also be provided.

Nanak Chand Pandit, the member of the Legislative Council who introduced the bill, offered three reasons for its submission, relating directly to three increasing scales of contextualization. At the local scale, existing laws did not provide sufficient provisions to either punish or protect. At the state scale, it was argued the following provinces and states already had similar legislation: Bombay, Bengal, Burma, Madras, Ceylon (though a separate colony), United Provinces, Puddakottah, Travancore, and Cochin. Similar legislation was also said to be under consideration in the Central Provinces, Mysore State, the Northwestern Frontier Province, Assam, and Delhi. At the international scale, the League of Nations report on *Commission of Enquiry into Traffic in Women and Children in the East* was cited as evidence that the brothel is the central market, transit zone, and focusing point for such trade. The bill was designed to suppress these centers of traffic, in line with legislation in operation in other parts of India and "the rest of the civilised world." In debating the bill, Chand insisted that the aim was not to enforce morality, but to join part of an international effort to target vice. Despite the foregoing evidence that there was little if any international involvement in the trade in the Punjab, Chand suggested that stricter regulation in the West had forced unscrupulous people to Indian ports, and that better laws were required to face this challenge. While carefully debated in council and amended by the Select Committee, the Punjab SITA was passed on 21 November 1935 (Act IV). Following the established SITA template, the act provided punishment in the following sections for:

1. Keeping a brothel
2. Living on immoral earnings
3. Procuration
4. Importation
5. Detention
6. Seduction of a girl under eighteen years old

As with the other SITAS, however, the implementation of the act proved difficult. As the chief commissioner of Delhi discovered when he was pressured in 1935 to apply a similar SITA to Delhi, the act had not been applied in the Punjab itself by February 1936.[97] The reason for this had been the government's unwillingness to apply section 4, which would necessitate closing down every brothel in the Punjab and finding a place for the "rescued" girls to be housed.

Having observed the problems in Madras due to the lack of rescue homes, Meliscent Shephard had taken a keen interest in the Punjab SITA. She served on the Select Committee which reviewed the bill in June 1934 and campaigned with Nanak Chand in October 1934 to encourage popular support.[98] Shephard also reported on the efforts that were already under way before the passing of the bill to ensure a rescue home for Indian non-Christian girls and to appoint a suitable warden for the Anglo-Indian Girl's Home. Despite this, campaigners were still having to work in 1936 to convince the Punjab authorities that there would be suitable provision for rehousing non-Christian girls should the ban be carried out. However, when the SITA was finally enforced in 1937 it was only applied to the larger municipal areas and was executed without section 4 which, as the police report of 1937 suggested, deprived it of much of its value.[99] As such, the League of Nations report for 1938–39 shows that under 10 people had been charged under the SITA, while 137 were charged under the IPC.[100] The AMSH was still campaigning in the Punjab in 1939 to get the restrictions on section 4 removed but, as experience elsewhere had shown, during the war years the motivation to fund rescue homes, the condition for brothel closure, evaporated incredibly quickly.[101]

During the time since the passing of the Punjab SITA, the annual police reports had continued to comment on the porous nature of the border with the United Provinces in terms of trafficking. The report of 1936 commented that women sold by gangs in the United Provinces had been detected in the Gurgaon, Jhang, and Multan districts of the Punjab, while the report of 1937 confirmed that United Provinces women were regularly sold to Jat Sikhs. This was four years after the United Provinces SITA (VIII of 1933) had been passed and reflects the strikingly similar fate of the act. Its provisions, despite a more detailed set of measures against brothels, were similar to those in the Punjab, offering penalizations, under the following sections, for:

3. Keeping a brothel
4. Allowing premises to be used as a brothel
5. Letting out premises for a brothel
7. Importation

8. Detention

9. Procuration

10. Soliciting

11. Removal of girls under the age of eighteen from a brothel

By 1936, however, the United Provinces SITA had still not been fully applied. Meliscent Shephard met with Sir Jwala Prasad Srivastava, minister for education in the United Provinces, in March 1936 to discuss the matter.[102] He stressed that the act would only be enforced by degrees and in city areas, but not in Benares, Lucknow, Agra, or other larger places, where there was still great opposition by interested parties. Shephard suggested that the Legislative Council in the United Provinces also opposed the act because it had been proposed by a Christian, Ahmad Shah. As such, the League of Nations summary for 1936–37 could only report an incredibly patchy and partial application of the SITA. Section 11 had been extended to the municipal areas of Cawnpore, Benares, Allahabad, Agra, Lucknow, Naini Tal, Saharanpur, Meerut, Etawah, Gorakhpur, and Alligarh from March 1937. Meanwhile, the enforcement of sections 3 to 9, the main body of the act, was still under debate.[103]

As such, the United Provinces annual police reports make no mention of the SITA in their summaries of actions against prostitution, which continued to be confined solely to the operation of the IPC.[104] In terms of the grand total of true cases between 1934 and 1945, the annual figures averaged between 600 and 800, peaking in the early war years at around 840 and dipping to 550 toward the end of the war. The commentaries within the reports display remarkable similarities to those made earlier in the Punjab.

The reports insisted that trafficking for prostitution did exist, but went unreported and undetected. There were also cases of violence and abuse; for instance, the report of 1938 told of a raided house in Ballia which had found six girls aged between seven and thirteen from Gorakhpur, in the eastern United Provinces, two of which were actually locked up in a box. Yet the concern with "willing wives" was also apparent. The report of 1936 insisted that many women were not unwilling victims and suggested that "many of them are better married than they would have been had they remained at home and interference in such cases is not a kindness." The report of 1939 stressed that many women who may have been reported as kidnapped may have simply eloped with someone they preferred to their husband. Such confusions reinforced the seemingly widespread distrust of police statistics, although the United Provinces forces did seem determined to tackle the problem. The report of 1935 noted that because of the lack of faith in the statistics, all districts had been instructed to submit to their central Criminal Investigation Department a list of reported disappearances and the related police action. The report of 1936 detailed further action, including the displaying of photos of supposedly kidnapped children in cinemas. Despite this, in the face of an assumed growing professionalization of trafficking, the report of 1938 still insisted that the figures for kidnapping were of little value.

Of the trade that was detected, there was also a belief in the United Provinces that this was part of what the report of 1938 referred to as a "remedy for the disproportion of the sexes." As the Punjab reports had suggested, the trade was largely northwestward toward that province, but women had also been found in Ajmer en route to Rajputana and Bombay in 1938, while Punjabi women had also been found in Lucknow in 1942. In the face of this movement and the police's lack of knowledge of it, the common conclusion of the reports was that trafficking was as much a social problem and that, as the report of 1940 concluded, while "many social and communal societies are doing much useful welfare work, more is possible."

Despite the flaws of the Punjab and United Provinces SITAs in practice, their passing inspired further legislation. In 1934 the North-West Frontier Provinces, which bordered the northern Punjab, introduced an Anti-Prostitution and Suppression of Brothels Bill.[105] The slight variation in the title of the bill was matched by a succinct change in tone from the internationalist concern with trafficking, which was reflected in the penalizing sections that were eventually passed into law. In explaining the objects and reasons of the bill its proponent, Allah Nazaz Khan, declared both brothels and the existence of prostitution to be the enemy of the province. The days were said to be passed when brothels could be defended either as good for health or useful for civilized society. They were said to promote venereal disease and to be detrimental to the morality of youth. Concluding his introduction, Khan described the prostitute as a "ready made hell" and insisted that "our youth must be made to realise the dreadful havoc that is played by demon brothels. We want to save our children from this social, moral and economical evil." The act (III of 1937) provided sections to penalize the following:

3. Soliciting
5. Living on the earnings of prostitution
6. Procuration
7. Importation

8. Detention

9. Keeping a brothel or allowing premises to be used as a brothel

However, despite the language which went beyond prevalent abolitionist discourses in that it targeted the prostitute more than the orchestrators of commercialized prostitution, the act had more lenient clauses than abolitionists had insisted on. They were, however, in the light of problems in the Punjab and United Provinces, more pragmatic. While section 9 penalized brothel keeping, the law stressed that this would only take place if three or more persons occupying separate premises in the vicinity of the brothel were to make a complaint, although a district magistrate reserved the right to order the discontinuance of a brothel also. This counter-narrative to the spatial politics of abolitionism was also demonstrated through the Assam Disorderly Houses Act (IV 1936). It updated the Eastern Bengal and Assam Disorderly Houses Act (II of 1907) to allow the closure of any brothel that was

a. in the vicinity of any educational institution or residential accommodation used by students

b. of annoyance to inhabitants of the vicinity

c. near to a cantonment

This was followed by the even more extreme Bihar Suppression of Prostitution and Immoral Traffic Bill, which was submitted to the Bihar Legislative Council on 23 January 1939.[106] Though based on the Punjab and United Provinces SITAs, the bill also aimed to tackle illicit sexual intercourse more broadly by targeting adultery by unmarried women and widows. In addition to the standard SITA clauses, it also proposed the punishment of prostitution itself and of illicit intercourse between man and woman. In proposing his bill, Mr. Tajamul Hussain described prostitution as undoubtedly irreligious, immoral, unhealthy, and unhygienic. Despite this approach, which went against the abolitionist defense of the prostitute as victim, Hussain was aware of League of Nations publications, citing their definition of a "pimp." The bill met with skepticism during its first reading and does not seem to have resurfaced before independence. Indeed, the Delhi SITA of 1940 seems to have been the last passed in the colonial period. However, as the previous chapter showed, the Delhi Municipal Committee was operating segregationist policies throughout the interwar period, and the segregated zone on GB Road would survive the years of the Delhi SITA with ease.

The examples above have sought to demonstrate the dangers of reading policy decisions on governmentalities without due attention to their regional variation or manner or implementation. It has also drawn attention to the ways in which governments can attempt to conduct the conduct of agencies which they hope will govern on their behalf: whether this be local legislatures prompting civil society into action, campaigners encouraging local governments to legislate, or central governments prompting local bodies to act.

In terms of the latter, the central government refused to be dragged into any debates about the SITAS, or lack thereof. On 5 October 1936 a question was posed in the central Legislative Assembly by Mr. M. Ananthasayanam Ayyangar asking why Delhi did not have something like the "Brothels Act" of Madras, to which Sir Henry Craik replied: "This appears to be more a matter for private or municipal enterprise than Government action."[107] Despite its access to annual police reports, the government of India could even use this as an excuse for not filing its annual reports on time in London, which were destined for the League of Nations. The Home Department wrote in apology on this matter to the secretary of state in London on 22 December 1936, claiming that "the Government of India are not directly in touch with the administration of measures designed to suppress the exploitation of prostitution and had, therefore, to consult the local Governments."[108] The same response was deployed in 1944 in relation to a proposed question on the lack of extra measures to suppress immoral traffic, which had increased over the last five years.[109] The question itself was disallowed, but the internal notes stress clearly that, from a law-and-order perspective, this was an issue for the provinces, and the central government did not know if it had taken special measures.

### Conclusion

The foregoing discussion has shown that abolitionism did not seep into India as an ethereal discourse, nor was it an abstract legal principle that was debated centrally and enforced locally. Rather, it was a hard campaigned-for *network* of sites, which built on the scandals of regulation to legitimate experimental sites that would demonstrate the utility and morality of suppression over segregation. It was the material and social contexts of these sites from which new legislation emerged, while simultaneously drawing upon clauses and lessons from other sites. These lessons were very much dependent upon *nominalist* processes of naming and categorizing. The brothel had been delegitimized through sexological literature that cast it as a site of perversion and disease. But the category of India was also one in flux: prostitution was cast as a local not national problem, for which sites would have to invent their own solutions. While an integrated and diffuse network of experimental legislating sites emerged, the move to both segregation and suppression was dominated by the axis of Bombay and Burma for over twenty years. In 1901 the Burma government had looked to the Bombay City Police Act for ways of tackling procuration, while both Rangoon and Bombay cities adopted segregationist powers in 1902. In 1917 Shuttleworth was sent from Rangoon to Bombay, among other cities, to investigate the regulation of prostitution, just as the Association for Moral and Social Hygiene's campaign in Burma reignited, and the murder scandal in Bombay broke out. The amendments to the Bombay City Police Act of 1918 inspired the Burmese Suppression of Brothels Act in 1921, which itself was drawn upon in the Bombay Prevention of Prostitution Act in 1923. While the Burmese act was antisegregationist, it did not provide powers to tackle all the elements of trafficking, while the Bombay Act included provisions against traffickers but continued to allow segregation. The anti-trafficking and antisegregationsit elements of these acts were combined in the Calcutta SITA of 1923 which set the template that would be adjusted but not fundamentally altered as the SITAs spread through much of British India over the next seventeen years (see table 2.2).

Impressive as these clauses look, when they were put into practice it was obvious which of their two objects (the closure of brothels and the protection of the victims of trafficking) was prioritized. As the *Stri Dharma* article of 1935 pointed out, of the 448 women evicted from brothels in Madras, only 7 had been sent to rescue homes. Evidence from the working of the first suppressionist legislation, the Burma Act of 1921, could have provided forewarning of this. Reports to the League of Nations show that between 1929 and 1934–35 the number of persons dealt with for offenses directly related to trafficking and the orchestration of commercial prostitution (living on the earnings of prostitution, procuration, and importing) was greatly overshadowed by the number dealt with for those offenses that related to the impact of prostitution on the respectability of urban space (brothels, soliciting, and the act of prostitution itself). While only 98 persons were dealt with for the former, 1,402 were dealt with for the latter (see table 2.3).

One should be wary of inserting a false critical divide between prostitution and trafficking, or the domestic and the international, as the government had tried to erect (Legg 2009b). Brothels *would* have created demand for more women that could have been met through trafficking. But the complete failure to apprehend those involved in trafficking as opposed to the women involved in prostitution itself is telling. As a former female inspector of police from Rangoon commented in 1938, up to 1935 the Burma

**TABLE 2.2 Clauses included in abolitionist legislation 1921–40**

| Section | Burma 1921 | Bombay 1923 | Calcutta 1923 | Madras 1930 | Bengal 1933 | UP 1933 | Punjab 1935 | NWFP 1937 | Delhi 1940 |
|---|---|---|---|---|---|---|---|---|---|
| Brothel keeping | 11 | 8b | 3 | 5 | 4 | 3 | 4 | 2a | 4 |
| Unlawful detention of women | 10 | 8a | 9 | 10 | 11 | 8 | 8 | 8 | 8 |
| Living on earnings from prostitution | 7 | 5 | 6 | 8a | 8 | | 5 | 5 | 5 |
| Procurement | 8 | 6 | 7 | 11 | 9 | 9 | 6 | 6 | 6 |
| Soliciting | 4 | 3 | | 12 | 7 | 10 | | 3 | |
| Importing | 9 | 7 | 8 | 9 | 10 | 7 | 7 | 7 | 7 |
| Segregation | | 9 | | | | | | | |
| Removal of underage girls | | | | 6 | 13–15 | 11 | 12 | | 12 |

TABLE 2.3 **Cases under the Burma Suppression of Brothels Act, between 1929 and 1934–35**

|                                      | 1929 | 1930 | 1931 | 1932 | 1934–35 |
|--------------------------------------|------|------|------|------|---------|
| Brothels                             | 1    | 2    | 49   | 57   | 50      |
| Soliciting                           | 234  | 147  | 153  | 201  | 206     |
| Prohibitions for prostitution        | 175  | 123  |      |      |         |
| Living on the earnings of prostitution |    |      | 25   | 35   | 31      |
| Procuration                          |      |      | 2    | 10   | 2       |
| Importing                            |      |      | 2    | 4    | 1       |

Suppression of Brothels Act was used almost entirely to prosecute prostitutes, not traffickers (Niccoll-Jones 1938). This was in part due to untrained police officers, in part due to the difficulty of securing witnesses, but no doubt in large part due to the nominalist stigmatization of the prostitute and the networking drive to clear the city of brothels so as to present the image of ordered, natural, civil cities.

However, because these statistics were grouped together under an act that self-proclaimed itself as for the Suppression of Immoral Traffic, the government of India could internationally proclaim itself as taking part in the battle against trafficking in women and children. Its reports to the League of Nations were filled with individual cases whereby women or girls had been rescued from traffickers. On 14 February 1934 Meliscent Shephard commented of this tendency that "from the 'official' replies sent in to Geneva one would think that India was the most moral place in the world. I do so wish Govnt would see that this whitewashing of conditions does harm in the end for it makes other nations say 'poor, dear India: if they were only allowed to govern themselves, how happy they would be, and how good.'"[110]

This comment exposes the nature of the statistical reports passed between New Delhi and Geneva, but also Shephard's contentious political positioning in relation to nationalism and imperialism. Both scalings out, via Shephard to happenings within the imperial core, and via the League of Nations to international developments, were vital to the emergence and evolution of the sitas in India, as eventually applied in Delhi. The following chapter will continue to track the spatial genealogies of segregation and suppression through these more extended networks.

# Three

# IMPERIAL MORAL AND SOCIAL HYGIENE

This chapter confronts most directly the problem, and potential, of narration. It simultaneously narrates a woman, an institution, and a boundary between civil society and the colonial state. In so doing it also, necessarily, intermeshes with other narrations: of feminism, in its imperial and Indian manifestations; of segregation and suppression; and of the scientific and cultural framings of medicine. But it also poses new problems of archiving and power. The majority of the material in this chapter was drawn from the Association for Moral and Social Hygiene (AMSH) papers at the Women's Library in London. The papers concerning India were largely deposited, and composed, by the AMSH's representative in India between 1928 and 1947, Meliscent Shephard. She campaigned tirelessly to abolish tolerated brothels and to spread suppressionist legislation through the political landscapes of dyarchy, from 1919 to 1935, and of provincial self-government, from 1935 to 1947. But the AMSH material is also already narrated and inflected by a place and period-specific form of feminism, hygiene, and racialism. It attests to the belief in an imperial civil society, a domain of *naturalistic* improvement that brought with it certain responsibilities in terms of colonial public health. The interwar world saw the emergence of "hygiene" as the most efficient technology for this venture, but the tensions between its moral and social variants hinted at the broader tensions that harried the concept of the imperial "civilising mission."

After exploring these broader contexts, the chapter will then consider Shephard's time in India through three periods: her first three years in Calcutta, four years in Delhi with independent funding, and the remaining years in Delhi while partly subsidized by the state. These periods will be examined through the three analytical lenses of her networkings, her stance on moral hygiene, and her racial politics. This will expose how Shephard exploited *nominalist* techniques of branding to contingently recast herself as a campaigner of local, national, imperial, or international significance. The way she exploited the potential of self-naming and branding will be explored in terms of her philosophy, policies, and practices. But Shephard can also provide us with insights into how the local and national overturning of the toleration of brothels was part of, but not solely explainable by, an imperial *network* of campaigning. These networks will be analyzed in terms of law, funding, and institutions.

Unlike the other chapters, the focus here is on one institution and its changes during a particular period. To provide insights into the common rationalities across the AMSH's different types of work, and to allow comparisons of that work over time, the analytical categories from the governmentality literature will be used to present the empirical data (as in Legg 2007b, 12), namely, the techne that allowed sites and networks to be constructed and analyzed, the sense of identity informing the AMSH's nominalist conduct of conduct, and the racial and politicized ethos that was behind the problematization of Shephard's work, and her eventual undoing.

### New Imperial Histories of Civil Society and Colonial Public Health

As this book's introduction suggested, studies of imperial history, new and old, have shown that imperial circuits and networks very much surpassed the state. ~~Empires~~ were as much made by traders, missionaries, travelers, scientists, and humanitarians as by the formal agents of a state. But how should these agents be framed and understood? As part of a heteroglossic imperialism, whose strength lay in its diversity and whose coherence, to the extent that it existed, lay in its dispersion of contradictions and productive tensions? Or would this be to subsume willfully independent organizations within an imperial framework upon which they depended, but in many ways they rejected? Capitalist markets, Protestant or Catholic missionaries, scientific explorers, or humanist campaigners could complement or thwart colonial projects or imperial Great Games.

Market, state, and civil society have often been posed as an epistemological trinity of independent though related domains, forming a semiautonomous system of *natural* orderings. These units have been applied to the international as much as the domestic domain, with a transnational civil society posited between global markets and an international sphere of states by contemporary theorists of nongovernmental organizations and grassroots movements. However, such analyses have mistakenly posited civil society as a separate sphere, ignoring the transfer of knowledge, personnel, and responsibilities between markets, states, and non-state/non-market actors (Pieck and Moog 2009, 418). This relationship is increasingly acknowledged as one of dependency and accountability, in which civil society is constituted *through* its relationship with market and geopolitical forces. This was, however, as much a product of colonial liberal governmentalities as of the neoliberal world economy.

As the first chapter illustrated, colonial civil society was in many senses overdetermined by the colonial state even, indeed more so, when it was critical of the effects of imperialism. Harald Fischer-Tiné (2007), for instance, has shown how the Salvation Army was surveyed and harassed by the police and the Bombay government after it arrived in India in 1882. Only in the atmosphere of anticolonial violence and nationalism in the 1900s did its mantra of obedience and discipline gain approval within central government, which offered financial support from the 1920s onward. As will become clear in this chapter with regards to the Rockefeller Foundation, however, any civil society organization that was felt to challenge the interests of the colonial state, or to be too closely linked to the interests of another state, found its operations blocked or curtailed (Kavadi 1999).

As the previous chapter has shown, the turn from segregation to suppression in interwar India cannot be understood solely through the lens of military prerogatives, as with much nineteenth-century prostitution legislation in India, nor was it solely a medical matter of reducing venereal diseases. The military and the medical contexts *do* provide important backgrounds for understanding the AMSH campaign, recurring as they did in lingering practices of examination and anxiety (indeed, one of the most strikingly recurrent features of the archive is how Shephard had to fight against subversive practices of military inspection and toleration into the 1930s). Any inspection of this vexed nexus between the soldiery and the sanitary, the colonial population and the politics of health, must situate itself within the historiography on colonial medicine. Since the 1980s a substantial body of literature has emerged that not only questions "what is colonial about colonial medicine" but also investigates resistance, hybridity, indigenous medicine, and the translation of medical paradigms around the world (Ernst 2007). Such incitements are in evidence throughout this book, where the reaction of prostitutes to their regulation, the role of Indian women's movements and organizations, and the varied reaction to venereal disease statistics are considered.

This chapter is, however, more concerned with the emergent sense of colonial public health. The switch from segregation to suppression was conditioned by the realization that the state had to adopt some level of welfarist concern for the health of the Indian population. This movement "out of the enclave" (Arnold 1993a, 96) of the colonial state's disciplinary archipelago of barracks and jails marked a radical extension of the types and numbers of bodies the state would, in all its diversity, attempt to "colonize." From a curative stance that responded to biopolitical problematizations, the state would now haltingly engage in experiments in preventative medicine. The political furor resulting from the failure to deal effectively with plague outbreaks from the 1890s resulted in the Sanitary Resolution of 1912 which pushed the government closer toward controversial sanitary intervention and preventative medicine (Arnold 1993a). Previous grounds for exceptionalist arguments against intervention, such as the backwardness of the Indian people, fears of intervention in local cultural and religious traditions, and administrative barriers, were all being undercut. Nationalist and natural scientist commentators were suggesting that colonial underdevelopment, not racial biology, accounted for any "backwardness" of the Indian people (Zachariah 1999); the colonial state was increasingly seen as the barrier, rather than channel, to social development (Sinha 2006), while the Government of India Acts removed obstructions to provincial investment in public health. The act of 1919 instituted dyarchy, which transferred control of sanitary infrastructure, vital statistics, and public health to provincial administration, building upon moves made in the 1870s–80s toward local self-government in medical relief and sanitation (Kavadi 1999, 9). Here, administrative experiments by innovative colonial officials could drive moves toward investment in the broader population (Amrith 2006; Hodges 2008), although dyarchical provincial developments *were* also marked by a continuing preference for cheaper, curative methods, and a lack of national coordination. Financial restraints also forced these branches of the late-colonial state into their characteristic "openness" (Darwin 1999) and to collaboration with voluntary organizations.

This combination of openness to non-state expertise and lack of coordination has been commented upon in other areas of late-colonial biopolitics. In terms of birth control, neo-Mathusian and eugenicist debates were common among some of India's middle classes, but the state failed to produce any sort of coherent policy on the matter (Ahluwalia 2008; Hodges 2008). When Britain's military presence in India was threatened by venereal disease, the state famously reacted with a coordinated, if generally ineffective, registration policy (Ballhatchet 1980). The rate of venereal disease among the military peaked in 1895, at 522 per 1,000, but by 1913 had declined to just 53 per thousand (Arnold 1993a, 87). While the Indian Contagious Diseases Acts had allowed for civilian populations to be brought within the military's purview, this was more the extension of military medicine than the emergence of sexual public hygiene. Where the broader population was considered before 1914, it was to speculate on the rampant infection of common women, as well as prostitutes, with venereal disease, and its severe tropical manifestations (Levine 1994, 590). It was only after the Royal Commission on Venereal Diseases in the United Kingdom in 1916 that the policy of free treatment of, and education about, venereal diseases for all started to percolate into colonial India (Legg 2009a, 461), though hospitals remained reluctant to administer such treatment toward the poorer classes (Roy 1998). This combination of curative and preventative measures would be configured through a newly emergent medico-moral complex that was slowly supplementing the nineteenth-century belief in sanitation as the foundation of public health. The National Council for Combating Venereal Disease, which had campaigned for Britain's Royal Commission and was charged with implementing its findings, embodied this shift when it renamed itself in 1925 as the British Social Hygiene Council (BSHC).

## Social, Moral, and Imperial Hygiene

The following definition was provided in a foreword to the BSHC's *Empire Social Hygiene Year-Book*, "Social Hygiene focuses attention on those factors essential to 'the good life' which depend on the inherent quality and the personal behaviour of the individual and the race. It aims at securing a standard of positive health and of personal behaviour such as will endow the individual and the race with a true appreciation of the values of the good life and with capacity to live that life" (Blackett and Grigg 1935, 19–20). This definition made explicit the linkages that were thought to exist, although they were deemed inadequate, between the individual and the population, as conceived through the bloodline of the race. Regardless of the definition of a "good life," it was thought to necessarily depend upon mental and physical health. Venereal diseases were singled out, in the foreword as in the BSHC, as a prime example of the suffering and racial damage caused by ignorance and a lack of conscience. In response, social hygiene provided for the social protection of the "defective," the treatment of the sex delinquent, the relations of the family to the state, the training of the young in responsibility, questions of nutrition, migration, and miscegenation. This task was said to be much harder in the empire, due to the lack of social services more broadly. This dense summary of the import of hygiene in the 1930s can be appreciated through its situation in genealogies of the body, national variations in hygiene practices, and the interrelations between social and moral hygiene.

Hygiene can be productively situated at a pivotal moment in the emergence of liberal governmentalities. The latter depended upon a play of freedoms, conducting the conduct of individuals upon whose calculations and decisions the laws of society, economy, and demography depended. Yet while such individuals were conceived of through aggregates such as race, population, people, or multiplicity, the laws which supposedly operated in these autonomous domains presupposed a certain subject: one that could work, one that made rational decisions, one with a conscience and preferably a regulatory soul. A thoroughgoing liberal governmentality would inculcate a population of individuals that were self-regulating, in terms of their work ethic and productivity, their devotion to society and their sense of self, and their contribution to a vigorous race through personal health and hygiene. The latter would supplant earlier models in which the economy eroded the health of the workforce, while the state attempted to create an infrastructural urban milieu able to sustain life and reproduce social labor. As such, David Armstrong (1993) has suggested that biopolitical spaces of public health are intimately tied to the "fabrication of identity" (also see Bashford 2004). Augmenting the quarantine model, in which places became infected, and that of sanitary science, in which the interface and flows between the body and soils, climate and buildings, had to be monitored, came the model of personal hygiene. Outside of the intense surveillance of disciplinary institutions, people had to learn how to govern and conduct themselves such that their own personal needs would be fulfilled and the effects of climate and environment overcome. Warwick Anderson (2007, 4) has highlighted hygiene's biopolitical but individual focus by contrasting it to the technique of the vaccine, which targets the social body in order to regularize a population, being a technology of security;

hygiene, in contrast, produces an individuation, being a technology of the drill. Rose (2001, 1), among others, has situated this very general progression within the evolving biopolitical management of life itself, both of the population as a vital order and the individual as a living subject: "Politics now addresses the vital processes of human existence: the size and quality of the population; reproduction and human sexuality; conjugal, parental and familial relations; health and disease; birth and death. Biopolitics was inextricably bound up with the rise of the life sciences, the human sciences, clinical medicine."

This chapter will later return to sexology as the emergent human science that united medical and moral concerns around venereal disease, but this literature was also synonymous with the turn to hygiene. Rose identified hygiene as one of two great state-sponsored biopolitical strategies emerging across Europe, North America, and their colonies in the early twentieth century (the other being eugenics). Sanitary infrastructural interests were supplemented with individualized attention to habits conducive to physical and moral health, which were tied from the Boer War onward to anxieties about the imperial longevity of the British "race." Greta Jones (1986) has shown how British social hygiene broadly overlapped with social medicine, focusing holistically on human mental and biological well-being, as investigated by a new generation of experts. But social hygiene also had an attachment to statistical analysis, as well as structural affiliations with eugenics and its desire to engineer population change through regulatory and ameliorative work. At its most assemblage-like, therefore, social hygiene targeted birth control, family policy, nutrition, industrial efficiency, social policy, and "mental hygiene," especially of the poor.

Social hygiene varied greatly, however, by location. David Pivar (2002, xiv) has shown that in the USSR it was associated with environment and public health, and in Germany with feminist organizations and racial hygiene. In the United States it was closely associated with sexual regulation, prostitution, and the control of venereal diseases, and after the war it became less influenced by feminism and liberal purity campaigners and more modeled upon military hygiene, business methods, and state fears over prostitutes and venereal disease. Via J. D. Rockefeller Jr.'s support for the American Social Hygiene Association, and after the establishment in 1918 of a State Interdepartmental Social Hygiene Board, a neo-regulationist system was erected that saw coercive police action overshadow techniques of moral suasion (Pivar 2002, 212; for comparable movements under the influence of hygiene thinking in France, see Corbin 1978 [1990], 339). Alison

Bashford (2004, 168) has explored imperial hygiene in Australia, examining the way in which colonial formations of social hygiene reinvented quarantine spaces for prostitutes amid a broader racialization of hygiene thought. Here it becomes obvious that Armstrong's teleological progression, with its implicit assumption of a progression from sovereign to disciplinary to biopolitical power relations, must be triangulated (also see Braun 2007). Coerced segregation, consensual segregation, and education, Bashford shows, coexisted as modes of spatial practice in imperial hygiene.

Warwick Anderson's study of the American Philippines has provided the most thorough exposition to date of the role of hygiene in attempts at racial transformation, exploring "how the political rationality of American colonialism became manifest in a technical discourse on bodily practice, mundane contact, and the banalities of custom and habit" (Anderson 2006, 2; for comparable work on prostitution see Briggs 2002). The object here was the constitution of racial capacities, which was increasingly important as new germ theories made it clear that it was conduct and contact, not the tropical environment, that threatened the colonial population. Mark Harrison (1999, 21) has argued that the nineteenth century saw a similar change of approach to the Indian environment within the mentalities of its European rulers and explorers. From adapting to the locality and avoiding disease, the emphasis came to lie on managing the environment, especially as urban settlements came to display ever more pungent reminders of colonialism's deleterious urban effects. As European standards of hygiene rose, so did the consensus regarding the unhygienic Indian. From the exclusion and *cordons sanitaires* of the plague, policy in India finally turned to education in elementary hygiene (Harrison 1990, 29; Prakash 1999). The BSHC established an office in Bombay and attempted to extend its campaign to India (Legg 2013). While it did expand its remit to include marriage and promiscuity, the BSHC's origins meant that, like American social hygienists, it remained wedded to the campaign against venereal disease. Sarah Hodges (2006b) has, however, shown how hygiene spread as a model through Indian women's education, health, and reform organizations. But social hygiene was also hybridized with other movements (see Heath 2010, on obscene publications in Indian and imperial networks). In one hybridization it was combined with longer-standing concerns regarding inequality and justice, and pulled away from its focus on statistics and disease, to emerge as *moral* hygiene.

While "moral hygiene" does not have the same common recognition or historiography as social hygiene, its influence emerged in various strands of hygiene thinking more generally. In Cecil Hutt's (1927) discussion of conferences addressing venereal diseases in *International Hygiene*, for instance, it was noted that increasing attention was being paid to the legal responsibilities of causing venereal infection, and to equal standards between men and women. The latter was the key feature of moral hygiene as applied to the problem of prostitution and marked out its origins in the social purity movements of the nineteenth century. It combined tenets of these movements with the new science of social hygiene in an uneasy alliance, displacing feminists with the new breed of hygiene experts (Hunt 1999, 103). The surviving tenets of the purity movement amount to what Hunt terms "moral regulation." The conduct of conduct was, as with social hygiene, the objective, but the basis of that conduct would not be what was simply clean or safe, but what was ethical or moral. The government of *others*, to reduce their risk, had thus to be fundamentally tied to the government of the *self* (Foucault 1982–83 [2010]). Moral hygiene was thus less amenable to legislation and state administration, and relied more upon the capillary circulation of norms and judgments, and the multifarious assemblage of organizations, beliefs, people, faiths, and campaigns in civil society, to "structure the possible field of action of others" (Hunt 1999, 4, citing Foucault 1982, 221).

Regarding prostitution, much of what we can term "moral hygiene" literature in the twentieth century focused on the "white slave trade," or trafficking in women and children. The philanthropist and social writer Sir James Marchant's (1917, 309) *The Master Problem* (i.e., trafficking), for instance, suggested that "hygiene is on the lips of every would-be reformer of the twentieth century" and acknowledged the need for individual physical health. But he also stressed the need for social, mental, moral, and even spiritual hygiene, which effectively combined the government of self and others: "Social health, too, results from this free interplay of mind on mind as much as from improved sanitation, public libraries, the green fields, and the songs of birds" (Marchant 1917, 309). This moral hygiene reforged the pastoral equation of health and holiness ("no morals, no health," but also "no morals, no man"): "The question of Moral Hygienics steps beyond the personal, while also comprehending it. An individual is trained to personal cleanliness of soul and thought, but as useful and necessary a part of the 'hygienising' process is to remove the contaminating elements from the reach of the individual, and especially the young, venturesome, and ill restrained products of latter-day civilisation. . . . Hence a growing part of moral and social hygienics has been to hedge round with wise restriction some part of that much worshipped god, 'the liberty of the subject'" (Marchant 1917, 314).

Marchant's open declaration that the object of these measures be "social purity" makes clear the origin of moral hygiene, but also hints at the means by which it would be achieved. Articulating with great clarity the liberal play on freedoms and regulation, Marchant laid plain the logic by which prostitutes would be "removed" from the reach of vulnerable populations as a way of protecting the public. But this urge was also in tension with the growing acceptance that the prostitute herself was a *woman*, who should not shoulder all the blame for venereal diseases or man's infidelity. This was a realization fought for by first-wave feminists who stressed the equality of prostitutes with other women, as well as for women and men. This equality was, however, tested when stretched across space and race. Shephard would bring together social, moral, and imperial hygiene into a unique hybrid; this will be explored in detail through a reading list she supplied to the government in 1935.

While Shephard's campaign can be fitted into a broader shift toward social and moral hygiene, it must also be understood within a tradition of "imperial feminism" (see Burton 1994; Legg 2010). Shephard self-consciously sought to continue the work of Josephine Butler who had fought for, and in the name of, Indian women, while still defending the broader imperial project and incorporating racialist assumptions into her campaign. These assumptions would be challenged by Indian female social reformers in the 1930s and would force Shephard closer to the state that she had originally come to India to campaign against. In this sense, Shephard fits into a long tradition of liberal reformism and philanthropy within and beyond India (Lambert and Lester 2004). It was directed from the metropolis but organized within a colony; it was simultaneously critical of yet protected by the colonial state; and it hybridized universal-humanist claims against abuse of women with regionalist-racial claims about cultural and biological difference. Yet Shephard also stands out for the duration and intensity of her campaigning, for the breadth of her networking (from municipal committees to viceregal councils), and for the outdated imperialism of her feminism.

As with the other chapters in this book, scalar politics infuse the material that follows. The AMSH was a distinctly imperial organization, being based in the Westminster area of London, but conducting campaigns across the British Empire. Rather than operating in some reified imperial sphere, or in a horizontally transnational civil society of smooth space, it excelled at grasping the empirical specificity and stickiness of place. As Meliscent Shephard became familiar with the politics of governmental negotiation, she also came to appreciate the benefits of being labeled "international" (through collaborations with the League of Nations), "local" (through connections with provincial governments), and eventually "national" (by accepting a stipend from the central government).

As such, Shephard's campaign in India also fits into the three narratives of imperial and transnational civil society, social and moral hygiene, and imperial feminism. The AMSH drew its lineage from the antistate, but proimperial, feminist campaigns of the nineteenth century. Rather than campaign solely from London, the AMSH worked in India for nearly twenty years. As with other institutions in colonial India, it gradually became entangled with the government, and as such this chapter provides a narrative of the symbiotic boundary between civil society and the state. Secondly, Shephard updated Victorian purity campaigns to the newer hygiene sciences. While concerned with venereal diseases, her emphasis was very much on moral hygiene and the ethical compunction to close tolerated brothels and to encourage abstinence. This chapter will also, therefore, provide a narrative of the AMSH as it fought for survival against both the central state, which was a reluctant abolitionist, and against neo-regulationist vigilance associations or hygiene councils. Finally, this chapter will chart Shephard's very personal experiences as an imperial feminist. Her achievements, as a woman in an intensely patriarchal colonial society, were phenomenal. She was, however, imprinted with the imperial racialism of her time, and was on occasion actively racist, which debilitated her attempts to engage with the Indian social reformers who were pursuing similar aims. This tension erupted shortly after she arrived in Calcutta in 1928 and dogged her throughout her remaining nineteen years in India.

### Calcutta and the AMSH

As detailed in the previous chapter, Calcutta had passed the first Suppression of Immoral Traffic Act in 1923. The failing operation of this act led to the Bengal SITA replacing it in 1933, but only after sustained local campaigning. While the All Bengal Women's Union was central to this campaign (see Southard 1995), the AMSH also had a history in the city. The two organizations had worked in sync to forge a more effective SITA, but in the fractious political atmosphere of the early 1930s Shephard struggled to summon the tact and sympathy to negotiate Bengali politics and was, as she explicitly viewed it, hounded out of the city in 1931. After establishing the existing context of prostitution and the Vigilance Association in Calcutta, the first section of this chapter will explore the association's request for a worker and Shephard's acceptance of this role.

In a 1926 article in the *Shield* entitled "Vice Areas in Bombay and Calcutta," the AMSH laid out its claim to a long genealogy of work against recognized prostitution in India.[1] Propaganda carried out by its predecessor organizations had pressured the government since the 1880s, while the investigations of Bushnell, Andrew, and Dixon had all also been funded by its predecessor bodies. The AMSH's support of Cowan's campaign against the situation in Rangoon was recounted, as was the association's campaigning against the government, and with Indian women's organizations, for the Burma Act of 1921 to become a national legislative template. However, the significant ramifications of the Government of India Act of 1919 were also acknowledged. Dyarchy meant that the issue was one for Legislative Councils in Bombay and Calcutta, and that the best the AMSH could do was to provoke public discussion. One topic of debate would be the malfunctioning of the Calcutta SITA, which provided powers to remove some of the suspected two thousand girls aged between nine and thirteen from brothels, but provided nowhere for them to be housed.

It was to this later task that the Calcutta Vigilance Association (CVA) applied itself. Unlike the Association of Moral and Social *Hygiene* with which it would come to collaborate, the CVA explicitly stated its object to be that of social *purity* (Hunt 1999, 161).[2] While vigilance associations shared with the AMSH the belief in rescue work and educating public opinion, they also aimed to initiate, promote, and amend regulations by the police, which the AMSH often viewed as anti-prostitute and illiberal. However, the collaboration of the institutions was made possible by the CVA recommending that Calcutta adopt regulations that were abolitionist, on the model of the Burma Act of 1921. While the Calcutta SITA of 1923 required places in which "rescued" women or children could be placed, the CVA realized that Christian missions would be out of the question, anticipating accusations of converting vulnerable young girls. As such, the CVA launched a fundraising campaign and was able to announce the opening of the Greaves Home in 1927–28.[3]

In its first year it housed twenty-six girls aged eight to thirteen and focused on instruction in Hindu religion and vocational training. While the CVA was an independent body, the extent to which the home formed an unofficial part of the governmental regime was clear. The government of Bengal had not introduced the SITA, but had looked on the private member's bill with "benevolent sympathy." Lord Lytton had presided over the Rescue Home Fund Committee, which resulted in the Mayor's Fund for Minor Girls being merged with the CVA. He also passed on to Geneva a request by the CVA that the League of Nations Trafficking in Women and Children Committee visit India. Despite this glamorous patronage, the CVA struggled for money, raising only a third of the lakh (one hundred thousand) rupees it desired. The association did, however, receive a donation of a property, which opened in 1929 as Govinda Kumar House, and could accommodate seventy girls (see figure 3.1). The report of 1928 was also able to announce that it had decided to celebrate the centenary of Josephine Butler's birth by requesting the AMSH in London to send a worker for three years to concentrate on the brothel problem.[4]

The Lord Bishop of Calcutta, president of the CVA, wrote to the AMSH on 17 May 1928.[5] His request was discussed by a subcommittee in London, and on 20 July the secretary of the AMSH, Miss M. Turner, wrote to Meliscent Shephard inviting her to help in a project to close all public brothels in Calcutta. Born in December 1885, Shephard had been educated in Hampstead and, though not poor, grew up within the environs of a thoroughly middle-class London. After training as a secretary she held various posts in the medical sector and civil service, before moving to the Josephine Butler Memorial House in Liverpool where she was prepared for her struggle against vice and for the uplift of women. Shephard had already deposited her curriculum vitae with the AMSH, writing from her then position at the Manchester Diocesan Association for Preventative and Rescue Work. The scale of her ambition was clear from the start; she was amused that the secretary of the AMSH, Alison Neilans, presumed her to be "pure Lancashire" to begin with. She had turned down offers "up north" because she wanted to do *national* church work: "I *can't* think in terms of parishes! Sometimes I wonder if I have not been foolish to refuse Rachel Crowdy's suggestion of work in the League."[6] Crowdy was head of the Social Questions Section of the League of Nations between 1919 and 1931, and Shephard shared her internationalist aspirations.

Shephard replied to the AMSH's invitation on 23 July accepting the offer, and a week later she received a letter from the chairman of the AMSH. Dr. Helen Wilson acknowledged Shephard's nervousness, but stressed that no lesser figure than C. F. Andrews (ex-member of St. Stephens College

FIGURE 3.1. The Govinda Kumar House, from the *Calcutta Vigilance Association Report 1929–31* (Union Press, Calcutta), courtesy of the Women's Library at the London School of Economics (file reference: WL/3AMS/C/5/1).

in Delhi and confidant of Gandhi) was emphatic that the subcommittee choose her. Shephard's experience in public health (social hygiene) and rescue work (moral hygiene) must have appealed widely to the AMSH, but her experiences had also left her with little personal wealth and a long list of demands. After an autumn of frantic correspondence and budgetary wrangling, the AMSH hosted a farewell meeting for Shephard on 23 November. En route Shephard docked at Karachi and Bombay in December before finally reaching Calcutta to begin her campaign in the new year. Her first brush with colonial culture left her disparaging of Britain's creation of so many social problems in India, keen to start her campaign against military-medical inspection of brothels, but also convinced that "these entrenched Hindus cannot be moved in a day."[7]

### Vigilance in Calcutta: 1929–1931

Shephard's time in Calcutta between January 1929 and September 1931 was phenomenally productive. The AMSH archive offers up a cacophony of documents, reports, and correspondences that give evidence of the energy with which Shephard approached her task. The story of her Calcutta years will be told first by examining the geographies she analyzed and constructed, in terms of case studies and networks that were legal, financial, and institutional. Secondly, Shephard's approach to moral hygiene will be explored, as abstract principle, policy, and practice. Finally, her political engagements will be introduced through a discussion of her racialism and the backlash it provoked.

*Techne: Networks*

CASE STUDIES

Shephard's methodology immediately upon arrival in Calcutta centered on intense, local investigations. The case studies she compiled convinced her, and her London sponsors, of the severity of Calcutta's brothel problem, and allowed Shephard to come to her own conclusions about the causes of prostitution in India. Yet she always situated her investigations within national and international contexts. For instance, her first letter from Calcutta to Neilans, on 1 January 1929, requested that she investigate whether the League of Nations planned to come to India during its investigations into trafficking in the East and asked that the proceedings of the most recent Imperial Social Hygiene Congress be sent on. She also stressed, however, that she had been meeting chiefs of police, nationalist Congress workers, and "leading Indians" which had been "most exciting."[8]

Shephard did have various data sets on which she could draw while compiling her study of Calcutta. Following the passing of the SITA in 1923, the City Corporation appointed a a subcommittee in March 1925 to consider which main thoroughfares should have brothels and houses of ill fame removed from them.[9] Because this practice controversially gave the impression that prostitution was allowed elsewhere, the subcommittee decided to complete a thorough investigation of the geographies of prostitution in Calcutta so as to determine the true volume of commercialized vice.

This was done by comparing census and police records to map the "brothel nuisance" ward by ward, as well as showing which streets had already successfully been declared. Census data alone, it was noted, was not accurate because as the census reports grew in detail, the number of women self-identifying as "disreputable" had fallen (from 34,910 in 1891 to 10,814 in 1921). The report listed thirty-four chief streets in which Calcutta's brothels were located and then provided a ward-by-ward description of census and police information.

Reverend Herbert Anderson had been working in collaboration with the CVA and helped Shephard settle in during her first year, handing over "to her all my papers, books, charts, the result of more than thirty years' investigation" (Anderson 1930, 75). His advice to Shephard was that "studying the situation is a most important and a most difficult task," and that this was more difficult for a foreigner in a great "Eastern City" of one million people, fifty-seven languages, and half a dozen tolerated areas of vice. Despite this, Anderson was impressed with Shephard's vigor in investigating the city, which had "brought her face to face with what are the darkest and saddest problems of commercialised vice. . . . Once or twice she has been up against very ugly situations, but her wisdom has brought her through."

Within six weeks of arriving in Calcutta, Shephard sent her first report to Neilans and Turner from her base at St. Stephen's Parsonage in Kidderpore. Her investigations had been carried out in private, although an unsolicited article about her had appeared in the *Statesman* newspaper. Its report that Shephard advocated a radical change in Indian thought had done her untold harm, she suggested, and had shut the door among leading Hindus to her. She admitted that she felt its claims were true, however, and held out little hope for the CVA's rescue home: "They say they can do it with Hinduism, so they must be allowed to try."[10] Despite this patronizing attitude toward her contemporaries, Shephard's initial case study of Calcutta provided a varied and insightful social geography of the brothel districts. Shunning traditionalist, biological, or cultural explanations of prostitution in Calcutta, Shephard laid the blame firstly on socioeconomics. The root problem was signaled out as Indian women's lack of safe employment or occupation other than marriage. The key to the economic question was that of wages. While she (surely over-) estimated that prostitutes could earn Rs 1 lakh over five years, tea garden work paid Rs 4–9 per month, jute mill work Rs 10 per month, while toiling in the coal fields brought just 8–12 anna per day.

Loyal to Josephine Butler's doctrine of gender inequality, Shephard also argued that the purdah system repressed fellow female understanding while Indian men viewed sexual intercourse as central to manhood and relied upon a caste system that condoned male action, yet chastised women for any lapse. The tradition of separated castes and trades was also associated with tolerated areas of segregated prostitution. Shephard believed that the geographical congregation of castes in specific areas meant that "therefore it is natural to the Indian to have his prostitutes living in the same street, and to allow separate areas for them." In Calcutta, each of the city's thirty-three wards was said to have tolerated areas, with the largest being in wards 1 (Shampookar) and 3 (Bartola), for Indian clients; Japanese prostitutes in ward 21 (Ballyganj Park Circus) for the use of Europeans; and a large zone in ward 25 (Watganj) for the use of the English. On 21 April 1929 Shephard sent back photographic evidence of these zones, which now constitutes an exceptionally rare visual archive of these tolerated brothels. Shephard composed two sheets for display in poster format. The first, entitled "Karaya Road, Calcutta. European Brothel Quarter," drew attention to the lavish style and architecture of the bungalows, but contrasted this to the barbed wire enclosing two of the pictured compounds. Cages and wiring were common features in descriptions of Indian brothels, although many commentators conceded that these were to protect the women inside rather than to keep them hostage. The abnormal nature of the dwellings was also stressed by their usage; both were shut in the afternoon to allow the women inside to sleep, ahead of a night's work. While the European prostitutes tended to serve a wealthier clientele, the Japanese prostitutes charged less and were open to a wider range of customers. The second poster, depicting "Watganj Street, Calcutta. Japanese Brothel Quarter," made this contrast clear. Images were provided of open sewers in the street, uncowed "touts," and dilapidated brothels (including the "Nagasaki Roof Garden" brothel containing forty-five "girls") surrounded by makeshift trade stalls (see figures 3.2 and 3.3).

In addition to photographing the brothels, Shephard also investigated seven of them, five of these visits being at night. She found that the army had arranged for three brothels in the Japanese area to be medically inspected, with soldiers at Fort William being told they could go there. This became the focus of Shephard's attentions over the summer and on 29 November she sent a "plain, unvarnished statement about Watganj Street" to London.[11] She claimed that her investigations had been delayed because she

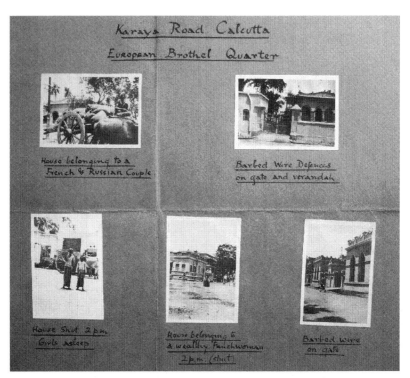

FIGURE 3.2. Karaya Road, Calcutta. European brothel quarter. Courtesy of the Women's Library at the London School of Economics (file reference: WL/3AMS/C/5/2).

had become known to procurers on that street, meaning she had to abandon her nighttime visits. The street was described as one of brick houses interspersed with basti (slum) shops and pukka (permanent) houses. It was located between the docks and the Maidan park and, though not served by a tram, had to be passed through to reach the docks directly. The occupants were mostly Japanese, with at least five houses being brothels, despite there being a police *thana* (post) on the street itself. At about 5:00 p.m. the streets began to "wake up," with girls being taken out to visit customers in garden houses for the night. Although military police paraded the road, they admitted to Shephard that they were forbidden from preventing men entering house 11c, even if in uniform. On further inquiry she found that the medical officer at the Fort inspected women at houses 11c and 50. An Indian medical officer was persuaded to let Shephard accompany him while visiting a maternity case at 11c, during which she got to speak to two of the seventeen women living there. The Japanese women admitted that they gave all their money to their "mistress" and got food, kimonos, and lodg-

FIGURE 3.3. "Watgang" Street, Calcutta. Japanese Brothel Quarter.
Courtesy of the Women's Library at the London School of Economics
(file reference: WL/3AMS/C/5/2).

ing in return. They could only receive "Tommies and Jackies" (soldiers and
sailors), who paid just Rs 2–3 each time, and the women were medically
inspected by a doctor from the Fort. They would take up to ten men a night,
and two to three on a "'bad' night." The local police sergeant deputed to this
work had been instructed not to interfere with soldiers unless there was a
row, in which case he was to call the military police. Shephard presented
these facts to the bishop of Calcutta who consulted the military authorities
in Simla, resulting in the closure of militarily inspected brothels on Watganj
Street by August 1929.

During the year Shephard began to engage in publicizing the plight of prostitutes in Calcutta, although without drawing attention to her own work. They appeared in the *Calcutta Diocesan Review*.[12] The three published articles each focused on a different "race" in Calcutta, starting with the Anglo-Indian community. Those women with "predominantly European" blood were said to be particularly vulnerable to "moral problems."[13] This was attributed to socioeconomic factors, such as high rents, bad housing, and low wages, as well as cultural conditions, such as "irresponsibility of temperament," lack of education, and the temptations of European men. Misled women initially found themselves not in brothels but in apartments, where they were maintained by a British man until he tired of her or left the country. Shephard suggested that after this betrayal Anglo-Indian women's love turned to scorn and hate, leading them to seek revenge on men, and financial survival, through lower forms of prostitution (see Blunt 2005, for a critique of popular tragic and eroticized narratives of Anglo-Indian women). They would ply this trade in European brothel quarters like those described in her previous reports and portrayed in her photographs: "One or two storied bungalows, with barbed-wire entanglements around the walls and gates. All day the streets have a dead look; shutters are closed, men servants asleep on the verandahs, the women asleep within" (see figure 3.4).

Melodramatically, an incident was related in which Shephard had been interviewing a prostitute within one of the brothels when two drunken Europeans entered. Shephard supposedly hid in a back room long enough to hear them haggle a price, then slipped out a back entrance: "Why should the men be free to live where they will, and the women obliged to live in 'known' areas? Who will do rescue work amongst men? Courage was needed in the War years by both men and women. Courage, physical, mental, and spiritual is needed in these after-War years if this hydra-headed monster of lust and greed is to be slain."[14]

Speaking of the European community, Shephard considered why men lived immoral lives in Calcutta.[15] She blamed social factors, such as loneliness, economic factors, such as wages being too low to allow more sociable activities, and cultural pressures toward drinking and loose living. It was also apparent to her that European men treated Indian women differently because of their nationality, in the face of which she made a case for the immorality of sexual relations for payment, irrespective of race. Shephard continued to appeal to Christian morality against such temptations to European men. This was a continuation, however, of her first published article

Barbed Wire Defences
on gate and verandah.

FIGURE 3.4. Brothel on Karaya Road, the European quarter, with barbed-wire defenses. Courtesy of the Women's Library at the London School of Economics (file reference: WL/3AMS/C/5/2).

on the Indian community. She suggested, anonymously, that Indians lacked high moral standards in relation to extramarital relations. This could not be separated from her comments on religious communities, where Shephard suggested that Hindu customs reinforced man worship and child marriage, while Muslims allowed men sexual indulgence but insisted upon servitude and seclusion of women. Only through equal partnership at the level of the home, the nation, and the international could the real genius of Indian thought be given to the world: "And this genius will not find its outlet until the Indian man and woman together kneel at the Feet of the Incarnate Christ."[16] It is this combination of racial and Christian condemnation of Calcuttan society that would bring Shephard's time in the city to an ignominious end.

While charged with investigating the Calcutta scene by her employers, Shephard also investigated other case studies in India and beyond. In 1930 she helped establish a Moral Welfare Association in Bangalore, which offered free advice on venereal diseases and performed propaganda using film and social hygiene handbooks. She also spent March to April 1930 in Ceylon, where she investigated the effects of the abolition of segregated brothels in Colombo in 1913.[17]

While these local studies were part of the campaign that Shephard would work toward over nearly twenty years to spread AMSH principles across India, they also served the purpose of highlighting comparisons and connections across India. In July 1931 Shephard wrote to Turner from Bombay, where she had been inspecting the workings of the Bombay Prevention of Prostitution Act (XI of 1923, amended 1930) since her visit on arrival in India in December 1928. She remarked that "the change is MOST marked" since brothels had effectively been criminalized by the amendment.[18] Richer prostitute zones had been cleared while poorer prostitutes had been saved from the worst abuses of madams and procurers. While the Bombay model was obviously more effective than the Calcutta SITA in comparison, it was also connected, as prostitutes were leaving the former city and traveling to the latter. As Shephard commented, "The girls, barriwallahs and pimps know the law better than anyone else!" It was to these broader networks that Shephard would also turn during her remaining time with the CVA.

CONNECTIONS: LAW, FUNDING, AND INSTITUTIONS

While Shephard would continue her local investigations during her time in India, it was as a networker that she would really excel. While her social networking lacked grace and tact, and was at times incredibly offensive, her spatial networking was much more effective, in terms of the *law*, her *finances*, and *institutional* negotiations. As detailed in the previous chapter, Shephard contributed throughout the 1930s to spreading the SITAS, province by province, across British India. Her time in Calcutta was spent familiarizing herself with existing *laws* across India and assessing their comparative merits. The result was a typed set of "NOTES, comparing the Acts concerning the Suppression of Immoral Traffic in Calcutta, Burma (Rangoon) and Bombay."[19] The existing legislations were compared across fourteen categories, including local extent, definitions, powers to close brothels, procuration, removal of minors, and magisterial powers. The Bombay Act of 1923 was held up as a model, building upon the Burma Act of 1921 as it had done, for its thorough definitions, while the existing Calcutta SITA was shown to be deficient in terms of powers to close brothels, to challenge solicitation, and to punish unlawful detention. On the basis of this work the legal subcommittee of the CVA submitted suggested amendments to the Calcutta SITA that would make brothels illegal, punish those over sixteen living off the earnings of the prostitution of another person, punish procurers and traffickers, and safeguard public places from acts of prostitution. These would be the bases for Shephard's campaign to overhaul Bengali legislation, which she would continue to pursue from Delhi after she left the city in 1931.

While Shephard was fascinated by the legal connections and comparisons within India, she was constantly aware that she was also strung between imperial and internationalist networks. This was especially apparent in terms of her *funding*, which was dependent upon the AMSH in London, but which could not compete with generously funded projects from across the Atlantic. In January 1931 Alison Neilans tentatively raised the issue of Shephard's future by suggesting she might want to stay on with another vigilance association in India, as finances were not looking good in London.[20] In the context of the Great Depression, most voluntary organizations were struggling financially, but the Rockefeller Foundation continued to invest both in its headquarters in New York and in ever-increasing spheres of influence internationally (Farley 2004; and Pivar 2002, 123, on Rockefeller, prostitution, and social hygiene in the United States). Shephard had recently been to Lahore where she had met Ruth Woodsmall, who was executive secretary of the Young Women's Christian Association (YWCA) in the Near and Middle East. Woodsmall was on a Rockefeller Foundation traveling scholarship that was financing a fact-finding trip to India and Persia, and Shephard admitted that if she could get such funding she would like to stay in India.[21] Woodsmall had obviously opened Shephard's mind to a very different type of funding and of campaigning. In addition to Rockefeller funding, she was also supported by the National Layman's Missionary Movement and the American Social Hygiene Association (ASHA, itself a recipient of Rockefeller funding). Shephard's initial description, in a letter to the AMSH in February 1931, suggested a certain naïveté regarding the complex intersection of economics and politics in the emergent field of international health: "The idea is that business men with interests in other countries want to do something to improve the place so invest money. They see if missionaries have done all they can and what more needs to be done." Woodsmall's two years in Persia had, thus, resulted in America sending out teachers of social hygiene based on her recommendations. Shephard obviously shared, however, the suspicions of those, then and since (see Brown 1976), who suspected the Rockefeller Foundation of being facilitated by, and facilitating, America's expansive informal imperialism. As she explained: "You see, America is keen to capture all the YWCA and YMCA work here, and as many of the missions and schools as possible are being interpenetrated by American teachers. I don't know whether America wants to be 'Top Nation' (as *1066 and All That* calls it!) in India, but certainly she soon will be unless some of us from other Nations stay and do the jobs which are simple opening up all over the place."[22]

Shephard claimed that, having heard her talk, Woodsmall had said, "Gee, you get your story across." Shephard continued: "Well, I want to continue 'getting it across' and there are plenty of anti-Abolitionist folk who want a different story." In her eyes, Americans simply went to a country with a heap of funds, stayed a few months, issued a large questionnaire, soaked up that atmosphere, then went home to an army of typists and dictated a book: "Thus America is bound to be 'Top Nation' one day, though whether that will be 'a Good Thing' is not for me to say!" (Walter Sellar and Robert Yeatman's *1066 and All That* [1930] parodied nationalist historians' division of history into "Good" or "Bad Things," and their tendency to place their country of origin as "Top Nation.") Even Shephard's old friend Dame Rachel Crowdy did not appear immune to the charm of the United States. Upon retiring from the league she had apparently agreed to lecture in America, where she would earn as much in one year as she would during five at the league ("a comparatively easy way of making a fortune").[23] As such, Shephard requested that the AMSH approach the National Layman's Missionary Movement on her behalf, while Woodsmall herself had backed the idea of a cooperative scheme to support the All India Vigilance Association that would have drawn funds from the American National Christian Council, the League of Nations Union, and the ASHA.[24] Neilans, however, sent a pessimistic reply. She had previously expressed her dislike of the repression of prostitutes in New York as encouraged by the ASHA and the Committee of Fourteen (Gilfoyle 1994, 305). She suspected they had blackballed the AMSH's work in Shanghai five years previously, as part of an attempt to discredit British rule. She continued: "I must say in confidence that I do distrust all these reports and all this capturing of the YM and YWCA Mission work by Americans within the British Empire. I am quite sure a good deal of it is political and it is quite hopeless to imagine that the Americans are friendly to the British Empire, and particularly to Great Britain, at this time."[25]

Neilans suggested that funds from the League of Nations would be more likely, as the American hygiene organizations did not have the motivation, and the British Social Hygiene Council did not have the money, to support them. This combination of political defensiveness over the British Empire, which was a recurrent feature of imperial feminists no matter how anticolonial they could appear, combined with a perceived threat to abolitionism by American regulationism, obviously stirred the AMSH in London. At Shephard's request, the association agreed to extend her work in India for two years, and in June wrote to her requesting details of her envisaged role.[26] Shephard replied that her role should be totally independent of other organizations, and that her work would be legal, educative, and consultative. While Woodsmall had suggested more lecturing, as American hygienists did, Shephard insisted that "personally I am not in favour of further Americanising this over-Americanised country."[27] That Neilans should have put so much effort into keeping Shephard in India was evidence not just of Shephard's accomplishments, but also of their growing friendship, and the war which Shephard and Neilans felt they had to wage against neo-regulationist forces not just from America, but from rival institutions based in the United Kingdom and India.

Even before leaving for India, Shephard had expressed her reservations about the National Vigilance Association and its affiliated bodies in India. During her correspondence with Alison Neilans her *institutional* links to London became closer, while the AMSH's links to the NVA became ever more strained (see Laite 2008, for a discussion of similar tensions in Britain). Shephard came across some of the AMSH's correspondence with Mr. F.A.R. Sempkins, the general secretary of the NVA, during her first few weeks at the CVA, and was told by Neilans in January 1929 that the NVA was at heart regulationist and wanted special controls, though not medical examinations, for prostitutes.[28] Neilans reiterated in October that the NVA had become the "official defender of the police," calling for special regulations against prostitutes, and warned Shephard about assuming any official role with the vigilance associations.[29] In January 1930 she went further, having been provoked by a series of attacks made on the AMSH in the *Vigilance Record*. The NVA members were denounced as "queer people" for accepting public opinion and constantly attacking prostitutes while remaining silent on male conduct. She even went so far as to align the AMSH *with* prostitutes, hinting at the fundamental differences between the abolitionists and regulationist NVA, who had been "using column after column of their paper to attack the AMSH and prostitutes. Probably they think neither of us is strong enough to hit back, but as the New York Report shows the prostitute certainly can hit back against her suppressors,[30] even if indirectly; and I venture to think that the AMSH has still power to put the Vigilance people in their place, if it chose to use it, but I rather imagine we shall ignore them."[31]

### Identity: Naming Moral Hygiene

While Neilans and Shephard condemned the NVA for siding with the law and the police, Reverend Anderson (1930) concluded of Shephard's first year in Calcutta: "The Police and the Law have also been her staunch friends." While Neilans willingly aligned the AMSH with the perspective of the prostitute, Shephard campaigned for almost twenty years to get their brothels and places of habitation closed down across India, and to eradicate the tolerated areas that may have housed networks of support, not just of abuse (Tambe 2006). The riddle of these ambivalences lies at the heart of the *philosophies*, *policies*, and *practices* of the AMSH, which was liberal yet abolitionist, committed to medical treatment of disease, but more so to the eradication of the desire for promiscuous sex and gender inequality. As the quote below from one of Shephard's letters in March 1929 suggests, the AMSH wanted to pass abolitionist laws, but to do this as part of a more thoroughgoing project of social normalization. That is, the aim was not just one of science, sex, and social hygiene, but of education, gender, and moral hygiene. This was an explicitly *nominalist* policy in which Shephard was fighting to shift the terms of the debate about prostitution. Over her first three years in Calcutta Shephard worked to clarify the philosophy, policy, and practices of the AMSH and to adapt them to her specific needs. "We realise fully, of course, that one does not make black things white by passing a law, but the great point is that directly one challenges an evil openly and puts the supporters of the evil on the defensive, one begins to change the whole public attitude on the subject."[32]

In terms of more abstract principles and *philosophy*, Shephard reflected back and summarized her stance in her report on 1928–31 to the CVA.[33] Her aim was said to have been to investigate areas of tolerated vice, and to work toward abolition and education. Her principles, derived from Josephine Butler, were that all races at all times deserved justice, that all deserved freedom unless condemned, that there should be a high standard of sexual conduct for all, and that one should uphold dignity and the human spirit. The role of hygiene as an instrument of governing self-conduct was obviously central to Shephard's interpretation of AMSH governmentalities. She deployed techniques from across the whole scalar range of nominalism, branding herself as imperial and internationalist while gathering intensive local knowledge and focusing on the intimate scale of the body. In an article from August 1930 in the *Statesman* entitled "Self-Government Is Self-Control," Shephard suggested this was a more appropriate topic for discussion than to "govern."[34] Drawing attention to the work of vigilance associations, rather than political parties, across India, she illustrated the campaign to free "unpitied slaves" of segregated vice areas across the country.

Shephard's principles had been tied to the active study of tolerated areas, devadasis, child marriage, selling children, "unnatural vice," and the failure to treat for free those suffering from "social diseases." However, it was tolerated brothels that consumed most of Shephard's attention, and in July 1930 she circulated a printed letter to her friends wherein she admitted that the aim of the Bengal SITA she was drafting was "clearing the segregated vice areas within a certain number of years."[35] Similarly, when the first draft of the Bengal SITA was distributed in January 1932 only one of the five reasons for the bill related directly to trafficking, the others focused on the relation between tolerated brothels and vice, youth corruption, venereal disease, and exploitation.

While the AMSH in India would pursue this policy with dogged determination, in the United Kingdom the AMSH fought to defend the rights of women arrested as prostitutes (Laite 2008, 210). This is evident in the archive through the various moderating messages sent by Neilans to Shephard (discussed below), but also through occasional interventions on issues of principle. The president of the AMSH, Dr. Helen Wilson, wrote in October 1930 that an early drafted amendment to the Calcutta SITA risked suggesting that no one could legally allow a prostitute in any house at all, leaving her with nowhere to live: "It amounts to almost the same thing as punishing prostitutes as such,—a method to which we are firmly opposed. And since it cannot possibly be applied even in all known cases, it puts too much discretionary power in the hands of the police, and that means 'Regulation.'"[36]

Dr. Wilson would also intervene on less abstract issues of *policy*. On 17 December 1929 Shephard wrote to Neilans admitting that she had gotten into financial trouble after paying women to help reclaim them.[37] She had helped a Russian who contracted a venereal disease and was left paralyzed after being mistreated, while she also took in an eighteen-year-old Anglo-Indian as a typist. She insisted that rescue work was not her aim, but that it was difficult not to give a little money when she knew it would place them out of the hands of procurers.[38] Wilson wrote sternly to Shephard in April 1930 that she had authorized another grant to level her finances, but that she had to stop such charity as it would have no effect.[39] At nearly halfway through her time in Calcutta, Shephard was told to conclude her investigative work there and start drafting an abolitionist bill following the example of Bombay, spending the rest of her time rallying public support for the bill. Wilson desired Shephard's bill to be the peg on which to hang all future works toward the abolition of (tolerated) brothels.

Shephard took this advice to heart, and her *practical* work focused on spreading the SITA legislation through India for the next ten years. She did this through direct intervention, but also by encouraging the establishment of affiliated or compatible organizations. She claimed in July 1929 that her tactics on first arrival in India had been to keep in the background, make friends, teach individuals in pivotal positions, and attempt to understand Indian social work.[40] Her view of the latter did not greatly shift from that expressed in a circular to her friends of March 1929 when she claimed that "one of the great hindrances here, as I foresaw in England, is the fact that, with immense wealth and spasms of great enthusiasm, India has but little sense of cooperative service."[41] As demonstrated in the first chapter, India was not felt to have a civil society, and the AMSH's hygiene programs were thought to contribute to the institutional and individual material of the "social." Shephard later tried to work with the All India Vigilance Association, becoming its joint secretary in 1930 and attempting to set up a branch in Lahore, although this did not prove a harmonious union, as will be discussed in the following section. Her campaigning for SITA introduction and reform was, however, more successful. Within three months of arriving in Calcutta she had begun campaigning for more than the existing nineteen roads to be notified, while she highlighted faults with the Madras SITA of 1930 which had failed to include a clause against third parties living on the earnings of prostitution. In reviewing her time in Calcutta Reverend Anderson (1930) had drawn special attention to the excellence of Shephard's propaganda work, and she proved a tireless public speaker and publisher. For instance, in November 1929 an article was published in the *Statesman* covering a speech she had given at the Calcutta Legislative Assembly. She had denounced segregated vice areas for incentivizing trafficking, spreading venereal diseases, punishing women while tempting men, and profiting pimps and procurers.[42]

Shephard's other enduring focus, which she had inherited from Josephine Butler, Elizabeth Andrew, Katharine Bushnell, and Katherine Dixon, was the military. Among her first reports to the United Kingdom were those of the medically inspected Japanese women in Calcutta, with similar cases having been confirmed in Lahore, Karachi, Quetta, and other cities.[43] She could report in 1931 that the brothels had been closed and the Japanese women repatriated. In 1929 Shephard prepared a circular to be distributed by the metropolitan of India to the chaplains of the Indian Ecclesiastical Establishment alerting them to the challenge against military-inspected brothels and the necessity of promoting moral welfare among the troops. In February 1930 Shephard visited Bangalore where she met army officers, after which she wrote: "I am not at all happy at the distinct tendency out here amongst officers in command to regard regulation as the only way out. But I AM happy, so far, at the delightful way in which they change their minds, and borrow papers to read. As one said, when returning my things, 'We are quite obviously about 30 years behind the times out here; I shall certainly support 'your' side in future."[44] The extent to which the military followed through on this pledge disappointed Shephard's high expectations, though in the war years after 1939 even her determination on this issue faltered. This was, however, in a period of heightened nationalist sentiment, to which Shephard had made herself especially susceptible after years of highly controversial racialist comments regarding her work and the country in which she had found herself.

### Ethos: Politics and Race

#### RACIALISM

Aged forty-three when she traveled to India, Meliscent Shephard had been educated during the years of high imperialism in Britain. While many of this generation shook off their Victorian and Edwardian heritage to embrace notions of racial equality and self-rule, Shephard did not. Yet unlike many of her metropolitan colleagues who espoused racial harmony and self-improvement from the imperial core, Shephard experienced these phenomena in India itself, for nearly twenty years. The comments she made during her initial investigations show that, on arrival in India, she was of the opinion that the source of many of India's social ills were European, and that the colonial economy structured the problem of prostitution. While she clung to these principles during her stay in Calcutta, it also became obvious very quickly that Shephard was not able to transfer these observations into an antidote to her ingrained racialism.

This became obvious within a month of her arrival in Calcutta, when she wrote to Grace Human, her colleague in the United Kingdom. Human forwarded the letter to Neilans at the AMSH in February 1929, with a note expressing her hope that these views would not become staples of Shephard's thought.[45] The letter had described Shephard's opinion of the Indian scene after only two weeks, and she was scathing. She described the views of many English that if India was to be part handed over to "the muddled administration of Indians" it was worthless to spend further strength during British rule and suggested that witnesses could be bought outside the court. The Calcutta SITA was damned and the rescue homes criticized for not retraining its girls: "There is a danger, I feel, of catching the general spirit of depression, and of *hating* the Indian people—I must love them and hate their religion and customs, or I can't hope to be of any service."[46] She created concern amongst Neilans's colleagues in England by suggesting in her correspondence that Katherine Mayo (1927) had spoken the truth in her controversial book, *Mother India*. Mayo had criticized Indians for the treatment of their women, neglecting to consider the influence of the colonial state, creating an international scandal (Sinha 2006). In other letters Shephard reproduced crude racial stereotypes of ethnic groups in India, although she professed to believe that Europeans were the real problem.

This suggestion was, however, contradicted by her increasing defense of the colonial state. She admitted in November 1929 that the Criminal Investigation Department was increasingly asking her to investigate "doubtful places; this is good experience, and I think makes them see that our idealism is also practical."[47] In a summary of her work from 1929 that she sent to the AMSH in London, she stressed how important it was that she got abolitionist principles into the heads of responsible leaders in major cities. Sir John Simon had been dispatched to India in 1928 to make recommendations on constitutional reform, and his report was to be issued in 1930. Shephard suggested that "it would be a most unfortunate coincidence if, when the Simon Commission reports, and much is handed over to Indian responsibility, the then ruling Indian class could point to our British administration and show that our authorities did not keep their own rules."[48] Similarly, in October 1929 Shephard requested Neilans not to publicize her closing of military-inspected brothels, just as she had not informed the CVA, "as in India Swarajist [self-rule] propaganda would be made out of such an incident."[49] During the Civil Disobedience nationalist campaign of 1930 Shephard commented that Bengal was in a ferment politically, with useful Bengali politicians in jail or not elected for being pro-British: "Politically, India seems to be trying Ireland's methods. Alas, though the Irish were ready for self-government, India is not."[50] Given her campaign against British military brothels, the hypocrisy of the following statement to Dr. Helen Wilson, president of the AMSH, is astounding: "In talking to individual Bengali men, my main argument has always been that a race that regards tolerated vice areas as an amenity and a necessity is not fit to govern itself; a race which keeps women as slaves can hardly expect to be given independent status amongst the free nations; but one has to be careful with whom these things are said. However, I believe some of the Abolitionist ideas are slowly percolating through, especially amongst Moslems."

As suggested in the previous chapter on the SITAS, campaigners like Shephard were increasingly faced with a fractured legislative landscape that impressed upon them the heterogeneity of the subcontinent just as, ironically, nationalists like Jawaharlal Nehru (1946) were beginning *The Discov-*

*ery of India*. In a letter to Neilans in July 1930, Shephard insisted that the political situation in India was not helped by the press at home in the United Kingdom. Shephard stressed that there was no such thing, in her mind, as an Indian nation or an Indian person. This could only come about if they all became Christian, Jewish, Muslim, Hindu, Parsi "or any ONE sort of religion instead of about three hundred sorts, and sixty thousand sects in every one of those three hundred sorts."[51] She blamed the likes of C. F. Andrews for perpetuating the image of the spiritually minded, lofty, idealistic, united, nationally conscious person, prevented from his destiny by a repressive government: "The 'Indian' simply does not exist in that sense. There are spiritually minded Hindus, Buddhists, Moslems etc, etc, but they are only caste-conscious as yet: and far from a united mind on anything, unless it be a unity of hate and suspicion for anyone not of their own particular caste, creed or sect, well, a united mind does not exist either." In this context, Shephard gave the British response to the mass movement her full backing; the alternative to her was unthinkable: "Once the British leave off governing India, then open warfare will ensue at first between Moslem, Sikhs and Parsis, with Hindus; and later on, between the North and more Southerly places. India will be a shambles." It was believed that Indian women could not possibly want the British to leave, who were supposedly despised for having seen through Indian menfolk, whom their women were supposed to worship. Despite this, Shephard insisted that she did not delve into politics, except to say that (political) self-government would need moral self-government (a Gandhian point she later made to the man himself). This could not be said to exist while lakhs of rupees were spent on prostitution but little on female education; and while committees to deal with drainage, venereal disease, and tuberculosis were canceled so that resolutions could be passed sympathizing with Gandhi, while the rest of the day was spent "twiddling taklas" (spinning cloth).

These comments were fairly incendiary, suggesting that Indians were incapable of self-government due to their political commitments, in the year when the Simon Commission's report, recommending how the dyarchy system would be superseded, was being published. While these views had been expressed in private correspondence, the trouble for Shephard began when she expressed similar sentiments in a printed circular letter sent to her friends, issued a week after the letter to Neilans above. A copy of the letter was forwarded to Neilans by Elizabeth Abbots, a contributor to the Calcutta Fund supporting Shephard, accusing her final paragraph of being a very serious matter.[52] Here Shephard suggested that India would descend into barbarism without the British, that Gandhi's policies were destructive not constructive, and that she had seen a side of Hinduism in Benares that was "utterly revolting."[53] Neilans mentioned the letter to Shephard and the objections she had received, and asked that she make it clear that such letters did not express the views of the AMSH.[54] Remarkably, Shephard replied with a vociferous defense of her right to free speech, insisting that her correspondence with her friends was not written as a worker, and that she lacked no sympathy with "honest" Indians. However, she still stressed that she felt Christian ideals were essential to government, and that India realized it was not yet a nation. It was this uncompromising approach to her beliefs that provoked the growing numbers of commentaries, reproaches, and an eventual controversy that contributed to her departure from Calcutta in 1931.

*Problematization: The Backlash*

Given the political context in which she was operating, it was unlikely that Shephard's views would go without comment, and after her first year's work she gave a hint of the animosity her approach was creating: "This is all confidential. But it IS not easy to keep friendly with Indians when one knows what they are saying and doing behind one's back, and they are only too eager to snatch every little bit of evidence of English bad government to broadcast it everywhere."[55] In April 1931 she wrote to Neilans stressing that, despite accusations against her, she had only ever tried to help India. She suggested that the source of peoples' criticisms of her was her combination of loyalty to English traditions, police, and government, as well as a willingness to engage Congressmen on a polite basis.[56] Going further, she suggested her aim was to cause Congressmen themselves to adhere to Gandhi's principles of nonviolence, truth at all costs, and abandonment of caste. Shephard fancied herself as a signpost for Indian men who were parting from old traditions, customs, and religious ceremonies. In August she wrote of having had a forty-five-minute chat with Gandhi, during which he had promised his support for her campaign.[57] She also met the prominent Congresswoman Sarojini Naidu in July, when they spoke about the abolition of customs, ceremonies, or laws that would deny women their "fundamental rights as ordinary citizens."[58]

However, despite these efforts to appeal to Indian nationalists, in mid-1931 Shephard sent a confidential memo to the AMSH in which she reported that a movement was afoot among Bengali Hindus to spread rumors that she was really "behind Miss Mayo."[59] However, displaying yet again her refusal to accept that her opinions might be to blame for this animosity,

Shephard suggested the campaign was a result of an article in the AMSH's *Shield* that suggested she would publish her results at a later date. Yet in the same letter she detailed how she had alienated her own employers in India, the CVA, such that she was desperate to split away and form her own AMSH in India. She had found them so unpleasant that she could not see why the public would cooperate with them, and protested against a memorial they had submitted to the metropolitan, asking him what her "motives" were in collecting so much information. Although she signed off the letter by reassuring Turner that this was the only circle in Bengal that was hostile to her, in September she wrote to Neilans that she was facing the opposition that "had faced Josephine Butler."

Relating to her work on treating venereal disease she claimed that "as part of the organised propaganda against me, certain Congress members of the [Calcutta] Corporation are questioning the reliability of my facts and figures."[60] The Ladies Advisory Committee for the Govinda Kumar Rescue Home had also turned against her after Civil Disobedience in 1930. The Indian Congress ladies of the committee apparently believed Shephard had "Miss Mayo's mind and methods" and objected to her abolitionist principles as "Christian domination" of Hindu religions and customs. Seven of these ladies also signed the memorial submitted to the metropolitan who, after several meetings with Shephard, suggested she resign from the CVA, which she did on 23 July 1931. While she was hopeful that the criticisms might draw attention to her campaign, it was obvious that her position had become untenable. She claimed that they were out to "destroy," not face her with any alleged crimes, and that they had descended into insinuations and distortions of phrases and deliberate omissions of vital sentences in reproductions of papers she had printed. It was also apparent that the animosity was personal as well as one of principles: "I am sorry because it must be so unpleasant for them to meet me socially; indeed, with two of the ladies in question, I have had to insist upon normal courtesies at tea parties! It is simply ridiculous for these gentle Indian women to cut me dead now when in the past they have come to tea with me and been friends."

In June 1931 Shephard had received news that the AMSH would fund her for another two years in India, and she promptly resigned from the CVA in July. Following this she used the above letter to further outline how she envisaged her independent career developing. She sought approval to stay in Bengal until the new SITA bill had been carried forward, while continuing to lecture at conferences or group meetings in India when requested, to write press reports, and to continue in her roles with bodies such as the National

Council of Women in India, the National Christian Council of India, and the YWCA. However, if an All India SITA was to be pushed for (which at this point was still being debated) Shephard had been advised by Lady Willingdon, the vicereine, that a move to Delhi might be required (and Shephard added in pen to her typed letter "I want to get the Govt of *India* interested and instructed!") This suggestion was taken seriously by the AMSH in London and was considered during Shephard's yearlong vacation and furlough in the United Kingdom from September 1931. During this time she worked to raise the profile of the campaign in India, addressing in just six weeks after 1 May 1932 the Council of Women Workers in Lewisham, Barnet Church Schools, the National Council of Women in India's London Committee, and the British Commonwealth League Conference, while also attending four other meetings and interviewing eight prominent female social reformers, including Dame Rachel Crowdy.[61] Shephard (1932) also published an article in the *Shield* describing "The India I Have Seen." In addressing the future she mentioned that a League of Nations traveling commission of inquiry into trafficking in women and children had been to India in her absence, but that it was only permitted to discuss the *international* traffic, while India's traffic was *interracial*. Shephard suggested that the only way to be of real help, unlike investigators from New York or Geneva, was to live alongside the people, and to profit from abolitionist experiences in other countries. In October 1932 Shephard returned to India to resume her campaign, in both a spirit and letter seemingly unaffected by her violent rejection by the Congress ladies of Bengal: "We need to let more light into these very dark places, studying the local vice area conditions, promoting wise laws, adequate educational and medical policies, promoting social services, and then to trust that men and women in India will endeavour together to build a world in which it is safe and happy for little children to be born" (Shephard 1932, 74).

### Law Making in Delhi: 1932–1936

In May 1932 Shephard attended a meeting of the AMSH's India subcommittee (including C. F. Andrews, Reverend Paton, Helen Wilson, and Alison Neilons) in London to discuss her future.[62] Andrews stressed that after the Calcutta Bill was passed Shephard should leave the city in the background unless invited. There were other cities such as Nagpur, Bombay, or Madras that needed help, as did many cantonments across north India that were reintroducing the "worst sort of practices." But it would also be important for Shephard to find not just the right place to study, but also the "right centre and the right committee." This would be an institutional location for coordinating a nationwide campaign and would thus need rail links, local people who could offer guidance, and local work that needed to be done. Andrews suggested Delhi, and Reverend Dixon, who had been based in Delhi and had campaigned with his wife Katherine Dixon against military brothels, agreed that Delhi would be perfect for working with the government, and against military inspections of brothels. A consultative committee was agreed for Shephard, the advice from which she had to follow unless it contravened the principles of the AMSH. It included the bishop of Lahore, the metropolitan of India, Dr. Ruth Young, and Lady Bhore.[63] Shephard soon wrote to Neilans that she looked forward to their advice and support, but that she would tolerate no restrictions on her investigations. She returned to India in October 1932 and, after trips to Bombay, Calcutta, and Lahore, established herself at 6 Rajpur Road, in the Civil Lines north of Old Delhi, from where she immediately refamiliarized herself with the practice of investigating and coordinating the AMSH's various geographies in India.

*Techne: Networks*
CASE STUDIES

As chapter 1 has illustrated, Shephard showed just as much enthusiasm for local reform in Delhi as she had done in Calcutta. She soon argued her way onto influential positions on a subcommittee of the Delhi Municipal Committee, the Delhi Women's League, the Central Social Services League, and the Delhi Children's Aid Society. She would continue with this work until the passing of the Delhi Act in 1940, following her help in establishing the rescue home necessary to enable the activation of the SITA. Yet during the early 1930s Shephard would also coordinate activity along AMSH lines throughout India, whether through direct investigations herself or through coordinating the work of others. While Shephard's work was constrained mostly to British India, there was also work done in the princely states. Mabel Pillidge (1934) reported in the *Shield* the activities of the AMSH branch in Mysore State, South India.[64] Like Shephard, Pillidge had trained at Josephine Butler House in Liverpool and proudly announced to the AMSH of the Mysore branch's formation, *"and so we became your first child in India"* (Pillidge 1934, 101). She reported that her task was to challenge traditional inequality between man and woman, seeking to take advantage of India's opening up as a nation and the impact of modern science. She had convened groups to campaign on law, publicity, medical issues, houses, and education, and the Mysore State Association had eventually come to assimilate branches in Bangalore, Mysore, Kolar, and Tumkur. The association participated in the campaign for a Suppression of Traffic in Women and Children Act, which was eventually passed in 1937 (Nair 2008).

Shephard did, however, continue her own investigations, of newer and older sites. Whenever she returned to India she would travel through Bombay and, in October 1934, she consulted with local leaders and found that conditions had continued to improve and that girls were being well housed in a rescue home run by the National Council of Women in India.[65] From Bombay Shephard moved on to Lahore, which she had previously visited in November 1930, January–February 1931, October 1932, and February 1934. In September 1929 Shephard had identified the city as one with the potential to pass abolitionist legislation for the Punjab and had campaigned with the help of Miss Daisy Mackenzie on this issue.[66] During her visit in 1930 she had addressed meetings of Christians, swarajists, and institutional leaders, and helped Mackenzie secure the honorary secretaryship of the Lahore Vigilance Association.[67] In 1933 she was asked by S. P. Singha, registrar of the university and honorary secretary of the Lahore Vigilance Association, to help with the redrafting of a municipal amendment bill so as to remove its segregationist intent.[68] Shephard circulated a memorandum and suggested to Neilans that if her meeting with the local self-government minister did not result in him renouncing his segregationist policies, a question should be asked in the House of Commons about this policy.[69] In 1934 she joined MacKenzie in pushing for a Punjab SITA in Lahore, visiting a further two times in 1935, joining the bill review Select Committee on the second visit before it was passed in November of that year.

Her move to Delhi made central and north India much more accessible, and the United and Central Provinces received much greater attention by the AMSH after 1932. Shephard first visited the United Provinces (UP) in March 1935, two years after it had passed its own SITA. In an indication of her changing social circles (as addressed below), she stayed with Sir Harry and Lady Hague at Government House in Lucknow, and thus had instant access to top officials, with whom she planned an educational and medical scheme.[70] Having toured Allahabad, Cawnpore, and Benares, a UP branch of the AMSH was established, with Lady Hague as patron. Shephard spent most of August and September in the Central Provinces staying, again, at Government House in Nagpur with Sir Hyde Gowan. Here she focused on discussions with educational leaders and workers in the Women's Jail.

Having established local contacts and assessed the situation, Shephard decided in February 1936 to make direct appeals to the central government.[71] She forwarded to them a letter she had sent to the home member to the UP government reporting on conditions encountered during her recent tours. In Etawah she found that the UP SITA was not being enforced, while municipal bylaws were being used to exclude prostitutes from certain areas meaning that, as in Delhi, they were slowly forced into unofficially tolerated zones. This resulted, Shephard argued, in families being forced to live on one side of streets that now faced open brothels. The SITA could be used to forbid such open solicitation and to close down the brothels. In reference to Brindaban, Shephard went way beyond her usual remit. She had visited the Ranji, Shiva, and Gobinji temples, having heard that young widows had "disappeared" in that area. In the Shiva temple she believed she had found 450 widows, while the priest claimed there were 870 widows in another house under the age of sixteen. Her investigations led her to believe they were Bengali girls, some of whom had been sold for Rs 40–1,000. She also reported a rumor, without any caution as to its veracity or origin, that when a tank outside the town was drained eighteen months previously, the remains of four hundred baby skeletons had been found at the bottom. The priest suggested that the daily routine of the girls was dawn to 10:30 a.m. chanting in the Shiva temple; 10:30 a.m.–2:00 p.m. given a handful of food and sent out to beg; 2:00 p.m.–5:30 p.m. chanting in the temple; 5:30 p.m. given three pice and locked out of the temple to find lodgings. Shephard commented that "I make no comments on this arrangement (I don't need to!) . . . I realise that, under the Victoria promise, the Government will be unable to take any action." Shephard had, however, raised the issue at a recent conference with "Mrs Kamla Devi Chattopadhyay," who had promised she would investigate.

In March 1936 Shephard stayed with the Haigs again in Lucknow, where she was informed by the UP government that the Education Department would draw the attention of local magistrates to the relevant clauses of the SITA, and encourage them to enforce those clauses progressively.[72] The influence of interested parties meant, however, that there was no hope of immediate implementation in Benares, Lucknow, Agra, or other big places. Harry Haig offered general support but stressed that without popular backing, governments such as his could not push through the enforcement of the SITA. Through Shephard's traveling and her establishment of communications with organizations of various different hues she was able to claim a wide reach for the AMSH in India. In a printed AMSH pamphlet of 1936 a map was included (figure 3.5) that gave the impression of a near-nationwide network, although the points actually indicated places visited, as well as those in which AMSH work was taking place. A more transparent breakdown had been given in a memorandum of 1934 to the government when the places later represented on the map were differentiated. The first category included those provinces in which groups were working out a constructive policy to tackle prostitution (although the role of the AMSH here was still vague, the listed provinces were Punjab, Bombay, Bengal, Madras, United Provinces, Ceylon [though a separate colony], Travancore, Mysore, Puddakottah, Cochin, Delhi Province, and "Burmah"). The second category included places Shephard had visited to try to encourage rescue and education work (Poona, Benares, Simla, Assam, Bangalore, Calcutta, Bombay, Madras, Kandy, Nuwara Eliya, Colombo, Calle, Bangalore).[73] This flexibility with her interpretation of verifiable AMSH influence would later draw criticisms from various quarters that Shephard was colonizing the work of others and claiming the existence of a fictitious network of AMSH influence.

While local investigations would continue to be a driving passion for Shephard, she increasingly devoted her attention to places that were significant for networks of different sorts. Between July and October 1934 she traveled to Europe, spending time in Geneva where she attended the assembly and interviewed members from the Social Questions Section, to discuss trafficking in women and children (TWC), the International Labour Office, and the Institute of International Education. In Paris she spoke at the International Council of Women, and in London spoke at a preparatory meeting for the Conference on TWC in the East that was being planned.

In March 1936 Shephard wrote to Mr. J. A. Thorne in the Home Department of the government of India, addressing places that she believed were central to the networks that she had discussed in Europe in 1934.[74] She forwarded her "notes on special local conditions which favour Traffic in Women and Children and may be of some use to you." While Shephard didn't order or compartmentalize her eleven locations, they can be seen to fit into four commonly recurring tropes, namely, those relating directly to trafficking, and those concerning economics, morals, and religion. Conditions relating to trafficking included demand by Chinese men (Darjeeling), supplies to vice areas in Calcutta (Bogra in north Bengal), and police corruption (Gurdaspur in the Punjab). Poverty was said to influence the selling of women by indebted Muslim *ryots* (land cultivators, in Decca, Bengal) and the procuration of poor women from the Assamese hills for

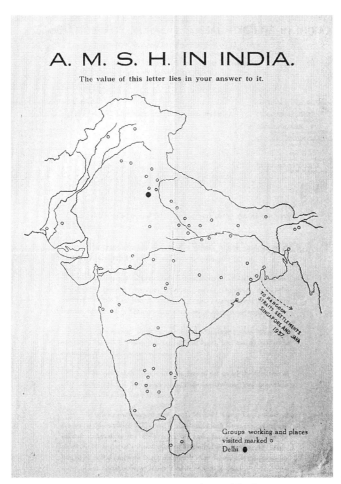

FIGURE 3.5. Frontispiece to an AMSH printed pamphlet from 1936
requesting subscriptions. Courtesy of the Women's Library at the
London School of Economics (file reference: WL/3AMS/C/5/1 folder 1).

men on the tea estates. Low morals were to blame among the zamindari
landowners in Decca, for unnatural vice in Assam ("recently three Hindus
were killed in a sodomy affray"), and for elopement in Ferozepur (Punjab)
due to a low standard of family life and a "rather coarse type of manhood
with whom the women do not want to live." Finally, religion was blamed
for the kidnapping of boys for temple work in Rawalpindi (Punjab), for
red-light tents at *mela* festivals in Bogra, for Sadhus (holy men) supposedly leading off women and boys as disciples for trafficking at Ujjain (Central Provinces), for devadasi temple prostitution in Bilaspur in the Central

Provinces, for suspect low-caste marriages in Yeotmal (Berar), and for immoral and promiscuous dancing in Dondi (Central Provinces). The sources for these accusations were unclear yet they conform to many of the spatial tropes identified in the trafficking discourses covered in chapter 2. The northeast of India was depicted as a trafficking source of supply to Chinese men and Calcutta, while other women were victims of the landed classes (whether zamindari or tea estates men). The Punjab was depicted as part of a structured trafficking network for transporting "willing wives" from areas of female over- to underpopulation, through a corrupt police force and the custom of elopement. Meanwhile, religious prostitution, though noted in melas and temple service in the northeast and the Punjab, characterized the central states, far away from the coastal cosmopolitanism of Karachi, Bombay, Madras, Calcutta, and Rangoon. Here the defining actors and victims were thought to be Sadhus, devadasis, low castes, and dancing boys and girls. Shephard's interest in trafficking, rather than in brothels, was slowly developing, but it increased during the 1930s as her interest in the League of Nations, and its influence over the government of India, grew.

### CONNECTIONS: INSTITUTIONS AND LAWS

As with her time in Calcutta, Shephard can be seen to have engaged in *institutional*, *legal*, and *financial* networking in her first four years in Delhi. As her sources of funding increasingly came from the government of India, this necessarily impacted upon the politics of her work, as will be assessed at the end of this section. *Institutionally*, Shephard's rivalries with both the British Social Hygiene Council and the National Vigilance Association came into bitter fruition (see Legg 2010), but her real object of institutional interest during this period, besides the government of India, was the League of Nations.

The league had experienced varying fortunes in India (Legg 2014). It accepted India as a founding member, thus proffering it some hope of equal standing on the international stage, but was discredited as a white men's club in the late 1920s and early 1930s. Thus Shephard had to temper her personal enthusiasm for the organization with a pragmatic awareness of its utility as an ally. Neilans had encouraged Shephard in June 1930 to promote the league as an agent for change, but also as a forum in which India risked being portrayed as having ruthless trafficking and vice areas frequented by more Indians than Europeans.[75] From this point on Shephard started to reference the league more regularly. In August 1930 she concluded a *Statesman* article by citing league reports that proved tolerated brothels created steady demand for new girls: "How is this demand met? By unspeakable cruelties, by forced obedience, by buying children when mere babies and bringing them up to the life, by false marriages, by jalpani [cheap food]; and by drink and drugs the victim-child is kept quiet."[76] However, after the league's nonintervention during the repression of the Civil Disobedience movement of 1930, its esteem plummeted in India. When outlining her future plans after leaving the CVA in June 1931, Shephard stressed that she no longer spoke of the league in India, where it was viewed as a "magnified Miss Mayo, so far as their Commission of Enquiry is concerned."[77] More than this, it was perceived as a League of European Nations, which Shephard felt to be largely true.

However, the issuing of the league's TWC report on the East was greeted with much curiosity. Although Shephard regretted there was so little about India in it due to its lack of *international* trafficking, she admitted that the chapter on the role of the brothels would be great for propaganda.[78] The AMSH in London was also keenly advertising its links with the league, having printed an article in the *Shield* in 1934 that highlighted its involvement in Geneva since 1920 and the abolitionist resolutions that the league had passed.[79] By this time Shephard had overcome her reservations and was desperately keen to be on the TWC Committee of the Social Questions Section of the league. In December 1933 she learned that the league had requested a representative for India to visit Geneva, but the government decided that the representative had better be Indian. Shephard wanted to be in Geneva so that she could challenge Mr. F. A. R. Sempkins, who had secured representation for the British National Vigilance Association in the Social Questions Section of the league, but also so that she could challenge the government of India's own representations of trafficking and prostitution in India. This was not, however, intended as an attack on the British state in India, as Shephard's warning against the government whitewashing its reports to Geneva at the end of the last chapter suggested.

The government sent Mrs. Kailash Radhabai Subbarayan, a prominent Madras feminist campaigner and Congress supporter, to Geneva in September 1934, while Shephard herself also attended. She wrote to Neilans that Subbarayan had made a good impression but needed specialist advice on technical questions, which Shephard thought she should provide.[80] On her return to India Shephard's faith in the league seemed to have been galvanized. She spoke about it to students in Bombay and Delhi, the latter of which apparently said that she made the league "live" for them.[81] In November she learned that the league had confirmed that a conference would take place in the East to discuss TWC, and in December she could report that she had been recognized as the central authority for league work on TWC in India.[82]

In March 1935 Shephard published an article in the *Statesman* outlining the conference plans. She intended to embark on a preparatory tour of regional conferences to raise publicity for the league, taking in Agra, Lucknow, Benares, Allahabad, Cawnpore, and Jubbulpore. She aimed to collect information on tolerated brothels, trafficking, and obscene publications; the legal position; medical care; education; child protection; and finance.[83] She was limited, however, in the amount of information she could gather due to people's reluctance to answer questionnaires: "Too many Blue Books have been made and people are wary of a second Miss Mayo."[84] By May 1935 Shephard could report that she had provincial conferences organized in Bengal, Madras, and Nagpur, while other organizations like the National Council of Women, the Women's Indian Association, and the All India Women's Congress were also circulating information. While doing this work Shephard continually pushed for more formal recognition from the league because, as she put it in April 1935: "For the League principles are our principles, and I have created already considerable interest for the League of Nations."[85] The extent of Shephard's networking capabilities was delimited, however, by the scalar nature of her commission, and by the tensions that existed between the imperial and international aspirations of Britain and the league.

The government of India had tried to delimit the league's traveling commission of inquiry in TWC in the East when it visited India between November 1931 and January 1932 (Legg 2009b). The government had articulated its objections to what it saw as interference in its internal affairs through the particularly scalar language of international and domestic spheres. As Neilans wrote to Shephard: "The real truth about the Commission's work in India is that they were held up by the terms of reference, namely, that they were to investigate International traffic and not Inter-State and Inter-racial traffic."[86] The league had to accept this delimitation, although its reports were expertly written to undercut the scalar ontologies that they were confined by. On other matters, however, the league's hands were tied more firmly. Eric Ekstrand, head of the Social Questions Section of the league, wrote to Shephard in February 1936 acknowledging her request to be represented at the league, but he regretted to say that "only *international* associations and not national can be represented."[87] This must have been a bitter blow to Shephard, but this scalar logic was one with which she was familiar and had even deployed herself. During 1935

Shephard was still fighting off Sybil Neville-Rolfe's attempts to spread British Social Hygiene Council influence in India, which she felt lacked expertise and experience in that country. While Rolfe had influence at the League of Nations, Shephard stressed that this only gave her the right to challenge international traffic and, as the league had pointed out, India had very little of this, only interracial and interprovincial traffic.[88]

Yet with the government of India, the scalar argument also came to be used against Shephard's aspirations. In order to prevent abuses in ashrams she had suggested that the government give them *all* grants such that they could also be inspected. Thorne replied from the Home Department in August 1934: "I fear the matter is one for local Administrations. There is no provision of law under which the Govnt. of India could frame such a rule: and the Govnt. of India have no power to insist that any local Administration either give grants to Ashrams of this kind or require their inspection."[89] Thus Shephard found herself delimited in terms of her international work and faced with a government unwilling to intervene locally. In response to this scalar positioning of her work, Shephard focused on the nation-state and, through this, managed to have an impact at both the international and local level, but at a dire cost for her racial and political standing in the eyes of Indian nationalists.

In terms of *legal* networks, Shephard's first four years in Delhi saw her accept that, in an age of dyarchy and political sensitivity to the encroachments of the central state, an All India SITA was unlikely. Shephard accepted this after taking advice from Sir Lancelot Graham, the chief of the Legislative Department in the viceroy's central government in May 1933. Following the Simon Commission and in consultation with Indian politicians a new Indian constitution was being drawn up that would replace the system of dyarchy from 1919 with the Government of India Act of 1935. This would see extended local self-government and elections that would enable Congress to take power in vast swathes of the subcontinent. In this context an All India SITA was felt to be in advance of public opinion and would be handled by different personnel in 1935. The home member Sir Harry Haig apologized on behalf of himself and Graham for sounding like "a horridly unsympathetic Conservative," but Shephard admitted to Neilans in May 1933 that "as my own feeling and knowledge of conditions and thought brings me to the same conclusion, I could only say that I felt the present policy, (of proceeding Province by Province), is the right one.[90]

Accepting that the transition from dyarchy to provincial self-government would even further restrict her campaigning, Shephard opted to support the passing of provincial SITAs. This period saw the eventual passing of the Bengal SITA (1933) with which she had been so involved, and those in the United Provinces (1933) and the Punjab (1935). At a London conference organized by Neville-Rolfe's BSHC in July 1934, Shephard continued to emphasize the interconnectedness of her five lines of work, namely, law, education, medicine, recreation, and rescue work: "The *law* is useless unless public opinion marches alongside. Law should be but the crystallisation of the best public opinion; therefore legislation must be slow, and must be used as a peg upon which to hang education."[91] She stressed that there were laws in seven provinces and presidencies, as well as Ceylon and Burma, in line with League of Nations recommendations: "This legal network penalises the keeping of brothels, procuration, living upon immoral earnings (whether as landlords or as souteneurs), and protects women and children." Her attempts to tighten the *legal network* so as to remove gaps through which "traffickers can jump" would remain her policy throughout her remaining time in India, during which her other *philosophies*, *policies*, and *practices* altered accordingly.

### Identity: Naming Moral Hygiene

At Neville-Rolfe's London conference of July 1934 Shephard had a chance not just to differentiate the AMSH's position from that of the BSHC, but also to reflect on her *philosophy* and principles after five years' work on India. In particular, she emphasized the nominalist capacities of education to craft subjects and policies in her image. She had made her stance crystal clear in a letter to Neilans in January 1934. Having described the inactivity of the BSHC's branches in Bengal, Bombay, Madras, and Mysore, she stressed that she wanted to develop India on "MORAL and social hygiene lines, not just social hygiene," which meant the policy of abolition, not just of curing venereal disease. As shown above, Shephard's belief in using the law in an abolitionist, nonregulationist manner was affirmed. But so was her belief in education, medicine, recreation, and rehabilitation. Education had to focus on different cultures in India, not so as to transfer Western culture to the East, but so as to help Indian friends translate Western ideas into the vernacular. Medical training was necessary to help with the treatment of venereal diseases, while recreational monitoring was necessary to censor some films and increase the circulation of educational media. Rehabilitation work had to be indigenous; "we must believe that Eastern cultures can regenerate themselves."[92] While these comments mark an increasing awareness that Shephard's aim had to be to encourage India's own legislation, science, and culture, she still could not restrain herself from commenting that, as she had felt about the CVA rescue homes, she believed that only the Christian faith could offer rehabilitation, but she would not say that her Hindu, Muslim, Parsi, and Buddhist friends had to think that. This attempt to incorporate Indian thinking and initiative into the AMSH project, while remaining fundamentally committed to a racialist hierarchy of capacities, marked Shephard's evolving moral hygienist thought in this period.

She pursued this objective by seeking out affiliations and collaborations, rather than by preaching directly and local campaigning herself. In March 1934 Shephard submitted a memorandum to the government of India explaining her project, her investigations, and her hopes for future work.[93] She stated: "Miss Shephard's plan so far has been to seek individuals, themselves leaders in their own communities, and get them to consider whether their own sphere of influence can be used to promote a challenge against the low standards of conduct between the sexes." She claimed thus to have encouraged subgroups to be formed within organizations such as the National Christian Council, the Women's Indian Association, and the AIWC to study local conditions from the segregated area point of view, and then from the legal, medical, educational, and rescue angles. Such claims would doubtless have infuriated those in Indian women's organizations who had been working on related topics for decades, but so would Sempkins have been astonished to hear Shephard claim that it was due to her that local vigilance associations were joined together to form the All India Vigilance Association.

At the provincial level Shephard suggested her goal had been to secure comradeship over creedal or political differences. Such comradeship was the result of gradual education, not "showy platform speeches," and individual teaching not propaganda. Thus statistics (so favored by organizations like the BSHC) were less useful in the AMSH's line of work. Shephard insisted on the value of long-term workers like herself who she claimed have made "real friendships in Indian homes, and who therefore are trusted, as *friends*, and not merely as social workers of another race." However, she concluded that such work was necessary so that India could throw off some of the vile customs that bound it. This inherent denigration of Indian culture was also hinted at in the slightly different wording she used to describe her project in a letter to Mr. Butler at the India Office in London in July 1934: "Our policy has also been to work through indigenous organisations by penetrating their minds with principles."[94]

However, when this approach was put forward to a more critical audience, it became quickly apparent how specific to the AMSH mind-set it was. At the ninth annual session of the AIWC in Karachi between December 1934 and January 1935, Shephard attended as a member of the Delhi delegation. A resolution was moved by Mrs. N. C. Sen on the abduction of women and the need for rescue homes and SITAS. Indian social workers were summoned to follow the example of the League of Nations and target trafficking. Shephard moved certain amendments but also insisted that there had to be an emphasis on constructive moral education in addition to work on sexual hygiene and medical care. However, the ardent nationalist Kamladevi Chattopadhyay responded with a statement suggesting that economic distress lay at the root of the problem of moral lapses and TWC. She claimed that 80 percent of erring women went that way because they found it hard to make a living: "If you suppose you can solve the problem merely by education, you are jolly well mistaken."[95]

This public rebuke chimed with the divergence in views on the causes of prostitution in contemporary literature. This was, however, a literature with which Shephard was well acquainted and which she used in the mid-1930s to propagate her cause. Rather than target the reading public directly, Shephard had been urging the Education Department to train its teaching staff in matters of social and moral hygiene, as advocated by the AMSH and the recent publications of the League of Nations. Shephard wrote to Neilans in October 1935 that ministers of education in three provinces had asked for a list of satisfactory books to educate their teaching staff with.[96] The list contained thirty-seven publications, which give an insight into the sources of Shephard's thinking as well as the worldview she was hoping to inculcate in India's teaching and nursing staff. This drew upon yet augmented the basic European sexology literature from the turn of the century, which had been influential in government circulations during the tipping point from segregation to suppression in the postwar years (as discussed in chapter 2). The list exposes the wide-ranging literatures that Shephard was consulting and emphasizes the hygiene assemblage that she was constructing, stringing together personal experience, legislative campaigning, governmental projects, and international correspondence.

In terms of topic, the literature covered most of the areas one would expect for a feminist campaigner against trafficking, venereal disease, and unequal moral standards in colonial India. On the traffic in women and children there was Abraham Flexner's (1914) *Prostitution in Europe*, the pivotal text that had been commissioned by the Rockefeller Foundation and, on the basis of Flexner's personal investigations, found segregation to be at the heart of the problem of prostitution. Shephard also included a translation of André Londres's (1928) *The Road to Buenos Ayres*, and H. W. Harris's (1928) *Human Merchandise*. Shephard's feminist philosophy was referenced in works by and about Josephine Butler, as well as reviews of female emancipation (Challoner and Mathews 1928) and women's position under English law (Crofts 1925). Such writings were tailored to "social history and custom" through works on Indian women (Rathbone 1934; Vaughan 1928), though both of the authors were English (the list excluded recent Indian works by, for instance, Mukherji 1934 or Sinha and Basu 1933). Various texts were included on biology and sex, but more were included on psychology and morality. These ranged from those that explicitly aimed to explain psychoanalysis such as Geraldine Coster's (1926) *Psychoanalysis for Normal People* to those that drew more upon the increasingly popular social psychological work of North Americans such as William James and George Herbert Mead. It was the latter work, as it merged with that on moral, mental, and racial hygiene that most obviously influenced Shephard's work.

In terms of content, several traits recur among the readings. Ben Lindsey and Wainwright Evans (1925) spoke of the need to break the taboo surrounding sex and remove ignorance of health and sexual science, while Leslie Weathershead (1931, xviii) spoke of the need to rescue sex from Victorian curse and taboo, which had made it, for his generation, "a murky and furtive secret." The approaches to this task ranged from those that emphasized parallels between human and animal or plant life, and took the biological or social hygienist approach, to those that emphasized ethics and personal relations. Norah March (1936, first issued in 1915) had combined both views in her handbook on "racial health" by providing chapters on "nature studies in the service of sex instruction" next to guidelines on "ethical training." In the latter she insisted that sexual hygiene had to combine an interest in the physical and the psychic, the body and the mind. At the intersection of these two realms lay what was the key question for many of the authors: "From [man's] behaviour in meeting the claims of sex—the egoistic—and of race—the altruistic—emerges social conduct" (March 1936, 168).

For those, like Shephard, who believed that the object of social reform should be changed behavior, not reduced disease, "conduct" was a central concept. The means of conducting conduct was, however, much debated. Shephard recommended two books by Thomas Pym, chaplain to the king and fellow of Balliol College, Oxford. In *Conduct* Pym (1933) attempted to guide his readers through questions of right and wrong in the postwar world of pessimism, depression, and communism. This was done in accordance with the "standards of Christ," which had been applied to "biological urges" in his *The Place of Sex in Life* (Pym 1928). Leslie Weathershead acknowledged that, alongside the Victorian taboo, early Christian thought had also been to blame for associating sex with sin but he also insisted, in *The Mastery of Sex* (1931), that religion was the great molder of behavior and had to take its place alongside psychology. He insisted upon the clear education of children about biology and sex, and worked out a hybrid of religion and psychology in his guidance on marriage, birth control, celibacy, and "mishandled sex lives" (including masturbation, homosexuality, and venereal disease). Others, however, focused on a more solely scientific guide to conduct. Some insisted that freedom of action was the key to authentically right conduct (Lindsey and Evans 1925, 97), while others suggested it was the antisocial nature of unbridled sexual desire that forced each individual to contemplate the integrity or selfishness of his or her conduct through the powers of reasoning and choice that evolution and civilization brought (March 1936, 168). This concern with the "welfare of the race" did not amount to sexual repression, which could lead to "perversion"; rather, sexual energy should be habitually sublimated: "Self-discipline as a well-established habit will lead to moderation—temperance in all things" (March 1936, 172). This restraint in conduct would be brought about through mental hygiene and harnessing the powers of the imagination through the production of literature or poetry. Others took a more scientific approach. James Hadfield's *Psychology and Morals: An Analysis of Character* (1923 [1955]) aimed to advise professionals on how to practically direct individuals in regard to questions of "life and conduct." Drawing on psychological theory developed from studies of shellshock victims after the First World War, Hadfield examined the relationship between physical and moral causes and symptoms. This necessarily brought the descriptive science of psychology into dialogue with the ethical and normative science of moral conduct; but this was a distinction Hadfield dismissed: "If psychotherapy aims at curing abnormal individuals, it has already set up a standard or norm. For what is an abnormal individual? Before we can speak of the abnormal we must already have a conception of the normal" (Hadfield 1923 [1955], 4–5).

He went on to relate biological instincts to environmental influence through the complexes, sentiments, and subsequent conducts that they created. Misfunctions were located at four levels between the biological and the willed, with illustrative examples given from the domain of sex (Hadfield 1923 [1955], 50–61):

a. Organic diseases with physical causes (e.g., venereal disease leading to insanity)
b. Nervous disorders with physical symptoms (e.g., early sexual trauma leading to physical inability to have sex)
c. Moral diseases from repressed complexes (e.g., early sexual trauma leading to sexual perversion)
d. "Sins": deliberate choices to accept low ideals (e.g., sexual excess)

Hadfield did not make recommendations for regulation in such matters, but did suggest that those who could infect the conduct of others should be restrained from affecting others. But it was exactly this sort of stigmatization that others railed against. March (1936, 237) drew on research by the AMSH's Dr. Helen Wilson into 669 cases of prostitution in London which had concluded that, rather than being driven by a sex inclination, the majority of prostitutes found themselves in the trade due to bad housing, desertion, low wages, compulsion, or grief. Weathershead (1931, 187) similarly pointed out the role of sexual assault, "worthless men," and "evil women" in dragging women into prostitution, and the gendered double standard that kept them there.

Shephard's one concession to Indian opinion on the list, however, challenged many of the assumptions of the European authors listed above, even while confirming many of their central contentions. Shephard had listed a collection of Gandhi's (1927b) essays entitled *Self-Restraint versus Self-Indulgence* which contained his thoughts on morality, sexuality, and purity. He spoke of his increasing correspondence on private conduct and of being inspired by contemporary sexological literature. From a selective reading of this material he found evidence for his spiritual belief that sex was never justified except for the reproduction of the race. Moral indiscipline drained the race and was inspired by theater, cinema, and the press, which was delivered minute by minute through cable, steamers, and their cargo: "The voluptuousness of the West comes to us with lightning speed and with all its variegated enchantment dazzles and blinds us to the realities of life" (Gandhi 1927b, 37). Gandhi's solution was monogamy, as a step on the path to Brahmacharya (complete control of one's senses), not the modern liberal's defense of freedom (see Prakash 1999, 154, on Brahmacharya's religious heritage and modern, scientific revival). While he valued the sober voices of the West, he also wrote: "Let us beware of the strong wine of libertinism that the intoxicated West sends us under the guise of the new truth and so-called human freedom" (Gandhi 1927b, 50, foreshadowing

Foucault's problematization of the sexual revolution). Thus, while the parallels between Indian social reformers and Victorian sexual morality are stark (Whitehead 1995), on the topic of sexuality in general, and prostitution in particular, Gandhi and European liberals were poles apart. During the 1930s Shephard would edge closer to the government and, with this shift, closer to those who emphasized the regulatory power of the state. This was not the regulatory power to register prostitutes, but the legal power to punish their abusers. While this would slowly eat into Shephard's emphasis on education and conduct, the influence of the authors listed above in bolstering her belief in conducting the conduct of the general population, rather than of solely targeting prostitutes themselves, was clear.

In terms of shifts in *policy*, Shephard did invest more time in education and propaganda and attempted to work behind the scenes on legislation. In December 1932 she returned to Calcutta but did not want to "butt in" on the Suppression of Immoral Traffic Bill that was still being debated, although she met the member who had proposed the SITA and attempted to talk around a member who had made an anti-abolitionist amendment in private.[97] Shephard wrote to Neilans when the bill was passed "without a division, and the Home Member, in supporting it, said that the Government 'regarded such Bills with benevolence,' which is a useful sentence when we are struggling with others in the Punjab, UP, NWFP and Delhi Provinces."[98] Neilans was delighted, and wrote offering congratulations on having achieved the act so quickly, suggesting that Shephard may have been taking considerably more credit for the SITA than was due. Neilans also wrote to Reverend Anderson to acknowledge his contribution, but made it clear that the AMSH would not be publicizing the SITA as she believed that the All Bengal Women's Union did not want anyone else's name connected to it.[99] She did, however, illustrate how Shephard's policies were self-consciously situated between the scales of the world, the national, vice areas, tolerated houses, and the personal: "It is, of course, true that world opinion has come much more rapidly towards Abolition in the last five years, and many intensely Nationalist countries feel that it has a bearing on their national prestige, as indeed it has; but the fact that the world is now more favourably disposed to the abolition of vice areas and tolerated houses does not in the least detract from the personal credit which is due to you for your very strenuous work and for the helpful ways in which you have assisted at the final stages of the Bill."[100]

In practice, Shephard continued to travel widely, and by 1936 was in correspondence with fifteen rescue homes throughout the country. But she had also continued her work in relation to the *military*. Having read a report by Shephard on the armed forces in India, the Military Department of the India Office in London sent a statement to the AMSH in July 1932 stressing that any state advertisement or recommendation of brothels, or the medical inspection of prostitutes, was contrary to government orders.[101] This was confirmed in an interview with the Indian commander in chief in March 1934, when he promised to make investigations on Shephard's recommendations without using her name and said how useful it was to have her as a stream of information regarding the activities of his troops.[102] Despite this, Shephard received reports throughout 1933 of brothels being used by the military in Lahore and Madras, with prostitutes in the latter being paid to follow the troops when they moved to Bangalore. She understood the problem to be as follows:[103]

1. Men are fed and trained to the highest pitch of physical efficiency.
2. Few are allowed to marry.
3. Education and moral work undermined by telling men to take prophylactic packets.
4. Officers fear men going to villages for trouble unless provided alternative arrangements.
5. Low-wage rate and economic depression of Anglo-Indian community.
6. Imitation by the Anglo-Indian community of the dancing girls caste which makes it difficult to prove if a place is a brothel.

Shephard would continue to work against this problem, which she understood as biological, social, political, and economic, with dogged determination over the next three years. In June 1936 she could report that a brothel in Jubbulpore was closed within four days of her reporting it to the military secretary to the commander in chief, as had been a brothel in Agra which remained closed. This growing proximity between the AMSH and the military was evidence that, as has been shown in Delhi, the armed forces were finally becoming convinced that regulation did not reduce venereal disease rates and that the SITAS were the best solution to the problem of prostitution. But this proximity was also evidence of Shephard's growing closeness to the state.

### Ethos: Politics and Race
#### RACIALISM

"I hope the Committee was not offended by any of my comments about 'Indians'! Some will think me very British and anti-Indian. I am neither.

I am facing the ugly facts, and trying to help some of these people, (whom I like in spite of their naughty ways!) to correct their own characteristics and backbonelessness."[104] This quotation comes from a letter Shephard sent to Neilans in November 1933. It shows that she was obviously aware of the controversial nature of many of her comments, but also reveals her continued infantilization ("naughty") and emasculation ("backboneless") of the Indian people. This tendency had always been latent in her thought, and became manifest in many of her writings while at Calcutta. Her understanding of prostitution had formerly balanced assumptions about Indian culture and tradition with an understanding of the influence of the colonial state and economy. However, in April 1934 this balance was upset in a memorandum to the government in which she sought financial support for the AMSH in India. That the colonial state and economy should be portrayed more favorably in such a report should not be a surprise, but the shift in emphasis was one that would be sustained throughout Shephard's remaining time in India.

Shephard outlined her considered opinion of prostitution based on her local investigations and interviews with the women themselves. While her reports from 1929 had identified Europeans and poor female wages as the main problem, the report from 1934 identified the cause, for Hindus, as the "fundamentally patri-lineal and false idea, with its consequent subjection of womanhood to the whims of man, and the worship of man by woman" as well as the fatalistic outlook of Hinduism which supposedly regarded human actions as dependent upon a previous life.[105] A third cause was admitted to be economic, but Shephard explicitly stated that this cause was less prevalent than expected. Prostitutes, instead of being drawn from the migratory and exploited working classes, were thought to be early widows and deserted wives, and to come from castes devoted to prostitution. In an astonishing comment Shephard questioned the effects of women coming out of purdah to picket on the streets as part of the Civil Disobedience campaign, warning against the vulnerability of these women to brothels. Confirming her earlier emphasis on education, she said teaching in the family led to male worship, thus the close cooperation of Indian friends in education was made clear.

Despite both this subtle shift toward blaming Indian culture for prostitution, not the material conditions of the colonial state or the gendered and sexual biases in its legislative framework, and her racialist outbursts, Shephard did seek out collaborations with Indian nationalists. She followed up her earlier meetings with Sarojini Naidu, requesting a statement showing that the reasons behind Gandhi's fast (against untouchability) in 1933 were the same as those of which Josephine Butler spoke, that is, the unity of moral law and the quality of all human souls before God.[106] With the suspension of Civil Disobedience, Gandhi had turned toward social uplift work which Shephard felt would allow a greater number of people to support her work without the fear of being branded pro-government.[107] Though still in prison, Gandhi had responded on 4 March 1933 to a five-page letter from Shephard of 27 February.[108]

Following the collapse of the second Civil Disobedience movement of 1932–33 Gandhi had turned to community cohesion and social uplift work. Shephard pleaded that an appeal for prostitutes, whom she likened to the untouchable class, be part of this campaign. Men were said to waste money and energy on prostitutes, which put their families at risk, as modern science had proven beyond doubt. This also made "India" suffer internally, but also in the eyes of the world. Shephard insisted that the solution lay in self-conduct: that a true man was self-controlled; that "self-control *is* self-government"; and that the low expectations of male conduct must be challenged. No doubt drawing on her own experiences, Shephard insisted: "Nothing can be of more moment than to heal racial bitterness," yet concluded with a typically imperial metaphor: "India needs light in her darkest places. Will your lamp of life help the Truth to shine in those dark places?"

Addressing her as "My dear sister," Gandhi replied that he was glad she was back in India, but that her appeal for him to join her in her quest was superfluous. Gandhi wrote of finding himself in the house of a prostitute at the age of fifteen but of being deprived of the "animal instinct," to his shame then but to his great pleasure ever since (see Gandhi 1927a [2007], 37, on this incident and a further four others, from which he was also saved). He had worked to eradicate this evil of man misbehaving toward women ever since, although his work was limited in prison, and he felt unable to address the topic directly in his journal *Harijan*. He continued: "You have no need to apologize for being a foreigner doing this service. When people realize that you have no other motive, but the simple motive of serving these fallen sisters of India and through their service also serving the fallen men of India, they will forget that you are a foreigner. Those who have other ends to serve under the guise of humanitarian service will always be treated as foreigners, whether they wear the white skin or the brown skin."[109]

These words of encouragement marked a brief high in relations with Indian nationalists and social reformers. In January 1936 Shephard attended the meeting of the International Council of Women in Calcutta, where two resolutions were passed. In July of that year she could confidently report to the government of India that she was in contact with leading Indian female campaigners, including Rajkumari Amrit Kaur, Aruna Asaf Ali, and the All Bengal Women's Union, which she claimed was now asking her for help, after Shephard had suffered at their hands in Calcutta in 1930.[110] Yet despite this support, Shephard admitted in April 1936 that "the political situation is such that it is practically impossible now for any Nationalist group of men or women to say that they want a society with roots in England to stay here."[111] Amidst this growing sense of a threat from nationalist sentiment, Shephard would draw closer and closer to the state over the following years. This did not, however, mean that her policies lost their critical edge, as she made clear in March 1935: "Personally and privately, I feel that Government does not WANT this work to go on as I am trying so hard to do it, for more than couple of years, because it is having permanent results in opposition to municipal and military and often official policies. The women's movements are up against many things, including some of their own husbands who serve on these municipal and military boards; it is therefore not a bit easy to carry on, IF the Government's money means a limitation of the scope of my work."[112]

### Problematization: Funding

The money she was referring to was the prospect of the government of India stepping in to make up the shortfall of funds that the AMSH had left Shephard with. The association had initially hoped that provincial charities and associations would be able to support her costs. Seventeen voluntary associations and clerics were approached regarding the value of Shephard's work and whether they would be willing to contribute. Almost all welcomed her return to India in 1932 but most, especially those in Bengal, stressed that there were Indian bodies now doing this work. Twelve offered no funds, and those that did offered only minimal support.[113] Due to this lack of funds both from London and from provincial India, Shephard was forced to approach the government for support in 1934. The Home Department consulted Lieutenant Colonel Russel, the public health commissioner, in April 1934, who suggested that the AMSH had laid foundations in so many places it would be unfortunate if they were not built upon.[114] After a meeting with Shephard and members of her committee the government agreed to send a letter from the viceroy to all provincial governments circulating Shephard's memorandum (as discussed above) and suggesting amounts they contribute to her, totaling Rs 6,300. While Madras, the Central Provinces, the Northwest Frontier Province, and Delhi agreed, the other replies were disappointing and only Rs 4,000 was raised.

However, Shephard had worked hard over the previous five years to penetrate the upper crust of Indian society, and this stood her in good stead. In 1933 she stayed with Viceroy Irwin in Simla, and he continued to offer her personal support. She also kept up her close relationship with the Haigs, had Vicerine Willingdon declared patron in 1936, and cultivated close relationships with figures like Thorne in the Home Department. In January 1936 she could claim to Neilans that the government had been "using me quite a lot" but would still not give her the recognition that would make her an assessor for Geneva. She approached Thorne personally in April 1936, and he requested figures on Shephard's finances, which the AMSH in London sent on in May. The details he received for 1935 showed how desperately Shephard had been pulling together her funding. The majority was from provincial governments, responding to the viceroy's letter of 1934, although donations also came from twenty-four other sources, including vigilance associations, individuals, and charities.[115] When circulating these figures around the Home Department for comment in July 1936, Thorne attached a lengthy note making clear Shephard's claim for financial assistance. He stressed that Shephard was spoken well of by the viceroy, Mr. R. A. Butler the undersecretary of state for India and Sir Abdul Qadir, who represented India at the League of Nations that year. He also made clear that he had most contact with Shephard and that it would be a great pity if her work ceased: "It is true that the provincial Governments are mainly concerned with coping with the actual facts: but our position *vis-à-vis* the League of Nations . . . renders it important that we should have someone at the Centre who is in touch with what is being done. Moreover, it is a fact that Miss Shephard's initiative is responsible for a lot of what has been done in the provinces. The foundations have by no means been consolidated yet: and I submit that there is a good case for Government assistance for a limited period."[116]

Shephard was thus explicitly pitched as a figure who would be both non-provincial and non-international, but who would work to consolidate local foundations and report to the League in Geneva and advise on their initiatives. It was this capacity to network the local and the international into the apparatus of the government of India that won Shephard central funding of Rs 5,000 for three years from 1 January 1937. In July 1936 Shephard met her Delhi-based AMSH Committee to discuss the offer made by the government. The funding was dependent on the AMSH becoming a registered association and having its accounts audited by the central government. She claimed to Neilans: "We will state our principles when we register so they shall not be thrown overboard. This grant is not enough, but is the first of its kind in Indian history."[117] While this deal seemed innocuous enough, it effectively allowed the government to outsource many of its league-enforced responsibilities to the AMSH, while also semi-internalizing an organization that had often deeply embarrassed the colonial state in the past. While this harmonious coupling was very much not the case in reality, for those wishing to attack Shephard during the politically charged atmosphere of the late 1930s, that was exactly how it was portrayed.

### An Adjunct of Government? 1936–1939

Shephard's acceptance of governmental funding coincided with a number of other seismic shifts in the broader political landscape. The Government of India Act of 1935 had removed many of dyarchy's central reservations and replaced them with provincial self-government. The entailing elections in 1937 for these autonomous provincial governments would see the Indian National Congress swept to power in 44 percent of the 1,585 available seats by the newly enfranchised electorate, which numbered 30 million (14 percent of the population), making it the largest party in seven out of the eleven provinces (Schwartzberg 1978 [1992], 222). The need for Shephard to successfully cooperate with Indian social reformers was thus greater than ever, but India's new local and national governors were understandably wary of an at times unabashed imperial feminist. In terms of trafficking and brothels, the government would come under increased pressure by the League of Nations to show that it was taking measures to enforce its commitments, even though it had refused to sign the league's convention of 1933 which had abolished the age limit on prosecuting procuration from another country. Negotiating these obstacles and opportunities as someone in the pay of the imperial government would be Shephard's greatest challenge in this period. Before the war limited what she could hope to achieve and forced the resignation of Congress elected officials, Shephard would be faced with a dramatic challenge to her authority that altered her ambition and scope for her remaining time in India.

*Techne: Networks*
CASE STUDIES

While Shephard would continue to be faced with distractions from her abolitionist crusade, even with the benefit of government funding, she maintained her interest in specific campaigns and investigations. In December 1936 she visited Karachi and claimed to Neilans that she had convinced the municipality to reverse its policy of keeping a medically inspected, segregated quarter for brothels.[118] As the case of Delhi showed, well into the 1930s there were municipalities that resisted the tide of national legislation and clung to regulationist policies. In Karachi Shephard blamed the failure of the governor of Sind to adopt abolitionist legislation on the action of the chief secretary, a Hindu, who associated abolition with his Muslim and Parsi opponents. However, the newly elected Congress Ministries, in line with Gandhi's sexual prohibitions, proved to be "prohibitionist" and denied requests from English officials for a segregated brothel area in Karachi.[119] Yet Shephard was faced with regulationism within her network of AMSH branches, when she heard that the Etawah branch was backing segregation and medical inspection. She informed them that they could not be a member of the AMSH while backing segregation and placed Etawah on her tour itinerary for summer 1937, which also included Bihar, Orissa, Benares, Lucknow, and Agra. Shephard forwarded notes on AMSH and League of Nations policy to the Indian National Congress and Gandhi but received no reply, admitting that she found it difficult to see what the future held for her after the elections.

Being close to her base of Delhi, Shephard often visited the Punjab and became closely involved with the workings of the AMSH base in Lahore. She reported on the establishment of a Rescue Home to enable the working of the Punjab SITA, on the formation of ladies' committees to meet with university students, as well as general efforts to provide suitable accommodation and recreation for students.[120] Shephard was critical of the SITA which, in its passage through the legislature, had had the clause penalizing brothel keepers removed, nullifying much of its power. The local AMSH campaigned to have the restrictions removed, as well as for local provision of free treatment for venereal diseases. Closer to home was, of course, Delhi. This was the area on which Shephard lavished her most intense efforts, which greatly helped the passing of the Delhi SITA and the establishment of a rescue home, as recounted in the first chapter.

The temporary provision of prostitutes elsewhere in India was also investigated, and Shephard sent on to Neilans details of 242 prostitutes who were provided at an annual mela camp in Sonepur, Bihar, in January 1938.[121] The women were divided into three classes relating to their fee, with a letter "D" next to their name denoting a history of venereal disease. The list included the prostitute's name, home address, age, religion, number of attendants, rent for her tent, and usual fee per visitor. There were 19 "A" class women listed, ranging from thirteen-year-old Kaniz from Muzaffarpur to thirty-two-year-old Krishnaker from the same location. The average age was eighteen and the average charge was Rs 4. The list contained 91 "B" class prostitutes, who displayed a similar age range but whose average age was twenty-six and whose fee was between 1 and 2 rupees, 28 of whom were marked with a "D." The number of class "C" women totaled 132 but had an average age of thirty-three, ranging from Rambatia and Manrajia and Roserah aged forty-five, with a fee of 4 annas, to twenty-year-old Buchi from Patna who charged the same fee of 2 rupees. Sixty-three of these women had a history of venereal disease. While the veracity of the list must be called into question due to the ages usually being rounded to the nearest five, it does hint at a system of organization that Shephard insisted the government must have been aware of it.

CONNECTIONS: THE LEAGUE OF NATIONS
AND MILITARY NETWORKS

As the above evidence attests, Shephard kept in touch with the regulation of prostitution, or its abolition, in local cases through extensive networks of correspondence. As the Punjab AMSH put it in its 1937–39 report: "Constant correspondence is part of the work undertaken by [the] Association [for] Moral Social Hygiene, in India, from the headquarters in New Delhi, and this aspect of the work, often involving research and legal opinion, is difficult to summarise."[122] Shephard's networks continued to reach well beyond the Punjab, and India, as she maintained her interest in the *League of Nations*. Following on from the recommendations of the TWC commission's report in 1932, a league conference was held in Java in February 1937 to discuss the specific challenges of trafficking in the East. Shephard attended, with the support of the government, but only to represent the AMSH. The government had made it clear that it desired an Indian representative, so Mrs. S. C. Mukherji acted as the official delegate. Shephard's participation was curtailed by a bout of appendicitis on the fifth day. In this time she had, however, been able to address the conference and censor a statement by Neville-Rolfe which Shephard felt had overplayed the contribution of the BSHC to abolitionist legislation in India.[123]

Just as Shephard has used the league report of 1932 into TWC in the East to propagate the work of the AMSH in India, so it was with the Java report. It recommended an information-coordinating bureau in the East that would also recommend measures to governments to reduce trafficking, and it declared abolition as the shared final goal of the participants, to be achieved through cooperation with voluntary organizations and women officials. Shephard wrote to Mr. R. F. Mudie in the Home Department in September 1937, inspired by discussions at Java to reengage the scale question while challenging trafficking networks. The government has passed to Shephard a press communiqué it planned to issue stating that, as international trafficking was still not a major problem for India, the Java conference was not of much interest. Shephard insisted Mudie cut a sentence that suggested that the abolition of tolerated houses was not immediately practicable in India, and stated: "It was made clear to us all in Java that the internal as well as the external questions were part of our work, especially for those countries signatory to the 1921 Convention."[124] The government did not respond, however, to this provocation, and Shephard's supporter Thorne even wrote to rebuke her for suggesting that league conventions committed governments to the abolition of tolerated brothels, which was in the spirit but not the letter of the league.[125]

Despite Shephard's concerted action over her seven years in India, and repeated statements from the commander in chief on the subject, the *military* inspection of brothels continued. In September 1937 Shephard wrote to Neilans passing on information about a brothel that had opened, and closed, recently in Quetta.[126] She had received a report from the senior chaplain in Quetta reporting that the district commander had built the brothel, ordering the construction of a house with seven rooms specifically for this purpose in the compound of the ruined house of the army commander, which had been abandoned after the earthquake of 1935. It was apparently heavily used by British units and although the district commander was furious at the interference, he ordered it to be shut when the chaplain presented him with the facts. An unauthorized brothel soon sprang up outside the cantonment, but by private enterprise, not military decree.

In 1935 Shephard had produced a "Rough Record" of AMSH dealings with the British Army in India since 1858. However, by January 1938 she felt that she had received so much information about brothels being used by British troops that she produced an updated version.[127] Location, description, and action taken were provided for the following:

- LAHORE (December 1935): house opened under authority of the military; letter sent to the military secretary to the commander in chief
- JUBBULPORE (July 1936): brothel outside cantonment for troops, who were instructed to use it by their officer; after complaint the order was retracted, but the brothel continued to exist on a private

basis and the four Punjabi prostitutes were reported to have permits allowing them into the military area

- MULTAN (July–October 1937): eight women resident in the jungle outside the cantonment in a house run by the station; unsuccessful attempts to close
- AMBALA (June 1936–July 1937): a house maintained by the station outside the cantonment; Shephard spoke to military officials and requested another public statement outlining the official military line on brothels

A statement was issued by the army in India confirming what it had told the AMSH in 1932, namely, that advertisement, inspection, or recommendation of any brothel was contrary to government policy. In addition to passing on information collected by others regarding regulation, Shephard also completed her own investigations. This has been an ongoing passion since her investigations of Calcutta in 1929; she later recalled her happy stay with Sally Niccoll-Jones of the Rangoon police en route to the Java conference in 1937 "going with her to the vice areas, where we raided brothels together" (Shephard 1948, 41). In February 1938 she was invited by the Punjab branch of the AMSH to give a lecture in Lahore, but was informed by a member of the audience at the YMCA that everyone knew of a brothel used by British troops that was medically inspected. At 10:00 p.m. that evening she convinced a Dr. Cairns to accompany her to the house. The house was located in the scrub, but was accessible by tonga and was brilliantly lit by lights on the veranda. The house contained many men in uniform. Provost Sergeant Johns, within whose beat the brothel lay, soon approached on his bicycle. He did not deny medical inspection of the house and insisted what a "rotten job for a married man like himself" he had.[128] Shephard made inquiries at brigade headquarters the next day, to the military's obvious discomfort and annoyance. She returned to the house that afternoon with her friend Mrs. Ingles, who raised the curtain on one room to reveal four soldiers in the company of six girls. The men insisted that the brothel had been declared "in bounds" by a notice in the orderly room in Napier Barracks, although this was denied again at headquarters. Shephard passed her report on to the bishop of Lahore, but took no further action herself.

Yet it seems that, just as she was campaigning and sending confidential reports to Neilans about military brothels, Shephard had a crisis of faith regarding this longest-standing campaign of the AMSH and the Ladies National Association before it. She wrote on 14 February 1938 that her campaigning could lead to a crisis by both turning the army against the AMSH in India, after much collaboration on the SITAS, and also by forcing Shephard to see the logic of its arguments. Shephard increasingly agreed that military men were safer in guarded houses than in the bazaars where they could be "murdered or robbed," while women would wander into cantonments or pester men on the street without a brothel anyway. Abolition also risked British men having affairs with Anglo-Indians, marrying them, and then resigning from the army in order to stay in India permanently without being forced to take home leave. Shephard soon fell back on environmental discourses of tropicalism as well as traditionalist explanations of prostitution:

> I am quite clear in my own mind that our PRINCIPLES are right; but I also see quite clearly that the conditions of this country are different from those in any other country in the world. The caste rule precludes these women from living any other life, and they are better off in a guarded house than in a rough and tumble life in the bazaars. I am NOT going over to the enemy, as you may think. I am only trying to be fair, and to realise that 5% or 7% of the men who [sic] will lead this life anyhow. Whatever is done to interest them in other things, [they] are the very men who . . . cannot be trusted to look after themselves in open bazaars; and in any case, Indian life is more difficult than in any other country, with the heat and pests and fevers. . . . Do not think that I am a failure, will you? I am simply trying to be wise, and to take the action which seems to lead to the most practical results. It is obvious that my representations to Colonel Ranking have resulted in nothing satisfactory.[129]

Shephard professed to not having the money or energy to carry on investigations such as those conducted in Lahore and felt the work would best be left to the chaplains and bishops. After this point Shephard sent back no notice of further work on military brothels. This may have been, in part, due to the onset of war in 1939. All abolitionist measures had ceased during the First World War, and the AMSH may simply have accepted this again, although Miss Fernley Powell did report some success on this front in Calcutta, having been recruited by the AMSH for the then bishop in February 1944.[130]

### Identity: Naming Moral Hygiene

In May 1938 the AMSH in London issued a pamphlet with the *Shield* that described the association's mission.[131] It gave five summary examples of its work:

1. The AMSH engaged in research, criticism, advisory work, and propaganda for a high and equal standard of moral responsibility.
2. It is not repressive against the individual but works to crush the third party exploiter of vice (i.e., the brothel keeper, souteneur, and procurer).
3. The AMSH had worked most consistently toward abolition in India and the Crown Colonies.
4. The association had worked to reduce venereal disease rates in HM Army.
5. It had campaigned for free and confidential treatment for the civilian population.

Shephard herself continued to publicize her principles and philosophy in India, although there was a noticeable shift in the tenor of her publications after she accepted her stipend from the government. She submitted a statement for the Eighth Imperial Social Hygiene Congress, held in London during July 1937, entitled "Co-operation of the Voluntary Social Services with the Health and Educational Services." Shephard claimed straight away that the object of the AMSH was the overthrow of all forms of official regulation and commercial exploitation of vice. But she followed this by stressing that the General Committee in India was fully representative of both the voluntary and official agencies dealing with such questions in the country; members included the marchioness of Linlithgow (the vicerine) as patron, the chief commissioner of Delhi as president, and members of the advisory committee from the Indian Civil and Medical Service and the Inspectorate of Prisons, as well as Hindu, Muslim, and Christian leaders of women's Indian groups. As has been stressed in the first chapter, this work blurred the boundaries between civil society and the state, while constitutively reshaping both in the process. Cooperation with the Home Department and Military Commands was stressed to be vital, and the annual grant from the central government, as well as donations from provincial governments, was said to avoid overlapping work. This work concerned five main areas: investigation and research, legislative work, education, public health and medical propaganda, and rehabilitation of women and children. Running through these tasks was a clear nominalistic sense of the identities of the people who were being targeted, and the best way of altering their behavior: "The Association, realising that public *opinion* can be aroused emotionally, and yet have little effective action as a result, has always sought to appeal to the public and private *conscience*; to stimulate real thought, by producing accurate information as to actual conditions; and to build upon those high principles of justice, liberty with responsibility, and equality as between men and women, which are common to the best religious and national thought of all civilized races."[132]

She concluded the pamphlet with an explicit argument that replaced the state as the enemy of the AMSH with fascist ideologies sweeping Europe in the late 1930s, while reaffirming a commitment to targeting individual conduct: "It is not without significance that the Association should stand steadily for reverence for the individual personality, whether men or women, and for equal justice for both. In days when certain nations are tending to eliminate individual choice of action, and to train masses of men to be herds, dominated by propagandist ideas, the workers of the Association for Moral and Social Hygiene, in India as elsewhere, are helping to give guidance to individuality expressed in creative action." In her pamphlets for an Indian audience Shephard was less explicit in outlining her tactics and focused more on conduct. In one document from this period entitled *The Challenge against the Traffic in Women and Children*, she claimed, "Moral and social hygiene is concerned with questions arising from the possession of the creative instinct, and its right use, whether in the spiritual, mental, or physical spheres. The ultimate goal of moral and social hygiene is the preservation of a wholesome personal and family life."[133] Here Shephard made clear that the nature of the project transgressed the boundary between state and civil society (official and voluntary organizations) across the five types of work she identified the AMSH with in India. The responsibility for each was identified with the following:

1. Investigation and research: official and voluntary agencies
2. Legislation: magistrates, the police, and Legislative Department; voluntary protective agencies
3. Education: family, college, school, "religious sects," and groups such as the scouts, guides, and religious community organizations
4. Medical measures: Health Department, hospitals, and voluntary welfare organizations
5. Rescue work: Municipal Committees, but mostly social agencies and women's organizations

In the same publication Shephard reminded readers that the "official" sector in India went beyond the "state." Reprinting an article she had published in the *Statesman* newspaper on 25 March 1935 she chastised the public for judging the League of Nations as an institution that was failing to make the world a happier place to live in. This was said to overlook the unostentatious but invaluable work done regarding conditions of labor, trafficking in drugs and, not least, women and children. Shephard remained loyal to the league due to its abolitionist stance in the report of 1932 and the conference in 1937 on traffic in women and children in the East. But this may also have been due to the league's vital role in keeping her funded by the government. In August 1939 the government reviewed whether it would renew the AMSH's annual grant of Rs 5,000 which was promised for three years from the beginning of 1937. The association was shown to have abided by the set terms (to level its finances, be registered with the government, and provide annual reports) and, more importantly, Shephard's reports showed that she was helping the government to meet its obligations under league conventions. The Home Department concluded: "The Govt. of India have already recognised that Miss Shephard's work is of real value and deserves some financial support from Central Government."[134]

However, just as the AMSH had done when renewing Shephard's contract, the central government inquired in the provinces as to her value and their willingness to offer support. The Home Department was informed that the AMSH had done no work in Madras, Bombay, the Central Provinces, Assam, and Sind, although Orissa and Bihar had benefited from Shephard's work and offered joint grants of Rs 1,500. These results were found to be discouraging, and Mr. Lillie in the Home Department questioned how Shephard's work quite related to the league's mandate. This was understood to relate to TWC, which Shephard was not thought to be directly associated with. With the provinces being nominally self-governing the only work the central government could fund was that in centrally administered territories such as Delhi. Luckily the chief commissioner gave evidence of Shephard's work, but because her linking of abolition of brothels to cutting off the demand for trafficked women was not widely accepted in central government (Legg 2009b) many questioned her claim on funding. The doubters were defeated, however, by a spirited argument that the reason so many provinces no longer needed her was because they were operating practices she had helped put in place, and her funding was assured. This positive appraisal of her work was not, however, mirrored in the outside world.

*Ethos: Race and Politics*

As has been made clear above, Shephard drew the AMSH in India closer to the state through financial dependence and increasingly cooperative policies. The vicereine and chief commissioner of Delhi were confirmed as patron and president respectively in March 1937 and this circle of friends and colleagues must have been beguiling given the political excitement that followed the elections of 1937. As Shephard wrote to Neilans in December: "My problem is to get the subject of justice in relationships between men and women across to thousands of people who are all interested in something else: political independence."[135] This frustration did occasionally boil over into statements as offensive as those when she first arrived in Calcutta. Shephard sent to the AMSH in London her report of the AIWC meeting in Nagpur in December 1937, of which she wrote: "I came away with the impression that the Conference had shown how clamorous Indian women can be when they are swayed by political emotion, and of how little comparatively has been *done* in the 12 years of the life of the Conference, apart from self-education."[136] Such comments would prove to be an incendiary combination with her reception in 1937 of three medals from the government, in honor of her social work. As Shephard wrote to Neilans in August 1937: "They have given me a Coronation Medal as well as the Jubilee, and the KiH [Kaisar-i-Hind] so now I have all three: all in a few months; almost embarrassing."[137] Reflecting later on the consequences of the awards, however, she confessed to Neilans: "I am afraid the Kaiser-i-Hind will condemn me in Congress eyes as they automatically view with disfavour anyone who accepts honours from the British gov.'"[138]

These were obviously fears shared by Neilans in London. She had commented on the high circles that Shephard was moving in during her legal work in 1933, but conceded: "Had the work been, as it was 15–20 years ago, in direct opposition to the government's policy it might have been unwise to have relied so much on the results of contacts with influential people."[139] The policy was now that of keeping the "generally sound government policy" on the right lines. However, with the provinces increasingly run by Indian officials, Neilans became much more concerned for Shephard's prospects, just as Shephard herself had admitted in September 1937 not knowing what the future held for her after the elections. Neilans consulted C. F. Andrews who replied on 28 October 1937 that Shephard was felt to take the "Government view" and had lost the confidence of "national India."[140] Neilans also contacted her colleagues Agatha Harrison and Grace Lancaster, both of whom commented on Shephard's awkward character and views. Her attempt to advise Shephard was met by a furious rebuttal, in which the latter claimed that she had given all her money, health, and happiness to her cause, which she compared to crucifixion; that Neilans's advisers should come out to India and work on the spot; and that others "attribute to my work motives which are Mayo-like in character, and which have NEVER BEEN MINE."[141]

Shephard spent May to October 1938 on furlough in the United Kingdom, staying at the family cottage in Cornwall. While there she wrote an article for the *Shield* entitled "Bridge-Building in India." She opened by recounting a recent compliment paid to her in Madras and used this bridge metaphor for her work in India. She acknowledged that AMSH work was based on a strong spiritual movement that had started in India with Keshan Chandra Sen, and flowed through Bushnell, Andrew, and Dixon to Shephard. From this had come the sketch plan for the bridge, which was built on foundations of justice and equal moral standards. Future builders, in the form of Indian AMSH workers, were acknowledged to be essential. Extending the metaphor to include her recent experiences, Shephard dismissed those who watched scornfully the building of this bridge, as she dug away at its foundations in the mud on her knees. Purportedly speaking of the view from her window, Shephard wrote: "The seas are running at high spring-tides; there has been a great storm at sea; the rain has been lashing against the windows. But just now, as I finish this little comment on a conversation in Madras, there is a glorious rainbow across the Bay. Perhaps that is a symbol, too, of the Bridge and the Invisible Builders" (Shephard 1938, 68).

### Conclusion: Wartime Hygiene, 1939–1945

Shephard's furlough was extended due to ill health and she spent much of 1938 in England. When she returned to Delhi in October she set to doing what work was possible, organizing a paper to be presented at a rural reconstruction conference and visiting Indore. In January 1939 she wrote to Neilans and Turner at the AMSH in London that she hoped the horror of self-inflicted war would be deflected. Following Chamberlain's appeasement with Hitler in September 1938, German troops had occupied the Sudetenland in October, leading to the resignation of the Czech government, which was followed by Kristallnacht in November. Shephard had earlier commented that she had heard that Hitler had a mental defect, a retribution for his ghastly persecution of the Jews.[142] During the following year, Shephard's activities were conducted under the gathering clouds of war. Her work was mostly confined to her immediate locality, and she focused her attention on the Delhi SITA and Rescue Home, as detailed in chapter 1. Her approach to military brothels was unchanged, and in May 1939 she requested that the AMSH in London only raise the matter with the India

Office in a friendly and face-to-face manner. The army in India was said to be aware of its folly and to be providing recreation for the troops. However, showing how clearly she now took the military perspective, she related the case of several troops who had recently attacked a village, killing a man and woman, concluding that a supervised house was better than killing villagers. She promised to take action if it remained open, but argued that the women were caste prostitutes and were better cared for than they would be in a bazaar house.[143]

Shephard luckily had her funding agreed to before the outbreak of war in September 1939 and the resultant effective suspension of the league. She offered herself for war service and tried to get back to England but was told that only people under forty were desired. She also offered herself to the Red Cross, but was turned down in favor of "some rich, unexperienced person who didn't need paying" so told the government of India that she would go anywhere and do anything, but she was not called upon.[144] In October 1939 Congress's elected officials had resigned over the British government's failure to consult Indian officials over its declaration of war on the country's behalf. Gandhi would announce the courting of individual arrests in late 1940 as a small-scale *satyagraha* protest at war, before the announcement of the Quit India mass movement in mid-1942. Before the satyagraha phase there was much political activity in New Delhi, and Shephard used this opportunity to meet with the nationalist elite. She contributed to research on prostitution and abolition by the Indian National Planning Committee, which had been formed by Congress in 1938 to craft a vision of India's future. Shephard also claimed to be making progress on convincing nationalists that she had no political agenda, which she suggested Gandhi himself appreciated when she met him in Delhi. Between 1940 and 1945 Shephard's main traceable work was local and in Delhi. An annual report for 1941–42 listed key foci as the Indianization of AMSH work, some health lectures, and publicity, although she also had to report the unavoidable closure of the rescue home in Delhi. The 1943–45 report admitted that Indianization of the AMSH was not possible due to all desirable Indian staff being in the war services.[145] Contrary to her confidential letters to Neilans, Shephard insisted that the AMSH was still against the military use of brothels, even in wartime. Her ability to travel was greatly curtailed, although she was able to visit Calcutta in 1942, 1943, and 1944. Shephard had the government reissue its condemnation of military brothels, and reported that Miss Fernley Powell was doing good work on the AMSH's behalf. Fifteen years after first doing so, Shephard found herself suggesting adjustments to the Bengal SITA to enable a crackdown on the brothel quarter, which still existed in Calcutta. Karaya Road was still thriving, with the deputy commissioner apparently sending women for medical inspection. Shephard even met some familiar faces, reporting that old acquaintances Marla, Carmen, and Yvonne were still there but now lived in their own houses as "madames."

The AMSH in London was informed in March 1946 that Shephard was in a run-down and nervous state because of the war and that a successor should be appointed within a year.[146] In October 1946 Shephard informed the AMSH that she had found her successor, Dr. Cama, who had a background of social service in Bombay. The *Shield* announced Shephard's replacement in 1946, insisting that "it is impossible for us to realise how much she has accomplished, what difficulties she has had to overcome, nor how arduous these years must have been."[147] Over the winter of 1946–47, Shephard helped train Dr. Cama in Delhi and toured the country with her, introducing AMSH work in the provinces, before returning to England (Shephard 1948).

During her time in India Shephard had emerged as both an exceptional figure of empire, in terms of her commitment and her imperial feminism, but also as one of the last in a long line of liberal campaigners that had sought to remake India in their image. Shephard had faced many challenges: crafting her moral-hygiene concepts to a fast-changing sexual and cultural economy; tempering her racial views while politically negotiating the boundary between civil society and the state in a dyarchical landscape that was hostile to imperial feminist intervention; and orchestrating a *network* of activities that combined local investigations, national networks of abolitionist legislation, communications with the imperial core of London, and a yearning for internationalist recognition. This was in part an institutional desire; the AMSH had petitioned the league from its outset to adopt an abolitionist position. But this was also a personal passion for Shephard, who had turned down Crowdy's invitation to work in Geneva, but doggedly pursued the attentions of the league throughout her time in India. She had defended the league to the central government against the suspicions of unwarranted interference, had tried to become the league's central correspondent or liaison officer, and had organized conferences to support its work. The authority she gained from being able to associate herself with the powerful *nominal* category of the "league" and "internationalism" secured her both government funding and criticisms of attempting to speak on behalf of the silent Indian subaltern on the international stage. But the league also depended upon figures like Shephard to circulate its reports and pamphlets within the territory of the largely indifferent government of India. It is to these multiply scaled geographies of the individual, the urban, the national, the imperial, and that international that we will return in the following brief conclusion.

# CONCLUSION

———·—·———

## WITHIN AND BEYOND THE CITY

This book has exposed the spatial genealogies of a shift from segregation and toleration to abolition and suppression in interwar India. The brothel went from being a site of social and biological safety and visibility to one of risk and occlusion. Tolerated zones of prostitution came to be seen as signs of incivility, disease, and sexual slavery. The scalar methodology I have deployed here has highlighted how this process had discrete yet interlinked logics within urban, national, and imperial networks. Within these, the nominalist forces of a city, a state, and an empire were put to work to civilly abandon prostitutes and their dwellings and to enforce the naming power of civil society, the Raj, and imperial hygiene. At each scale these powers were challenged by, and hybridized with, the resistance of prostitutes themselves, Indian women's social reform groups, nationalist ideologies of development, and emerging internationalist apparatuses in opposition to trafficking and sexual exploitation. These regulations and complex sociopolitical engagements show how assumptions about the natural orderliness of urban civil society, of a legislating and civilizing colonial government, and of a cleansing and improving domain of imperial hygiene were (and still need to be) problematized.

The brief concluding comments below will summarize the turn to suppression at these scales and draw out some of the methodological and theoretical lessons we can learn from the interpretive frames of apparatuses and assemblages, along with a scalar appreciation of natures, networks, and nominalism. I will then sketch out some of the legacies of these developments in independent India to contribute to a dialogue about colonial and postcolonial forms of sexual governmentalities.

### Beyond Colonial Delhi

I began in the first chapter by showing how Delhi's women were civilly abandoned not by government initiative alone, but in response to local petitioning as a result of urban congestion and a modernizing municipality. In line with emerging discourses of the time, the women were stigmatized as moral and social pathogens. Coinciding with ongoing governmental concerns about venereal disease and the military, public prostitutes were forced out of the city into variably marginal spaces. Through the Delhi administration and its Municipal Committee, the state outsourced responsibility for these women to a dense network of civil society organizations, which it partly funded and explicitly supported. Despite the eventual introduction of a Suppression of Immoral Traffic Act, however, Delhi remained explicitly segregationist, resulting in the abandonment of prostitutes in GB Road's civil space of exclusive inclusion.

Delhi came late to the suppressionist legislation that had been spreading throughout India since the early 1920s, as chapter 2 chronicles. The two scandalous sites of Rangoon and Bombay had finally discredited tolerated brothel zones. The experimental legislation in these sites laid the template for the SITAs, yet, as would happen later in Delhi, the enforcement of these acts worked to alter the constitution of brothel areas, not to abolish their existence. The spread of the SITAs depended upon the constitutional legal geographies of dyarchy (1919–35) and provincial self-government (1935–47), which defined prostitution as a "local" issue, to be legislated by the provinces, though with ongoing stimulation and suggestion from central government. Indian women's reform groups and broader civil society organizations campaigned in these legislative debates and reviews. In line with different traditions regarding prostitution, marriage, and trafficking, the powers and expectations embodied in the SITAs reproduced the geographical imaginaries and realities of the cosmopolitan coastal ports and the inland provinces.

Imperial concerns with military inspection and the use of brothels were continuous, as the final chapter showed, but the new hygienist manifestation of philanthropy created unexpected alliances between the army and the Association for Moral and Social Hygiene. Meliscent Shephard struggled for nearly twenty years to network together the interests of the military, the government of India, and the League of Nations with the increasingly influential interests of Indian nationalists, women's groups, and urban politicians. The impressive scope of the AMSH's influence belies the racial tensions involved in an unabashedly imperial feminist attempt to import an empire-wide abolitionist campaign into a country where the state, to which Shephard became increasingly attached, was seen as the obstacle to, rather than the engine of, social reform.

The narrative cohesion of these scales has allowed a series of complex networks to be explored, at the necessary cost of inattention to scales of different lengths. Throughout this book, the brothel has been a consistent and contested site. In Delhi, it was disparaged for its effect on neighborhoods and the reputation of the city, yet the women as well as the deputy commissioner defended its existence as a space in which women had a right to dwell. In cities across India, the brothel was re-branded as a site of slavery and violence (Bombay), of intergenerational disease risk and immorality (Rangoon), and of the disgracing of the military (Calcutta), yet the women's right to live somewhere and practice their trade was defended within the tradition of liberal individualism.

The province also emerged here as the vital frame of a network through which supporters hoped abolitionist legislation would spread. As the testing ground for democracy and self-government, provincial legislation was used to prove that Indians could govern their own health, education, and sanitation, though operating under the supervision and benevolence of governors in council and the central state. "India" here emerged as a contested, fraught, and anxious amalgam of states that jostled for patronage, prestige, and solutions to the interminable question of the sexually disobedient public prostitute.

Finally, the League of Nations extended influence through two channels. As a founding member of the league, India signed up to the legal conventions of the Advisory Committee on Trafficking in Women and Children, which made it directly committed to efforts against trafficking and, indirectly, encouraged it to quell the demand for prostitutes. Secondly, and more influentially, the league worked beyond international law and through international governmentalities to change the terms of debate about prostitution itself. Definitions of the problem, investigations of worldwide efforts to reduce abuse, and incitation to action were quoted and invoked in debates throughout the country, during which international incursions into local, national, and imperial discussions often proved pivotal. The league's influence was often temporary and unpredictable, drawing upon hopes for an international order or fears of traffickers. This influence had a greater impact than the staid dictates of committees in Geneva, as an assemblage as much as an apparatus of internationalism.

### Assemblage, Apparatus, and Scale

The apparatuses and assemblages throughout this book have drawn attention to the diverse ways through which sexual activity was being regulated. In Delhi, the apparatus of the state was apparent through the overlapping institutions of the Delhi administration, the Delhi Municipal Committee, as well as the Delhi Improvement Trust and the health officer. But the apparatus of civil society also worked to construct the "social," not as an oppositional body against the state, but often as part of the colonial mission of civilization. The Delhi Health and Social Service Union, the Central Social Services League, and the local branch of the AMSH worked alongside women's groups like the Delhi Women's League to build a consensus around a large range of smaller organizations that inclusively excluded women from the city. But these organizations also drew sustenance from and were forced to mold themselves around temporary assemblages that drew together biological pathogens, social stigmas, and abstract notions of what was "just." Equally as important was the persistence of male desire for what prostitutes could offer and these women's insurgent claim to the right to dwell. Most powerful of all was their refusal to explain their difference (Chatterjee 2010, 229), which they realized simply by being unchanging and unmoving.

At the state level, the apparatus of the government of India reforged itself around the part-devolved, part-democratized dyarchical constitution of 1919, encouraging and pressing for experimentation and legislation that would protect the imperial military apparatus and the internationally surveilled reputation of the Raj. But these apparatuses had to deal with the swarming assemblage of scandals that crippled the colonial consensus on segregation in the war years and continued to haunt the state with traffickers who were more mobile, and at times even more fictitious, than the vast assemblage of the Raj itself. Publicly debated bills brought in the signatures of petitioners, the campaigns of editors and reformers, the interdictions of a Mahatma, and the population myths of gendered geographies and "willing wives" into the formation of the SITAs.

The apparatus of the AMSH emerged as a fiercely critical, yet always impe-rial, campaigner for women's rights, as defined in London. It strung together district offices, occasional financial subscribers, and various advisory boards to create a diffuse apparatus that situated itself at the boundary between a colonial state and an international civil society. Too local for the League of Nations and too imperial for Indian nationalists, the AMSH became a state-level apparatus and, increasingly, was absorbed into the official mind of em-pire. However, Shephard was, to quote one of her contemporaries, "no boot-licker" (see Legg 2010, 89). She drew on a remarkably diverse assemblage of actors, events, and theories: from psychoanalysis to Christian theology, from Gandhi's Brahmacharya to texts on sexology, hygiene, and feminism. She decried what she saw as the policing statism of the British Social Hy-giene Council while applauding the output of the League of Nations.

These reflections have emerged from a series of arguments that at-tempted to demonstrate the value of a scalar methodology to colonial and imperial analysis. It drew upon an implicit logic in Foucault's 1977–79 lec-tures that suggested that we should be wary of claims to natural orderliness and should challenge such claims with an analysis of the existence and ef-fects of networks and nominalism. In Delhi, the orderly associations of civil society were shown to be exclusionary and to abandon those who did not comply with a series of sexual norms. Attempts to create a "civil" society necessitated intense networking efforts, which exposed the focused interest of the state in this social apparatus. But this also exposed the different ap-proaches of the various associations that were networked together and cre-ated new contexts for the mobilization of prostitutes themselves. The power of naming was demonstrated by municipal decrees that the city was to be a prostitute-free zone, anxieties over Delhi as a "byword for immorality," and the stigmatization of the prostitute. Although this was a label these women would contest, it soon attached itself to the segregated district of GB Road.

The legitimacy of the colonial state in India depended upon law and order. The natural orderliness of the colonial state had long justified its claims on the basis of saving women from sati, from child marriage, or from temple prostitution. Shying from the political controversy of cen-tral social legislation in the twentieth century, however, the government of India depended upon networking together provincial experiments in suppressionist legislation. Though in private the government had called its policy "segregation," it was forced to condemn these policies and benevo-lently support suppressionist experiments in an attempt to defend the name of the Indian Empire.

Countering the fear and reality of imperial syphilization, the AMSH traded upon the idea of a natural and cleansing domain of international civil society. The ill-fated dependency of this project upon the self-conduct of stubbornly non-self-regulating subjects (of whatever nationality) forced the AMSH to employ a range of scientific theories, from sexology to moral hygiene, in an attempt to enfold biological nature within the smothering embrace of a resolutely puritanical subjectivity. Shephard attempted to summon this enterprise into being by networking the empire into India, stringing together laws, institutions, and finance across and within the landscapes of dyarchy and anticolonial nationalism. The AMSH's philosophy, policy, and practice named gender inequality, not prostitution per se, as the problem, but early attempts to fault the colonial economy and society later gave way to a racialized nominalism that ultimately blamed Indian culture. This fated Shephard to obsolescence as Indian civil society forged its own form of hygiene within the context of a Gandhian resolution of the prostitution question.

### Futures Past

As has become clear, central to an understanding of the move from segregation to suppression is an awareness of the specificities of local urban politics, as well as a detailed empirical reading of the connections between local, national, imperial, and international shifts toward abolitionism. This was not a unilinear movement, but one through which we have seen regulated spaces diffuse, evolve, stall, surge, calcify, and collapse. India's turbulent democratization and development in the sixty-five years since independence eschews any easy suggestion of links between then and today. But the urge of spatial genealogies to think out, and in, should not displace the inherently political premise of genealogies to work toward histories of the present. Debates on tolerated sex zones continue to vacillate between segregation and suppression, in ways that demand a historical-comparative reading (see Howell, Beckingham, and Moore 2008). The postcolonial afterlife of regulatory policies, and the zones that survived suppression, demand further study, some of which I hint at below.

Delhi's GB Road stands as testimony to the stubborn residuality of colonial governmentalities. It remains one of India's most notorious red-light districts. The occasional raids and "rescue" attempts attest to the politics of abandonment that excludes these women from the city while they remain included with the powerful sovereign remit of the police (Sankar and Nair 2004). But the occupants of this zone continue to display resilience, both to stigmatization and to governance as practiced in the 1930s (Govindan 2013).

The SITAS, likewise, have survived and exceeded both their colonial and provincial origins. Jean D'Cunha (1987) has demonstrated how the All India SITA of 1956 reproduced the assumptions of female vulnerability and fortified the powers of a patriarchal society in independent India. While surpassing the provincial limitations of interwar legislation, the act was directly indebted to international legal governmentalities because it adhered to India's signing of the UN Suppression of Trafficking Convention of 1950. Rajeswari Sunder Rajan (2003, 117–46) has highlighted how the updated Immoral Traffic Prevention Act (1986) failed to resolve the questions regarding female agency, women's work, and the public/private divide (also see Kotiswaran 2008). Just as in Delhi, many of the segregated areas that emerged in the late nineteenth and early twentieth centuries endure, most notably in Mumbai's Kamathipura (Shah 2006) and Kolkata's Kalighat, Kidderpore, and Watganj districts (Sleightholme and Sinha 1996).

While the AMSH survived into postcolonial India, it has been superseded by successive generations of international civil society organizations that have attempted to "rescue" Indian prostitutes, often without consulting local women's organizations, or in direct conflict with them. Bodies like the International Justice Mission, a well-funded American Christian NGO, have pioneered the "raid and rescue" techniques of the "new abolitionists" (Govindan 2013). These operations raise questions about race, liberty, and sexuality that are all too familiar from the AMSH's campaign. But there are also highly organized and successful bodies representing sex workers, like the Veshya Anyay Mukti Parishad (VAMP) network (see Kole 2009). The contemporary assemblage of trafficking, prostitution, feminism, and neoliberal economic liberation versus sexual liberation is gaining increasing attention (Shah 2004), and I hope this book can provide some historical contextualization for that work.

The hypermobilities of neoliberal globalization, for all their virtuality and time-space compression, raise similar methodological and geographical quandaries as did the imperial and internationalist globalization of the interwar years. Prominent among them, I would suggest, is the dilemma of scale. What I have argued is that we have to simultaneously sustain an acknowledgment that the scales of the city, the state, and the empire existed as networks of particular lengths and as naming effects of particular force. But the co-constitution of these scales by their insides and outsides warns us against any easy assumption about the natures of the urban, the national, or the imperial, just as wider scholarship has disbanded any notion of autonomous scalar domains of the social sphere, economics, or the population.

I have tried to show that sustaining the productive contradictions between these approaches to scale can be done through a type of erasure: the ~~city~~ of internally agonistic networks and outside relations; the ~~state~~ of provincial blocks and imperial connections; and the ~~empire~~ of radical heterogeneity and uneasy engagement with new, ~~international~~ outsides. These difficult but rewarding moves will, I hope, present us with new ways of thinking about late colonialism, early internationalism, and the persistent civil abandonment of women who work with sex.

# NOTES

———•—•———

## INTRODUCTION

1. League of Nations, *Traffic in Women and Children: Summary, Prepared by Secretariat, of Annual Reports for the Year 1930* (Geneva: League of Nations, 1932), 7.

2. The photograph was taken by Bourke-White in c. 1946 and is catalogued under the title "Indian prostitutes peeking out fr. doorways of their brothel" in Lahore. Although she published widely on her experience of working in India (Bourke-White 1951, 1963, chapters 24 and 25), this image goes without comment, just as it does not appear in a collection of Bourke-White's Indian works (Kapoor 2010). Most attention is drawn to her famous photographs of Gandhi and of the aftermath of partition violence. The women depicted on this book's cover (and the just visible male in the second room) remain inscrutable.

3. See League of Nations, *Commission of Enquiry into Traffic in Women and Children in the East: Report to the Council* (Geneva: League of Nations, 1932), 344.

4. "Victory in India: The Cantonment System Crumbling," *Shield*, 3rd ser., 2, no. 2 (1919): 79–85.

5. Delhi State Archives (henceforth DA)/Chief Commissioner's files (henceforth CC)/Education/1928/6(26)B.

6. DA/CC/Public/1939/8(95).

7. *All India Women's Conference, Diamond Jubilee, 1927–87* (All India Women's Conference, New Delhi, 1987), 27.

8. Nehru Memorial Museum and Library (henceforth NMML)/ Delhi Criminal Investigation Department files/IV/20.

9. "Delhi Women's League: At a Glance, 1927–2004," in *Platinum Jubilee and Women Achievers Awards: 20 April 2004* (All India Women's Conference, New Delhi, 2004).

10. Thanks to Dan Clayton for drawing my attention to the scalar dimensions of subaltern historiography.

## CHAPTER 1: CIVIL ABANDONMENT

1. Pramatha Banerjee, "The Social and the Political: A History in the Light of Today," a paper presented at a "South Asian Governmentalities" workshop organized by myself and Deana Heath at the Jawaharlal Nehru Institute of Advanced Studies, JNU, New Delhi, 11 November 2011.

2. Delhi State Archives (henceforth DA)/Lock Hospital files (henceforth LH)/1873/74.

3. DA/Chief Commissioner's Files (henceforth CC)/Local Self Government (henceforth LSG)/1940/2(97).

4. DA/CC/LSG/1940/2(97).

5. DA/LH/1870/27.

6. DA/CC/Home/1919/70B.

7. DA/CC/Home/1919/70B.

8. National Archives of India (henceforth NA)/Home/Police/1916/December/64–67A; "Regulated Prostitution within the British Empire," *Shield*, 3rd ser., 2, no. 4 (1919): 152–58.

9. DA/CC/Education/1928/4(16)B.

10. Municipal Corporation of Delhi files (henceforth MCD)/Special meeting/9 January 1929. Thanks to Anish Vanaik.

11. MCD/Special meeting/9 January 1929.

12. DA/CC/Education/1929/6(11)B/Volume II.

13. DA/CC/Education/1930/6(16).

14. DA/CC/LSG/1940/2(97).

15. Editorial, *Delhi Social Service* (Organ of the Central Social Service League) 1, no. 1 (1931).

16. DA/Deputy Commissioner's files (henceforth DC)/1927/64.

17. DA/CC/Education/1931/4(30)B.

18. DA/CC/Education/1931/4(30)B.

19. DA/CC/Education/1931/4(30)B.

20. DA/CC/Education/1931/4(30)B.

21. Memorandum and appendix submitted to Mr. A. P. Hume, 20 June 1936, Delhi Public Library. For contextualization of this report see Legg (2006).

22. Legislative Assembly/27 February 1938/1217.

23. DA/CC/LSG/1938/821.

24. India Office Records and Library file, the British Library (henceforth IORL)/V/8/213.

25. IORL/V/8/209.

26. DA/CC/LSG/1939/2(3)/Volume II and III.

27. *Hindustan Times*, 2 June 1939.

28. DA/CC/LSG/1940/2(97).

29. DA/CC/LSG/1939/2(3)/Volume IV.

30. *Hindustan Times*, 9 July 1939.

31. *Hindustan Times*, 9 July 1939.

32. *Hindustan Times*, 18 July 1939.

33. *Hindustan Times*, 21 July 1939.

34. DA/CC/LSG/1939/2(3)/Volume V.

35. DA/CC/LSG/1939/2(3)/Volume V.

36. DA/CC/LSG/1939/2(3)/Volume VII.

37. DA/CC/LSG/1939/2(3)/Volume VII.

38. DA/CC/LSG/1940/2(97).

39. Legislative Assembly/21 November 1944/1106.

40. DA/DC/1944/15.

41. DA/CC/Home (Education)/1917/18B.

42. DA/Confidential (Home)/1918/46.

43. DA/CC/Education/1928/6(26)B.

44. DA/CC/Education/1929/6(11)B/Volume II.

45. DA/CC/Education/1930/6(13)B.

46. DA/CC/Education/1928/6(26)B.

47. DA/CC/Home/1935/66B.

48. The Women's Library, London (henceforth WL)/3AMS.C.5.6/1933: Meliscent Shephard (henceforth MS) to Alison Neilans (henceforth AN), 6 February 1933.

49. WL/3AMS.C.5.6/1933: AN to MS, 15 February 1933.

50. WL/3AMS.C.5.6/1933: AN to MS, 15 February 1933.

51. WL/3AMS.C.5.6/1933: AN to MS, 22 February 1933.

52. WL/3AMS.C.5.6/1933: MS to AN, 9 March 1933.

53. WL/3AMS.C.5.6/1933.

54. WL/3AMS.C.5.6/1933: MS to AN, 28 April 1933.

55. NA/Home/Judicial/1936/536/36.

56. *Hindustan Times*, 21 July 1936.

57. NA/Home/Juridical/1937/56/20/37.

58. WL/3AMS/C/5/9, original emphasis.

59. NA/Home/Judicial/1936/563/36.

60. DA/CC/Home/1935/147B.

61. DA/CC/Home/1936/85B.

62. DA/CC/General/1938/694.

63. DA/CC/General/1938/237.

64. DA/CC/LSG (Medical)/1938/724.

65. DA/CC/General/1938/237.

66. DA/CC/General/1938/237.

67. Legislative Assembly/5 October 1936/2317–318.

68. DA/CC/General/1938/237.

69. NA/Home/Judicial/1939/142/39.

70. WL/3AMS/C/5/13.

71. NMML/CID/IV/22.

72. WL/3AMS/C/5/9.

73. DA/CC/LSG(Public Health)/1939/46B.

74. DA/CC/LSG(Public Health)/1939/46B.

75. WL/3AMS/C/5/13.

76. DA/CC/Public/1939/8(95).

77. NA/Home/Judicial/1938/218/38.

78. NMML/AIWC/1939/44.

79. DA/CC/Public/1939/8(95).

80. DA/CC/LSG/1939/2(3)/Volume V.

81. DA/DC/1935/10.

82. DA/CC/Public/1939/8(95)A.

83. DA/CC/Public/1939/8(95).

84. DA/CC/Judicial/1938/173/38.

85. DA/CC/Public/1939/8(95)A.

86. DA/CC/Public/1939/8(95).

87. DA/CC/General/1940/8(66).

88. DA/CC/Judicial/1938/173/38.

89. DA/CC/General/1940/8(66).

90. DA/CC/General/1940/8(66).

91. DA/CC/Miscellaneous/1941/8(157)I/B.

92. NA/Home(Police)/1945/204/45.

93. NMML/CID/IX/20.

94. "Association for Moral and Social Hygiene in India: Summarised Biennial Report, 1943–45," *Shield*, 5th ser., 10, no. 1 (1945): 11–22.

95. NA/Home/Police/1945/12/4/45.

96. NA/Home/Police/1945/11/2/45.

97. NA/Home/Police/1945/11/2/45.

98. NA/Home/Police/1945/11/2/45 DA/DC/1943/283.

99. DA/DC/1943/283.

100. DA/DC/1944/52.

101. DA/Reports/1945/324.

102. DA/Reports/1945/324.

### CHAPTER 2: ASSEMBLING INDIA

1. Women's Library, London (henceforth WL)/3AMS/C/5/2: Meliscent Shephard (henceforth MS) to Alison Neilans (henceforth AN), 20 August 1930.

2. National Archives of India, New Delhi (henceforth NA)/Home(Legislative)/1901/6–9A.

3. WL/3/AMS/D/37/02.

4. *Public Prostitution in Rangoon: Report to the Association for Moral and Social Hygiene on Brothel-keeping, Prostitution, Segregation and Immoral Conditions in*

*Rangoon and Other Towns and Stations in Burma* (London: AMSH, 1916), 8; WL /3AMS/D/37/02 or India Office Records and Library, British Library (henceforth IORL) /L/P&J/6/1448(2987). Henceforth referred to as *Public Prostitution in Rangoon.*

5. WL/3/AMS/1/3/02.

6. NA/Home(Police)/1917/84–87A/February.

7. NA/Home(Political)/1915/378–381A/June.

8. Office of the Superintendent (Rangoon), *Report on the Administration of the Rangoon Town Police for the Year 1915* (Burma: Government Printing, 1916), section 13.

9. NA/Home(Police)/1916/64–67A/December.

10. *Public Prostitution in Rangoon*, 3.

11. *Public Prostitution in Rangoon*, 3.

12. *Public Prostitution in Rangoon*, 8.

13. *Public Prostitution in Rangoon*, 13.

14. "Burma: Conditions 1915–1919," *Shield*, 3rd ser., 2, no. 4 (August–September 1919): 155–57.

15. NA/Home(Police)/1920/24–29A/January.

16. IORL/1/P&J/6/1448(2987).

17. IORL/1/P&J/6/1448(2987).

18. NA/Home(Police)/1920/24–29A/January.

19. NA/Home(Police)/1920/24–29A/January.

20. NA/Home(Police)/1917/128–130A/December.

21. NA/Home(Police)/1917/128–130A/December.

22. Reverend Frank Oldrieve was secretary of the mission to lepers in India until 1923.

23. NA/Home(Police)/1919/173–189A/April.

24. NA/Home(Police)/1918/19–20A and K-W/November.

25. NA/Home(Police)/1919/173–189A/April.

26. WL/3AMS/C/4/2–3.

27. "Victory in India: The Cantonment System Crumbling," *Shield*, 3rd ser., 2, no. 2 (1919): 79–85.

28. NA/Home(Police)/1919/327B.

29. "Regulated Prostitution within the British Empire," *Shield*, 3rd ser., 2, no. 4 (1919): 152–58.

30. NA/Home(Political)/1916/358–360B/August.

31. NA/Home(Police)/1919/327B.

32. NA/Home(Police)/1919/327B.

33. NA/Home(Police)/1919/327B.

34. NA/Home(Police)/1902/20A/June.

35. NA/Home(Police)/1920/24–29A/January.

36. NA/Home(Police)/1918/87–88A/October.

37. "Regulated Prostitution within the British Empire," 152–58.

38. NA/Home(Police)/1920/24–29A/January.

39. NA/Home(Police)/1921/153–161A/April.

40. NA/Home(Police)/1921/153–161A/April.

41. NA/Home(Police)/1921/153–161/April.

42. IORL/1 /P&J/6/1448(2987).

43. NA/Home(Police)/1923/75/II.

44. NA/Home(Police)/1923/24/VI/23.

45. "Vice Areas in Bombay and Calcutta," *Shield*, 3rd ser., 5, no. 1 (1926): 9–12.

46. The following analysis is based on published records, from the *Annual Report on the Police of the City of Bombay for the Year 1923* (Bombay: Government Central Press, 1924) to *Annual Report on the Police of the City of Bombay for the Year 1941* (Bombay: Government Central Press, 1942). .

47. *Annual Report on the Police of the City of Bombay for the Year 1928* (Bombay: Government Central Press, 1929).

48. NA/Home(Police)/1925/24/XII.

49. NA/Home(Police)/1930/24/II.

50. *Annual Report on the Police of the City of Bombay for the Year 1931* (Bombay: Government Central Press, 1932).

51. WL/AMS3/C/5/4: MS to Miss M. Turner (henceforth MT), 11 July 1931.

52. See IOR/1 /P&J/7/261.

53. *Calcutta Vigilance Association Report 1925–26*, WL/3AMS/C/05.

54. *Bengal Legislative Council Proceedings* 8, no. 183 (17 August 1923).

55. IOR/1 /MIL/7/13899 (collection 315/84).

56. *Legislative Assembly Proceedings* 7, part 1 (27 January 1926).

57. NA/Home(Police)/1928/11/XV.

58. NA/Home(Police)/1929/24/XI/29.

59. "Social Evil in Madras," *Stri Dharma* 8, no. 12 (October 1925): 180.

60. "Rescue Homes," *Stri Dharma* 10, no. 6 (April 1927): 81.

61. "Traffic in Women and Children," *Stri Dharma* 10, no. 8 (June 1927): 186.

62. "The Social Evil," *Stri Dharma* 10, no. 9 (July 1927): 130.

63. "Crucified Women," *Stri Dharma* 7, no. 1 (November 1928): 1–3.

64. NA/Home(Police)/1930/24/IV.

65. *Stri Dharma* 8, no. 7 (May 1930): 295.

66. "The Madras Brothels Act: Women's Deputation to Home Member," *Stri Dharma* 14, no. 7 (May 1931): 297–301.

67. NA/Home(Police)/1931/24/IV/31.

68. "The Madras Government and the Act for the Suppression of Brothels and Immoral Traffic in Women and Children," *Stri Dharma* 15, no. 10 (August 1931): 458–59.

69. "Enforcement of the Madras Act for the Closure of Brothels and Suppression of Traffic in Women and Children," *Stri Dharma* 15, no. 2 (May 1932): 352–54.

70. *Report on the Administration of the Police of Madras Presidency 1932* (Madras: Government Press, 1933), 50.

71. WL/3AMS/C/05/06: MS to AN, 12 November 1933.

72. "Report of Vigilance Association," *Stri Dharma* 17, no. 3 (January 1934): 121–22.

73. "Home for Women," *Stri Dharma* 17, no. 6 (April 1934): 252–53.

74. "Suppression of Immorality Act," *Stri Dharma* 18, no. 4 (February 1935): 172.

75. *Report on the Administration of the Police of Madras Presidency 1936* (Madras: Government Press, 1937), 62.

76. *Report on the Administration of the Police of Madras Presidency 1938* (Madras: Government Press, 1939), 60.

77. Annual reports from *Advisory Committee on Social Questions: Summary of Annual Reports for 1937–38, Prepared by the Secretariat* (Geneva: League of Nations, 1939) to *Advisory Committee on Social Questions: Summary of Annual Reports for 1943–44, Prepared by the Secretariat* (Geneva: League of Nations, 1945).

78. *Report on the Administration of the Police of Madras Presidency 1945* (Madras: Government Press, 1947), 37.

79. "A Bill in the Travancore Council for the Suppression of Immoral Traffic in Women and Children," *Stri Dharma* 14, no. 11 (September 1931): 505–6.

80. "Mysore Bill for the Suppression of Traffic in Women and Children," *Stri Dharma* 16, no. 1 (November 1932): 3–4.

81. WL/3AMS/C/05/06.

82. NA/Home(Police)/1923/24/III.

83. WL/3AMS/C/05/02.

84. Delhi State Archives (henceforth DA)/Deputy Commissioner's files/1927/64: secretary of the Naik Sadhar Sabha of Nainital to the deputy commissioner, 5 January 1934.

85. BL/ IOR/1/PJ/7/355.

86. *Advisory Committee on Social Questions: Summary of Annual Reports for 1933–34, Prepared by the Secretariat* (Geneva: League of Nations, 1935).

87. Data taken from published records, from the *Annual Report on the Police Administration of Calcutta and Its Suburbs for the Year 1933* (Alipore: Superintendent of Government Printing, 1934) to the *Annual Report on the Police Administration of Calcutta and Its Suburbs for the Year 1940* (Alipore: Superintendent of Government Printing, 1941). Henceforth *Reports on the Police Administration of Calcutta.*

88. *Advisory Committee on Social Questions: Summary of Annual Reports for 1930, Prepared by the Secretariat* (Geneva: League of Nations, 1931).

89. *Advisory Committee on Social Questions: Summary of Annual Reports for 1931, Prepared by the Secretariat* (Geneva: League of Nations, 1932).

90. *Reports on the Police Administration of Calcutta.*

91. Data taken from published records, from the *Report on Police Administration in the Punjab for the Year 1920* (Lahore: Superintendent of Government Printing, 1921) to the *Report on Police Administration in the Punjab for the Year 1939* (Lahore: Superintendent of Government Printing, 1940).

92. "Mussumat" was an honorific term used for North Indian women (with thanks to Rohit De).

93. NA/Home(Police)/1927/85/II/27.

94. Many thanks to Veena Oldenburg for these translations.

95. *Statistical Abstract Relating to British India from 1910–11 to 1919–20* (London: His Majesty's Stationary Office, 1922), available at http://dsal.uchicago.edu/statistics/index.html, accessed 3 September 2009.

96. IOR/1/P&J/7/753.

97. DA/Chief Commissioner's files/Home/1936/85B.

98. NA/Home(Judicial)/1936/175/36.

99. *Report on Police Administration in the Punjab for the Year 1937* (Lahore: Superintendent of Government Printing, 1938).

100. *Advisory Committee on Social Questions: Summary of Annual Reports for 1938–39, Prepared by the Secretariat* (Geneva: League of Nations, 1940).

101. NA/Home(Judicial)/1939/90/39.

102. NA/Home(Judicial)/1936/175/36.

103. *Advisory Committee on Social Questions: Summary of Annual Reports for 1936–37, Prepared by the Secretariat* (Geneva: League of Nations, 1938).

104. Data taken from published records, from the *Report on the Administration of the Police of the United Provinces for the Year 1934* (Allahabad: Superintendent of Printing and Stationary, 1935) to the *Report on the Administration of the Police of the United Provinces for the Year 1945* (Allahabad: Superintendent of Printing and Stationary, 1947).

105. IOR/1/P&J/7/966.

106. NA/Home(Police)/24/3/39.

107. *Legislative Assembly Proceedings* 8 (5 October 1936).

108. NA/Home(Jails)/1938/43/3/38.

109. NA/Home(Police)/1944/11/27/44.

110. WL/3AMS/C/05/07: MS to MT, 14 February 1934.

### CHAPTER 3: IMPERIAL MORAL AND SOCIAL HYGIENE

1. "Vice Areas in Bombay and Calcutta," *Shield*, 3rd. ser., 1, no. 1 (1926): 9–12.

2. Women's Library (henceforth WL)/3AMS/C/05/1: *Calcutta Vigilance Association (CVA) Report 1925–26.*

3. WL/3AMS/C/5/1: CVA Report 1927–28.

4. "The Problem of the Vice Areas in Indian Cities," *Shield,* 3rd ser., 5, no. 4 (1928): 167–69.

5. WL/3AMS/C/5/1: Lord Bishop of Calcutta to the AMSH, 17 May 1928.

6. WL/3AMS/C/5/1: Meliscent Shephard (henceforth MS) to Alison Neilans (henceforth AN), 17 January 1928, original emphasis.

7. WL/3AMS/C/5/2: MS to AN, 3 January 1928.

8. WL/3AMS/C/5/2: MS to AN, 1 January 1929.

9. WL/3AMS/C/5/3: A copy of the report was forwarded by MS to AN, 28 April 1930.

10. WL/3AMS/C/5/2: MS to AN, 17 May 1929.

11. WL/3AMS/C/5/2: MS to AN, 29 November 1929.

12. WL/3AMS/C/5/2: undated typed manuscript by MS.

13. "A Challenge. 2. The Anglo-Indian Community," *Calcutta Diocesan Record* 18, no. 6 (1929): 166–68.

14. "A Challenge. 2. The Anglo-Indian Community," 166–68.

15. "A Challenge. 3. The European Community," *Calcutta Diocesan Record* 18, no. 7 (1929): 192–94.

16. "A Challenge. 1.," *Calcutta Diocesan Record* 18, no. 5 (1929): 139–41.

17. WL/3AMS/C/5/1: *Summarised Report to the Council of the CVA for the Years 1928–31, by Meliscent Shephard, Representative in India of the AMSH* (henceforth *CVA 1928–31*).

18. WL/AMS3/C/5/4: MS to Edith Turner (henceforth EET), 11 July 1931.

19. WL/3AMS/C/5/3.

20. WL/AMS3/C/5/4: AN to MS, 5 January 1931.

21. WL/AMS3/C/5/4: MS to AN, 27 January 1931.

22. WL/AMS3/C/5/4: MS to ET, 1 February 1931.

23. WL/AMS3/C/5/4: MS to ET, 1 February 1931.

24. WL/AMS3/C/5/4: MS to AN, 25 February 1931.

25. WL/AMS3/C/5/4: AN to MS, 9 March 1931.

26. WL/AMS3/C/5/4: AN to MS, 16 April 1931 and 12 June 1931.

27. WL/AMS3/C/5/4: MS to AN, 24 June 1931.

28. WL/AMS3/C/5/2: AN to MS, 25 July 1929.

29. WL/AMS3/C/5/2: AN to MS, 2 October 1929.

30. Neilans doesn't refer elsewhere to this report, but it is most likely the annual report for 1928 issued by New York's Committee of Fourteen anti-prostitution body. The report was the product of an undercover investigation into prostitution in Harlem, describing the sheer variety of locations and types of prostitution that had flourished in Progressive-era New York. It led to 1,293 arrests and the hospitalization of women with venereal diseases (Robertson 2009).

31. WL/AMS3/C/5/2: AN to MS, 21 January 1930.

32. WL/AMS3/C/5/2: MS to Grace Brown, 20 March 1929.

33. CVA 1928–31.

34. "Self-Government Is Self-Control," *Statesman*, 19 August 1930.

35. WL/3AMS/C/5/3: MS printed circular, 16 June 1930.

36. WL/3AMS/C/5/4: Dr. Helen Wilson (henceforth HW) to ET, 26 October 1930.

37. WL/3AMS/C/5/2: MS to AN, 17 December 1929.

38. WL/3AMS/C/5/2: MS to AN, 12 February 1930.

39. WL/3AMS/C/5/3: HW to MS, 14 April 1930.

40. WL/3AMS/C/5/2: MS to AN and ET, 14 July 1929.

41. WL/3AMS/C/5/2: MS printed circular, 13 February 1929.

42. "Moral Status of Calcutta: Plea for Reform," *Statesman*, 22 November 1929.

43. WL/3AMS/C/5/8: *A Rough Record 1858–1935 on the Work of the AMSH, in Connection with the British Army in India* (henceforth *Rough Record*).

44. WL/3AMS/C/5/2: MS to AN, 8 February 1930.

45. WL/3AMS/C/5/2: Grace Human to AN, 28 February 1929.

46. WL/3AMS/C/5/2: MS to Grace Human, 18 January 1929.

47. WL/3AMS/C/5/2: MS to AN, 14 November 1929.

48. WL/3AMS/C/5/2: "Draft Statement on Miss Shephard's Work in Calcutta," n.d.

49. WL/3AMS/C/5/2: MS to AN, 22 October 1929.

50. WL/3AMS/C/5/3: MS to AN, 28 April 1930.

51. WL/3AMS/C/5/3: MS to AN, 8 July 1930.

52. WL/3AMS/C/5/3: Elizabeth Abbots to AN, 10 November 1930.

53. WL/3AMS/C/5/3: MS printed circular, 16 July 1930.

54. WL/3AMS/C/5/3: AN to MS, 5 December 1930.

55. WL/3AMS/C/5/2: MS to AN, 12 February 1930.

56. WL/3AMS/C/5/4: MS to AN, 18 April 1931.

57. WL/3AMS/C/5/4: MS printed circular, May 1931.

58. WL/3AMS/C/5/4: MS to ET, 11 July 1931.

59. WL/3AMS/C/5/4: MS to ET, 11 July 1931.

60. WL/3AMS/C/5/4: MS to AN, 16 September 1931.

61. WL/3AMS/C/6/1: MS to AN, 10 June 1932.

62. WL/3AMS/C/5/5.

63. Dr. Young (1884–1983) trained in medicine in Dundee, Vienna, and Dresden, before taking up a lecturing post in Ludhiana in 1910. She later lectured in Delhi and worked for the Women's Medical Service of India and the Indian Red Cross. From 1936 to 1940, she was the principal of Lady Hardinge Medical College in Delhi. Her archives are held at the University of Dundee (GB 0254 MS 31). Lady Bhore (1884–1946) was the wife of Sir Joseph William Bhore. Margaret Bhore (née Stott) was also trained in medicine in Dundee and had worked in Berhampore Baptist Missionary Hospital.

64. Also see 3AMS/C/09/03.

65. NA/1936/Home(Judicial)/175/36.

66. WL/3AMS/C/5/4: MS to AN and ET, 11 September 1929.

67. WL/3AMS/C/5/3: MS to AN, 5 November 1930.

68. WL/3AMS/C/5/6: S. P. Singha to MS, 7 March 1933.

69. WL/3AMS/C/5/6: MS to AN, 16 March 1933.

70. NA/1936/Home(Judicial)/175/36.

71. NA/1936/Home(Judicial)/175/36: MS to J. A. Thorne, Home Department, 14 February 1936, forwarding letter from MS to Sir Maharaj Singh, Home Member, UP Government, 14 February 1935.

72. NA/1936/Home(Judicial)/175/36.

73. NA/Home(Judicial)/1934/624/34.

74. NA/1936/Home(Judicial)/175/36: MS to J. A. Thorne, 13 March 1936.

75. WL/3AMS/C/5/3: AN to MS, 24 June 1930.

76. "Self-Government Is Self-Control," *Statesman*, 19 August 1930.

77. WL/3AMS/C/5/4: MS to AN, 24 June 1931.

78. WL/3AMS/C/5/6: MS to AN, 31 May 1933.

79. "The Association for Moral and Social Hygiene and the League of Nations," *Shield*, 5th ser., 3, no. 2 (1934): 53–56.

80. WL/3AMS/C/5/7: MS to AN, 22 September 1934.

81. WL/3AMS/C/5/7: MS to AN, 18 October 1934.

82. WL/3AMS/C/5/7: MS to AN, 5 December 1934.

83. "Traffic in Women and Children: Conference Plan: Efforts to Check Evil in India," *Statesman*, 18 March 1935.

84. WL/3AMS/C/5/8: MS to AN, 15 March 1935. Blue Books were the quantitative and qualitative surveys put together by the government of India to assess conditions across their territories.

85. WL/3AMS/C/5/8: MS to AN, 6 April 1935.

86. WL/3AMS/C/5/6: AN to MS, 14 June 1933.

87. WL/3AMS/C/5/9: Eric Ekstrand to MS, 6 February 1936, original emphasis.

88. WL/3AMS/C/5/8: MS to AN, 8 March 1935.

89. NA/Home(Judicial)/1936/563/36, J. A. Thorne to MS, 12 August 1936.

90. WL/3AMS/C/5/6: MS to AN, 31 May 1933.

91. WL/3AMS/C/6/1: *Traffic in Women: Official and Non-Official Action in Combating the Traffic in the East: REPORT of a Conference of British and International Representatives, London July 1934* (London: British Social Hygiene Council, 1934, henceforth BSHC REPORT 1934).

92. BSHC REPORT 1934.

93. NA/Home(Judicial)/1934/624/34.

94. WL/3AMS/C/5/7: MS to Mr. Butler, 30 July 1934.

95. *All India Women's Conference Ninth Annual Report* (Karachi, 1935).

96. WL/3AMS/C/5/8: MS to AN, 26 October 1935.

97. WL/3AMS/C/5/6: MS to AN, 6 February 1933.

98. WL/3AMS/C/5/6: MS to AN, 2 April 1933.

99. WL/3AMS/C/5/6: AN to Reverend Anderson, 21 April 1933.

100. WL/3AMS/C/5/6: AN to MS, 12 April 1933.

101. *Rough Record.*

102. WL/3AMS/C/5/7: MS to AN, 26 March 1934.

103. WL/3AMS/C/5/7: MS to AN, 20 December 1933.

104. WL/3AMS/C/5/6: MS to AN, 12 November 1933.

105. NA/Home(Judicial)/1934/624/34.

106. WL/3AMS/C/5/6: MS to AN, 31 May 1933.

107. WL/3AMS/C/5/7: MS to AN, 8 November 1934.

108. My sincere thanks to the Sabarmati Gandhi Ashram in Ahmedabad for sending me a copy of Shephard's letter.

109. *Collected Works of Mahatma Gandhi* Vol. 59, 439–40 (New Delhi: Publications Division, Ministry of Information and Broadcasting, Government of India, 1958–); NA/Home(Juridical)/1937/56/20/37: M. K. Gandhi to MS, 4 March 1933.

110. NA/Home(Judicial)/1936/563/36.

111. WL/3AMS/C/5/9: MS to AN, 14 April 1936.

112. WL/3AMS/C/5/8: MS to AN, 12 March 1935.

113. WL/3AMS/C/5/5.

114. NA/Home(Judicial)/1934/624/34.

115. NA/Home(Judicial)/1936/175/36.

116. NA/Home(Judicial)/1936/175/36: J. A. Thorne note on file 8 July 1936.

117. WL/3AMS/C/5/9: MS to AN, 24 August 1936.

118. WL/3AMS/C/5/10: MS to AN, 12 August 1937.

119. WL/3AMS/C/5/10: MS to AN, 29 September 1937.

120. NA/Home(Judicial)/1929/90/39: "Brief Summary of Work Undertaken in the Punjab 1937–1939 by the AMSH in India," by R. Stott for the home secretary to the government of the Punjab.

121. WL/3AMS/C/5/12: MS to AN, 12 January 1938.

122. NA/Home(Judicial)/1929/90/39.

123. WL/3AMS/C/5/10: MS to AN, 19 February 1937.

124. NA/Home(Juridical)/1937/56/20/37.

125. WL/3AMS/C/5/12: J. A. Thorne to MS, 11 January 1938.

126. WL/3AMS/C/5/10: MS to AN, 29 September 1937.

127. WL/3AMS/C/5/12.

128. WL/3AMS/C/5/12: MS to AN, 14 February 1938.

129. WL/3AMS/C/5/12: MS to AN, 14 February 1938.

130. WL/3AMS/C/5/13: MS to ET, 5 March 1945.

131. *Shield*, 5th ser., 6, no. 1 (1938).

132. NA/Home(Juridical)/1937/56/20/37.

133. NA/Home(Juridical)/1937/56/20/37.

134. NA/Home(Judicial)/1939/142/39, Note on file, 26 August 1939.

135. WL/3AMS/C/5/10: MS to AN, 3 December 1937.

136. WL/3AMS/C/5/10: MS to ET, 23 December 1937.

137. WL/3AMS/C/5/10: MS to AN, 12 August 1937.

138. WL/3AMS/C/5/10: MS to AN, 25 October 1937.

139. WL/3AMS/C/5/6: AN to MS, 20 June 1933.

140. WL/3AMS/C/5/10: C. F. Andrews to AN, 28 October 1937.

141. WL/3AMS/C/5/12: MS to AN, 2 December 1937.

142. WL/3AMS/C/5/12: MS to AN and ET, 2 January 1939.

143. WL/3AMS/C/5/12: MS to AN, 27 May 1939.

144. WL/3AMS/C/5/13: MS to AN, 14 January 1940.

145. WL/3AMS/C/5/13.

146. WL/3AMS/C/5/13: W. L. P. Pens to Denys Pilditch, 22 March 1946.

147. "News from AMSH in India," *Shield*, 5th ser., 10, no. 2 (1946): 76–78.

# REFERENCES

Aalberts, Tanja, and Ben Golder. 2012. "On the Uses of Foucault for International Law." *Leiden Journal of International Law* 25 (3): 603–8.

Agamben, Giorgio. 1998. *Homo Sacer: Sovereign Power and Bare Life*. Stanford, CA: Stanford University Press.

———. 2005. *State of Exception*. Translated by K. Attell. Chicago: University of Chicago Press.

Agnes, Flavia. 1999. *Law and Gender Inequality: The Politics of Women's Rights in India*. New Delhi: Oxford University Press.

Ahluwalia, Sanjam. 2008. *Reproductive Restraints: Birth Control in India, 1877–1947*. Urbana: University of Illinois Press.

———. 2012. "Scripting Pleasures and Perversions: Writings of Sexologists in the Twentieth Century." In *Sexualities Studies*, edited by Sanjay Srivastava, 24–45. New Delhi: Oxford University Press.

Amrith, Sunil. 2006. *Decolonizing International Health: India and Southeast Asia, 1930–65*. Basingstoke, UK: Palgrave Macmillan.

Anderson, Ben, and Colin McFarlane. 2011. "Assemblage and Geography." *Area* 43 (2): 124–27.

Anderson, Herbert. 1930. "Miss Shephard's Campaign in Calcutta." *Shield* 6 (2): 73–78.

———. 1933. "Changes in the Outlook on Prostitution in India." *Health and Empire* 8: 203–15.

Anderson, Warwick. 2006. *Colonial Pathologies: American Tropical Medicine, Race, and Hygiene in the Philippines*. Durham, NC: Duke University Press.

———. 2007. "Immunization and Hygiene in the Colonial Philippines." *Journal of the History of Medicine and Allied Sciences* 62 (1): 1–20.

Armstrong, David. 1993. "Public Health Spaces and the Fabrication of Identity." *Sociology* 27 (3): 393–410.

Arnold, David. 1993a. *Colonizing the Body: State Medicine and Epidemic Disease in Nineteenth-Century India.* Berkeley: University of California Press.

———. 1993b. "Sexually Transmitted Diseases in Nineteenth- and Twentieth-Century India." *Genitourinary Medicine* 69: 3–8.

Aslanian, Sebouh David, Joyce E. Chaplin, Ann McGrath, and Kristin Mann. 2013. "AHR Conversation How Size Matters: The Question of Scale in History." *American Historical Review* 118: 1431–72.

Ballhatchet, Kenneth. 1980. *Race, Sex and Class under The Raj: Imperial Attitudes and Policies and Their Critics, 1793–1905.* London: Weidenfeld and Nicolson.

Banerjee, Sumanta. 1998. *Dangerous Outcasts: The Prostitute in Nineteenth-Century Bengal.* Calcutta, India: Seagull Books.

Barry, Kathleen. 1995. *The Prostitution of Sexuality: The Global Exploitation of Women.* New York: New York University Press.

Bartley, Paula. 2000. *Prostitution: Prevention and Reform in England, 1860–1914.* London: Routledge.

Bashford, Alison. 2004. *Imperial Hygiene: A Critical History of Colonialism, Nationalism and Public Health.* Basingstoke, UK: Palgrave Macmillan.

Basu, Amrita, Inderpal Grewal, Caren Kaplan, and Liisa Malkki. 2001. "Editorial: Globalization and Gender." *Signs* 26 (4): 943–48.

Basu, Aparna, and Bharati Ray. 1990. *Women's Struggle: A History of the All India Women's Conference 1927–1990.* New Delhi: Manohar.

Belcher, Oliver, Lauren Martin, Anna Secor, Stephanie Simon, and Tommy Wilson. 2008. "Everywhere and Nowhere: The Exception and the Topological Challenge to Geography." *Antipode* 40 (4): 499–503.

Bell, Ernest A. 1909. *War on the White Slave Trade.* Chicago: Charles C. Thompson.

Bell, Shannon. 1994. *Reading, Writing and Rewriting the Prostitute Body.* Bloomington: Indiana University Press.

Bigo, Didier. 2008. *Terror, Insecurity and Liberty: Illiberal Practices of Liberal Regimes after 9/11.* London: Routledge.

Birla, Ritu. 2009. *Stages of Capital: Law, Culture, and Market Governance in Late Colonial India.* Durham, NC: Duke University Press.

Blackett, Basil, and Edward Grigg. 1935. "Foreword: The Implications of Social Hygiene." In *Empire Social Hygiene Year-Book 1935*, edited by British Social Hygiene Council, 19–25. London: George Allen and Unwin.

Bloch, Iwan. 1908. *The Sexual Life of Our Time in Its Relations to Modern Civilization.* London: William Heinemann.

Blomley, Nicolas. 2008. "Making Space for Law." In *The SAGE Handbook of Political Geography*, edited by Kevin Cox, Murray Low, and Jenny Robinson, 155–67. London: Sage.

Blunt, Alison. 2005. *Domicile and Diaspora: Anglo-Indian Women and the Spatial Politics of Home*. Oxford, UK: Blackwell.

Bonner, Thomas Neville. 2002. *Iconoclast: Abraham Flexner and a Life in Learning*. Baltimore: John Hopkins University Press.

Bourke-White, M. 1951. *Interview with India*. London: The Travel Book Club.

———. 1963. *Portrait of Myself*. New York: Simon and Schuster.

Braun, Bruce. 2007. "Biopolitics and the Molecularization of Life." *Cultural Geographies* 14 (1): 6–28.

Briggs, Laura. 2002. *Reproducing Empire: Race, Sex, Science and US Imperialism in Puerto Rico*. Berkeley: University of California Press.

Brown, E. Richard. 1976. "Public Health in Imperialism: Early Rockefeller Programs at Home and Abroad." *American Journal of Public Health* 66 (9): 897–903.

Browne, Kath, Jason Lim, and Gavin Brown. 2007. *Geographies of Sexualities: Theory, Practices and Politics*. Aldershot, UK: Ashgate.

Bryant, Herbert. 1931. "Abolitionist Victory in Bombay." *Shield*, 3rd ser., 7 (1): 31–32.

Bryder, Linda. 1998. "Sex, Race, and Colonialism: An Historiographical Review." *International History Review* 20 (4): 806–22.

Burchell, Graham. 1991. "Civil Society and the 'System of Natural Liberty.'" In *The Foucault Effect: Studies in Governmentality*, edited by Graham Burchell, Colin Gordon, and Peter Miller, 119–50. London: Harvester Wheatsheaf.

Burton, Antoinette. 1994. *Burdens of History: British Feminists, Indian Women, and Imperial Culture, 1865–1915*. Chapel Hill: University of North Carolina Press.

———. 2007. "Not Even Remotely Global? Method and Scale in World History." *History Workshop Journal* 64 (1): 323–28.

Butler, Lawrence J. 2002. *Britain and Empire: Adjusting to a Post-Imperial World*. London: IB Taurus.

Calarco, Matthew, and Steven DeCaroli. 2007. *Giorgio Agamben: Sovereignty and Life*. Stanford, CA: Stanford University Press.

Candy, Catherine. 2000. "Competing Transnational Representations of the 1930s Indian Franchise Question." In *Women's Suffrage in the British Empire: Citizenship, Nation and Race*, edited by Ian C. Fletcher, Laura E. Nym Mayhall, and Philippa Levine, 191–206. London: Routledge.

Cell, John W. 1986. "Anglo-Indian Medical Theory and the Origins of Segregation in West Africa." *American Historical Review* 91 (2): 307–35.

Chakrabarty, Dipesh. 2000. "Subaltern Studies and Postcolonial Historiography." *Nepantla: View from the South* 1 (1): 9–32.

Challoner, Phyllis, and Vera Laughton Mathews. 1928. *Towards Citizenship: A Handbook of Women's Emancipation*. London: P. S. King and Son.

Chatterjee, Partha. 1993. *The Nation and Its Fragments: Colonial and Postcolonial Histories*. Princeton, NJ: Princeton University Press.

———. 2004. *The Politics of the Governed: Reflections on Popular Politics in Most of the World*. New York: Columbia University Press.

———. 2010. *Empire and Nation: Selected Essays*. New York: Columbia University Press.

———. 2011. *Lineages of Political Society: Studies in Postcolonial Democracy*. New York: Columbia University Press.

Chattopadhyay, Swati. 2005. *Representing Calcutta: Modernity, Nationalism and the Colonial Uncanny*. New York: Routledge.

Cohen, Jean L., and Andrew Arato. 1994. *Civil Society and Political Theory*. Cambridge, MA: MIT Press.

Coleman, Mathew. 2007. "Review: State of Exception." *Environment and Planning D: Society and Space* 25 (1): 187–90.

———. 2011. "Colonial War: Carl Schmitt's Deterritorialization of Enmity." In *Spatiality, Sovereignty and Carl Schmitt: Geographies of the Nomos*, edited by Stephen Legg, 127–42. London: Routledge.

Collier, Stephen J. 2009. "Topologies of Power: Foucault's Analysis of Political Government beyond 'Governmentality.'" *Theory Culture Society* 26 (6): 78–108.

Comaroff, Jean, and John Comaroff. 2003. "Ethnography on an Awkward Scale: Postcolonial Anthropology and the Violence of Abstraction." *Ethnography* 4 (2): 147–79.

Cook, Matthew. 2006. "Law." In *Palgrave Advances in the Modern History of Sexuality*, edited by Harry G. Cocks and Matt Houlbrook, 64–86. Basingstoke, UK: Palgrave Macmillan.

Cooper, Melinda. 2004. "Insecure Times, Tough Decisions: The Nomos of Liberalism." *Alternatives* 29: 515–33.

Corbin, Alain. 1978 [1990]. *Women for Hire: Prostitution and Sexuality in France after 1850*. Cambridge, MA: Harvard University Press.

Coster, Geraldine. 1926. *Psychoanalysis for Normal People*. Oxford: Oxford University Press.

Crofts, Maud I. 1925. *Women under English Law*. London: National Council of Women of Great Britain.

Crowdy, Rachel. 1925. "The Work of the Advisory Committee in Relation to Prostitution." In *Imperial Social Hygiene Congress*. London: National Council for Combating Venereal Disease.

Dalrymple, William. 2002. *White Mughals: Love and Betrayal in Eighteenth-Century India*. London: HarperCollins.

———. 2006. *The Last Mughal: The Fall of a Dynasty, Delhi, 1857*. London: Bloomsbury.

Darwin, John. 1999. "What Was the Late Colonial State?" *Itinerario* 23 (3/4): 73–82.

Dass, Jamna. 1929. *The Torch of Light, or, the Regeneration of India*. Delhi: Qaisar-i-Hind Press.

Davidson, Arnold I. 2006. "Ethics as Ascetics: Foucault, the History of Ethics, and Ancient Thought." In *The Cambridge Companion to Foucault*, edited by Gary Gutting, 123–48. Cambridge: Cambridge University Press.

D'Cunha, Jean. 1987. "Prostitution in a Patriarchal Society: A Critical Review of the SIT Act." *Economic and Political Weekly*, 7 November 1919–25.

DeCaroli, Steven. 2007. "Boundary Stones: Giorgio Agamben and the Field of Sovereignty." In *Giorgio Agamben: Sovereignty and Life*, edited by Matthew Calarco and Steven DeCaroli, 43–69. Stanford, CA: Stanford University Press.

Deleuze, Gilles, and Félix Guattari. 1987. *A Thousand Plateaus: Capitalism and Schizo-phrenia*. Minneapolis: University of Minnesota Press.

Derrida, Jacques. 1976. *Of Grammatology*. Baltimore: Johns Hopkins University Press.

Edkins, Jenny, and Véronique Pin-Fat. 2004. *Sovereign Lives: Power in Global Politics*. New York: Routledge.

Edwardes, Stephen Meredyth. 1924. *Crime in India: A Brief Review of the More Impor-tant Offences Included in the Annual Criminal Returns with Chapters on Prostitution and Miscellaneous Matters*. London: Humphrey Milford.

Eley, Geoff. 2007. "Historicizing the Global, Politicizing Capital: Giving the Present a Name." *History Workshop Journal* 63 (1): 154–88.

Ellis, Havelock. 1910 [1925]. *Studies in the Psychology of Sex*. Vol. 6, *Sex in Relation to Society*. Philadelphia: F. A. Davis.

———. 1912 [1927]. *The Task of Social Hygiene*. London: Constable.

Ernst, Waltraud. 2007. "Beyond East and West. From the History of Colonial Medi-cine to a Social History of Medicine(s) in South Asia." *Social History of Medicine* 20 (3): 505–24.

Escobar, Arturo. 2001. "Culture Sits in Places: Reflections on Globalism and Subaltern Strategies of Localization." *Political Geography* 20 (2): 139–74.

Farley, John. 2004. *To Cast Out Disease: A History of the International Health Division of the Rockefeller Foundation (1913–1951)*. Oxford: Oxford University Press.

Farrell, Gerry. 1993. "The Early Days of the Gramophone Industry in India: Historical, Social and Musical Perspectives." *Ethnomusicology Forum* 2 (1): 31–53.

Ferguson, James. 2004. "Power Topographies." In *A Companion to the Anthropol-ogy of Politics*, edited by David Nugent and Joan Vincent, 383–99. Oxford, UK: Blackwell.

Fischer-Tiné, Harald. 2007. "Global Civil Society and the Forces of Empire: The Salva-tion Army, British Imperialism, and the 'Prehistory' of NGOs (ca. 1880–1920)." In *Competing Visions of World Order: Global Moments and Movements, 1880s–1930s*, edited by Sebastian Conrad and Dominic Sachsenmaier, 29–67. Basingstoke, UK: Palgrave Macmillan.

Flexner, Abraham. 1914. *Prostitution in Europe*. New York: Century.

Forel, August. 1908. *The Sexual Question: A Scientific, Psychological, Hygienic and Sociological Study for the Cultured Classes*. London: Rebman.

Foucault, Michel. 1970. *The Order of Things: An Archaeology of the Human Sciences*. New York: Vintage Books.

———. 1972. *The Archaeology of Knowledge*. London: Tavistock.

———. 1975–76 [2003]. "*Society Must Be Defended*": Lectures at the Collège de France 1975–76. Translated by David Macey. Edited by A. I. Davidson. London: Penguin.

———. 1977a. *Discipline and Punish: The Birth of the Prison*. Harmondsworth, UK: Penguin.

———. 1977b. "Nietzsche, Genealogy, History." In *Language, Counter-Memory, Practice: Selected Essays and Interviews by Michel Foucault*, edited by Donald F. Bouchard, 139–64. Ithaca, NY: Cornell University Press.

————. 1977–78 [2007]. *Security, Territory, Population: Lectures at the Collège de France 1977–78*. Basingstoke, UK: Palgrave Macmillan.

————. 1978–79 [2008]. *The Birth of Biopolitics: Lectures at the Collège de France 1978–1979*. Edited by Michel Sennelert. Basingstoke, UK: Palgrave Macmillan.

————. 1979. *The History of Sexuality*. Vol. 1, *The Will to Knowledge*. Translated by Robert Hurley. London: Allen Lane.

————. 1982. "The Subject and Power." In *Michel Foucault: Beyond Structuralism and Hermeneutics*, edited by Herbert Dreyfus and Paul Rabinow, 208–26. Chicago: University of Chicago Press.

————. 1982–83 [2010]. *The Government of Self and Others: Lectures at the Collège de France 1982–1983*. Basingstoke, UK: Palgrave Macmillan.

Foucault, M., H. L. Dreyfus, and Paul Rabinow. 1983. "On the Genealogy of Ethics: An Overview of Work in Progress." In *Michel Foucault, Beyond Structuralism and Hermeneutics*, 229–52. Chicago: University of Chicago Press.

Foucault, Michel, Jean Le Bitoux, Nicolae Morar, and Daniel W. Smith. 2011. "The Gay Science." *Critical Inquiry* 37 (3): 385–403.

Fraser, Nancy. 2010. *Scales of Justice: Reimagining Political Space in a Globalizing World*. New York: Columbia University Press.

Gandhi, Mohandas Karamchand. 1927a [2007]. *An Autobiography, or The Story of My Experiments with Truth*. London: Penguin.

————. 1927b. *Self-Restraint versus Self-Indulgence*. Ahmedabad, India: Navajivan Press.

Gane, Mike. 2008. "Foucault on Governmentality and Liberalism." *Theory Culture Society* 25 (7–8): 353–63.

Gedge, Evelyn C. 1931. "Modern Social Work in Bombay." *Shield*, 3rd ser., 7 (1): 33–35.

Ghosh, Durba, and Dane Kennedy. 2006. *Decentring Empire: Britain, India and the Transcolonial World*. London: Sangam Books.

Gibson-Graham, J. K. 1996. *The End of Capitalism (As We Knew It): A Feminist Critique of Political Economy*. Oxford, UK: Blackwell.

Gilfoyle, Timothy J. 1994. *City of Eros: New York City, Prostitution and the Commercialization of Sex, 1790–1920*. New York: W. W. Norton.

————. 1999. "Prostitutes in History: From Parables of Pornography to Metaphors of Modernity." *American Historical Review* 104 (1): 117–41.

Glover, William J. 2007. "Construing Urban Space as 'Public' in Colonial India: Some Notes from the Punjab." *Journal of Punjab Studies* 15 (1): 1–14.

————. 2008. *Making Lahore Modern: Constructing and Imagining a Colonial City*. Minneapolis: University of Minnesota Press.

Golder, Ben, and Peter Fitzpatrick. 2008. *Foucault's Law*. London: Routledge.

Gordon, Colin. 1991. "Governmental Rationalities." In *The Foucault Effect: Studies in Governmentality*, edited by Graham Burchell, Colin Gordon, and Peter Miller, 1–52. London: Harvester Wheatsheaf.

Goswami, Manu. 2004. *Producing India: From Colonial Economy to National Space*. Chicago: University of Chicago Press.

Govindan, Padma. 2013. "Rethinking Emancipation: The Rhetorics of Slavery and the Politics of Freedom in Anti-Trafficking Work in India." *Interventions: International Journal of Postcolonial Studies* 15 (4): 511–29.

Grace, Wendy. 2009. "*Faux Amis*: Foucault and Deleuze on Sexuality and Desire." *Critical Inquiry* 36 (1): 52–75.

Gramsci, Antonio. 1971. *Selections from the Prison Notebooks of Antonio Gramsci*. New York: International Publishers.

Grant, Kevin, Philippa Levine, and Frank Trentmann. 2007. *Beyond Sovereignty: Britain, Empire and Transnationalism, c. 1880–1950*. Basingstoke, UK: Palgrave Macmillan.

Gregory, Derek. 2004. *The Colonial Present*. Oxford, UK: Blackwell.

———. 2007. "Vanishing Points: Law, Violence and Exception in the Global War Prison." In *Violent Geographies: Fear, Terror and Political Violence*, edited by Derek Gregory and Allan Pred, 205–36. London: Routledge.

Guha, Sumit. 1993. "Nutrition, Sanitation, Hygiene, and the Likelihood of Death: The British Army in India c. 1870–1920." *Population Studies: A Journal of Demography* 47 (3): 385–401.

Gupta, Charu. 2001. *Sexuality, Obscenity, Community: Women, Muslims, and the Hindu Public in Colonial India*. Delhi: Permanent Black.

Gupta, Narayani. 1981. *Delhi between Two Empires, 1803–1931: Society, Government and Urban Growth*. Delhi: Oxford University Press.

Hacking, Ian. 2002. *Historical Ontology*. Cambridge, MA: Harvard University Press.

Hadfield, James Arthur. 1923 [1955]. *Psychology and Morals: An Analysis of Character*. London: Methuen.

Hall, Catherine. 2002. *Civilising Subjects: Metropole and Colony in the English Imagination, 1830–1867*. Cambridge, UK: Polity.

Hall, Stuart, and Bill Schwarz. 1985. "State and Society 1880–1930." In *Crises in the British State 1880–1930*, edited by Mary Langon and Bill Schwarz, 7–32. London: Hutchinson.

Hannah, Matthew G. 2008. "Spaces of Exception and Unexceptionability." In *War, Citizenship and Territory*, edited by D. Cowen and E. Gilbert, 57–73. London: Routledge.

Hansen, Thomas Blom, and Finn Stepputat. 2005. *Sovereign Bodies: Citizens, Migrants, and States in the Postcolonial World*. Princeton, NJ: Princeton University Press.

Harcourt, Bernard E. 2011. *The Illusion of Free Markets: Punishment and the Myth of Natural Order*. Cambridge, MA: Harvard University Press.

Harris, Henry Wilson. 1928. *Human Merchandise: A Study of the International Traffic in Women*. London: Ernest Benn.

Harrison, Mark. 1990. "Towards a Sanitary Utopia? Professional Visions and Public Health in India, 1880–1914." *South Asia Research* 10 (1): 19–40.

———. 1999. *Climates and Constitutions: Health, Race, Environment and British Imperialism in India 1600–1850*. New Delhi: Oxford University Press.

Hazareesingh, Sandip. 2007. *The Colonial City and the Challenge of Modernity: Urban Hegemonies and Civic Contestations in Bombay City, 1900–1925*. Hyderabad, India: Orient Longman.

Heath, Deana. 2010. *Purifying Empire: Obscenity and the Politics of Moral Regulation in Britain, India and Australia*. Cambridge: Cambridge University Press.

Herod, Andrew. 2011. *Scale*. Abingdon, UK: Routledge.

Hershatter, Gail. 1997. *Dangerous Pleasures: Prostitution and Modernity in Twentieth-Century Shanghai*. Berkeley: University of California Press.

Hindess, Barry. 2004. "Liberalism—What's in a Name?" In *Global Governmentality: Governing International Spaces*, edited by Wendy Larner and William Walters, 23–39. New York: Routledge.

Hodges, Sarah. 2005. "Looting the Lock Hospital in Colonial Madras." *Social History of Medicine* 18 (3): 379–98.

———. 2006a. "Indian Eugenics in an Age of Reform." In *Reproductive Health in India: History, Politics, Controversies*, edited by Sarah Hodges, 115–38. Delhi: Orient Longman.

———. 2006b. "Towards a History of Reproduction in Modern India." In *Reproductive Health in India: History, Politics, Controversies*, edited by Sarah Hodges, 1–22. Delhi: Orient Longman.

———. 2008. *Contraception, Colonialism and Commerce: Birth Control in South India, 1920–40*. Aldershot, UK: Ashgate.

Hoops, Albert Launcelot. 1928. *Present Day Public Health in India: A Report on the League of Nations Interchange of Health Officers in India, 1st January–18th February, 1928*. London: John Bale, Sons and Danielsson.

Hosagrahar, Jyoti. 2005. *Indigenous Modernity: Negotiating Architecture and Urbanism*. London: Routledge.

Howe, Stephen. 2010. "Introduction: New Imperial Histories." In *The New Imperial Histories Reader*, edited by Stephen Howe, 1–20. Oxon, UK: Routledge.

Howell, Philip. 2000. "Prostitution and Racialised Sexuality: The Regulation of Prostitution in Britain and the British Empire before the Contagious Diseases Acts." *Environment and Planning D: Society and Space* 18 (3): 321–39.

———. 2007. "Foucault, Sexuality, Geography." In *Space, Knowledge, and Power: Foucault and Geography*, edited by Jeremy Crampton and Stuart Elden, 291–316. Aldershot, UK: Ashgate.

———. 2009. *Geographies of Regulation: Policing Prostitution in Nineteenth-Century Britain and the Empire*. Cambridge: Cambridge University Press.

Howell, Philip, David Beckingham, and Francesca Moore. 2008. "Managed Zones for Sex Workers in Liverpool: Contemporary Proposals, Victorian Parallels." *Transactions of the Institute of British Geographers* 33 (2): 233–50.

Hubbard, Philip. 1999. *Sex and the City: Geographies of Prostitution in the Urban West*. Aldershot, UK: Ashgate.

Hunt, Alan. 1999. *Governing Morals: A Social History of Moral Regulation*. Cambridge: Cambridge University Press.

Hussain, Mohammad. 1931. "Prostitution Problem in Delhi." *Delhi Social Service* 1 (1): 6–10.

Hussain, Nasser, and Melissa Ptacek. 2000. "Thresholds: Sovereignty and the Sacred." *Law and Society Review* 2: 495–515.

Hutt, Cecil William. 1927. *International Hygiene*. London: Methuen.

Hyam, Ronald. 1990. *Empire and Sexuality: The British Experience*. Manchester, UK: Manchester University Press.

Isin, Engin. 2007. "City.State: Critique of Scalar Thought." *Citizenship Studies* 11 (2): 211–28.

Jessop, Bob, Neil Brenner, and Martin Jones. 2008. "Theorizing Sociospatial Relations." *Environment and Planning D: Society and Space* 26 (3): 389–401.

Joardar, Biswanath. 1984. *Prostitution in Historical and Modern Perspectives*. New Delhi: New India Publications.

Jonas, Andrew E. G. 2006. "Pro Scale: Further Reflections on the 'Scale Debate' in Human Geography." *Transactions of the Institute of British Geographers* 31 (3): 399–406.

Jones, Greta. 1986. *Social Hygiene in Twentieth-Century Britain*. Wolfeboro, NH: Croom Helm.

Jones, Martin. 2009. "Phase Space: Geography, Relational Thinking, and Beyond." *Progress in Human Geography* 33 (4): 487–506.

Jordan, Kay K. 2003. *From Sacred Servant to Profane Prostitute: A History of the Changing Legal Status of the Devadasis in India, 1857–1947*. New Delhi: Manohar.

Joyce, Patrick. 2002. "Introduction." In *The Social in Question: New Bearings in History and the Social Sciences*, 1–18. London: Routledge.

———. 2003. *The Rule of Freedom: Liberalism and the Modern City*. London: Verso.

Kalpagam, Umamaheswaran. 2002. "Colonial Governmentality and the Public Sphere in India." *Journal of Historical Sociology* 15 (1): 35–58.

Kapoor, P. 2010. *Witness to Life and Freedom*. New Delhi: Roli Books.

Kapur, Ratna. 2005. *Erotic Justice: Law and the New Politics of Postcolonialism*. London: Glasshouse Press.

Kapur, Ratna, and Brenda Cossman. 1996. *Subversive Sites: Feminist Engagements with Law in India*. New Delhi: Sage.

Kaufman, Reginald Wright. 1911. *Daughters of Ishmael*. London: T. Werner Laurie.

———. 1912. *Broken Pitchers*. London: Stephen Swift.

Kavadi, Shirish N. 1999. *The Rockefeller Foundation and Public Health in Colonial India 1916–1945: A Narrative History*. Pune, India: Foundation for Research in Community Health.

Kearns, Gerry. 2007. "Bare Life, Political Violence and the Territorial Structure of Britain and Ireland." In *Violent Geographies: Fear, Terror and Political Violence*, edited by Derek Gregory and Allen Pred, 9–34. London: Routledge.

Keith, Robbins. 2009. "The 'British Space': World-Empire-Continent-Nation-Region-Locality: A Historiographical Problem." *History Compass* 7 (1): 66–94.

Kiersey, Nicholas J. 2009. "Neoliberal Political Economy and the Subjectivity Crisis: Why Governmentality Is Not Hollow." *Global Society* 23 (4): 363–86.

Kiersey, Nicholas J., and Jason R. Weidner. 2009. "Editorial Introduction." *Global Society* 23 (4): 353–61.

Kole, Subir K. 2009. "From 'Veshyas' to 'Entertainment Workers': Evolving Discourses of Bodies, Rights, and Prostitution in India." *Asian Politics and Policy* 1 (2): 255–81.

Kolsky, Elizabeth. 2010. *Colonial Justice in British India: White Violence and the Rule of Law*. Cambridge: Cambridge University Press.

Kotiswaran, Prabha. 2008. "Born unto Brothels—Toward a Legal Ethnography of Sex Work in an Indian Red-Light Area." *Law and Social Enquiry* 33 (3): 579–629.

Kumar, Radha. 1993. *The History of Doing: An Illustrated Account of Movements for Women's Rights and Feminism in India 1800–1900*. New Delhi: Zubaan.

Laclau, Ernesto. 2007. "Bare Life or Social Indeterminacy." In *Giorgio Agamben: Sovereignty and Life*, edited by Matthew Calarco and Steven DeCaroli, 11–22. Stanford, CA: Stanford University Press.

Laite, Julia Ann. 2008. "The Association for Moral and Social Hygiene: Abolitionism and Prostitution Law in Britain (1915–1959)." *Women's History Review* 17 (2): 207–23.

———. 2012. *Common Prostitutes and Ordinary Citizens: Commercial Sex in London, 1885–1960*. Basingstoke, UK: Palgrave Macmillan.

Lambert, David, and Alan Lester. 2004. "Geographies of Colonial Philanthropy." *Progress in Human Geography* 28 (3): 320–41.

Lecky, William Edward Hartpole. 1926 [2004]. *The Substance of History of European Morals from Augustus to Charlemagne*. Whitefish, MT: Kessinger.

Legg, Stephen. 2006. "Governmentality, Congestion and Calculation in Colonial Delhi." *Social and Cultural Geography* 7 (5): 709–29.

———. 2007a. "Beyond the European Province: Foucault and Postcolonialism." In *Space, Knowledge, and Power: Foucault and Geography*, edited by Jeremy Crampton and Stuart Elden, 265–88. Aldershot, UK: Ashgate.

———. 2007b. *Spaces of Colonialism: Delhi's Urban Governmentalities*. Oxford, UK: Blackwell.

———. 2009a. "Governing Prostitution in Colonial Delhi: From Cantonment Regulations to International Hygiene (1864–1939)." *Social History* 34 (4): 447–67.

———. 2009b. "Of Scales, Networks and Assemblages: The League of Nations Apparatus and the Scalar Sovereignty of the Government of India." *Transactions of the Institute of British Geographers*, n.s., 34 (2): 234–53.

———. 2010. "An Intimate and Imperial Feminism: Meliscent Shephard and the Regulation of Prostitution in Colonial India." *Environment and Planning D: Society and Space* 28 (1): 68–94.

———. 2011a. "Assemblage/Apparatus: Using Deleuze and Foucault." *Area* (2): 128–33.

———. 2011b. "Security, Territory and Colonial Populations: Town and Empire in Foucault's 1978 Lecture Course." In *Postcolonial Spaces: The Politics of Place in Contemporary Culture*, edited by Sara Upstone and Andrew Teverson, 146–63. Basingstoke, UK: Palgrave Macmillan.

———. 2012a. "'The Life of Individuals as Well as of Nations': International Law and the League of Nations' Anti-trafficking Governmentalities." *Leiden Journal of International Law* 25 (3): 647–64.

———. 2012b. "Stimulation, Segregation and Scandal: Geographies of Prostitution Regulation in British India, between Registration (1888) and Suppression (1923)." *Modern Asian Studies* 46 (6): 1459–1505.

———. 2013. "Planning Social Hygiene: From Contamination to Contagion in Interwar India." In *Imperial Contagions: Medicine and Cultures of Planning in Asia, 1880–1949*, edited by Robert Peckham and David M. Pomfret, 105–22. Hong Kong: Hong Kong University Press.

———. 2014. "An International Anomaly? Sovereignty, the League of Nations, and India's Princely Geographies." *Journal of Historical Geography* 43: 96–110.

Legg, Stephen, and Colin McFarlane. 2008. "Ordinary Urban Spaces: Between Postcolonialism and Development." *Environment and Planning A* 40 (1): 6–14.

Leira, Halvard. 2009. "Taking Foucault beyond Foucault: Inter-state Governmentality in Early Modern Europe." *Global Society* 23 (4): 475–95.

Lemke, Thomas. 2001. "'The Birth of Bio-Politics': Michel Foucault's Lecture at the Collège de France on Neo-liberal Governmentality." *Economy and Society* 30 (2): 190–207.

———. 2005. "'A Zone of Indistinction'—A Critique of Giorgio Agamben's Concept of Biopolitics." *Outlines: Critical Social Studies* 7 (1): 3–13.

Lester, Alan. 2010. "Imperial Networks: Creating Identities in Nineteenth-Century South Africa and Britain." In *The New Imperial Histories Reader*, edited by Stephen Howe, 139–46. Oxon, UK: Routledge.

———. 2013. "Spatial Concepts and the Historical Geographies of British Colonialism." In *Studies in Imperialism, 100th Edition*, edited by A. Thompson, 118–42. Manchester, UK: Manchester University Press.

Levine, Philippa. 1993. "Rough Usage: Prostitution, Law and the Social Historian." In *Rethinking Social History: English Society 1570–1920 and Its Interpretation*, edited by Adrian Wilson, 266–92. Manchester, UK: Manchester University Press.

———. 1994. "Venereal Disease, Prostitution, and the Politics of Empire: The Case of British India." *Journal of the History of Sexuality* 4 (4): 579–602.

———. 1996. "Rereading the 1890s: Venereal Disease as 'Constitutional Crisis' in Britain and British India." *Journal of Asian Studies* 55 (3): 585–612.

———. 2003. *Prostitution, Race and Politics: Policing Venereal Disease in the British Empire*. London: Routledge.

Limoncelli, Stephanie A. 2010. *The Politics of Trafficking: The First International Movement to Combat the Sexual Exploitation of Women*. Stanford, CA: Stanford University Press.

Lindsey, B., and W. Evans. 1925. *The Revolt of Modern Youth*. New York: Boni and Liveright.

Londres, André. 1928. *The Road to Buenos Ayres*. London: Constable.

Macey, David. 1993. *The Lives of Michel Foucault*. London: Vintage.

MacKirdy, Olive, and W. N. Willis. 1912. *The White Slave Market*. London: Stanley Paul.

Mahood, Linda. 1990. *The Magdalenes: Prostitution in the Nineteenth Century*. London: Routledge.

Manderson, Lenore. 1996. *Sickness and the State: Health and Illness in Colonial Malaya*. Cambridge: Cambridge University Press.

Mani, Lata. 1998. *Contentious Traditions: The Debate on Sati in Colonial India*. Berkeley: University of California Press.

Mann, Michael. 2007. "Delhi's Belly: On the Management of Water, Sewage and Excreta in a Changing Urban Environment during the Nineteenth Century." *Studies in History* 23 (1): 1–31.

Manto, Saadat Hassan. 1985. "The Black Salwar (trans. Tahira Naqui)." In *The Life and Works of Saadat Hassan Manto*, edited by Leslie A Flemming, 206–19. Lahore, Pakistan: Vanguard.

March, Nora H. 1936. *Towards Racial Health: A Handbook for Parents, Teachers, and Social Workers on the Training of Boys and Girls*. London: Routledge.

Marchant, James. 1917. *The Master Problem*. London: Stanley Paul.

Marston, Sally A., John-Paul Jones III, and Keith Woodward. 2005. "Human Geography without Scale." *Transactions of the Institute of British Geographers* 30 (4): 416–32.

Massey, Doreen. 2005. *For Space*. London: Sage.

Mayo, Katherine. 1927. *Mother India*. London: Jonathan Cape.

McClelland, Keith, and Sonya Rose. 2006. "Citizenship and Empire, 1867–1928." In *At Home with Empire: Metropolitan Culture and the Imperial World*, edited by Catherine Hall and Catherine Rose, 275–97. Cambridge: Cambridge University Press.

McFarlane, Colin. 2008. "Governing the Contaminated City: Infrastructure and Sanitation in Colonial and Post-colonial Bombay." *International Journal of Urban and Regional Research* 32 (2): 415–35.

———. 2011. *Learning the City: Knowledge and Translocal Assemblage*. Oxford, UK: Wiley-Blackwell.

Merlingen, Michael. 2006. "Foucault and World Politics: Promises and Challenges of Extending Governmentality Theory to the European and Beyond." *Millennium—Journal of International Studies* 35 (1): 181–96.

Metcalf, Thomas R. 1994. *Ideologies of the Raj*. Cambridge: Cambridge University Press.

———. 2007. *Imperial Connections: India in the Indian Ocean Arena, 1860–1920*. Berkeley: University of California Press.

Metzger, Barbara. 2001. *The League of Nations and Human Rights: From Practice to Theory*. Unpublished doctoral thesis, University of Cambridge.

Minca, Claudio. 2006. "Giorgio Agamben and the New Political *Nomos*." *Geografiska Annaler, Series B: Human Geography* 88b (4): 387–403.

Mitchell, Tim. 1999 [2006]. "Society, Economy, and the State Effect." In *The Anthropology of the State: A Reader*, edited by Aradhana Sharma and Akhil Gupta, 169–86. Oxford, UK: Blackwell.

Moore, Adam. 2008. "Rethinking Scale as a Geographical Category: From Analysis to Practice." *Progress in Human Geography* 32 (2): 203–25.

Mort, Frank. 1987. *Dangerous Sexualities: Medico-Moral Politics in England since 1830*. London: Routledge and Kegan Paul.

Mufti, Aamir R. 2000. "A Greater Story-Writer Than God: Genre, Gender and Minority in Late Colonial India." In *Community, Gender and Violence: Subaltern Studies XI*, edited by Partha Chatterjee and P. Jeganathan, 3–36. London: Hurst.

Mukherji, Santosh Kumar. 1934. *Prostitution in India*. Calcutta, India: Das Gupta.

Nair, Janaki. 1996. *Women and Law in Colonial India: A Colonial History*. New Delhi: Kali for Women.

———. 2008. "'Imperial Reason,' National Honour and New Patriarchal Compacts in Early Twentieth-Century India." *History Workshop Journal* 66: 208–26.

Nehru, Jawaharlal. 1946. *The Discovery of India*. London: Meridian Books.

Neilans, Alison. 1921. "Prostitution in Bombay: Editorial." *Shield*, 3rd ser., 3 (4): 161–63.

Neocleous, Mark. 1996. *Administering Civil Society: Towards a Theory of the State*. Basingstoke, UK: Macmillan.

Niccoll-Jones, S. 1938. "Ten Years' Work in Rangoon." *Shield*, 5th ser., 6 (3): 104–9.

Nietzsche, Friedrich. 1888 [2007]. *Twilight of the Idols*. Ware, UK: Wordsworth Editions.

Norris, Andrew. 2005. *Politics, Metaphysics, and Death: Essays on Giorgio Agamben's Homo Sacer*. Durham: Duke University Press.

Ogborn, Miles. 1998. *Spaces of Modernity: London's Geographies, 1680–1780*. London: Guilford Press.

———. 2007. *Indian Ink: Script and Print in the Making of the English East India Company*. Chicago: University of Chicago Press.

Oldenburg, Veena Talwar. 1990. "Lifestyle as Resistance: The Case of the Courtesans of Lucknow, India." *Feminist Studies* 16 (2): 259–87.

———. 2007. "Sita's Epic Journey: Reflections on the Violence in the Lives of Hindu Women in India." In *Violence Against Women in Contemporary World Religion: Roots and Cures*, edited by Daniel C. McGuire and Sa'diyya Shaikh, 153–73. Cleveland, OH: Pilgrim Press.

Orsini, F. 2002. *The Hindi Public Sphere 1920–1940: Language and Literature in the Age of Nationalism*. Delhi: Oxford University Press.

Patton, Paul. 2007. "Agamben and Foucault on Biopower and Biopolitics." In *Giorgio Agamben: Sovereignty and Life*, edited by Matthew Calarco and Steven DeCaroli, 203–18. Stanford, CA: Stanford University Press.

Pedersen, Susan. 2006. "The Meaning of the Mandates System: An Argument." *Geschichte und Gesellschaft* 32 (4): 560–82.

Peers, Douglas M. 1998. "Privates off Parade: Regimenting Sexuality in the Nineteenth-Century Indian Empire." *International History Review* 20 (4): 823–54.

Phillips, Richard. 2006. *Sex, Politics and Empire: A Postcolonial Geography*. Manchester, UK: Manchester University Press.

Philo, C. 1992. "Foucault's Geography." *Environment and Planning D: Society and Space* 10: 137–61.

Pieck, Sonja K., and Sandra A. Moog. 2009. "Competing Entanglements in the Struggle to Save the Amazon: The Shifting Terrain of Transnational Civil Society." *Political Geography* 28 (7): 416–25.

Pillidge, Mabel. 1934. "The Work of the AMSH in an Indian State." *Shield*, 5th ser., 3 (3): 100–106.

Pinch, William. 2013. "Prostituting the Mutiny: Sex-slavery and Crime in the Making of 1857." In *Mutiny at the Margins: New Perspectives on the Indian Uprising of 1857, Volume I: Anticipations and Experiences in the Locality*, edited by Crispin Bates, 61–87. London: Sage.

Pivar, David J. 2002. *Purity and Hygiene: Women, Prostitution, and the "America Plan," 1900–1930*. Westport, CT: Greenwood Press.

Poovey, Mary. 2002. "The Liberal Civil Subject and the Social in Eighteenth-Century British Moral Philosophy." In *The Social in Question: New Bearings in History and the Social Sciences*, 44–61. London: Routledge.

Prakash, Gyan. 1999. *Another Reason: Science and the Imagination of Modern India*. Princeton, NJ: Princeton University Press.

———. 2002. "The Colonial Genealogy of Society: Community and Political Modernity in India." In *The Social in Question: New Bearings in History and the Social Sciences*, edited by Patrick Joyce, 81–96. London: Routledge.

Pratt, Geraldine. 2005. "Abandoned Women and Spaces of Exception." *Antipode* 37 (5): 1052–78.

Pym, T. W. 1928. *The Place of Sex in Life*. London: Ernest Benn.

———. 1933. *Conduct*. London: Student Christian Movement Press.

Raj, Sundara M. 1993. *Prostitution in Madras: A Study in Historical Perspective*. Delhi: PVT.

Rajan, Rajeswari Sunder. 2003. *The Scandal of the State: Women, Law, and Citizenship in Postcolonial India*. Durham, NC: Duke University Press.

Ramusack, Barbara. 2004. *The Indian Princes and Their States*. Cambridge: Cambridge University Press.

Rathbone, Eleanor F. 1934. *Child Marriage: The Indian Minotaur. An Object-Lesson from the Past to the Future*. London: G. Allen and Unwin.

Reddy, S. Muthulakshmi. 1930. *My Experience as a Legislator*. Madras, India: Current Thought Press.

Ringdal, J. R. 2004. *Love for Sale: A World History of Prostitution*. London: Atlantic.

Robertson, Stephen. 2009. "Harlem Undercover: Vice Investigators, Race, and Prostitution, 1910–1930." *Journal of Urban History* 35 (4): 486–504.

Robinson, Jennifer. 2005. *Ordinary Cities: Between Modernity and Development*. London: Routledge.

Rose, Nikolas. 1999. *Powers of Freedom: Reframing Political Thought*. Cambridge: Cambridge University Press.

———. 2001. "The Politics of Life Itself." *Theory Culture Society* 18 (6): 1–30.

Roy, Ananya. 2009. "Civic Governmentality: The Politics of Inclusion in Beirut and Mumbai." *Antipode* 41: 159–79.

Roy, R. Basu. 1998. "Sexually Transmitted Diseases and the Raj." *Sexually Transmitted Infections* 74: 20–26.

Russel, Ralph, and Khurshidul Islam. 1994. *Ghalib: Life and Letters*. New Delhi: Oxford University Press.

Said, Edward. 1993. *Culture and Imperialism*. London: Chatto and Windus.

Sankar, Sen, and P. M. Nair. 2004. *Trafficking in Women and Children in India*. Delhi: National Human Rights Commission, UNIFEM, and Institute of Social Sciences, New Delhi.

Sassen, Saskia. 1991. *The Global City: New York, London, Tokyo*. Princeton, NJ: Princeton University Press.

Schmitt, Carl. 1922 [2005]. *Political Theology: Four Chapters on the Concept of Sovereignty*. Chicago: University of Chicago Press.

———. 1950 [2003]. *The Nomos of the Earth in the International Law of the Jus Publicum Europaeum*. New York: Telos Press.

Schwartzberg, Joseph E. 1978 [1992]. *A Historical Atlas of South Asia*. Oxford: Oxford University Press.

Secor, Anna. 2007. "'An Unrecognizable Condition Has Arrived': Law, Violence, and the State of Exception in Turkey." In *Violent Geographies: Fear, Terror and Political Violence*, edited by Derek Gregory and Allen Pred, 37–53. London: Routledge.

Selby, Jan. 2007. "Engaging Foucault: Discourse, Liberal Governance and the Limits of Foucauldian IR." *International Relations* 21 (3): 324–45.

Sellar, Walter Carruthers, and Robert Julian Yeatman. 1930. *1066 and All That*. London: Methuen.

Selmeczi, Anna. 2009. "'We Are Being Left to Burn Because We Do Not Count': Biopolitics, Abandonment, and Resistance." *Global Society* 23 (4): 519–38.

Shah, Svati P. 2004. "Prostitution, Sex Work and Violence: Discursive and Political Contexts for Five Texts on Paid Sex, 1987–2001." *Gender and History* 16 (3): 794–812.

———. 2006. "Producing the Spectacle of Kamathipura." *Cultural Dynamics* 18 (3): 269–92.

Shephard, Meliscent. 1931. "The Moral Situation in Bombay." *Shield*, 3rd ser., 7 (1): 75–80.

———. 1932. "The India I Have Seen." *Shield*, 4th ser., 1 (2): 69–74.

———. 1938. "Bridge-Building in India." *Shield*, 5th ser., 6 (2): 63–68.

———. 1948. "Memories of the Association for Moral and Social Hygiene in India 1928–1947." *Shield*, 5th ser., 11 (1): 35–46.

Sherwell, Arthur. 1897. *Life in West London. A Study and a Contrast*. London: Methuen.

Simon, G. L. 1975. *A Place for Pleasure: The History of the Brothel*. Gateshead, UK: Northumberland Press.

Sinha, Mrinalini. 1995. *Colonial Masculinity: The "Manly Englishman" and the "Effeminate Bengali" in the Late Nineteenth Century*. Manchester, UK: Manchester University Press.

———. 2006. *Specters of Mother India: The Global Restructuring of an Empire*. Durham, NC: Duke University Press.

Sinha, S. N., and N. K. Basu. 1933. *History of Prostitution in India*. Calcutta, India: Bengal Social Hygiene Association.

Sleightholme, Carolyn, and Indrani Sinha. 1996. *Guilty without Trial: Women in the Sex Trade in Calcutta*. Piscataway, NJ: Rutgers University Press.

Smith, Neil. 2004. "Scale Bending and the Fate of the National." In *Scale and Geographic Inquiry*, edited by E. Sheppard and R. B. McMaster, 192–212. Oxford, UK: Blackwell.

Southard, Barbara. 1995. *The Women's Movement and Colonial Politics in Bengal: The Quest for Political Rights, Education and Social Reform Legislation, 1921–1936*. New Delhi: Manohar.

Spurr, David. 1993. *The Rhetoric of Empire: Colonial Discourse in Journalism, Travel Writing, and Imperial Administration*. Durham, NC: Duke University Press.

Stallybrass, Peter, and Allon White. 1986. *The Politics and Poetics of Transgression*. Ithaca, NY: Cornell University Press.

Steinberg, Philip. 2009. "Sovereignty, Territory, and the Mapping of Mobility: A View from the Outside." *Annals of the Association of American Geographers* 99: 467–95.

Stoler, Ann Laura. 1995. *Race and the Education of Desire: Foucault's History of Sexuality and the Colonial Order of Things*. Durham, NC: Duke University Press.

———. 2002. *Carnal Knowledge and Imperial Power: Race and the Intimate in Colonial Rule*. Berkeley: University of California Press.

———. 2009. *Along the Archival Grain: Epistemic Anxieties and Colonial Common Sense*. Princeton, NJ: Princeton University Press.

Stoler, Ann Laura, Carole McGranahan, and Peter C. Perdue. 2007. *Imperial Formations*. Sante Fe, NM: School for Advanced Research Press.

Strathern, Marilyn. 1991 [2004]. *Partial Connections*. Walnut Creek, CA: AltaMira Press.

Tambe, Ashwini. 2006. "Brothels as Families: Reflections on the History of Bombay's Kothas." *International Journal of Politics* 8 (2): 219–42.

———. 2009a. *Codes of Misconduct: Regulating Prostitution in Late Colonial Bombay*. Minneapolis: University of Minnesota Press.

———. 2009b. "Gandhi's 'Fallen' Sisters: Difference and the National Body Politic." *Social Scientist* 37 (1/2): 21–38.

———. 2009c. "The State as Surrogate Parent: Legislating Nonmarital Sex in Colonial India, 1911–1929." *Journal of the History of Childhood and Youth* 2 (3): 393–427.

Tambe, Ashwini, and Harald Fischer-Tiné. 2009. "Introduction." In *The Limits of British Colonial Control in South Asia: Spaces of Disorder in the Indian Ocean Region*, edited by Ashwini Tambe and Harald Fischer-Tiné, 1–10. Oxon, UK: Routledge.

Taylor, P. J. 1982. "A Materialist Framework for Political Geography." *Transactions of the Institute of British Geographers*, n.s., 7 (1): 15–34.

Terranova, Tiziana. 2009. "Another Life: The Nature of Political Economy in Foucault's Genealogy of Biopolitics." *Theory Culture Society* 26 (6): 234–62.

Tusan, Michelle Elizabeth. 2003. "Writing *Stri Dharma*: International Feminism, Nationalist Politics, and Women's Press Advocacy in Late Colonial India." *Women's History Review* 12 (4): 623–49.

Valverde, Mariana. 2009. "Jurisdiction and Scale: Legal 'Technicalities' as Resources for Theory." *Social Legal Studies* 18 (2): 139–57.

Vaughan, Kathleen. 1928. *The Purdah System and Its Effect on Motherhood*. Cambridge, UK: Heffers and Sons.

Waite, Louise. 2009. "A Place and Space for a Critical Geography of Precarity?" *Geography Compass* 3 (1): 412–33.

Wald, Erica. 2009. "From *Begums* and *Bibis* to Abandoned Females and Idle Women: Sexual Relationships, Venereal Disease and Redefinition of Prostitution in Early Nineteenth-Century India." *Indian Economic and Social History Review* 46 (1): 5–25.

Wallerstein, Immanuel. 1974. *The Modern World System*. New York: Academic Press.

———. 1991 [2001]. "Does India Exist?" In *Unthinking Social Science: The Limits of Nineteenth-Century Paradigms*, edited by Immanuel Wallerstein, 130–34. Cambridge, UK: Polity.

Walter, Ryan. 2008. "Governmentality Accounts of the Economy: A Liberal Bias?" *Economy and Society* 37 (1): 94–114.

Waters, Chris. 2006. "Sexology." In *Palgrave Advances in the Modern History of Sexuality,* edited by Harry G. Cocks and Matt Houlbrook, 41–63. Basingstoke, UK: Palgrave Macmillan.

Watt, Carey A. 2005. *Serving the Nation: Cultures of Service, Association, and Citizenship in Colonial India*. New Delhi: Oxford University Press.

Weathershead, Leslie D. 1931. *The Mastery of Sex: Through Psychology and Religion*. London: Student Christian Movement Press.

Whitehead, Judy. 1995. "Bodies Clean and Unclean: Prostitution, Sanitary Legislation, and Respectable Femininity in Colonial North India." *Gender and History* 7 (1): 41–63.

Woollacott, Angela. 1999. "Inventing Commonwealth and Pan-Pacific Feminisms: Australian Women's Internationalist Activism in the 1920–30s." In *Feminisms and Internationalism*, edited by Mrinalini Sinha, Donna Guy, and Angela Woollacott, 81–104. Oxford: Blackwell.

Zachariah, Benjamin. 1999. "British and Indian Ideas of 'Development': Decoding Political Conventions in the Late Colonial State." *Itinerario* 23 (3/4): 162–209.

# INDEX

campaigning target, 72, 104–5, 111–14, 131, 170; as policy, 10, 112, 129; of vice, 97, 112, 125, 194

Trafficking, 155–59, 206, 209, 210, 214, 226, 232

United Provinces, 17, 86, 116, 144, 152, 155–65, 204, 206; SITA (VIII of 1933), 88, 161–65, 212

Venereal disease: fears regarding, 12, 54, 92, 97, 101, 124, 126, 131, 163, 174; policies for, 14, 64–65, 76, 83, 102–4, 173, 177, 179, 201; rates of, 8, 76, 82, 102, 109–10, 124, 128, 225

Watgang/Watgunge Street, Calcutta, 115, 185, 187, 245

White slave trade, 3, 10, 106–7, 115, 131, 152, 157, 177

Young Men's Christian Association (YMCA), 14, 42, 58, 77, 109, 129, 133, 135, 191, 228

Young Women's Christian Association (YWCA), 191, 192, 202

Made in the USA
Monee, IL
04 November 2020